MY SONG OF LIFE

By
Rick Stanley
Copyright © 2016

http://saradainc.com

DEDICATED

TO MY WIFE AND TRUE FRIEND
Claudine

She has unselfishly supported me through 20 years of my creative work, both musical and literary.

And to my son **Brendan**, who tirelessly edited this book, never sparing my ego for the "sweet truth"

And to **Gwendolyn Rose Stanley**

my beloved daughter.

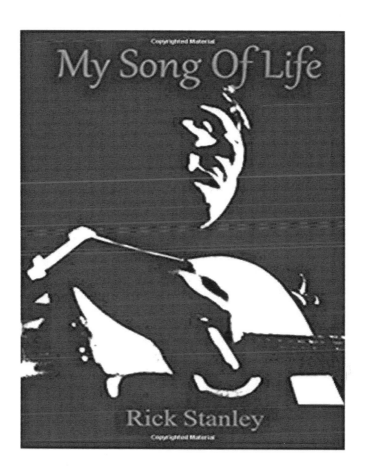

The 1st photo was taken by my mother,
Jean G. Stanley Jones

as I performed in a folk club in Heidelberg

1968

The book-cover photo of Maharishi was
taken by Alan Waite in India 1969

Thanks Alan!

INTRODUCTION

This book of memoirs relates the unusual stories of my life from birth to realization of the Divine. From my magical, Huckleberry-Finn childhood, to my adventures in the Navy, surviving 80-foot waves in a Typhoon over the Mindanao Deep; The real "Tonkin Crisis" in Vietnam, and a giant water-spout that nearly sank our ship and gave me a merging-with-the- afterlife experience. Then on to my life as a traveling folk singer, (near death at the hands of Hell's Angels) and the fulfillment of my childhood dream to become a professional recording artist with Columbia Records. Even better, to have the good fortune to record with the greatest American producer of the time, Terry Melcher, producer of "the Byrds" and "Paul Revere and the Raiders." Terry made magic with my group the "Gentle Soul" the album and singles were collector's items until "Sundazed Records" recently re-released the entire Gentle Soul discography on CD.

The final phase of this 32-year Odyssey is the fulfillment of the search of a seeker for the Truths of Life, how do we attain lasting happiness and enlightenment, why are we born on this Earth, to what purpose? From Divine Realization through my seven years of living, performing and traveling with the greatest spiritual master of our age. After the overwhelming experience on a California beach, the intimate communication with the invisible Divine, with God; I sacrificed my commercial music career, left Columbia Records, and became the musical expression of the Truth of Life with "The Song Of Life" album, written in India at the feet of His Holiness Maharishi Mahesh Yogi. If you're still reading this you've probably heard of me or you know me from the 60's Folk Renaissance album "The Gentle Soul" on Columbia Records or more likely the Celtic-Harp-Music world, or even more likely, from the TM Movement and the music I created, recorded, and performed for his Holiness Maharishi Mahesh Yogi. Maharishi inspired me to write songs infused with his knowledge and even gave me his teaching in poetic form so that I could more easily craft the lyrics and music:

"The truth of Life is eternal and the same everywhere,
the Light of Life is eternal and the same everywhere,
what is here is everywhere, what is not here is nowhere at all,
now begin from where you are, to find who you are."
(MMY)

He wrote down truths of life from the revelatory Insight of Brahman Consciousness, fathoming the depths of Vedic knowledge in phrases that I could spin into songs. Music made the teaching more compatible with my generation's love of lyrical beauty expressed in song. Bob Dylan, the Beatles, James Taylor, Cat Stevens and Joni Mitchell are a few of the artists who inspired us. I'll tell you many true tales of my adventures in the 60's and of my time with Maharishi with candor and insight that hasn't been officially picked over by any Censor or board of what-evers!

Book One
Memories From 1943 to 1968

THE SAMURAI VS JOHN WAYNE (DAD)

Lt. Dad

There was a World War going on and my father was scheduled for the Pacific and Japan. When he shipped off, he and his men were all jammed into a troop transport ship, I think they were called Liberty Ships. Being a life-long ocean-going sailor as a civilian, he was quite at home on the craft with its tendency to bob up and down like a cork in the water. The other men were constantly sea sick crossing the wide Pacific for Japan. Upon reaching Yokosuka the commanding officer gave him the order to go down the coast to convince a "Samurai" warrior-colonel to give up his command of several hundred seasoned marines.

He recently told me that this was also the base where the Kamikaze pilots awaited their doomed flights into the hereafter. Lt. Stanley was also ordered to bring back some US Navy wool blankets that the Japanese colonel had somehow come by. When Dad got to the Japanese base, he very quickly realized that these guys either hadn't heard the war was over or didn't care, and were probably going to fight to the finish. If he had been aware of the fact that Japanese troops were committing organized mass suicides all over Japan with the surrender of Hirohito, and that this was the likely outcome of his hazardous mission; after, of course, he and his men had been wiped out, he may not have been so bold.

The Samurai Colonel

So, my 5'8" lieutenant father raised a white flag and bravely walked into the hornet's nest to parley with Colonel Musashi Bushido. He figured that the only way to gain the respect of this old warrior was to be like John Wayne, totally fearless; so he puffed himself up and in his best Wayne impression, demanded that the Colonel give him his sword and the blankets and have his men surrender their weapons. He said "Let's all go home and take care of our families, there has been more than enough bloodshed." Well, the Samurai seemed shocked, and sat in silence, evaluating his options, and the little lieutenant. At last, after a nail-biting deliberation, the Colonel expertly drew his sword with a swish and placed it on the table in front of my father. It seems that he was impressed enough with the little lieutenant's bearing and bravery in the face of being vastly outnumbered and out gunned, that he felt no dishonor in this, his last action.

I'm sure he was aware that the war had ended with the Emperor's surrender and that if he wiped out these Americans all his men would soon be killed by even more Americans; still, there were many Japanese officers who made the opposite decision. Dad found out later that the real reason he was given this dangerous duty was to liberate those few hundred blankets that had been commandeered, for the enjoyment of his ranking officers.

I always wanted that Colonel's Katana, it was so substantial, so heavy and sharp. Whenever I visited my father I would check it out in his bedroom, that and the Japanese Luger in his sock drawer. I didn't like the pistol with its brass bullets, something about it was ominous, like it had a history. Dad had picked it up as a souvenir from a pile of surrendered officer's weapons before he left Japan. Anyhow, I always thought that one day my father would leave me his sword, you know, father to eldest son, passing on the warrior's power. However, my life story isn't quite romantic enough for my little fantasy to be realized, the sword was stolen long before my father died.

THE FAMILY

Ma & Mini-Me

Master Sailor Dad

Little Lord Fauntleroy (Dad)

Above are pictures of my Mother with "Mini-Me," the next is my father (Norm) on his teak decked, Marconi-rigged sloop, the "Harriet," looking like a handsome movie star, JFK, or the pampered son of some old money, Daddy Warbucks. The third one is Dad as a wee lad with Grammy in the background. My Mother was always very brave about acting on her feelings and intuition; at times her feelings would get the better part of a decision. As an attractive and intelligent Tufts University student, she was admiring the Harvard man from the pier, basking in the sun on the deck of his beautiful 30-foot sloop, and she wanted to meet him. She waved, and when he waved back, she dove into the water and swam to the side of his boat and he pulled her out of the sea like a mermaid.

That's how they met and how I, ultimately came into being. Unfortunately, for my mother Jeanne and the rest of us, my father wasn't rich. The sloop, his brand new Cadillac every year and his Harvard education were all gifts from his uncle Evy, who had married into money. Evy carried on the tradition our ancestor, John Stanley started when he married into the French Cadillac family who owned much of the land and islands around Mt. Desert in Acadia (Maine).

I should mention that Norm, was one of the most celebrated sailors in the 30's, winning trophies up and down the east coast and at the age of 14 sailed his sloop single-handed from Boston to Bar Harbor Maine and the Cranberry Islands, the ancestral home of the Stanley's. Uncle Evy had once been the Captain of the Ilesford and Cranberry Island's Rescue station, the first Coast Guard. In the 19th century Captain Franklin Stanley succeeded Captain Hadlock as commander of the Life Saving Station, and with his efficient crew of hardy surf-men, prevented many wrecks and brought much credit to the service. The story of John Stanley, the first resident of Little Cranberry Island is interesting but for now, let's just quote the history books; "John Stanley, who died in Great Cranberry in 1790, was the ancestor of many families of the Stanley name throughout Hancock County.

Captain Frank Stanley and his courageous life saving crew, the first Coast Guard

Grampa Stanley, one of three brothers from the Cranberry Isles, Mt. Desert, Maine. He's got some kind of supernatural thingy shooting out or into his left foot!

My mother's mother "Minnie Winnie" was from Montpelier Vermont one of those college educated ladies back when ladies didn't go to college. There were a few Irish sea captains from Boston and such before the Revolutionary War that we recently discovered, to my joy. My father's side of the family always prided themselves on being English even when his mother, my "Grammy" was totally Dutch (Ma said she was really German?). "Why do you sing all that Irish music? you're not Irish" dad would say. On Minnie Winnie's Dutch side, the Deboers arrived in the early 19th century; one of them became Senator of Vermont and died during his run for Governor, but my Yankee family tree has very little to do with me.

THE FOOD OF RATS & BUGS

I came into this world at Fort Bragg NC and moved to Fort Sill in Lawton Oklahoma where I can still vividly recall lying in my crib trying to fight off red bugs and a rat that was crawling all over my head. I remember crying a lot and nobody being there or responding to my cries. My right ear still has a few pieces missing from it, cartilage and all, that I'm sure provided a tasty snack for my crib buddy, "la rata!"

I remember managing to get out of my crib and escaping the house once, only to walk into a large construction hole in the dirt road in front of our house. My memory pictures it as around five feet deep but this is based on a toddler of about 24." Making allowances for size, I'd say it was probably about 3 feet deep, as it was deeper than I was tall. I can only remember being in it, not falling, and after awhile seeing people above me.

SOLITARY CONFINEMENT

I've often wondered when my parents broke up? as I have no recollection of ever seeing my father as a baby or a toddler, at Fort Bragg or after the war in Cambridge Mass. I know I was about two and a half years old when my little brother was born and Dad wasn't around then. We lived in the historic, Hyde/Taylor House at 96 Winthrop Street just across the cobblestone street from one of Harvard's stone edifices. The house has a colorful history of its own, including being the first "House Of Blues."

I really don't have any memories of my mother either, at least not until Cambridge, where I remember screaming from my crib and shaking it for long periods of time until she actually made an appearance, at least one time that I can recall. I do remember a few student babysitters. I remember somehow sliding out through a hole under the thin mattress and standing on the floor, looking down the long hall toward what I thought was my mother's room, and it was all dark and quiet. Now, I realize that she was probably sleeping a lot and recovering from delivering my little brother who is two and a half years younger than I. However, being confined to a crib all day and night at an age when you can walk, at least toddle, is like taking the keys away from a 16 year old who just got his new car!

The second time I managed to get out of my crib after hours of crying for attention, I peered down the dark hall again where I could feel that my mother must be sleeping. Then I walked rather "stumbley" down the steep stairs, one step at a time, holding onto the rail. I made it down to the first floor where the landlady, Miss Macmillan lived, and toddling further, found myself out on the street. Turning left, I Wandered down the winding cobble-stoned streets of Harvard Square. People stopped and stared at me as I purposefully made my little-naked way into a crowd of rush hour giants. Finally, a man took my hand and led me to the local police station where they gave me an ice cream cone and somehow were able to contact my mother.

She must have noticed that I wasn't in my crib and called them. She told me that the police really liked me. I should add the fact that not long after the above incident I was hit by a speeding sports car tearing down our tiny street. I was standing close to the edge of the sidewalk in front of my house waiting for Mrs. Tierney to pick me up for nursery school. There was a roar of his engine and the flash of a red MG heading right for me. I awoke to the sound of the young speeder whining like a child to my mother, professing his profound sorrow for hitting me. My mother was holding me in her arms and I think that was one of my happiest childhood moments...they never checked for a concussion, no 911, no hospital checkup, no insurance or cops, no money from the offender, and yet I was hit hard enough to knock me out. (the

Hyde/Taylor House at 96 Winthrop Street Cambridge

1940's!)

THE SHY AND THE BOLD

Ricky & Teddy at "The Barn" in New Hampshire

I was a very shy boy, the opposite of my younger brother Ted; I look at old photos of Ted and me, and he looks like "Spanky" the miniature toughy right out of "The Little Rascals." His little chest out and only one of the shoulder straps holding up his shorts with the diaper puffing them out and an air of total confidence all over him. I'm almost three years older and a foot taller, my arms all pretzeled up and my face scrunched like I'm in pain. I always looked real self-conscious when any attention was put on me. The photo above was taken when I was around 7 or 8 and I'm reminded of where we were and what was going on there.

We were on a kind of vacation, sleeping in a huge barn up in the hayloft; I think it was rural New Hampshire, 1950 or so, my mother was about 28. My mother's boyfriend at the time was a handsome Yaley grad.; with a name like Fenton Holmes would you expect any less? He asked me if I had ever had a beer and handed me his Schlitz bottle to give it a try. I acted repulsed at the idea, something my father and grandma had instilled in me. My father, who was until he died at 97, a dedicated non-smoker and non-drinker, a real old-time Yankee puritan. Fenton wasn't going to take no for an answer, and just about forced me to take a swig. When the bottle got as close as my nose (which rebelled violently at the fermented stench) I knocked it out of his hand and he swore, "shit" and said that I wouldn't be getting any more. I think that was when he stopped trying to get me to like him so that Ma would be more inclined to take him seriously. My mother never had any trouble finding boyfriends in spite of the fact that she was smarter than most of the men she met, or maybe it was because she was so intelligent that she attracted intelligent and sensitive men? She was an Ivy league college girl from Tufts, the female equivalent of Harvard at the time; at least that's what she told me. She had wavy blond hair and a Marilyn Monroe figure which probably didn't hurt her love life.

SENSITIVE OR PSYCHIC?

Ma used to tell me that there was a Brownie living in the big coal stove when we lived in Harvard Square, but I never saw him. I'm sure she didn't really believe in fairies and brownies, and I don't remember ever seeing one until 1976 at the Saboba TM Academy when Joanie-the-cook came out of the kitchen and walked over to my table. She opened her mouth and said something, but I wasn't listening as there was a tiny lady in a red sari moving about in front of her mouth. She was the first and the clearest wee Devi or Fairy, that I've ever seen, or that I can remember.

I am going to relate a lot of things that may give you the impression that I'm a spiritual mood-maker, or perhaps, a New Age fantasy writer! In fact, the only reason I'm writing down what I can remember of the first thirty-two years of my life, from 1943 to 1975 is that I'm afraid that at 74 I'm beginning to lose my short-term memory and I know it won't be long before the long-term becomes inaccessible. Basically, I think it has been an interesting life, connected with a host of famous characters of the 2nd half of the 20th century. There is one other reason, however, and that is, I feel it is important for those of us who spent personal time with Maharishi Mahesh Yogi to give our account of what he was like; so few of the Saints and Prophets of the past are characterized as both human and Divine. Humanity needs to know that everyone has a spark of God in their hearts and that just as Christ said: "The kingdom of Heaven is within you, seek ye first the Kingdom of Heaven within, and all else will be added unto you."

In other words, Christ came to teach us how to go within and find our own Christ-Consciousness, not to worship him like an idol or the only Son of God. We are all the sons and daughters of God and will all eventually find him in our hearts as Christ did, Buddha did, Ramakrishna did, Maharishi did and countless others over timeless-time. This is the reason we are here, to find our way back to our Divine Self that is God. But I digress!

The previous paragraph was meant to try and explain that I sometimes see and feel things that most folks don't. I guess some call that psychic, I'm not! it's really just a slight expansion of sensitivity to my environment. Anyway, when I was a kid I felt a oneness with the natural world around me. Back then, I couldn't relate very well to people but all the creatures and plants and smells and breezes, all of it felt like a part of me and me, a part of it. A good example was when I was alone, something I excelled at, I loved to scout around and get into all the secret places that most humans would never bother with. Here are a few memories that may give you a clearer idea of what I'm talking about:

NAGA CHILD

One day I had seen a hidden, shaded area of the pond by the

barn; it didn't have a path to it and I noticed it when my cousin Peter was rowing me around and I was trailing my arm in the water over the transom. I was watching a couple of water snakes who were intrigued by the movement of my hand above them, and when I looked up, I saw the shaded spot and what looked like grass on the pond's bank was alive and undulating. It was later that afternoon when I found my way there. I always walked silently and cautiously when I was in any kind of wild area and so when I came through the bushes and trees and saw a whole tribe of snakes of all sizes and colors I just froze and moved as if in slow motion into the gathering. I remember sitting there for around an hour until I heard the dinner bell clanging. The snakes made no show of fear or anger so I just gracefully moved out the way I came in. Looking back it's hard to believe their number and if it weren't for a similar experience a few years later I probably wouldn't believe it really happened.

My next snake encounter took place in Milton Mass when I was around ten. I was attracted to the ancient woods behind my grandmother's new home-the last house in a sub-division cut out of Milton's old growth forest. There had been a natural steep incline about 40 yards behind her home that had been bulldozed so that it was level all the way from the back of the house to the hill. I had to climb the open earth, a vertical cut of exposed rocky New England subsoil to get up to the woods. When I got up there I was amazed at how beautiful and deep the forest was; I think back then it went on for miles till it opened, in part, onto the mysterious "Quarry." The first thing I came upon was a freshwater spring that bubbled clear and deep. An old iron barrel had been put in it in the distant past; now the earth around it had become the color of rust leaving only the shape the old barrel as witness to its ever having been there. It must have been the water source for some pioneer although there was no trace of any kind of cabin anywhere around there.

I found the faint trace of an ancient pathway through the wood and followed it until it opened up into a creek area which I saw from around 30 yards distance through the trees. I noticed movement on the rocks above the creek and slowed myself and hid behind a large tree. I peeked out and squinted and I saw something hard to believe. On top of a boulder embanking the creek there was a huge snake coiled up like a cobra and he appeared as if addressing several creatures huddled below him on the rocks and the bank of the stream. He was facing me, and I could actually hear his hissing as he became aware of me and I walked on the path by his group of creatures whose "backs" were to me. Respectfully, I merely glanced over my shoulder once or twice, and they just seemed to carry on with their meeting. When I came back that way a half hour later they were all gone and I never told anyone about them.

MA I'M NOT RETAADED!

Strange, weird or perhaps the more politically correct "different," is how I was thought of as a kid. My parents assumed that I was mildly retarded because I had absolutely no interest in school. Most of my attention was focused out the window and so I was quickly left behind. Lost to the relevance and logical progression of the teaching, I felt like an outsider, like a Boston kid in a Chinese school. I didn't think I could ever catch up but somehow, my mother found the money to send me to a really cool private school for a few months where they had one-on-one tutoring so that I could learn to read. I loved this place! My teacher taught me how to make a weeping bird (a Cootie) by folding paper and putting it on my hand so that its beak would open and shut, he had no trouble teaching me to read; with him in my face, I couldn't look out the window and he was my first grownup friend.

Being held back in first grade and then again in third grade to the "well, it's not like we didn't expect it" reaction of my parents, must have done a number on my self-confidence.

I don't remember ever being punished or talked to about school which makes it obvious that they didn't really have high hopes for me and academia. My brother didn't help any by being so smart and cocky with a genius IQ of 154 that was proven accurate by his effortless honors. Finally, in fourth grade, my class took the IQ test and everyone was shocked that I got 148 on it. My brother was still the whiz-kid but now my teachers and parents all thought that I must be extremely lazy and had been fooling them all along. It wasn't true, I just found no interest in the lifeless tedium they were intent on feeding me. I'm sure that the power of my parent's convictions, that I was an intellectually inferior being, had a lot to do with my own low academic self-worth. I believed their feelings about me which supplanted any confidence I might have had in school.

When I was down at Grammy's, alone, out in the woods or the Sea, I was Me, one with my beautiful Nature. School bored me to death all day until I could get out into the air and the trees and wrestle and climb, be an Indian scout, and a spy hidden in the trees. One Christmas I got a brownie camera and I had a picture taken of me looking as if I had fallen down a 20-foot mini-cliff onto a pile of dead and dying trees. I used to call the place The Great Swamp. I made my arms, all crooked and twisted my legs as if they were broken. Like most people who have been loners and outsiders, I felt a compulsion to entertain if someone was paying attention to me. In most photos I'm making a face, the act of someone who doesn't feel interesting enough to show their real face.

I think of all the poor comedians who end up so depressed, the seemingly happy clowns who make everyone else laugh and seldom die of old age. They are so desperately dependent upon social approval and lacking in an intimate connection with the deeper joy of life, behind all the world's illusions, that lies in the very heart of all of us. I may have been destined for a similar fate, had Nature not been compassionate enough to open itself to me as a child.

SOMEBODY UP THERE LIKES ME!

I would never just be me in photos, always a character, a face-maker. But that very day in the Great Swamp, an hour or two after my photo-op, I was laying comfortably on the old trees and the sun felt soft and warm in the brisk winter air and I became aware of a consciousness that I felt looking down at me with fondness and reassuring love. It wasn't coming from my grandparent's apartment building; it wasn't merely a person. This being was huge and filled the sky above me; at least that was how it felt when I tried to locate the attention that was showering down on me. It was much the same as my Explorer Scout Voyageur on the Kennebec River in Maine; white water rapids canoeing. There, He was a reassuring father in the sky, banishing my fear of the thunder and lightning storm as we lay beneath out aluminum canoes by the wild river.

MOTHER HUBBARD'S CUPBOARD

I was a very thin and sinewy lad, we never had more than a can or two of Campbell's soup in the cupboard. On good days, there might be a box of cheerios and a quart of milk in the fridge, no fruit or fresh vegetables. So, it was cereal for breakfast, the few scraps they gave you at school lunch and then cereal when I came home from school and if we had it, maybe I'd fry up a burger for Teddy and me for supper. Ma wouldn't get home till late in the evening and she would already have eaten out somewhere since she had to work into the night running the Institute of Contemporary Art in Boston. I was skinny but wiry and strong like a Chimpanzee (you don't see their strength) spending much of my after-school time climbing trees and wrestling or playing sports. I believe that the food we'd get on weekends at Grammy Stanley's was the only reason we weren't malnourished and sickly.

ANTI-GOYIM-ISM

I was ambidextrous and could bat lefty and righty, it drove the pitchers nuts when I would switch on them after a few balls were thrown. I could hit really well but they always stuck me in the outfield; I wasn't a popular kid, I was strange. The outfield, especially left-field was boring--like school boring to me; I could never quite judge the ball's descent into my glove as I had a pretty bad astigmatism in one eye. I was fine infield, but only the cocky popular kids were entitled. I was one of the few, financially poor, non-Jewish kids in an almost entirely upper-middle-class Jewish school which my mother had purposely chosen to live next to because it had the best academic rep. I felt sorry for the little girl who sat next to me in fourth grade, Mrs. Tanner's class, with her freckles and bright red hair. She was used to her classmates snickering and rudely commenting on what they thought was ugly about her. She was from the poor Irish part of Brookline, 1950's Brookline Village.

THE LEGEND OF "PD"

It was like I lived in two different worlds; when I was in Brookline living with my mother and brother, I was the strange, odd kid and I felt like it was true until Minnie Winnie, my mother's mother, would pick us up and drive us down to Fort Point in North Weymouth where Grammy Stanley lived in a renovated summer house just up from the beach. At Grammy's, I excelled at everything. The toughest kid down there was PD; he was one of those kids who grow to physical manhood before everyone else. He had naturally huge muscles. He wasn't tall but was broad shouldered and good looking.

He had what I learned to describe later as a shit-eating grin. His father was a six-foot-six, 300 pound, Irish-American brute and a feared sergeant on the Boston Police force. Famous for fighting, he loved to drop into the bars on his beat and start fights with the biggest guys he could find. Local gossip had it, that he would always beat them mercilessly with a big grin on his face. PD's mother was 100% Apache Indian and almost as tall as his father. This was not your typical bully; the coward who picks on kids smaller than him. This was a real tough warrior. Talk about fierce people, Apache, and Irish Cop mixed! If you saw him coming you took another route because he would always stop you and mess with you. It was like a test that he enjoyed giving to anyone and everyone. He enjoyed torturing the Italian kids down the street; they were the sons of some of Boston's Mafiosi from the North End; they once had Rocky Graziano (legendary champion boxer) down for the weekend and I saw him practicing on a body bag filled with sand. The next day Michael, one of the family kids, showed me the hole that Rocky had punched right through the heavy canvas bag! The "Italians" had a summer house just up from Grammy's and you could smell when they were down for the weekend with all that Sicilian food cooking day and night.

PD would line us all up and light a candle and stand in front of each of us and sprinkle hot wax on our faces, arms and hands, and if you cried out or moved he would keep doing it until you stopped your whimpering. I put up with it one time to see if he could make me show any pain; he couldn't. The reason I didn't show any pain was that I was living my American Indian warrior persona at all times in those pubescent years. I'd go to the Fort Point store to buy candy and girls would be giggling; (this happened more than once) one would come up to me and say "can I pinch you? Maggie says you think your an Indian, and don't feel pain;" I would nod and she would pinch my peck with all her fingernail might. Of course, I could feel the pain but I had trained myself to be apart from it and ignore any mental cries of physical damage. The next time PD felt like burning us, one evening as we sat on the seawall, I got into a fight with him; we wrestled for around an hour until I got him in a serious choke hold, something I was good at. I didn't let him out of it until he said he "gave" and I loosened my arm. The moment I did, he got his legs around my ribs and I have never felt such strength, he was about to snap them when Grammy toddled up to us and said: "stop that right now PD or I'm going to your father."PD was deathly afraid of his father and mother and he knew that his father respected Grammy as she was the only righteous, Victorian Lady in those parts and she was fearless; everyone loved and respected Grammy, she was a "quality lady," a truly religious and compassionate Divine Mother.

Claudine Stanley - "Grammy"

One afternoon I was zooming around in my eight-foot pram - the little thing would row really fast - when PD came down the beach and signaled for me to come to shore. I was very leery about what he might be up to but I rowed in with my stern toward him. He bent over and picked up a huge rock, big enough to go right through the bottom of my precious little boat and without a word he threw it in. I went down with my little ship right there.

He ruined my beloved boat and I was too upset to even respond; all I could think to do was to pull her into shore and figure out how to patch her up. PD didn't expect this response and actually helped me get her onto the beach and even said he would help patch her; of course, he never did. Whenever hurricane winds were beginning to blow I would grab the big beach umbrella and head for the pram. One time, as hurricane Carol was on her way I attached the wooden umbrella stand to the front seat with rope and used one of my oars as a rudder. I could only go with the wind as I didn't have a keel or center-board, but good lord did I go. Some of the kids said it looked like was going about 25 or 30 knots.

We used to stand in the middle of Caldwell street and jump in the air as the wind gusted mightily. I remember jumping and landing about ten feet up the street from where I jumped. We loved wild weather! When I was around 15 all the boys my age were into girls and it was hard to get any of the Latvian brothers or anyone else to go on my adventures. I still needed to live out my warrior fantasies but at the same time, I had this crush on Susy Divine. I would go in and out of sleep much of the night, inventing dreams of how I would approach her, talk to her, but I never worked up the nerve in the waking state. She was PD's sister, the Irish looking one.

Anyway, PD was down at the beach with a guy we called "Flavo-fart" from Dorchester, a very tough neighborhood. He was in a gang there and would come down to Fort Point occasionally and stay with PD or some family member in the summer. Being from "Dot" he had to keep up appearances and would hang out with PD. The funny thing was that he was all front, about as tough as a Twinkie. I think most of the guys from the streets had two ways they would get their rep. or image: talk tough and be the first to kick the other guy in the balls. So, when I saw him trying to get close to Susy who was sitting in the sand in front of her big brother I said: "Hey Flavo-fart get up."

PD immediately realized that I liked his sister, and he got a big smile on his face and said: "Hey Flave, you gonna let him push you around?" Flavo was all about impressing PD and started tough-talking, coming up close in front of me, and PD said, "Rick, give me your hunting knife." I said "fine" but then he wanted me to give him the wooden knife I had in my belt. It was just a piece of cedar shingle I had carved into a long nasty looking red painted blade. Flavo wanted me to get rid of it but I said, "Aww this couldn't hurt anyone, it would just break."

So he continued to swear and tell me what he was going to do to me, but I just smiled, I had no fear of him at all. Suddenly, he took a swing at my face and I pulled back and then he kicked me in the crotch but missed and got my thigh which pissed me off big-time. I jumped him and got him in my choke hold until he started squealing like a little kid. I said "give and I'll let you go" and he started swearing again, so I really throttled him till he cried out "I give" half-crying. He was humiliated, he was about 6 inches taller than me and when he got up he immediately tried to kick me in the balls again, it was his only move but he wasn't very good at it, he kept missing. I pulled my wooden knife and stabbed it hard into his leg, I don't think it broke through his Jeans but it scared the crap out of him because he thought I'd keep coming at him; I was growling and acting crazy-mad. I had told PD when he wanted the wooden knife that I would hold on to it in case Flavo-fart started dirty fighting. Flave screamed when I pretended I was coming after him with it to finish him off, and he ran away crying and swearing. This all made PD's day, he loved it. Of course, Susy wasn't impressed and had gone home before the fight for her had even finished.

At 15, PD was a legend all over Boston and the South Shore. He was famous for the insanely dangerous, ballsy pranks and feats of daring he would perform, and for beating up full grown men in their 20's and 30's, and especially for humiliating men in front of their wives or girlfriends. The guys who would follow him on his exploits were the lowest dregs of humanity;

really sad looking skinny little pseudo-toughs with low slung garrison belts, sharpened buckles pulled to the side, and black motorcycle boots and greasy DA's combed with Murray's Pomade or Brylcreem. Poor Choma was the most memorable of them as it was said that he died in his attempt to dive off the Mystic River Bridge (Tobin) 254 feet high. They dove from around 180 feet, and PD made it look easy as he swan-dived and hit the water straight as an arrow with a sweet "thuck" sound. Then he called way up to Choma and said: "ca'mon chicken-shit, dive!" The little guy jumped and somersaulted all the way down and hit the water like it was cement. None of us ever found out anything more about him; I don't think he had anyone who would miss him at home. I'm sure PD must have tried to rescue Choma but the water is very dark and deep in the Mystic River. The truth is, we never found out if he lived or died?

PD AND THE JOCK

I was witness to one of PD's pranks that was extremely funny but very painful for the big lover-boy who was the victim. We were all sitting up front at the Quincy Drive-in Theater where the speakers sat on 2 x 2-foot cement blocks. There was a guy that looked like a tackle on the Hingham football team who was making out with a girl in front of all of us. It was kind of over the top in those days cause most of the kids up front were little, riding on the swings and playing tag and such. Of course, there was always a group of us on the ground on blankets staring up at the movie screen and some doing a little kissy-face. This guy was sitting with his girl on one of the cement speaker blocks up in front of everyone in the Drive-In. He was jamming his tongue down this rather petite girl's throat when PD suddenly appeared next to me and snickered as he held out a cherry bomb for me to see. I gasped, cause I knew how much damage one of these little bombs could do; I saw one blow a kids finger off as it exploded prematurely.

PD just walked up, lit the fuse and stuck it under the guy's butt crack, and ran back about ten feet. My heart stopped with the explosion and the scream, and then the guy with fire and fear in his eyes tear-assing after PD who had his escape route already figured out. The guy really must have been a footballer as he was fast coming up on PD and by this time they had gotten to the far end of the Drive-In, where, there was a dark trench that had been dug to allow for more speaker stands. When PD got to the trench he flew over it, about an eight-foot jump. The poor big guy couldn't see it in the dark and just went smashing down into it, face first. I don't really know how bad he was hurt but PD was thrilled with his latest misadventure.

THE RAFT

I'll give you one more PD story. One summer day most of us were at the sandy end of the beach, the Prospect Hill end. The Hill-gentry had paid for the sand and didn't like the Fort Point kids to swim there. The bathing part of the whole beach was only about a hundred yards long and was naturally covered with round and flat pebbles which I always preferred to sand. Anyway, we were either sitting in the sand or swimming. I remember peering at a newly arrived lady, probably around 28, who was wearing the skimpiest bathing suit any of us had ever seen. It was a two-piece "bikini," and this lady must have bought a petite teen-sized model as it was way too small - she was bursting out of the top. I had never seen a real lady with all her stuff so exposed before, and I couldn't stop staring. To make things worse, or perhaps better, she smiled at us as we ogled her, this row of 14 and 15-year-old horny-toads.

There we were, transfixed on the beach when PD sauntered up and said: "let's build a raft and go diving off it." At the time we didn't realize he intended to paddle all the way out to the channel in the middle of Quincy Bay. So, around seven or eight of us scoured the beach for wooden planks and drift-wood; we inflated inner tubes from home and ended up with a huge pile of raft parts to work with. I had to run barefoot back up the red-hot rock and tar street to Grammy's to get rope and hammers and oars. I think it took about two hours until the thing was finished, and we then had the obstacle of pushing the water-logged thing down the sharp muscle beds in our bare feet with PD flogging the backs of any who didn't give it all they had or complained of cut up feet.

Fortunately, the tide was on its way in and the raft was suddenly water born with the first sizable wave. PD jumped aboard and ordered us all to push the thing out deeper and deeper until we were up to our shoulders with the waves filling our noses and mouths with the cold salty brine. I pulled myself on and picked up an oar and started paddling. PD had been pushing us out Venetian-style with a long pole, and the others managed to scramble on as we slowly drifted out to sea. The raft would tilt to one side then another as PD had his fun trying to get us off balance so that we would fall into the water.

A couple of the kids knew this would probably end up badly for some of us and dove into the water and swam back to the beach. The rest of us braved it out until we were about half a mile out into the channel where the big ships sailed into Quincy Bay to the Naval shipyard. It was at this point that things could have gone very bad for me. PD said, "we are gonna have a contest to see who can swim all the way to the bottom and bring up a piece of seagrass as proof." We all expected PD to go first but even he wasn't crazy enough to do it and challenged me to be first.

You must understand that PD and I had been having an ongoing competition over who could swim the furthest underwater. He did eventually win due to his swimming strength; we were about equal in how long we could hold our breath. So, like poor old Choma I wanted to prove myself to PD and the others, plus I was curious as to what might be down there. PD had a really wild grin on his face; like he was going to thoroughly enjoy seeing me chicken out only a few feet down, spluttering up to the surface close to drowning. You see, the channel was over 35 feet deep, 40 and over in places, and very dark. I took a few deep breaths and dove in. I tried to gage how much breath I had to get back to the surface by how much it took to get down to the grass. When I got to the sea floor there was grass standing about 8 feet high and I thought, "well I should just grab some and not try to go the extra distance," which I did. I turned to make my way quickly to the surface as I was about to burst from lack of air.

THE MAN O' WAR

Facing upward and about halfway to the surface I noticed long tentacles just a few inches from my head and as I spun around to avoid them I realized I was just about to swim into a deadly 15 foot long, stinging Man O' War. They look like a jellyfish but are really thousands of small co-dependent creatures that float about near the surface. If I had swum into the thing I would surely have been paralyzed and unable to breathe or to swim the fifteen or twenty feet remaining to get to the raft. When I surfaced, after a total of about 4 or 5 minutes with my hand full of sea grass I noticed that even PD looked relieved. It turned out that they had almost given up on me and PD was about to dive in and check it out. This adventure secured my place as someone who PD could treat as a comrade in arms like his Mohawk Indian friend who could easily beat PD at wrestling. That kid had twisted me into a knot in about ten seconds when PD brought him into my back yard and challenged me to fight him. PD never again gave me any trouble, but our time as kids was nearing its end, and music soon took over my life. As for PD, the next time I saw him was in 1965; he was on leave from duty as an Army Ranger in Vietnam. I had just been honorably discharged from the Navy. He said, "hi Rick" and seemed so mild and humble; he had become a man.

Most of these memories were of my Fort Point days, when Dad would come down on an occasional Sunday and we would gather all the local kids and drive to some field for football, or a lake in winter, where we would play hockey. Dad would be on one team and Peter Hylan – my older first cousin - would head up the other.

THE STRANGE HERO

Being raised entirely by a strong woman seems to sometimes breed effeminate sons, of course, the opposite is also true; being raised by a strong man can have the same effect. In my case, being raised by a strong woman and almost no father bred a protector of women and girls. The guy who opens the door for them pulls the chair out and sits the lady down, sacrifices himself to honor and protect all women. It hasn't always met with supportive karma, and later in life, nailed me to a cross for fifteen years. But I remember one time when I was around 14, I was in the field north of Caldwell street with my war bow that I had carved from a hickory branch, and a couple of brass tipped target arrows in my belt.

There were actually several of us, two girls and me and Emans, one of my Latvian friends. We were all involved in a dirt bomb fight with several "tough" kids from Great Hill. It was a friendly fight at first. We would pull these plants up, roots and all and throw them at the opposing, stranger kids, and they would do the same. One of them started getting rough with one of our girls; he had come up to her and hit her with the plant. The hard caked dirt and stones had cut her face, and he was still coming after her. I picked up my bow and told him to get the hell out of our field, and he laughed at me and said: "oh your that kid who thinks he's an Indian, what are you going to do, shoot me with your toy bow and arrow?" I said "I'll give you to the count of three to go, one, two (he was laughing at me) three" I aimed for his chest and the arrow went sssshh-hhthuck and hit him dead center on his sternum. It hit with such force that the arrow made quite a sound on his bone and bounced off about ten feet.

He started shrieking for dear life, certain that the arrow had really hurt him. I'm sure that If it hadn't hit him in that solid bone it would have gone into him; as it was he was lying on the ground screaming. I looked at his injury, and the arrow had gone through his shirt and through his skin, bruising the bone. I was secretly very thankful that I had hit the bone, but I acted as if I did that kind of thing every day to kids who challenged me. The Great Hill gang never showed their faces again. I think I expected to be treated with some deference by the girls for my intervention but It didn't happen. I think they just thought I was strange, maybe crazy?

THE WITCH & THE GRAVEYARD

I'm writing this "memoir" as I remember the events, people and places, not necessarily in a chronological sequence. Time seems to end up being unimportant in relation to one's memories; they take on an order of their own, based on how much they meant to you or affected you with pleasure or pain. With that, I'm going back in time to when I was in third grade, we had moved to Waban just west of Newton, a long way for Ma to go to work on the buses. My mother found a house that sat right next to a huge graveyard, an eight foot tall, steel mesh fence ran along our back yard. The woman who rented the house to us lived in one room upstairs and she was almost never home. It was strange because she never used the kitchen or any other part of the house except the basement and we would never see her coming or going. Once I did see her by chance, and she scowled at me as she turned into her room. I took a fast look into it and saw all these metal looking tables with herbs and plants in them, they took up the whole room. Later, when I saw Rosemary's Baby I realized what they were, and what she was. I'm not kidding, that house was so strange I had to stop writing about it last night because I could feel a chill in the room and the hair on my arms was standing at attention.

My little brother was affected by the graveyard; he used to be very popular for his "PUS Stories." He would get an audience of local kids who would assemble by word of mouth, usually on full moon nights in the summer, and they would be hypnotized with his every word about the maggots and corpses and oozings. The background of the dark eerie graveyard definitely provided a convincing

set for his stories. In reality, the vibe from the graveyard and the Witch landlady was more than just fantasy, as you may agree after I tell you a few of my experiences during our time at the Old Victorian House in Waban.

OUR HAUNTED HOUSE

One of the most memorable happenings occurred just after school when I entered the house with three or four kids that wanted to see my Halloween tunnel. It was built around the dining room table and four chairs with sheets over everything. They were scrambling through when I heard heavy footsteps above me on the 2nd floor. I realized that they were coming from the Landlady's room. I told the kids to be quiet and we all listened as the steps went from the room just above and into the hallway and then disappeared into my mother's room. They were that audible, creaking the floor and all. One of the kids said "it must be your mother!" another said maybe it's Teddy? I called up the stair landing: "Ma? Teddy?" no answer. So, I signaled the kids to get behind me and we went up the stairway on tiptoes. When we got to the top, to the hallway, I called out again, silence, and now I was worried that we may have an intruder because of an incident that happened a few months earlier; I'll tell you about that later.

So, thinking we might have some scary deviant upstairs trying to hide from us we quickly ran into my mother's room and jumped on the bed. I led the kids into her room because I knew Ma had just got a 12 gauge shotgun that was beside her bed as a result of the last intruder. I was still unsure whether or not the landlady was around but couldn't resolve the fact that if she was, why had she gone into my mother's room? Anyway, I grabbed the shotgun and told the kids to stay behind me.

I yelled loudly, "if anyone is in the closet they had better come out, I'm gonna shoot through the door." Silence, then I said, "I'll count to three and then shoot." We all counted 1 2 3 and I pulled the trigger. Whammm!!! I was shocked by the force of the twelve gauge which knocked me over backward on the bed. The loudness had our heads ringing and our hearts pounding until we sat up and saw the four-inch hole in the door. I cautiously crept to the door and jerked it open; no one was there! Now it was quite clear who made the footsteps. The place was haunted and it was Halloween!! Ma got home some hours later but it took her a day or two to find the hole in the door. Much to my amazement, she wasn't mad at me, she realized she should never have left the gun loaded with two curious boys who were there alone.

Concerning, the intruder who inspired Ma to get the shotgun: It was late one night and we all awoke to a lot of crashing down in the kitchen; Ma ran into our room and led us into the bathroom. She told us to get into the steel bathtub and not open the door for anyone but her. She didn't have the shotgun yet, but bravely went to the top of the stairs and shouted in a kind of tough voice "who the hell is down there?" No answer but more crashing noise. She went down into the kitchen and the back door slammed before she could see anyone. One of the kitchen cabinets was open and cans and cereal boxes lay about the floor...it was strange! I have never forgotten how brave my mother was to face who knows what or whom?

I can't really explain in words the eerie, empty, other-worldly feeling of this place. Now I can understand why I always felt like things were watching me, even influencing me to do things - sometimes even cruel things - like forgetting to take care of Hammy the hamster until I discovered him covered with maggots, or dropping our cat from my tree-house to see if it was true that they always land on their feet. The place had no empathy.

BAD THINGS KEEP HAPPENING

One time I had just finished building the tree house, really just a platform, in the huge tree beside the front porch. The cat was crying from up there and thought he couldn't get down without my help. I climbed up and, remembering that cats could be thrown into the air or dropped and they would always land on their feet, I held him out and dropped him. I realized I had done something cruel the moment I let him go. As he fell in slow motion, I was frozen in the moment, trying to break his fall with my whole being. But he sailed down like a flying squirrel and landed without a hitch. He shook himself off and sauntered up to the path as if he had just got up from a snooze.

I was impressed because it was about a fifteen-foot drop. My next fiend-inspired move was to lower a quarter-inch-thick cotton clothesline from my perch. As I went over the side holding onto the planking with one hand I grabbed the clothesline with the other, but I couldn't get hold of it as it was much too thin to grasp. (Picture Tarzan swinging through the jungle on a 1/4" cotton clothesline!). Now, however, I was committed because I couldn't get back up; I was hanging by one hand with the other one holding the too-thin line. I decided to go for it and in an abrupt jerk of my right hand to catch the clothesline with both hands, I caught my wrist on a rusty nail instead, my full weight swinging in the air by the nail, I couldn't get my hand off of it.

Now, I'm hanging by the rusty nail in my wrist with one hand and the useless clothesline with the other. It seemed like a long time until my only choice was to let the nail hold me hanging while I grabbed for a better hold on the tree-house with my left hand, and I did manage to grab onto the plank again. Hanging there with one hand on the planking and the other with a rusty nail caught deep in my wrist, I managed to lift my right arm up enough to free it of the nail and then I grabbed with both hands onto the clothesline. I went down just as fast as the cat had and the line cut deep into my palms and burned all the way down. The bloody clothesline was of no help at all, too thin to hold, and I hit the ground hard, smashing down on my tail-bone without the help of my feet or legs as a cushion. I lay there for around fifteen minutes whimpering like a wounded dog. Finally, my mother came out, something unusual for her, and called down from the porch "Ricky are you alright?" I said, "No! Help."

When she saw the extent of my injuries she rushed me off to the nearest doctor; she had me looking them up in the phone book while she drove. We tried three doctors who all refused to see me as it was a Sunday. Finally, we found a good doctor who was quite friendly and gave me a tetanus shot for the rusty nail wound and wrapped my raw palms with bandages, that was about it. I must admit that the Doctor who agreed to see me was young and good looking and might have seen me as an ideal way to meet my mother. I actually felt really good at the time with my mother taking care of me like that. She seldom had any time to spend with us; going to the doctors was great attention, she really seemed to care about me!

LITTLE THIEVES

These happenings may not sound so very ominous but there were many more and they happened more often than any other place we ever lived. Once, the idea to steal money from Jack Sheehan popped into my head. He was a brilliant physicist who worked at Raytheon and was courting Ma. He came for dinner one evening and left his wallet on top of the upright piano that was in the large hallway that led to the kitchen. When he took it out of his back pocket I noticed a twenty dollar bill and, perhaps, fell under the influence of the house that

I could steal it.

I had never even thought about stealing anything in my entire ten years of life; I had never coveted anything that was someone else's! Somehow, I couldn't do it myself so I told Teddy about the money and that if he climbed up on the piano stool he could get the twenty dollar bill out of the wallet and we could go to the store and buy lots of candy and toys. Teddy got the twenty and we walked the mile or so to the local "general store," one of those places that have just about everything. This is when I discovered that Teddy was already an experienced shoplifter. While I was looking around for things to spend the money on he had already filled his pockets with candy bars. He came up to me and I saw the bulges in his shorts.

I wondered where he had picked up his guiltless and guileless aptitude to steal so easily and he said: "it's easy, just stand with your back to the candy display and reach behind and put them in your back pockets." So, I went over to the display and stood there with the owner staring at me; I reached behind and felt so self-conscious that I made all these guilty faces and moved so slowly that it was totally obvious what I was doing. The owner said what are you doing, trying to steal candy? I was flustered and pulled out the twenty and said here we have money.

He looked concerned about two little thieves with all that money. (Twenty dollars in 1953 would be like a hundred today). Still, he sold us about five dollars worth of candy and a few plastic toys. We walked back to the wild field in front of our house and hid in the "fort" we had made out of leafy branches, and we sat in there eating candy till it was dark. Then came the call from Ma to get home for dinner and we figured she didn't know about the money yet, so we went. They were in the kitchen when we walked in and I quickly put the money we hadn't spent in Jack's wallet and ate dinner.

When Jack was leaving he noticed the wallet had been moved and he looked inside. His twenty had turned into a ten and a five dollar bill. He didn't say anything to us but whispered in my mother's ear and she said "what? Ricky, you stole Jack's money, how dare you?" Jack tried to calm her down and smiled and said that we could do some little job for him someday. I felt humiliated and said Teddy actually took the money cause he wanted candy, but that didn't wash with Ma. She handed out some severe punishment that has long vanished from my memory but I never stole anything again since that time, except maybe "forgetting" to pay for a piece of pizza at Hy-Vee a year ago?

Teddy, on the other hand, became an adept purloiner with his light-fingered guru Johnny A., when both were in their teens. I can even remember many years later in Venice Beach California when we had no food and there were around five of us including Johnny and Ted. Johnny went into the small local market and loaded his pockets and coat sleeves with steaks for a fine feast for all of us; he did buy a six pack of beer to allay suspicion. I was quite thankful for his amazing ability at the time. Part of his success (he was never caught!) was his appearance. He was about 6'4" perfectly built, broad-shouldered and the most handsome young man any of us had ever seen. He had perfect Colgate teeth and a beguiling smile. No one facing him could ever imagine this guy would rob from them. He looked like a movie star or a top model, always impeccably dressed.

There are many stories from the Waban time that are all negative, for cxample I had whooping cough for several months and had to lie in my bed, alone in the house all day and every once in awhile I'd hear the witch coming in the front door and up the stairs and into her herbal room. Another memory from Waban happened when I was in the cub scouts, it was pretty uneventful except for the Den meeting when the den-mothers brat decided to pick us off with his BB gun from the 2nd-floor hallway as we sipped Welch's grape juice. No one really heard the pop, pop, with all the talking until a boy screamed in pain. He had actually been shot in the eye and ended up losing it.

I relate this because isn't that exactly what mother always told us? "you can't have a BB gun because you'll put someone's eye out!" I must have heard that phrase a hundred times in my young life before it actually happened to someone. I was never allowed a BB gun or any kind of gun.

BROOKLINE

We finally moved out of the Haunted House when I was in the 3rd grade. Brookline Mass. became our new town and Lawrence School, which was situated just across the field from our new home; an 18th-century Carriage House and Groom's quarters in the back of a huge English Tudor Mansion owned by a very rich Greek family. My mother had a wonderful imagination for fixing up our rentals and she soon turned this place into a sailing ship with rope railings that allowed for easy scaling of the almost vertical, ladder-like stairs up to the apartment. Most of the coach house was an enormous, empty area where all the carriages and horses had been kept half a century before.

Our part of the building only took up the area of a two bedroom flat on the second floor. We used to hear the fencing masters who rented rooms in the Mansion going at it down in the carriage area on Sundays when we weren't at Grammy's house in Weymouth. In Brookline, I spent most of my time after school outside, as I always had, by myself. Teddy always had friends but they were his age, and not into my "one with nature" life. There was an overgrown, fenced-in, eight-acre wood not far from the coach house that belonged to a huge stone mansion; Brookline was full of mansions.

The only way in was to scale the ten foot wrought iron fence that had sharp tips on top of it. I found that I could avoid the spears by climbing up a tree that stood next to one of the 4'x4' ten-foot tall brick and mortar corners that held the metal fence secure. I would often go there after school let out, and creep up to the mansion which had a very large picture window overlooking a stone patio and the secret wood. A few times I saw people sitting in there having tea and I was scouting from way up in a beautiful beech tree hidden in the foliage. Brookline had quite a few wooded parks, both public and private which I would spend time in. They used to call me "Tree Man."

TOMMY HAMILTON

Lawrence elementary school had an odd mix of kids, most were Jewish upper-middle class sons and daughters of doctors, lawyers, professors, and businessmen. Then there were the Gentile, poor to middling group which I belonged to. Your social status was decided by your parent's income just as it is now. My best friend and my best enemy was Tommy Hamilton, a tough kid with a Scottish mother and an American father. We used to have a no holds barred fight-until-one-gives about once a month; one time I would win and another time he would. This wasn't your fake TV wrestling; it was real street fighting: various positions of the choke hold; judo and jujitsu throws, and lots of creative offensive and defensive counterbalance pulls and throws that we discovered to be effective.

If your opponent tried to kick you in the balls you stood aside and grabbed his foot and pulled him toward you with a jerk. He would land on his back and you would land on him, legs on either side of his chest with your hands holding his arms down. Then you could pin one of his arms under your knee and either choke him until he gave, or if you were PD, drool a luggi down into his face and catch it before it landed if he gave, or you'd let it land and do it until they gave. That was PD's favorite humiliation-move!

Tommy and I would never "dirty fight," which usually meant

kicking in the balls, eye gouging or even punching in the face. If someone stood there in a boxing stance I would just rush them with my elbows in front of my face and grab an arm for a throw, or get behind them with a choke hold and bring them down. The elbow move really hurts a boxer's fists as they punch their brittle finger bones into the sharp points of the much larger and stronger elbow bones.

One memory stands out above all others when it comes to Tommy. It was coming on Christmas and we had just received our report cards; I was halfway across the field checking out my grades and noticed that I got three E's, something I didn't expect at all. I let out a loud oath and feeling completely miserable and a total failure, I heard Tommy say something and when I turned to look, I saw my brother Teddy going really fast on his bike out of the school yard and down the hill on the icy asphalt walkway. I could see Tommy quickly making a rock hard ice ball out of some slush and whipping it fast at Teddy. Thwaak, it hit my little brother with such force that he went crashing to the ground, all caught up in his bicycle and whimpering in pain. That pretty much did it for me, I had nothing to lose now. I screamed in bloody rage at Tommy and he screamed back at me and that set me totally off.

I threw down my books and ran screaming across the field to exact revenge for all my problems. I came full throttle flying at him with no idea what I would do, but he was good; he simply bent over at just the right time and I flipped over him, head over heels and landed with all that momentum on my back. It knocked the wind out of me and all the anger and frustration as well. We wrestled for a bit but finally, I just laughed and rolled over on my skinny butt. He chuckled too and I said, "why did you do that to my brother?"

He told me that Teddy had said something smart-ass when he rode by, thinking that he was safe, zooming down the hill on his bike, a big mistake to make with "Tommy the

Terrible."One other thing about Tommy; as I mentioned his mother was Scottish, she married his father when he was working in Scotland where Tommy was born. His father, a helicopter pilot, had gone back to finish some work for North Sea Oil and was due to come home after a year away from his family. His mother had a real handful with three boys, twin ruffian warriors, both 10 years old, and constantly fighting; and of course, there was Tommy.

I remember being in her house and feeling kind of sorry for her, she wasn't happy at all. Then the news came that his father had died, his copter crashed shortly before he was due to come home to his family and his mother's devastation was horrible to see. Tommy's mom wouldn't let anyone in the house after that, and one day when he and I were walking to the dining hall at Lawrence, Tommy put all his grief and substantial might into punching his fist through one of those heavy metal door windows with the steel mesh in the glass.

The door barely moved but Tommy's arm was shaved of skin, muscle, and veins; a bloody mush all the way up to his elbow. I had to help him pull his arm out with glass and steel mesh all buried in it. I found someone to call the ambulance and off he went; as if his mother needed another tragedy! When I saw him next he had a cast up to his elbow and it took forever for it to heal with great scars all over it.

TOMMY'S BALOON

We went on to Brookline High School and had a few classes together where he would do things to make me laugh out loud in class, like holding the wrist of his left hand back with his right, as if the left was trying to poke it's finger into his mouth with his cheeks all puffed up with air like a balloon. After much effort and struggle, the left would win out against the right, and his finger would puncture his balloon mouth as he made a hissing sound when the air burst forth. The funny thing was the struggle he had with himself not to let the left finger pop

49

his mouth. He would desperately turn his head to avoid the impending finger of doom. Last I heard, he was the owner of a Mercedes Benz dealership, having worked his way up from mechanic but I can't seem to verify the rumor or find him, at least not on Google?

SMOKEY AND THE BIKE

While at Lawrence Elementary School I joined Boy Scout troop 20 with Mr. Felder as Scoutmaster. He was a nice guy that Mr. Felder. He was the father of my brother's best friend David, an unusual pairing in those days of Jew and Gentile "and never the twain shall socialize," but Teddy had friends from every walk of life - from North-end gangs to millionaire's sons. One evening on my way to the Scout meeting at Lawrence, I took a long way around instead of crawling under the fence because I had on my Explorer Scout uniform. I was walking down the asphalt walkway - a steep hill that started from the street above â€" when, as I approached the bottom of the grade another Scout came racing down on his bike.

I looked again and realized that "Smokey," our Greek land-lord's dalmatian, was running at top speed just in front of the bike. I thought I could just move a bit to the side, when, without warning, Smokey ran me down and I fell to the ground directly in front of the oncoming bicycle. The bike was going much too fast to veer to the side or deviate from its trajectory, and "Smaack"- the sprocket, that middle part of the wheel, hit the back of my head with the force of a bullet and tore a groove about two inches long into my occipital bone. At the same time, the middle finger on my right hand was run over by his wheel. You would think that getting your finger run over by a bicycle tire wouldn't be a big deal but the nail on my right hand has never healed and always grows in black and dented like some weird mutation.

I lay on the hard cement with my head bleeding all over and my fingers doing the same. It took a long time for anyone to figure out what to do about me but when I came to, there was Mr. Felder being extremely sweet and compassionate. He carried me up to the ambulance and accompanied me to the hospital where they gave me a whole bunch of stitches that really hurt every time they stuck that needle in my head. I can still feel the scar outcrop that remains on the back of my head.

I remember several decades later as I was meditating in the Golden Dome in Fairfield IA., I felt a sudden fierce shooting, stabbing, unbearable pain, like a hot iron rod throbbing from the back of my neck up the back of my head and scar tissue. I felt as though It tore my whole physical being apart from the inner silence, and I screamed with everything I had for the pain of it. After lying down and recuperating for half an hour, I realized that all that silence had released the stress from those poor, numb nerves that had been pretty much dead all those years. They call it "un-stressing."

MUSICAL DHARMA

Maybe I should tell you a bit about how I got musical. My earliest memory of playing music was when I was about 8 years old, and I had a small record player and a 78rpm recording of a marching band playing the tune that goes with "be kind to your web-footed friends cause a duck could be somebody's mother." I also had a penny whistle, and I would sit for hours fitting the notes on the whistle with the ones on the record. I remember being able to play along with it quite accurately, at least my memory thinks so. I can't remember playing another instrument until my father gave me his silver trumpet. I joined the Lawrence school band and learned to read the sheet music and blow that trumpet with my fat lower lip vibrating a raspberry-like Dad had taught me.

My father was an exceptional drummer in the 30's when he was at Harvard. The famous jazz drummer "Philly Joe Jones" would have Dad sit in for him at some of his gigs in Boston when he was sick, on a break or whatever; so my father was more than just good. Anyway, jazz was a big influence in my childhood on my father's side, and Classical, Opera, and Sinatra on my Mother's. Ma only played the very best, the most beautiful music in those genres. I didn't like Opera until she put on a record that blew me away and I wasn't blown away again until I heard Pagliacci by Luciano Pavarotti five or ten years ago. Ma played piano and sang, and both my mother and father liked "Old Blue Eyes." In my teens, I grew to like him as well, especially after seeing him in his movies.

Dad The Big Band Swing Drummer

NIGHTMARE OF COSMIC INFINITY

When I was about 14 yrs. old we were living in a big apartment building near Commonwealth Ave. and Boston University. I would have a dream that seemed very real and scared me so much that I would wake up screaming. It happened two or three times; in the middle of the night. I would be floating in space with no place to touch, no world or place to stand on, no way to get my bearings or to be upright.

This space was filled with weird objects floating around like soft circular shapes and shapes of various sizes, but above all, it was endless, it was forever and infinite with no place to go or to be. This was the scariest dream I had ever had. I finally realized what the dream was when I had been meditating for a while and experienced something much like my dream while I was awake in meditation. I had actually been experiencing the infinite, unboundedness of consciousness and space and the star-filled universe itself. Not knowing what it was, and being powerless to get out of it, was the nightmare part. I was floating through unbounded space and awareness with no up

53

or down.

This Is Similar To What It Looked Like In My Waking Dream

MANFREDI

After Teddy and I passed on Jack the physicist, Ma soon fell in love and became engaged to marry Manfredi, the newly minted Italian Architect. We all became Catholic, and I did my first holy communion in a little white suit. Ma and Manfredi went to the Yucatan on a month long pre-marital honeymoon. They slept in hammocks in the trees beside the Mayan pyramids and took over 400 photos of them for his Architectural degree. Ma came back all tanned with a used hammock for me and an Indian machete knife sheath with no machete in it. Soon after, Manfredi left for Italy and although he had promised to send for Ma and Teddy and me, it never happened! poor Ma! Oh well she was too old for him and his Mommy probably put some sense into his romantic little Roman heart when he got home.

BOB

While we were still living in the small apartment near Commonwealth Ave., my mother married a guy that we thought we liked - we called him Jonsey, and he had fooled us into liking him. I'm sure that my mother had, had enough of losing prospective husbands because we didn't like them, and had tipped him off on how to win us over. She would always ask us if we would mind if she married so and so, and we would always reject the guy. There was Manfredi, the Italian Architect, and Jack Sheehan the brilliant physicist; we actually liked him but he didn't play football and therefore wasn't up to our standards for a step-dad. I felt like I could probably beat him up and I didn't want to be able to take my mother's husband.

Anyway, back to Jonsey; It was only after he moved in that we realized we had been duped, he sat us down and was suddenly a drill sergeant in charge of us. He demanded we call him Bob and he confiscated all my cap guns, water guns and even my bow and arrows and hunting knife. You see his problem was that he had miraculously survived those hill battles in Korea and had seen all his friends blown to pieces around him. So, we had to suffer for his miserable life. Of course, I should feel compassion for him, and I would If he hadn't ruined my teens, as if I were to blame for his being used as a "pawn in their game." We really disliked him. He was a total asshole - never smiled unless he was drunk. One big saving grace was that he was a singer of old popular songs and a ukulele player and he sang and played quite often. I didn't like his taste in honky-tonk songs, Al Jolson songs and songs of the late 19th century up to the 20s. But, since there was a ukulele I started learning to play it on my own.

He soon bought a Martin tenor guitar, it's like a big metal strung ukulele, and I enjoyed playing that much more. I was totally into the Everly Brothers and I learned to sing and play "Dream" and "Devoted to You," "Bird Dog," and "Problems" in no time. They asked what I wanted for Christmas and I said a guitar, and Bob bought me the cheapest piece of crap, Harmony guitar he could find. ($35.) I wasted three years trying to learn to play that thing, but could never get above the third fret with bar chords, because the action went from around 5/32nds of an inch at the first fret to a half inch 25 frets up.

For those not familiar with guitar speak, that means the strings were way to high off the neck to press down without cutting the tips of your fingers on all that steel. I did gain some powerful hands trying to play that thing, and some mighty thick calluses as well. Since I couldn't focus on bar chords I concentrated on finger picking styles that I was picking up from records and the coffee house folk and blues players.

UKULELE, TENOR-GUITAR, GUITAR

By the time I was in my late teens, the Everly Brothers came out with "Songs Our Daddy Taught Us" which was an album of Appalachian folk songs like "The Gambler" and "Barbara Allen." "Take a Message to Mary," which I loved, and was on the "B" side of their hit song "Problems," got me hooked on folk ballads. I got together with a classmate Johnny Oliphant, who also played the guitar, and he introduced me to the recordings of Pete Seeger and Pete's brother Mike of the "New Lost City Ramblers." We did our first concert at a church social event. The Oliphants' were Episcopalians and we were whatever Ma's religion of the day was; it all depended on who she was going to marry.

THE DRILL SERGEANT

As much as I grew to dislike Bob Jones, my stepfather, I do acknowledge him for disciplining me to use my brain in ways I hadn't thought possible. He would demand that I come into his presence like a drill sergeant and order me to give him 20 push-ups. Then he would tell me to get my math homework, and he would proceed to help me with it until I could correctly solve the sample problems he would invent. When I was able to pass his test, I was ordered to do my homework. To my great surprise the next day I would not only have 100% on my homework but would get 100% on the weekly test as well. My math teacher, Mrs. Elliot, was a bit shocked and at first she thought I must be cheating and chastised me in front of the class, but when she then gave me a test after school, and I got another perfect score; she asked how I was able to make such a turn around from class boob to top nerd. I told her about Bob, and she began to treat me like a human being instead of a dumb animal.

SANTA IS REAL!

At this point, I would like to tell you my true Christmas story. When I was around 12, Teddy, Ma and me, were all spending another Christmas eve at Grandma Mini-Wini's up-scale apartment, it was huge. It covered a whole floor of one of those significant brownstone apartment buildings in Brookline. Grampa Goss was a senior accountant for some big corporation, and he had a chauffeur who drove him to work downtown in his big new Lincoln Continental. I don't think I ever saw him smile, and although Mini-Wini would laugh, she'd sound like she was gargling Listerine after drinking and smoking all day in her tiny kitchen. Mini was dreadfully un-happy and only lived for 62 years.

Anyway, Teddy and I slept on the back porch which wasn't really a porch at all, it just had windows all the way around its rounded end. As usual, we checked out what was under the enormous Christmas tree in the dining room, knowing that by morning there would be twice as many presents and we put up our stockings in the TV room over the big fireplace. The grownups would always stay up late drinking and smoking and talking, and we would lie in our beds wishing they would go to bed because Santa wouldn't come as long as they were up.

It must have been around five in the morning when I heard someone calling, and bells, and thumping on the roof. I'm sure

I heard "whoa dancer" even though it was somewhat muffled. I jumped from my bed and opened the bedroom door, and very silently slid down the hardwood floor of the hallway into the living room, which was on the other side of the TV room. There were two glass doors, but I could see into the room, and I hid behind the sofa that was just in front of the glass doors. I knew that it wouldn't be very long before I would see him coming down the chimney, and I held my breath in expectation. Suddenly, there was a puff of colorful smoke from the fireplace and in a flash there stood a little man about three and a half feet tall with a pot belly and in his Santa suit, for real!!! He turned toward the presents that were piled up beside the hearth, and he sprinkled something that glittered as it fell on them. I know this all sounds silly, but in truth, it looked just like the pixie dust that Tinkerbell's wand would emanate. Then, he turned toward our stockings and did some more throwing of that shiny stuff. He then turned around sideways to me, and I could tell he knew I was there at this point.

He blinked his left eye in my direction, put his thumb to the side of his nose, and instantly turned into the red and white smoke again and up the chimney he went. I could even hear the bells again, and the thumping on the roof, and the calling of the names of the reindeer as he flew away. I'm sure this all sounds like I'm making it up or that I had a vivid dream from hearing the Christmas Story, but I promise you it all happened just as I have described it. When we got up a few hours later, Teddy and I looked into the room, and I could see everything sparkling with that joy dust that Santa had shared with us. We were not allowed to go in until all the grown-ups got into a long line, from youngest to oldest. It always took the longest time to get Grampa-Goss out of bed, but we finally had everyone lined up, and when we opened the glass doors and went into the room, I could see and feel the incredible joy of Christmas shining all over the stockings, and presents. It was then that I realized that Santa doesn't bring the gifts, he blesses them with pure joy, the joy of giving and receiving.

As a result of this experience I kept putting my stocking up every Christmas until I was 16 when my mother took me aside and said, "Ricky, you do know that there really isn't a Santa Claus don't you?" and I said "yes there is, he is a spirit, the spirit of the joy of giving. I saw him come when I was 12; I know he doesn't bring presents, he blesses them with joy for the receiver and the giver." My mother said, "well this is your last year for getting a stocking, it's time for you to grow up like we all have to do." This was when I made a conscious decision not ever to grow up if it meant that I had to lose my connection with the beautiful world of intuition and spirit; the invisible creations that are as real as any you can see or touch in this ephemeral world. And so I have remained open to everything in nature; there is nothing you can imagine that doesn't exist somewhere...that's what infinite means, God's infinite creation

Not This Guy! I Could Tell.

MY FIRST CONCERT

It wasn't very long after Bob had given me my first guitar. The instrument that I learned all the songs on the Everly Brothers

"Songs Our Daddy Taught Us" album, and most of their hit singles as well. The songs that moved me seemed to be the folksongs, not the "commercial" radio hits. I imagine the reason is that they were written by people with an emotional connection to what they wrote, something that had to come out from the heart in a song. "Take a Message to Mary" was one of those that made me weep with its selfless love expressed by a bank robber for his Mary. The Everly Brothers were the exception to my taste in Hit songs on the radio. They sang songs, even as commercial as "Dream" and "Devoted to You" in the traditional style and voice of the old Scot's/Irish ballads like Barbara Allen, that came over with their ancestors to the hills of North Carolina and Kentucky.

It was down at Grammy's during my 16th summer that a friend of mine heard me practicing and said I should play at the talent show over at the community center, and I did. I wasn't scared; I was too new at performing to realize that I should be if I were at all normal. I went up in front of around ten kids and adults and sang "Roving Gambler" and some of the kids came up when I was putting my guitar away and said, "Rick we didn't know you could play and sing." It was funny because I didn't think that I could either until then. A pretty 16-year-old girl from Quincy, the big city to most Fort Pointers,' came up and said she liked my playing and I turned pink with self-consciousness and said thank you. She asked my name and asked if I was going to the dance that night and I said "sure." We met that evening and danced for a while, and the next day the people she was staying with at their beach house must have told her about my reputation for still playing Indians; they didn't realize I was changing my priorities from a relationship with Nature to wanting one with these charming creatures called girls! She was off to Quincy before I could find out her phone number or last name, and that was that...my first potential groupie.

THE BOY SCOUT VIRGIN

Even with my newfound stage presence, I was a virgin until the age of 17. My younger brother said he was 13 when a 16-year-old girl sat in his lap in the movies, and supposedly took his boy cherry; if I may be so bold! The problem was that Teddy was a cute kid; his wit, IQ, ability to exaggerate convincingly, and his enviable self-confidence, got him whatever he wanted. I, on the other hand, had a pimply face with pits from squeezing the zits onto the mirror. If I look at my photos from that time, I must admit I wasn't a bad looking lad, but my zits and my academic, inferiority complex kept me shy with girls. I was sure of rejection, afraid of failure, doomed to sabotage whatever chances I had with girls. Well, I can't tell you everything, it would be even more boring than much of what I will tell you about my growing up. I was a Cub Scout, a Boy Scout and then an Explorer Scout. When you turn 14, you automatically pass the requirement for becoming a green shirt, an Explorer.

I made 1st class, but the myriad of merit badges you would have to earn to become an Eagle Scout was too much like school for me to take an interest in it. Anyway, the Explorer Uniform, my several merit badges, and the first class patch were enough for me. I was the only Explorer in our Troop. I remember one camping trip to the Blue Hills back when beautiful forests surrounded them. I was the troop bugler and would stand on top of an enormous boulder which overlooked our site and play taps at night, and reveille in the morning on my father's silver trumpet.

I enjoyed being the lone Explorer on top of the boulder playing my best; you could get emotional with taps. Once I went on a (Explorer Scouts only) four day, 30-mile canoe trip in the mountains of Maine and we had one of those guys that everyone likes; blond, muscular, loved by all girls and envied by all the boys, including me; a regular Aryan Ubermensch. Our leader was a 72-year-old forest ranger (my age as I write this) with legs like steel pistons. I remember following him up an almost vertical mountain panting like a dog, and he kept up his pace as we fell by the pathway one after another, and he finally looked back and saw that there were only pretty boy lugging our canoe behind him and me, and he said "I guess you boys need to rest."

I have never forgotten his legs, they looked like they couldn't be over 22 years old and yet his face was 72. When we made it down the mountain with all our canoes (did I mention that we were carrying them up on our backs?), we set out on the fun part of our adventure. That first night the clouds came up, and the thunder and lightning started at around three in the morning. We were all camping under our canoes in the sand, and I woke with a shock to a Clap of thunder and blinding light. Lightning hit the canoe next to me, and as I lay there wondering if I was next, I became aware of a presence way above me in the sky. I could see Him on the level of feeling, It was sort of like the way you would feel as a child when your mother was leaning over you as you lay in bed and she was whispering nighty-night, sweet dreams, only it felt like a giant male father kind of being, smiling and assuring me all was well.

Some kids were crying and screaming, and I couldn't help wondering why they weren't aware of the Big Dad in the sky. After four days of wild rapids, overturned canoes and camping on the mosquito and sand-flea infested sandy banks, we found ourselves out of the mountains and moving with the current into the forested outskirts of our first town since starting our voyage. The early signs of "civilization" were two canoes with smiling Girl Scouts who were paddling around just offshore from their camp area. My two canoe mates and I paddled up to one of the canoes with three girls and said "hi, where you girls from?" one of them said "Brookline" and my mate said, "Ricky here is from Brookline."

A quick glance and she knew I was shy and didn't want any part of me. I soon noticed that Pretty Boy had been grabbed up by one of the older girls and they were already making plans. It turned out that we were going to camp on the opposite shore from the Girl Scouts and several of the boys had already made dates to meet after taps. I longed for some female attention, but I had never even kissed a girl, and it all made me feel lonely. The next morning around the breakfast campfire, Pretty Boy, and a few others exchanged their conquest stories and waved goodbye to their one night stands across the river as we set out toward our final rendezvous.

BOB RE-UPS

When Bob re-joined the Army our family life forever changed. My dear Mother and little brother all flew away to Mannheim Germany where Bob was to be an editor for the Stars & Stripes newspaper. I was supposed to stay and live with my Father and my stepmother Barbara in a tiny house in the woods of Scituate Mass. Occasionally, Barbara let me use her convertible, a sweet car that she lent me so that I could go on dates or down to Weymouth to stay with Grammy on weekends.

A year or two before the move, when I turned 16, I bought a $40, '48 Ford with a '52 Pontiac straight-six engine in it. It looked odd because the engine didn't quite fit and was installed a little crooked. I got a gallon of fire engine red, gloss enamel from my father's paint store, the Hingham Paint Pot, where I worked during the summer. I didn't have a sprayer, so I hand-brushed the whole car, rough? Yes, but still fire-engine-red! I wanted to be able to pick up girls in it when we went to the Surf Ballroom in Nantasket. Brian Mason was my chick-magnet. He looked like a cross between a skinny Elvis and the diminutive James Dean. Brian had spent his childhood in the rough streets of South Boston and was a crazy-man street fighter. He must have weighed less than 130 lbs., and stood a strapping 5'7," but every inch of him was wiry and insane if you disrespected him. He would kick and fly at you like a wild cougar, hissing, and swearing, picking up whatever he could to kill you. A fight was always life or death with him. At least this was his reputation derived from a few confrontations when he first arrived in Fort Point from the South-End.

He had a rather homely, fellow grammar school dropout buddy named Dave, who was a muscle-bound carpenter. Dave considered himself Brian's best friend and bodyguard. Together, they made a considerable entourage of protection for me if I ever needed them. As it happened, they came in handy at least one time when a massive football jock from Hull didn't like me dancing with his girlfriend at the Surf. Little Brian came up and said, "this guy bothering you Rick?" The jock didn't back off from the little tough guy, but his whole demeanor changed in an instant when he looked above Brian's head and saw, huge, ugly, Dave with his menacing beady eyes. The jock suddenly become overly friendly, backing off and saying "nice to have met you guys" and "see you later." Usually, Brian was a quiet, calm guy, and yet he was fearless when it came to approaching girls. He wouldn't have to talk to them. Brian would glance their way, then turn his head back as if they bored him, and they would be attracted. Over the two years we tried to pick up girls we drove lots of them wherever they wanted to go, but never did sleep or even make out with any until one girl who knew what she wanted, found out where he lived and stalked him, and that was it. He got her pregnant and ended up marrying her.

There was a period, just after our Surf Ballroom times, that Brian expressed an interest in learning to play the guitar and going with me to the coffee houses in Boston. We were both attracted to the college girls and the music, so I began giving him finger-picking guitar lessons. Brian's interest in learning folk guitar meant that he was aspiring to socialize with the literary types that frequented these dens of non-conformists, artists, bohemians, beatniks, and students. I was the son of a non-conformist, bohemian, intellectual mother but Brian was 100% working-class, born and raised, and yet he was going to give it a go.

My girl-magnet friend practiced very hard on his guitar pick-ing, and we were about to begin working on his singing when one day I arrived at his home with my guitar and his mother said that he no longer wanted to play the guitar. When Brian came down from his room he didn't say a word, he just held up his right hand, and I looked closely and realized that he was missing his index finger, it was entirely gone! He said his mind wandered while operating a band saw at work and when he looked down at the piece of wood he was cutting, his am-putated finger lay there in a puddle of blood. He seemed to feel sorry for himself, and at the same time, I could tell that he was relieved. I guess he realized that he would either have to become an exceptional guitarist or get educated to be able to fit into the Folk Club world. I felt the same way, it didn't look like I was going to get into any college, but at least I had read most of the books that were required reading for the pseudo-intellectual. Poor Brian had a fourth-grade education and no adult role models to inspire him.

Now that I look back I realize that he could easily have con-tinued with the guitar by mastering flat-picking style, but at the time I associated that with electric rock n' roll and coun-try-picking; a world away, I thought, from the Coffee Houses. Later the 47 club featured groups like The Kentucky Colonels and The Charles River Valley Boys, both with flat-picking gui-tarists like Clarence White, the best in the world at the time. Anyway, that was the end of our friendship as I was heading off for Germany and my last year of high school. Last I heard of him, he was making his living as a heavy equipment operator and was still married to his faithful stalker.

THE BOSTON/HARVARD-SQUARE FOLK SCENE

Those years before leaving for Germany in 1961 were filled with adventures in my new and exciting world of Music. I would go to the coffee houses that had folk music on weekends and (hoot nights) and learn the picking styles and songs of the performers that I liked. It was my music school - I never had to take lessons on guitar or voice - just studying the best folk singers and bluesmen for a few hours and then going home and trying to figure out what they had done was all I needed. There were Sonny Terry and Brownie McGhee, Jim Kweskin, Geoff Muldaur, Taj Mahal, Eric Von Schmidt, Joan Baez, Bob Dylan, Lightning Hopkins, Maria Muldaur, Buzz and Sally, The Kentucky Colonels, Josh White, Josh White Jr., John Hammond Jr. The Charles River Valley Boys, Mississippi John Hurt, Judy Collins, Tom Rush and many more. While landmarks such as San Francisco and Greenwich Village receive notorious acclaim for creating an American folk utopia during the 1960s, the eclectic roots of traditional folk music are grounded in the streets of Cambridge's Harvard Square. During the years of 1958-1968, 47 Mount Auburn Street in Cambridge, MA was the mecca for lovers of folk music who shared an intimate bond of passionately expressing what was real and meaningful in their lives through music.

Club 47 was founded in 1958 by two women from Brandeis University who initially imagined the club to be an artsy, Paris-inspired coffee house featuring only jazz music. Shortly following the opening of Club 47, the mission of the cafe quickly changed when 17-year-old BU student and folk singer Joan Baez walked through the doors. Although Baez received much skepticism from the club owners about performing folk music in a jazz club, she began playing at the club a couple of times a week. Within three weeks, Club 47 attracted masses of people who were mystified by Baez's graceful singing and sultry melodies. From Joan Baez on, Club 47 became an arena for extraordinarily talented musicians to gather together and share their genuine love for music, which ultimately hastened a metamorphosis in the American music scene. In addition to Baez, Club 47 also sparked the careers of legendary folk artists Tom Rush, Judy Collins, and notably Eric Von Schmidt, who became an emblem for digging up and recreating the instrumental sound of traditional folk music. Von Schmidt is also responsible for influencing a young newcomer to the folk scene who eventually became one of the most important figures in American music and culture -- Bob Dylan.

Once he showcased his talent to the club owners and fellow folk artists, Dylan began working closely with Eric Von Schmidt and soon became a valued performer at the club. More than 50 years following Dylan's Club 47 days, it is interesting to see how the counterculture's father of folk and all-around music legend once spent his early career, jamming with Cambridge artists who shared the communal bond of solely playing for their shared love of music. After ten riveting years of showcasing gifted folk artists, the life of Club 47 came to an end in 1968. The once not-for-profit club transitioned into a capitalist vacuum, making business expenses too overbearing to handle. Not only was the club too expensive to keep open, but the owners felt as though the club no longer served its original purpose of genuinely playing for the love of music.

Joan Baez at the "47"

Teddy Scourtis, one of my brother's friends who lived in an

enormous mansion in Brookline, had a talent for learning instruments and could afford the best. He and I could sing Everly Brothers harmony quite well, and either he or Brian, or my first music partner, John Oliphant, would be found frequenting the Golden Vanity, the 47 Mt. Auburn Club and many other folk clubs that used to be beatnik hangouts, mostly because we just loved the music and the scene.

Sometimes, on "Hoot nights" we would perform. One night I sang Dylan's "Mr. Tambourine Man" at a downtown, Boston folk club called "The Unicorn." The Hoot was broadcast live on the WBZ "Hootenanny" show with Jefferson Kaye. The next day when I went back to ask if they might hire me to open for some famous folksinger, the manager told me that he had gotten over thirty telephone calls wanting to know who I was and when I was going to be playing at the club. That was how timely Bob Dylan's music was; I could sing one of his songs and almost everyone listening to the program wanted to see me in person.

You see, almost no one outside the east coast "folk crowd" had ever heard of Dylan at that time. I had bought his first album before going to Germany for my last year of high school and had learned all his songs and even the harmonica while playing the guitar. That downtown Boston, folk club, Hootenanny got me a job! But I told the manager when he asked if I had more songs like that one, "I didn't write it" and was amazed that he didn't know about Dylan. So, I passed on that gig, not wanting to be known as a Dylan impersonator.

Little did I know at the time just how many Dylan clones were to manifest. Actually, a whole wave of singers - some of the biggest names in Rock & Pop - copied his ragged farmer/cowboy vocal style, which was actually adopted by Dylan from his study of Woody Guthrie: Mick Jagger, John Lennon, Bruce Springsteen, Patti Smith, Conor Oberst, Tom Petty, Neil Young, Jacob Dylan, Arlo Guthrie, Van Morrison's vocal phrasing & The Byrds for sure! Too many to list here.

He gave singers who couldn't sing "pretty," or didn't have a rich baritone like Frank Sinatra, the option of making it just as big as the previous generation of musicians. It became so prevalent that if you didn't sing with a rough growl, people didn't know what to do with you; they didn't think you were "real" or authentic. A good example is Springsteen who sounds unpleasant to me, but is considered "The Boss" by his followers, much like Sinatra was called "The Voice" by his. I guess it dates me to say that Sinatra's voice was profoundly soothing and could pierce the heart with its sincerity. Springsteen sounds sincere but intentionally crude and rough. Like a stocky, constipated Bob Dylan - his muscles all tight and rigid as he stretches his thick neck - veins popping out, trying to force out his rasp of a voice. He is a good pop songwriter; I'll give him that. I don't envy him! I envy Dylan, not for his voice but his lyrics, his pre-70's songs.

GERMANY!

So, at the end of my junior year at Scituate high school, my father drove me to Logan airport, and I boarded a noisy Icelandic Airline's Turbo-beater (not a jet), roaring and vibrating for fourteen hours with no cabin pressure and severe pain stabbing my eardrums. We finally landed in Frankfurt Germany, and Ma was there waiting for me. I was there to finish school and to see Europe, but aside from two school trips to see Sabicas and Montoya in Frankfurt, my last year of high school in Germany is a sore subject with me and I don't want to relive it here.

Then again, I did win a talent contest over there; Teddy won as well with his drumming and saxophone. Several of us who had won the talent show from different parts of occupied Deutschland - all Army brats, - were picked to put on a traveling exhibit for the troops. When we played Berlin, we had to go through the underground into East Germany and the remains of East Berlin. Teddy was a ballsy kid, and when a Russian Vopo (Guard) poked his head up to our open train window, Teddy held out his brownie camera and the Vopo took it and handed him a red hammer and cycle pin he had in his pocket. Teddy lost no time in grabbing and hiding it. I guess one of the GI's had let Ted in on the Vopo pin souvenir trade. I was freaked out that Teddy was gesturing to the Russian guard since we were told not to communicate with them as it was dangerous, and they might decide to search for spies or contraband of some sort.

Again, I wasn't going to say much about my year and a half in Germany, but I have begun remembering some things you might like to hear. We lived up in the hills of Unterflockenbach, just down from Oberflockenbach. Our two bedroom apartment was just above a Gasthaus owned by Frau Schmidt whose husband had been killed in the 2nd World War. One day, she left the glass door open which led from our apartment to another upstairs apartment down the hall. I was curious and peeked into a closet in the hallway and saw a framed photo of a dapper young officer in his storm trooper uniform, his name, Rudolf Schmidt signed under his picture. Then I remembered that they had a statue of several storm troopers in battle stance in back of the public fountain down the Strasse. They didn't like us there, and it was uncomfortable for me since I had already spent my childhood feeling that I didn't fit in anywhere! Except for Grammy's, of course.

THE FOREST FOLLOWER

Typically it was my job to take the strassenbahn (a miniature-sized train - like the trolleys in Boston only much smaller) from just outside of Mannheim, near the army base, all the way to Weinheim, which sat at the foot of a range of long sloping mountains. There were two area names I remember, both separated by a very long walk up the steep winding grade. Unterflockenbach, where I lived above the Gasthaus, and Oberflockenbach, which was two or three miles further up the road. Neither of these places had more than a Gasthaus and a bakery, and I couldn't even find their names on the Google map the other day. Sometimes, on a weekend when I didn't have to get home right after school, I would stay out late and catch the last strassenbahn to Weinheim. The only trouble with this was that I would miss the last bus up the hill from Weinheim to Unterflockenbach, and that would mean walking the five miles uphill with the dark woods on one side and the sealed-up houses on the other. It would take over an hour, and it was a chilly, misty, and sometimes scary walk with all the hill people in bed, and the wooden-slatted, window-shutters all let down. These hardwood shutters were impenetrable and couldn't help but remind you that things weren't always safe around here at night. They all had heavy steel doors that were bolted shut when they went to bed. I often wondered what had initially inspired all this need for protection. Well, it was on one of those chilly, wet nights that I missed my Unterflockenbach bus and found myself trudging up the long and winding road. I had drunk a few of those big steins of beer back in Mannheim and was still feeling slowed down, and not worried all that much about the long haul I had in front of me. I must have been about a mile or so up the road when I heard - over to my left in the dark woods - something or someone moving behind the trees, snapping sticks and crunching leaves as they crept along. It occurred to me that the sounds were timed to my stopping and going so I began to walk fast and then stop abruptly.

There it was - obvious - crunch, snap, crunch, and then nothing. But what in God's name was it? If it was a person I might be in deep shit; if it was some animal, no - they didn't have any animals of any size up there except cows and sheep! What if it was one of those creatures from the "Olde" German stories they told their children - you know - Werewolves and Witches and Vampires. As I continued along, I shouted out at it a few times - hoping to scare it away with loud curses and threats - and I would look to the houses hoping someone would wake up and open their door for me.

No such luck, and the thing wasn't trying very hard to conceal it's footsteps any longer either. I started running, sore feet and all; in fact, this was back when my fallen arches were causing me a lot of pain. When I ran, I would hear it running through the thickets, snapping branches and twigs, and it would get my heart pounding. When I could no longer run, I went over to the edge of the road by the woods and picked up a branch and made a four-foot walking stick out of it. Of course, my intention wasn't to use the stick for walking, but for my ultimate confrontation with whoever or whatever was following me.

After a long five miles of fear and pain, I was only about 300 yards from my Gasthaus apartment, and I didn't want "it" to know that I was almost home, since that might inspire it to break out of the trees and get me before I made it to safety. So, with lame feet, I stayed in the middle of the road so it would look like I still had a way to go. I took up a brisk and stately hiking march, and when I got to the Gasthaus, I ran like a rabbit up the porch stairs and the landing to my door. I peered into the woods across the street and never saw whatever followed me for four miles; it had two legs - maybe some madman who lived in the woods? I don't think so. Perhaps an ex-storm trooper or Dracula? To this day I believe it was one of those things that come out on full moons, but I have no idea which sort of thing that might be!

BOB AND THE BLACKSMITH

The Local Storm-Trooper Blacksmith

The local folks did not care for our presence in Unterflockenbach. In fact, on Christmas Eve, the local blacksmith and one of his cohorts knocked on the door and yelled out "Kris Kringle," and Bob opened the door and stood tall and menacing; maybe I didn't tell you that Bob was an Aryan blond, six-foot-five-inch powerhouse of Swedish meatball and weighed in at around 300 pounds. The two locals were dressed up in dodgy looking Santa Claus outfits, one was in a dirty white outfit, and the blacksmith was in black. This Blacksmith was the strongest man in the area but only about 5'8." They asked for Alex, Bob's son - my half brother - who looked like a perfect little Aryan candidate for the Hitler youth. Alex came to the door and the Black St. Nick said "Sie sind ein unartiger Junge, keine Weihnachtsgeschenke für Sie!" (that's high German, these guys used the local heavy slang) translated "You are a bad boy, no Christmas gifts for you!" Then the black Santa took a handful of charcoal dust from his canvas bag and a hardwood switch and went after little Alex. But Bob, with all his Thor-power, grabbed the burly storm-trooper in black. He picked him up and threw him off the porch, a ten-foot drop down onto the first level of hard concrete. The Black Santa went limping off swearing up a storm waving his fist at Bob. I understood the hill German and knew every one of the bad words he used, as I had worked in an Army laundry for awhile with the most foul-mouthed German ladies I have ever met. Anyone of them could pick me up and throw me wherever she wished; they were so strong, but they loved me and taught me their wonderfully foul language.

THE DIRTY LAUNDRY

That's right, I worked in the Army laundry, staffed by the manager down, with German civilians and a few army brats like me. The lower level manager used to pick girls he was attracted to and take them up into the piles of dirty soldier uniforms. He'd find a spot where no one could see him, and in ten minutes or so he would appear coming around the other side of the pile, and the girl would be seen climbing and falling out of the dirty clothes where he had taken her. My fellow workers would hiss at her, and yell out whore in German, and even spit in her direction. I felt a little compassion for the rape victims of this manipulative sex offender. It was well known that if a girl didn't go up there with him, she would soon be without a job, for some reason he would conveniently invent.

After six months at the laundry, I got a stock boy job at the non-commissioned officer's canteen. There was an SS wannabe with muscles named Wolf who hated Americans with an unusual passion. The German workers and I were all sitting having an amiable lunch break when Wolf, who always drank a few large bottles of Beer with his large Bratwurst, said something about how the Americans would never have won the war if it hadn't been for the Canadians, British, Australians, and all the other allies. He went on that Americans were soft pussies, and he could take any of us in a fight.

After years of street fighting and four years of high school wrestling, football and hockey, I had become unafraid of possible injury, and in this relatively fearless mindset I found it not to hard to make bullies beg off their initial challenge by merely being unafraid and playing with their ridiculous cliche's like, "You want a bloody nose?" My response might be "Not really! Why?" it would depend on the guy. Timing and calm, and a sense of humor underlying everything I said were always essential. Staring directly into their eyes with no fear would make them wonder "what has this guy got that makes him unafraid of me?"

It would also help to get the crowd with you, get them laughing at the bully's stupid statements so that he would feel like a fool proceeding with his attack. If he did attack in wild anger, he would be vulnerable like I was when I attacked Tommy Hamilton in a rage. The crowd was usually with me as I was often the underdog at 145 lbs and skinny. Bullies don't pick on guys their size, except for PD, of course. These days, this advice doesn't apply if the tyrant is crazed on methamphetamine or some other wicked drug.

TEDDY VS THE JAGER-MEISTER

Another bully was Yeager, an acne-pocked jock on the Mannheim American high-school football team. He was a tackle and had attained one of the most beautiful girls as his girlfriend. Teddy, as you know, was not afraid to approach girls, and he managed to get this beauty out in the countryside. As Ted told me later, they both took off their clothes and frolicked in the grass. He claims they made love and that she had the most beautiful body he had ever seen.

Well, all this would have gone unnoticed if it weren't for Teddy's big mouth, he challenged the 250-pound tackle to a fight across the street from the community center that our mother ran. Teddy asked if I would second him, we still had some leftover fighting rules from the 19th century back then, I guess? There they stood opposite each other with their arms up in a boxer's stance. My skinny little brother who was about four inches shorter than me at 5'11" him at 5'7" or so. The tackle was at least 6 foot 2" and big. He had a face like a moon, cratered with acne all over, even his arms and back; he was ugly as hell. Then it began, Yeager swung a round-house at Teddy and Teddy, in good form, quickly hopped onto his back foot which would have worked for him, but my dear little brother was never given mother's milk, and his bones were so brittle that his leg fractured and down he went onto the ground; all from jumping back with his 130 pounds of weight onto his fragile leg. The tackle couldn't believe that Teddy was hurt and started to kick him while he was down, holding his broken leg.

So I got up in Quasimodo's face and screamed, "his leg is broken, leave him alone. By then my mother had been told about what happened and arrived on the scene. She said we had to get Teddy to the dispensary, so I picked him up in my arms and carried him the fifty or so yards down the street. I don't think the girl would have gone with Teddy even if he had won the battle, she just wanted to be with the guy on the football team, and Teddy was the local intellectual and transcendentalist; the leader of the Geek Squad. She didn't even come to the fight that cost Teddy his ability to walk for over half a year.

BLOB VS. RICK

Teddy was drinking like a German on holiday. One evening he came up from the Gasthaus after downing 25 Steinhagers. That's like twenty-five shots of whiskey all going into the nervous system of a 16-year-old boy. When Teddy came in the front door, Bob met him and said: "you been drinking?" Teddy tried to talk, but his mouth didn't work too well, and Bob lost his temper and slapped my little brother across the face so that Ted smashed into the glass door and almost lost consciousness.

Bob, was our mutual enemy. He was an extreme alcoholic and had thrown my mother into a glass cabinet in the living room one night. That night he was entirely naked and was trying to get her to go to the bedroom with him, but she put up a valiant fight to ward him off, and he ultimately pushed her into the cabinet. Little Alex watched as his mother tried to extricate herself from the wood and glass which tore rips in her arms and legs and she was bleeding all over and crying. into the cabinet. Little Alex watched as his mother tried to extricate herself from the wood and glass which tore rips in her arms and legs and she was bleeding all over and crying.

Alex developed a severe case of Asthma from that experience, and I formed the intention to beat the living shit out of him if he ever became physical with anyone of us again. Well, here was my chance: I picked up my rock-maple baseball bat and started for "Blob" who was down the hall about to hit teddy again. I howled with the rage of a mother grizzly protecting her cub and Bob hardly believed what he was seeing and hearing. He had thrown down that one last straw that is supposed to break the camel's back, and I was out to protect my blood brother if it cost me my life.

Bob, became sober in those few seconds and he quickly left the apartment to defuse the situation. A few days later, Bob said he wanted to talk to me in the kitchen. Well, it was my time to leave home, and I could see that it was coming from my mother as well as from Bob Jones. He advised that I join the Navy; he had been in the army earlier in the 50's, and it had ruined his life to see all his close buddies blown up around him in N. Korea. He seemed to care about what he was telling me, and I did as he recommended; after all the draft was grabbing us all up back then, and I wanted to see the deep ocean and sail to foreign lands on a great ship - even if it didn't have sails.

MY SPAIN ADVENTURE

With all the money I had saved working in Mannheim and Heidelberg during my last year in Germany, I took a train to Barcelona Spain with the intention of buying a handmade flamenco guitar and taking some lessons. I got the guitar and a lesson from a gypsy guitarist in a flamenco bar. He was confused when I offered him money instead of his female dancer, who was supposed to get you to buy her drinks. He was pleasantly surprised to find a guitar student in this bar scene and proceeded to hand me his guitar, and after I showed him what I could do, he gave me some excellent guidance in the Soleares form of flamenco, my favorite.

When I left the bar, I was accosted on the street by a woman holding the hand of her little girl, five or six years old. She pointed at the girl and then looked at me and started to take the little girls hand to put in mine, and I got the gist. I was astounded that a mother could offer her child in prostitution to some strange American - to anyone for that matter! And I raised my hand as if to hit the woman, yelling at the top of my lungs for her to get the hell out of my sight!

I walked back to my hotel, and about a block away from it I noticed that two toughs about my age were following me closely. I was a little tipsy and thought I'll scare these guys with my German switchblade you know, you press a button, and the blade comes out with a dramatic swish and click sound. So I pull out my knife and turn around to face these two. I had some trouble getting the blade to switch as they stood there with amused looks on their faces. In a flash, they both drew knives and flicked them open with a twist of the thumb and then palmed them so that they held the blades with only an inch showing from their hands. This is the way they fight so that they don't kill you; they just cut you to ribbons. Then they both smiled and started toward me. By this time I realized that I was in way deeper than I had imagined, and made a run for my hotel, just a few hundred feet up the street. They came after me, but I flew into the hotel lobby just as they were grabbing for my shirt. What was I thinking bringing a knife to Spain? They are famous for their knife fighting; everyone carries a knife in Spain.

The next day I took the train back to Germany, where I hopped an Army transport plane for Boston and joined the Navy in the town of Quincy Mass. There are a few interesting stories I can tell about my time in the Navy. I went for basic training in the Great Lakes on a cold strip of land north of Chicago. I remember one night I was on guard duty with my little white summer cap and my shaved head, and wide open neck to the 20 mile an hour freezing wind blowing off the lake. I had to stand there feeling the 40 below zero wind-chill stiffening my body for four hours in one spot. I tend to follow my mother's constitutional weakness for bronchitis and pneumonia, and the next day I was sent to the base hospital. Two weeks of penicillin shots in the butt and a chest filled with endless mucus; you know, sick as can be.

Boot-camp Salon

They allowed me to wear a wool watch cap after that and a wool sweater under my jumper and pea coat. Two pairs of socks barely helped keep my feet from freezing, but I would try to walk about in a circle when there weren't any petty officers around. Not long before "graduation," they asked if any of us could sing and said there would be tryouts for the "Blue Jacket's Choir." I went in for the audition and I could hear the guy before me singing the melody from a piece of sheet music. I thought "Oh crap! I can't read music - maybe if I listen closely I can remember the melody and fake it."

My time came and I walked in and sat down in front of the petty officer, and he said to take the sheet music and sing the song. So, I picked it up and looked it over - as if I knew what I was looking at - and he blew a pitch pipe and I sang "mm mm" to it - then I began singing what I had heard the other guy sing. The P. Officer smiled and said, "very good. You will report to the Blue Jacket's Choir tomorrow" (at such and such an hour, you know 2300 hours or something?). When I got back to the barracks, the other guys were curious to know if I made it; if you did, it meant you got out of all kinds of crappy work details, like swabbing and scrubbing the bathroom "deck" endlessly until they gave you something else to do like march and march and march.

One of the recruits in our building turned out to be the choir leader. He had graduated music school from an Ivy league college, and the only reason he wasn't an officer was because he didn't want to commit to the added years he would have to be in the Navy as an officer. He had been given the option to become a 2nd class petty officer upon graduating from basic training. Anyway, he knew what he was doing and I was up with the baritones listening intently to my right and left for a clue as to what the sheet music indicated. It usually took a few times through the part for me to remember my part by ear.

Just Out Of Boot Camp

After a while, I could sing all my parts without listening to my neighbor. We were scheduled to go to Washington DC to sing for President Kennedy when I got that bout of pneumonia, and I missed out on the trip. I can't remember what happened after that, except that we were all tested and tested for days on end to find out what each of us was good at or could be useful doing for the Navy. They had a need for Radiomen at the time, and I really had no choice - they decided I would be a good radioman as I could already type and had an ear for music, which they thought might work for listening on headphones to Morse code and typing the code into or out of crypto hour after hour. So, they sent me off to Radioman 'A' school in Bainbridge MD. Before I officially reported to Radio school, I checked out the town off-base for any coffee houses that had Folk Singers on the weekends and found one good one. I auditioned one hoot night - they call them open-mic now - and right away they signed me up to open for Mississippi John Hurt in another month. I had learned a few Delta blues songs off of a John Hurt album earlier on and loved his finger-picking style.

MISSISSIPPI JOHN HURT

After an anxious month of expectation, the big night came, and I managed to get liberty. I figured I wouldn't play any blues when the master himself was present, so I brought my flamenco guitar and got up and played some pseudo-Solareas. Then I sang some of the ballads I loved, like "I never will marry" that I learned from Buzzy and Sally at the Golden Vanity coffee house in Boston when I was 17. I'm sure I probably did a few Dylan songs, trying as best I could to imitate him. I loved and respected his music too much to put my spin on it. After my set I went backstage and was talking to the owner of the club who was worried that Mississippi John hadn't shown up as yet; he wanted to know if I could fill up the rest of the evening for John.

I didn't have two sets of polished music, having just got out of boot camp where I wasn't able to play at all for three months. But I felt it was imperative that I try and save the day and come up with as many songs as I could remember of the two hundred I once had in my repertoire. Then I heard some loud talking and laughing coming from the front, and Mississippi John Hurt sauntered through the door with a big smile on his face. I stood up and shook hands with him, and noticed that my hand hurt from his grip, so I shook it out, and he said, "oh, sorry! I do a lot of farming, use my hands." He pulled out his Martin steel string and started tuning it up. He asked if I'd give him a D; I did, and he was in tune in about five seconds. He said, "play me some of that Spanish guitar," and I began doing my best. Then he said, "here try it on this," and he handed me his Martin. I couldn't even get one string to make a sound; the action of his strings was so far above the neck that you would have to have hands of iron to play the thing. He enjoyed my difficulty. Then he took it and started to play one of his sweet blues with all that alternating bass and his deep voice just rumbling like thunder like it was going through a bass amp.

RADIOMAN 'A' SCHOOL

Back to Radio School: Of course I had reported for duty a month before and was attending all my classes to become a Radioman. We had to learn typing, which I had already learned in high school, but here we were learning to translate Morse Code into numbers and the letters of the alphabet from our headphones to the typewriter keys. After a year of typing in rhythm to the same bloody song, "The Battle of New Orleans" by Johnny Horton, we went on to study electronics theory in depth. I had to take it for a second six months course as I couldn't concentrate on it. It was, perhaps the single most boring subject I have ever studied, or should I say ignored? Even though I barely passed electronics theory with a C, my typing skill and all the other things we studied were enough to get me out of Bainbridge and assigned to my next duty, the U.S.S. Eldorado, flagship to the seventh fleet out of San Diego, California. I remember those last few days of excitement as we waited to see our next duty-assignment up on the big board in the hall. We were all worried that we might get one of the only duties in the Navy at the time of Vietnam where you were likely to get killed by an enemy - the Mekong Delta fast boats, of Sec. of State, John Kerry fame. It was pretty well known to all of us that if you saw duty on one of them you were in deep shit. Those who did would often get picked off by Viet Cong, sniping from both sides of the river. Of course being a "Navy Frogman" (or "Navy Seal" in current terminology) was even more dangerous.

SAN DIEGO & THE ELDORADO

Before my ship sailed for the South Pacific from San Diego, I had been performing at the local folk clubs and making friends with the folk singers of southern California, especially in San Diego and LA. The first place I found was the Heritage, out in Mission Beach which was owned by two Irishmen. One weekend I opened for the Simon Sisters, Carly and Lucy. They were both cute and friendly, sang nice harmony, and were in the blush of their new career. I think I sang a mix of blues and ballads; I know I did one where I cupped the harp (harmonica) in my hands over the microphone so that it sounded like Paul Butterfield or John Hammond Jr. I'm sure I got the song from John Hammond; I used to emulate and imitate both Hammond and Dylan.

HOW TO MAKE FRIENDS AND IN-
FLUENCE MUSICIANS

To become friends with the musicians back then you had to prove you weren't a narc. The only way to do that when you looked like me - a Navy man with very short hair - was to go down to Tijuana, "score" some pot, bring it back for your new "friends," roll a joint and take the first toke. Otherwise, there would always be a barrier of suspicion between you and the others. Smoking a few joints with them had been my first experience with marijuana, so being a short-haired newbie, I agreed to make the trip if they supplied the car. One of them, a girl named Ann, volunteered to go with me, much to my relief.

We drove over the Mexican border and went to the Long-branch Saloon where Ann knew a guy who sold pot. We got our little bag - they called it a lid - and went into another bar for a beer; we hadn't been sitting more than five minutes when Ann spotted a Mexican cop peeking through the window of the bar. She told me to take the bag to the bathroom and hide it up in the water tank. I made my way back to the head and did as she said then flushed to make my actions more convincing. As soon as I sat down, the cop came through the swinging doors, not unlike an old western movie scene. He came right up to us and demanded to see our licenses. We were amazingly unafraid as he patted us down. We were all innocence and light, and he was perplexed that we had nothing on us or around us that could warrant our arrest.

So he just stood there going on about drugs in Spanish, and we held our hands up in the air as if we had no idea what he was on about. Finally, he left, looking both dismayed and disappointed. I guess he didn't have any pot on him that he could plant on us. I'll bet the guy who sold us the weed got an earful; both of them stood to make money had their gringo scam prevailed. We were worried that they knew our car, and had notified the border cops; so we drove up in the line and tried to make jokes and do a little kissy-face to keep from looking scared (fear, the dead giveaway).

I didn't know where Ann had stashed the pot! But sure enough they pulled us over, and Ann went with a lady cop for the pat down, and I went with a male; meanwhile, they searched the car, and scary thoughts of ten years in the Tijuana jail went through my mind. Well, they didn't find it, and I am still amazed that I made it out of that insane attempt at making friends without getting caught. As soon as we were on our way to San Diego, Ann put her hand under the seat and pulled out the pot! It was hidden in the springs of her seat; the seat cover had been cut to slide in the bag. I guess this wasn't her first run; I think she got off on adrenaline and danger. Since that day in 1965, I have never considered buying drugs!

When we got to Ted Stack's house and handed over the bag,

Ann showed me how to roll a joint, but I soaked the paper with my saliva to such a degree that she didn't want me to continue and rolled it herself. As soon as I had taken a deep inhale of this nasty stuff, they all seemed to relax and treat me like a fellow musician. Grass does enhance paranoia, especially if there is something to be paranoid about. There were five or six of us there - they were all in the kitchen making food, and I sat on the floor in the living room, playing my guitar and humming some melody that felt good with the chord progression. Something kind of magic was happening, and I turned on Stack's reel to reel tape recorder and closed my eyes; something beautiful was coming through me - much too beautiful to have been just me.

SUBCONSCIOUS MUSIC LEAKS OUT

When I came out of the reverie of musical possession, I turned off the recorder. Just then Stack and the others came into the room, and he said: "who was that you were playing on the recorder?" I said "me!" and he laughed and said "right, who was it?" I said, "it was me, I just recorded a song I was writing." He came over and turned the recorder on and played back what I had just recorded. He said "Shit! that is you, why haven't you played anything like that for us before?" I said, "it just came through me after that joint." I could tell that Stack was freaked out because he thought he had me nicely placed way below him, first as a swabby and second as a Dylan, John Hammond, mimic and not in the same league with the California singer-songwriters like him, and some of the others. It was about then that the girls in this little folk scene started to pay a bit more attention to me.

Jo Ellen and her sister were from a southern, music family; they could play banjo and guitar and sing Everly Brother's harmony. Their father had been a professional country musician way back when Country wasn't much different than the Scots/Irish mountain ballads brought over in the 18th & 19th centuries. I had a dreadful fear of getting girls pregnant or getting some nasty, creeping sexual scourge, something my mother had vigorously instilled in my nature. Having seen my 1st cousin get a 15-year-old girl pregnant when he was 17, made my fear like an adamantine lock on my privates.

"Poor guy" my father bemoaned about cousin Jack, hoping we would take his youthful indiscretion to heart and I did. The academically gifted lad, cousin Jack, was about to get a scholarship into the Ivy league and perhaps a straight path to financial and social "success," but back then there was no such thing as abortion or any way out of the situation other than to marry the girl and get a job. He worked the rest of his work-life in supermarkets, ultimately achieving the status of Butcher in the meat department of his local A&P.

Now, he's long since divorced and retired to Florida. Being of Viking heritage and a one time disciple of my father's family sailing passion, he has spent the last two decades sailing the islands from Key West to the Dry Tortuga's in his little sloop.

But again, I've rambled! I meant to say that the beautiful Jo Ellen made it clear she would like to share her bed with me after my pot induced song had revealed some latent-lady-attracting talent. I had heard some rumor about her and very demurely declined her sweet invitation, again fearing pregnancy or worse.

SHERRY CONCEIVETH

I have missed out on quite a few sailor's dreams due to fear of the responsibility of impregnation that my mother and father instilled in my young heart. I sometimes regret not being more open to these rare invitations for intimacy. Jo Ellen was one of those missed opportunities. Jo Ellen, Ted Stack, and several others were part of the San Diego folk music scene, centered around the Heritage and a few other Folk Clubs. There was a voluptuous singer - "Buxom Bonnie" I'll call her -

who could take the roof off with her big voice. She lived with two roommates: Ann, who I had the Tijuana adventure with, and Sherry (a sailor's dream), who I had once seen performing at a hoot. I ran into the whole crew when I came to visit Ann. It turned out Ann and Bonnie were going to the movies that night, which left me to get to know Sherry. I wasn't good looking enough for Sherry's taste - at least that's the impression I got from Ann when I asked her who that blond was, playing in the jug band the week before.

Sherry put on the new Bob Dylan album, "Bringing it all Back Home," with the song "She Belongs to Me" on it, and pulled out a joint, lit it and offered it to me. I couldn't believe how powerful Dylan's music was back then when it was indeed the back and foreground music of our lives. We started to slow dance and ended up on the couch. In what seemed like a moment, Sherry made a surprised squeal of delight and looked at me as if I had just given her a million dollars; then, almost on cue, Ann and Bonnie came in the front door and saw us entwined in the living room. Ann started to act like Sherry, and I had gone behind her back, but she knew very well that she had been treating me like an ignorant swabby, using me to temper her recent dumpage.

Her boyfriend, who was a talented songwriter, evidently didn't feel she was cool enough for him. I'd seen how he treated her, and yet she was still in love with him. That was a special night: Dylan and a joint, and a beautiful surfer girl with long blond hair, huge blue eyes and cream-soft skin. Sherry and I went to see Dylan when he came to the local college on his tour. Soon after, I was on my way to LA and destiny, I suppose! A relatively recent update to that evening with Sherry: I think that hour or so of intimacy created a beautiful child who I never knew was mine until almost half a century later!

ZOYA AND PAMELA

At about this time I drove my BSA, 650 motorcycle up to LA

with my guitar on my back. That was a long haul on a bike non-stop. When I got there, I went to the Troubadour, the meeting place and audition venue for most of us during the 60's. I had planned it so I would get there on a hoot night, and I ran into a girl named Zoya whom I had met at the Hermitage coffeehouse in San Diego. She offered me a place to sleep and gave me directions; it was way out in the Valley back when all there was around her father's Hacienda was desert, cactus, long grass and eucalyptus trees. Her father was Mr. Kruscamp, a Russian emigre who had gotten rich as a professional wrestler.

Pamela

The next morning Zoya played a few demos that Pamela Polland had given her. Pamela was a friend of hers, and Ry Cooder used to play with Pam at the Troubadour. These demos were of her and Ry, and I had never heard either of them before. I was amazed at Ry's guitar playing - way ahead of everyone else - and also Pamela's songwriting; it was just how I would have loved to be able to write and play the guitar. Another club on the outskirts of San Diego was a place I liked to play; I think it was called "The Bad Egg." Naw! It wasn't; I don't remember the name, there were so many little clubs back then. The owner would give me a percentage of his take for the night. This club was where I first saw Sherry performing with a jug band. One night I arrived to find Dino Valenti on stage. He had just started singing this song, "Get Together," which was later made famous by The Young-bloods...you know:

"C'amon people now smile on your brother;

everybody get together try to love one another right now."

This great songwriter and visionary grew up in a family of gypsies who owned a carnival. He could sing and dance and play any instrument you put in his hands. Dino was the lead singer for the "Quicksilver Messenger Service" of San Francisco after he had done two years for marijuana possession. To pay for his lawyer he sold "Get Together" the true anthem of the 60's, and at the time he figured he could just write another song. I was mind blown, as we used to say, sitting just in front of him I could hear the power of his soul and his words. For me, only Dino, Dylan, Tim Hardin, Judy Collin's voice and Pete Seeger's "Turn, Turn, Turn," moved me to the depth of my heart until Joni Mitchell, Cat Stevens, and James Taylor, the next generation of Masters, stole the show.

MORE SUBCONSCIOUS MUSIC

On weekend liberty, Sherry and I went up to LA for a Folk Festival at UCLA. Sherry had a friend who managed the Ash Grove Folk Club, probably second only to the Troubadour in its longevity and caliber of performers. We sacked out on a couple of sofas, and the next day we made it over to the campus. There were some of the greatest Delta blues players in attendance: Fred McDowell, Son House, and many others. We went out and sat in the grass for awhile. I started to play my guitar and hum as I did at Stack's house in San Diego, and after some time I heard a lot of clapping, and it seemed that it woke me from a dream. I opened my eyes and looked around to see that we were surrounded by students, maybe over a hundred or so all clapping and staring at me. I looked at Sherry and said what did I play? She looked puzzled, and I figured that my muse had struck again. When they wanted me to continue, I started to sing one of the songs I usually do and lost their interest during the first verse. What was this power that came from within? This was the second time it happened, and I knew I had to figure out how to conjure it up at will. It seemed like it must be something like this that came through Dylan; all he had to do was stand up there and sing with his Woody Guthrie-imitation-voice, those incredible drug-induced lyrics, his photographic memory, and as if by magic, he would communicate with our generation like some Svengali or force of Nature.

Of course, lots of stuff happened during my time in San Diego, before the Eldorado sailed for the south seas. Emo, my Marine buddy, and I rode our Bikes down to Mexico at crazy speeds! Emo seemed to think he was invincible, going 95 around mountain passes with pebbles all over the road. We flew down to Tijuana, through the mountains to Ensenada and back without incident. However, one evening he was speeding in downtown San Diego and caught the attention of one of those 6'6" motorcycle cops with the Nazi pantaloons. I happened to be on the back of his 750 Norton, and I screamed in his ear to pull over. Instead, he rev'd-round a sudden corner into a dark, narrow alleyway, and we found ourselves going 45mph, heading straight for a dead-end brick wall. Emo slammed his brakes on, but we were on gravel, and he just kept going straight for the wall. I figured I had better make a jump for it, and just pushed off the back footrests into the air, and came down on my hands and knees. I slid about 15 feet on my face. Emo deftly slide-turned and skidded an abrupt 90 degrees with gravel and dirt flying, and came to a perfect, Evel Knievel stop, six feet from the wall. I was on the ground, with my hands all bloodied and pierced with sharp gravel. Emo thought my attempt at saving myself was funny, and at the same time, he was a bit upset that I hadn't trusted his driving ability. I was pissed off, knowing that it would be some time before I would be able to play the guitar again. I still have a few of those bits of gravel permanently buried deep in my palms after almost 50 years, but we did shake the storm-trooper.

U.S.S. ELDORADO AGC 11

When I first arrived in San Diego, everything was so brilliant, so sunny, bright, and clean, and the ocean made me feel like a young tar back in the days of the wooden ships with square sails. I put on my dress blues, marched up the gangplank of the U.S.S. Eldorado, and got just a little nervous as I saw the officer on watch at the top. I thought, how will I salute him with my duffle-bag over my right shoulder? And I quickly switched it to my left, and just then I was in front of him. I said, "seaman apprentice, Radioman Stanley requesting permission to come aboard sir." He responded with "Your orders, seaman apprentice" "My orders sir." He looked them over for a second and saluted and said "permission to come aboard."

I can't remember what happened next, but I eventually made it down to the main radio shack, radio#1 Main Comm. There was a friendly Chief Petty Officer there who had a self-proclaimed, "old salt" seaman, show me down to my bunk and my 12"x 12" storage locker. The food was good! The best I'd ever had on a regular basis. Running up and down the ladders, with your hands and arms doing most of the work, gets your upper body in pretty good shape after several months. We were running messages up to the Captain and the Admiral. The Eldorado was the communications flagship for the 7th fleet. I think we first picked up our Admiral either, over in Subic Bay, Philippines, or maybe in Okinawa, not sure! But they made quite a formal festivity out of it when he came aboard.

The Admiral's staff came on first, with all of us assembled on deck at attention in our dress white's, trying not to turn our heads to look at the fancy officers and non-coms. They stood out, with their super starched whites and all that gold on the hats and arms of the Chiefs and the Officers. One old Chief had so many gold hash marks on his arm that they went from his cuff all the way up to his Master Chief insignia. (a hash-mark is a year of service, not a poop-stain) One of our petty officers said that the old Chief had been with this Admiral since the second world war when he saved his life.

Back then they were just seaman and Lt. JG. Now, the Chief was one of the most powerful non-cons in the Navy; he could get anything he wanted, and most of the officers treated him with great deference. When our Admiral came aboard with his entourage, the Gunnery Officer would no doubt have given him a 17 gun salute, but since we only had a few anti-aircraft guns, the two guns shot off seven or eight rounds in his honor. The Admiral showed up when we were about to go into maneuvers across the South China Sea, 800 miles to the coast of Vietnam, with a task force of the 7th fleet around us: destroyers, destroyer escorts and one of the largest aircraft carriers within striking range of us.

Time-jumping to now, I talked with a guy today at the Paradiso coffee shop in Fairfield Iowa, and he told me that I had been a part of the Tonkin Gulf crisis, which was the primary motivating factor for the massive buildup of the US war machine aimed at Vietnam. Well, I checked it out, and the Navy says that two destroyers were involved in a shootout with three Russian made PT boats, or fast boats as they call them now. The official story is that the PT boats attacked one of the destroyers, the Maddox, with a machine gun and left two bullets in the hull. The US responded by ordering another destroyer to help the Maddox to fight them off.

How can you hurt a destroyer with machine gun fire? You

can't unless you manage to hit some sailor standing out on deck. So, the destroyers scared off the fast boats, and the US president made it look like a major attack on our Navy by the North Vietnamese. Two bullets were the reason we went to war and killed millions of Vietnamese, who killed something like 50,000. of our young men. A big waste of my time as well! My direct experience of what they call the Tonkin Crisis was a different story altogether and one I wouldn't tell if anyone cared enough to shut me up after over half a century of post-Vietnam brainwashing.

MY EXPERIENCE OF THE "TONKIN CRISIS"

We were anchored a mile or so off Danang South Vietnam, with radio silence and all lights out. Most of the crew was doing four-on four-off, and I was getting off watch, and walking along the port rail when I heard a boat motor going alongside our ship. I knew very well that we were under total silence, which meant the whole task force, so this couldn't be any one of our boats motoring by. I looked out into the dark and couldn't see the craft, but it was very near us. I popped into the radar room, and all the guys on watch were playing poker, and not one of them looking at the radar screen. You had to stand up and look down to see it. I glanced at it and saw a blip right next to us, and I said "Jesus, you guys, there is a boat just alongside us check out the screen, it's on there, and I just heard it out there on the starboard side! Those guys stared at me like I must be playing a joke on them. They didn't know me, and I was a radioman - just a seaman at that. They were radar-men, and who the hell is this sparky telling us how to do our job? But the first class petty officer didn't want a radioman to get the credit for finding a potential threat on his very own radar screen. So he stood up and ambled over, very deliberate in his lack of emergency. He glanced down at the screen ready to blast me for messing with them, but instead, he howled out, "Fuck me! There's a boat to starboard," and he immediately called up to the bridge, taking full credit for the discovery.

The next morning I was again on watch when I was given orders to send to one of our destroyers. I sent the message, which was in code, so I didn't know what it was about until I was relieved of my watch and went on deck to see if there was any sight of the boat that passed us the night before. Well, there it was just offshore. It looked as if the sailors aboard her were trying to ditch her in a frenzy. Then, I heard the engines of a ship roar, and I looked toward our stern - off about five hundred yards there was that destroyer I had sent the morning's message. She was backing up like a fast car; I had never seen a ship backup fast like that. Then she turned and faced the PT boat, which was about a mile away, and lunged almost out of the water toward the hapless 62-foot craft. It only took a minute or so for the destroyer to come along broadside of the little boat, about a hundred yards from her. The big guns on the destroyer suddenly swiveled in unison as they automatically aimed at the target. Then "BLAM," they all went off together with a great fire and smoke and the destroyer almost turning over in the water with the force of the volley. I looked at the PT boat: what I saw was debris flying in a 360-degree circle from the point of where the craft had been. All that remained of her was a plume of smoke and fire, and the sea was dark and calm.

Now, what exactly did I witness? What had this to do with the Tonkin Gulf Crisis? Was this one of the supposed, three PT boats that had made a run from the fighter jets and the two destroyers, or the only PT boat involved? Johnson got us deeply involved in the Vietnam War using the Tonkin episode as his excuse. That little boat that went by us the night before didn't even fire a shot, and it didn't have any torpedoes on board either. I suppose our task force was ordered to destroy any Vietnamese PT boats if we came across them, and we certainly did. It seemed ridiculous at the time to send a destroyer after a little unarmed PT boat. We could easily have captured her! I wonder if she really had North Vietnamese aboard in the first place?

Maybe it was a couple of our UDT frogmen who had been ordered to sail her past us the previous night and sit and wait for our destroyer to blow her up? I did see a couple of men in her shortly before the destroyer blew her up; I'll bet they just jumped overboard in their froggy gear and swam away to shore under water. This probable scenario would go along with the general intelligence about Tonkin being just a ruse to give Johnson his excuse to upscale our involvement in the area dramatically. It turns out that the PT boat was Russian-made from WWII.

KOREA

We headed north toward South Korea and Japan after this and had a fun liberty in Incheon; the country pub-girls were so innocent and childlike. All the sailors sat around big round tables with colorful paper hanging decorations all around us. The pretty girls all giggling and lively, sat with us, and I don't think many of us even thought about sex. It was like a fun party with friends; these were not prostitutes but local country girls out for an evening of dancing, drinking, and flirting with a whole room full of very interested young men.

However, there must have been one lady of the night; as I passed a room on my way to the bathroom, I saw a sailor's shoes and a pair of elegant high heels placed in front of the door. I was a bit tipsy I guess because I took the girl's high heels and carried them on my way to the AAV (personnel carrier boat), which was almost due to take us back to the Eldorado anchored in the bay. Another sailor and I were walking the dirt path back to the harbor when two girls came up to us and spoke to us in very broken "Engrish." We understood the gist of it, and I said, "I don't have any money," and handed one of them the high heels, which greatly offended her. Still, she grabbed my hand and dragged me to what looked like an animal shelter, with a dirt floor and a makeshift cot on the ground.

She started to pull my shirt up and over my head, and I realized that she didn't believe me about not having any money, so I attempted to hand her the high heels again, and she yelled something at me in a very irritated tone. I threw the shoes onto her funky cot and walked out with her following and screaming Korean at me all the way back to the path. As we roared out to sea from shore I could still see her - she had the shoes, and she threw them into the bay and tromped off. Might I have transgressed some essential laws of Korean etiquette?

ENGRISH TEACH-O

As the sun came up, we docked for liberty in Seoul, a comparatively large city. My best buddy "Emo" - that was his last name - most of us called each other by our last names - that's the military way! Anyway, happy to be off the ship, Emo and I were walking in downtown Seoul when two little Korean men dressed in jackets and ties approached us. They asked if we would mind teaching English to their students, just for an hour today and an hour tomorrow. We said we didn't have any experience teaching, and they just laughed and took us to the school.

Emo was introduced to one classroom full of around forty students about 6th or 7th graders, and I was led to another. The teacher told me to draw a picture of whatever the word meant on the chalkboard and write the word next to it, then say the word in English and have the students say the word in Korean; I was to repeat the word in English several times, then have them do the same. I drew a picture of a side-view of a man's head. Then I wrote the word "head," and pointed to the picture and said "head." Well, I went on like this for awhile, and I got a lot of laughs at my attempts to draw things, and even more at my facial contortions, trying to pronounce the words in Korean.

Finally, a kid in the back, who had been irritating me by making faces and imitating my bad Korean, started yawning and making disruptive noises, probably out of boredom. I started imitating him and making the looks that he was making at me, and the whole class began doing what I was doing just when the real teacher came in. He thought that I must be doing something right as I had the entire class in an uproar of laughter. He wanted Emo and me to come back the next day, and so we did. We used up our liberty teaching English, instead of hanging out in the bars with the rest of our mates and made a lifelong memory of doing something constructive in the midst of the utterly destructive purpose of the war machine.

JAPAN

Next stop was Yokosuka, where the US Navy docked near Tokyo Japan. I only went to one bar in Yokosuka: it was one of those professional, rip-off-the-sailor ports with full-time waitresses who were masters of getting the poor swabbies to buy them drinks then talking trash to each other about how ugly we were in Japanese. They were extremely rude and angry. The next liberty I had, I went inland to Tokyo and walked the back streets, searching for Shinto shrines and old buildings for some remnant of the ancient Bushido culture. I didn't find much except a little working man's noodle house - with its room full of laborers sucking up noodles and broth from the deep bowls - just like I remembered in the Samurai movies I had seen. I ordered a bowl and imitated their eating technique.

We sailed down the coast to Kyoto, the ancient capital of Japan, and it was full of what I wanted to see. I walked to the old Imperial Palace, with it's sliding doors and beautiful wood frame, and the gorgeous gardens all around it. The Golden Pavilion, with its incredible gardens, from the highest period of Japanese garden creation, will always remain in my picture memories. The school kids were all in their clean-colorful uniforms chattering away as they came from class.

In Kamakura, another ancient capital of the Shogunate, I found myself in a beautiful park with Buddhist monks and tourists all wanting to climb into the giant Kamakura Buddha and light a candle. I waited in the line and climbed in; I never seem to forget the experience or the time. I watched a Shinto funeral ceremony in the cemetery nearby, with the only trees in this crowded place.

THE WATERSPOUT

So much for the travelogue! An impending, life-threatening, adventure was close at hand. Having given us our time off, after six months at sea, we were sailing over the Mindanao Deep - one of the largest and deepest trenches in the Pacific Ocean, in the world! I decided to climb up the 30-foot vertical ladder to the Crow's nest. This was where we had a radio tower, and you could climb through a small hole in the floor of the steel-walled, chest high, enclosure and see the vast ocean's curve on the horizon. I often came up here to get that feeling I used to get when I climbed the highest trees, pretending I was on a great sailing ship, looking down at the deck below as it went from the left to the right. But this time was extraordinary; I stood looking forward to the horizon when I noticed something moving like a tornado. Remember the one in "The Wizard of Oz"? It looked like It was the color of the clouds, and went all the way up and into them and seemed alive with its sinuous undulations. For a moment, I thought maybe I should warn the bridge because I knew from my childhood sea stories that it was a water spout, and it was heading directly for us. At this point, the spout was about five miles ahead of us and still coming our way when I noticed that we had changed course about ten degrees starboard. Now it was getting close, and what was really scary was that it had changed course to meet us with our change! I felt like this thing had a mind, or was being controlled by something that had intelligence.

Just when it looked like we were on a collision course, we changed our course again for around twenty degrees to port. It was only a minute or so when the bloody spout changed again to meet us!! I was starting to get anxious and thought I had better climb down and get below decks, but it was too late for that now. It was around a hundred yards away from hitting us - thousands of tons of ocean in the form of a Tornado, with the incredible power of wind and water circling like a whirlpool, ready to take us up or down at a whim. Just when I was sure this was how I was going to leave this world - holding on to the ladder inside the crow's nest with all my tiny might - I heard the thing roar by. It must have been fifty yards away, but it sounded like a jet engine, and I was soaking wet from its whirling spray. Somehow, it had decided to let us be on our way - and I'm not just projecting human consciousness onto a spout of water - I mean I saw that thing react to every move we made, and then, in the end, decide to stop playing with us. If you had been in the crow's nest with me, you wouldn't doubt a thing I've said!

AN EXECUTIVE BELLY-FLOP

After the Water Spout experience, I was amazed that no one I knew was speaking about it. I think the Captain and his officers on the bridge had probably just gone through a very traumatic experience, and what they go through never gets down to the enlisted men. Unless a message that isn't classified crypto - clearance is dispatched through us - only then would we be privy to our near misses and potential hazards.

Our Executive Officer, a commander and self-proclaimed man's man of around 50, decided we were all going to go swimming in the Mindanao Deep, 50 miles off Japan and seven miles (34,440 feet) to the bottom. Marine sharpshooters on the main deck were ready to shoot at sharks if they tried to grab us; in reality, the sharks would have just come up from under us and tore at our legs or dragged us down. The way bullets refract (up to 50 degrees when they hit the water at high velocity, and either break apart at a depth of six feet or become harmless at three), we were likely in more danger from the Marines than the sharks! To swim, we had to dive or jump 30 feet into the ocean and to climb back up; we had to work our way up that rope netting that the marines clamber up and down in the 2nd World

War movies.

Climbing Up The 30 Foot Rope Netting

Even   though I had climbed ropes and trees with just my arms I could barely get myself up, and the worst was the last part, trying to crawl over the top edge without help.

I had made my second dive and was floating about - out of the way of falling men - when I noticed way up above the main deck was an old man getting ready to jump off the superstructure, near the Bridge and the Admiral's cabin, about 45 feet up. He signaled for everyone to get out of his way and leaped out into the air; my heart stopped, and I held my breath as I saw him trying to right himself so that he would dive straight in. He made some last-ditch effort, wriggling like a snake, but landed with a loud smack on his belly. His had to be the biggest belly flop in history, and he just lay there motionless for a long time. The guys near him started to come to his aid when he suddenly took a deep breath - so loud they could hear it on the ship - and then he forced a big grin as if he had done just what he wanted to do. It was pretty apparent that the wind had been knocked out of him and that he was lucky he didn't break his neck. He must have had severe chest and tummy burns for a long time after that. I could tell that he wasn't able to move for some time and was pretending that he was enjoying floating about, poor guy! After about ten minutes of getting over his paralysis and smiling in pain, suddenly, his whole body jerked, and some monstrous force pulled him beneath the waves...just kidding!

TYPHOON OVER THE MINDANAO DEEP

We sailed on, east of Japan when we noticed a weather warning message in Main-Comm. Radio 1, directed to the Bridge. It mentioned a possible Typhoon directly ahead of us and recommended we change our current course. For some macho reason, I suppose, the Captain decided to ignore the warning, and it was on my 12 to 4 am watch that it hit us. At first, we tried to continue sending and receiving messages in Main-Comm. But soon the mimeograph machine fell over onto the floor, and the typewriters began to break loose from the tables. The ship was behaving like a huge bungee jump-line, down and up and side to side, and then all at the same time. It wasn't possible to stand or sit down without falling over, and our non-com in charge of the watch told us to go to our bunks once we had moved all the heavy equipment down to the deck. I stumbled out of the radio shack, falling from one bulkhead to the other, until I ran into Ortega, a Filipino 2nd class petty officer & veteran of WWII, who gave up being a Chief Steward so that he could do something other than serving the "bloody white officers on their linen table clothes."

He laughed at my seasickness like the old salts love to do, and I said something that changed his mood from elder brother to knife-wielding assassin. He sneered and hissed his threat that if I even spoke one more word, he would cut my throat, as he had done to many Japs, and in a flash, the knife was in my face. I don't think it mattered much to me in my dizzy, falling-down nausea; I just turned and fell forward toward the head. I guess I must have made fun of his Filipino accent since he was making fun of my seasickness. Anyway, I made my way to the head, which was just a deck above our sleeping compartment. After puking everything in me onto the steel-gray deck, I started to dry heave in spasms as I lay there.

The ship was like a little speck in this vast and deep ocean, 80-foot waves tossing us about like a toy boat with no power of movement. First, my legs would go vertical, and I would slide the length of the wet floor, then I would be as if standing upright, and I'd slide feet first to the other bulkhead or wall. It was so bad that I started to leave my body. It was a great relief, a feeling so sublime and sweet as I felt the presence of another dimension where everything was soft, calm and beautiful. Just as I was about to let go and give in to leaving this hell for a piece of heaven, the Captain piped up on the intercom and said, "well men, it's been good to know you; we just about capsized with that last wave and if we do that again with just one

more degree...Well, as I said it's been good serving with you."
Oh well! I thought I don't want to go through this any longer
anyway." Amazingly, we survived the typhoon. The relief I felt
upon finding out that the closer I got to death the more it felt
like a beautiful place to go was almost worth that wild and
crazy night.

ORDER OF THE GOLDEN DRAGON

Well, I can't leave the South Pacific without telling you the
story of our crossing of the Equator and the ceremony of "The
Order of The Golden Dragon." First let me give you someone
else's description of it: "No greater Naval tradition is there
worldwide than a line crossing ceremony. According to the
tradition, a polliwog is a sailor who has never crossed the
equator line." It was 1964 that I became a golden shell-back
(those who have crossed the Equator on the International
Date Line) through a line crossing ceremony. Afterward, I received my Domain of the Golden Dragon certificate. "Considered a rite of passage that tested upon the sailor's ability
to withstand a long ocean journey, many WWII sailors looked
forward to their line ceremony."

The day-long search for the polliwogs, who try to avoid discovery by hiding as best they can, began as a shell-back
dressed as King Neptune calls forth the polliwogs. During the
ceremony, the king of the sea interrogates the polliwogs that
have been found, through many embarrassing challenges, such
as being locked in a salt-water coffin, hair chopping, digging
through rotting garbage, locked in the stocks while shell-
backs throw mushy fruit at them, shocks on the testicles with
cattle prods, and other degrading behavior. After each event
through the series of obstacles, the polliwogs must declare
their allegiance to King Neptune. All of the humiliations are
meant to entertain the shell-backs by degrading the polliwogs. The brutality of the obstacles a polliwog must endure
depends upon the era in which the sailor lived. Up into the

1980's; beatings and severe brutality were so prevalent in the ceremony that many sailors found themselves in sickbay soon afterward. Some sailors lost their lives.

Even visiting dignitaries were not excluded from the line crossing ceremony. In November 1936, President Franklin Roosevelt endured the same harsh treatments when the USS Indianapolis crossed the Equator while he was on board. Our first class petty officer in charge of Main Comm. #2 was a black man named Grady: a man who had seen the worst of the racist attitudes of the whites by being beaten up and stripped of his rank several times because he had the self-respect to fight back. He liked me because I could sit and talk to him without a thought of race. My mother had encouraged me to date the only black girl in our high school of 2000 students, probably to teach me the lesson of our common humanity. We went to see Frank Sinatra in "Hole In The Head."

Anyway, when a fellow polliwog and I asked Grady if there was a secret place to hide during the search, he pointed up to the round hatch in the ceiling, and I stood on a table with a chair on top of it and turned the handle round counter-clockwise until it opened. I pushed it up so that I could climb through and into the "Secret" radio room above us. The two of us crawled up and hid in the darkroom under a desk, and listened to all the polliwogs running and screaming as the shell-backs chased them all over the ship. Many of the polliwogs volunteered to go through the hell on deck, probably out of fear of what the shell-backs would do to them if they had to drag them in fighting. I didn't care; I wasn't going to let them cattle prod me, or make me kiss the garbage covered belly of Neptune (some fat, sadistic petty officer, no doubt). As the yelling and chasing and sounds of scuffling wore down, the guy hiding with me began to worry that we would be the last to be discovered, and would therefore probably suffer some severe tortures. He opened the hatch and went down, and I told him not to tell anyone where I was, no matter what. Thankfully, he kept his word, and by evening, when the whole thing was over, Grady knocked on the hatch with a broomstick, and I went over to it, and he opened it from below and said "congratulations, Stanley!" He helped me down and said, "you are one of the few in the history of the ceremony that they couldn't find, and the rule is, that if you escape the shell-backs, you are eligible to be a member of The Golden Dragons." I was a bit worried to show my face at the mess hall, but Grady said: "they don't know you weren't caught." A few days later we all received our certificates, and I felt lucky and unique having braved out the fear-based ceremony of humiliation, thanks to good old Grady.

My Order Of The Golden Dragon Certificate

THE SEA MONSTER AND THE GRUNT

My best and only friend while in the Navy was Emo - the Marine radioman, farm-boy from the Sacramento area who taught English with me in Korea. After two weeks of kitchen duty, (a requirement of seamen) I told Emo about a stash of homemade wine I had made, under the direction of a third class kitchen cook who had been my boss. One evening we opened a bottle of the foul tasting stuff and got tipsy, falling about as we walked through the passageways to the forward, upper deck and into the Ocean air. I sat looking out to sea, past the wire rope railing, when Emo's (Marine) friend, a strikingly good-looking guy, about six foot two and very fit, came up the companionway. He had been a Golden Gloves boxing champion, and he didn't like me - after all, I was a swabby, and it was the tradition to hate us just as we hated Grunts. But his hate was more jealousy than Grunt/Swab hate; he was afraid I was stealing his Emo! He started to get belligerent with me as Emo, and I were laughing hysterically at silly things, especially at what the Grunt was saying. Once you got Emo laughing he couldn't stop, and he would end up on the deck in convulsions; this was one of those times. I decided to play one of my childhood pranks on the hostile, pretty boy. When we were kids, I would sometimes stop abruptly, looking off into the sky over my brother Teddy's head, as if I saw something coming from behind him. I would act out the part of a horrified victim witnessing some monstrous creature attacking. Then I would let loose an ear-splitting shriek, in my bloody, scared-to-death terror-voice, and poor Teddy would fall to the ground, panic-stricken, and I would laugh; not a very nice thing to do to your little brother, but in this case I thought it would be fun to see a bully scared enough to wet his pants.

So, I looked over his head as he was standing in a threatening stance in front of me. I calmly began to stare out to sea at the waves above his head, and very gradually changed my face into one of absolute terror. I cringed and moved as if to run from what I saw; then I screamed with all my soul and pointed at something behind him in the dark waves. As he turned to look, he cried out like a little girl and fell to the wet deck whimpering and pissing his beautifully pressed grunt-slacks.

Emo had run to the passageway and was looking out in wonder. He had been sure some monster was after us, and when he saw that his friend had peed his pants and was trying to get up off the deck, after sliding around in the sea water; Emo started one of his laughing fits and ended up on the deck as well. It was a great release to get to laugh so heartily after so long a time with no fun or joy. The Grunt didn't speak to me for the rest of the voyage; he probably didn't want to chance being reminded of his hidden fear again. I was just happy not to have him put one of his golden gloves in my face. Isn't it amazing how some of the toughest and biggest dudes have such crippling fear hidden under all that muscle and meanness?

THE SEALS & THE BEATLES

We sailed to Okinawa, and while we were docked at the pier, the USS George Clyburn rammed into us - a somewhat humiliating move for the Clyburn's Captain I would think, he rammed into the Admiral's Flagship! So we sat in Okinawa for a time, as they checked out our damages. Then it was back to Subic Bay in the Philippines, our base of operations while in the South Seas. There were still headhunters up in the mountains near Baguio at that time.

There were Huck's in the hills around the Army base and the one street we were allowed to travel on liberty. The Huck's were the so-called "Communists," and they would occasionally kill an unlucky sailor or marine who happened to leave the restricted street. While I was there, a sailor was found floating in the river which flowed out of the mountains and into the sea by our pier.

The first time I ever heard the Beatles' music was in a restaurant near the pier in Subic Bay. It was a Filipino group imitating their first album, the Pink one. I thought it was pretty good; I thought they had written all the songs and harmonies themselves at the time. Later, off of Danang, Vietnam, a UDT Frogman showed me the Pink Album, and played some of it one evening, down in the sleeping area. "Oh! so this is the group the Filipinos were copying, I thought."The Beatle's harmonies sounded like poor impressions of the Every Brothers, and their attempts at singing Little Richard and Chuck Berry songs were disappointing. They sped up the grooves and whitewashed the funk. Then the team leader of the UDT, or "SEALS," as they now known, asked if I had a guitar, and I said "sure." He took it and sat at the table and started playing and singing. We all joined in on some of the songs, but by morning they were gone. The Navy Seal singer was a huge guy and the leader of his UDT team. They had gone off before dawn in their little black rubber boat, and paddled off toward shore to do some demolition, or was it to procure the PT boats to initiate the Tonkin Crises? I wonder!

BLACK GUYS CAN BOX!

From my experience in the Navy and music world, black guys can dance and box and romance girls better than most white guys. I could go on in-depth about the characters in our crew, but as I want to move onto the adventures that came after the Navy, I'll relate just one more observation: We had quite a few black guys on our ship, and they were almost all decent boxers, one was actually a professional contender. Johnson was his name, a massive dude with massive shoulders and he stood about 6'4." He was a new radio-striker and shared a lot of my watches in Main-Comm. He would stand in front of the mimeograph machine copying messages, and he'd move his body as if he were shadow boxing - really graceful and powerful.

The black guys wouldn't talk much, if at all, when alone among whites, but I asked him if he was a boxer, and he turned and smiled and said "ya, I was about to go for the heavyweight title when I got my draft notice, so I joined the Navy to make sure I lived through the war." He never said another thing to any of us, and he didn't even participate in the big boxing match that took place not long afterward.

I think I can remember one white guy who entered the match, and he was knocked out in one or two rounds. All the other boxers were black, and they could dance around, and they had long arms and incredibly muscular bodies. Not long after the fight (with the winner getting a prize of some kind, probably increased liberty) one black guy, who was a friend of mine, told me that two of his friends went missing when we were four days out to sea, on our way to the States. He said the rumor was that one night they were pushed overboard after their watch, shortly after the white deckhand had been knocked out by one of them in the boxing match.

The deck hands are usually the most ignorant men aboard a ship because most of them can't do work that takes the ability to think somewhat clearly; otherwise they would have been sent to one of the specialty schools like Radioman, Radar, Sonar or ET. Their job is to keep the deck clean and shiny, and I suppose they check on the lifeboats and raise and drop anchor. There were some "deck apes," as we used to call them, from the deep south, who had been raised with the KKK belief system and may have even seen a lynching or two. I would occasionally overhear them disparaging their fellow black mates and laughing. There was never an inquiry made or even a search for the two black deck hands, but every man on the Eldorado knew about it except for the officers, and if they knew they certainly didn't let on.

We sailed by the Hawaiian Islands, and I would never have even noticed them if it weren't for someone on deck who pointed them out to me about fifteen miles off on the dark horizon. We made it across the Pacific, and as we approached the outer islands off of southern California, it all looked so beautiful from the sea. Sailing majestically into the harbor and Navy pier - we were all assembled on deck in our dress whites - and I thought, "no one even knows that I'm here; I wonder how many sailors won't have anyone to meet them on the dock?" When the lines were all tied down, and the gangway was in place, we were informed that all those who didn't have a watch could go on liberty. I looked over the rail onto the pier and searched for a familiar face but couldn't find any. Most of the crew were running down the gangway and hugging wives, mothers or girlfriends; so many tears of joy for loved ones; it made me feel pretty damn lonely walking down that plank.

MEDALS FOR ALL!

When I walked down the gangplank and stood on the stationary pier, my hard-earned sea-legs made everything sway as I tried to walk on solid ground after the two-week, Pacific crossing. I was pitching and weaving nauseously along the pier when a sailor came up to me and wanted to know where I got the medal; most seamen don't usually have medals pinned to the front of their dress whites. I had assumed that all the sailors who were in Subic and maneuvers off Vietnam had received the "Expeditionary Medal" but not so! He was jealous and couldn't see why he didn't get one. It was a status symbol, especially on a seaman. I found out later that the whole crew aboard the USS Eldorado had received the "Armed Forces Expeditionary medal" and the "Gulf Of Tonkin, Admiral's Trophy."

SAN DIEGO AGAIN

After returning to the States from the South Pacific, I hitched out to Mission Beach to see what was happening at the Heritage folk club. It was Hoot night, and I had just come down from the stage, having played a few songs, when a waitress approached me and asked if I wanted to drive up to San Francisco with her sister. It just so happened that I was thinking of hitch-hiking back east to Boston for the Newport Folk Festival, and to visit family, but San Francisco sounded interesting too. I asked why her sister wanted someone to drive her, and she said that she was afraid to drive alone at night.

I guess it seemed a bit odd to me, although it was over five hundred miles, a seven-hour drive. I assumed it would be a nonstop trip and questioned her further about why she asked me? She said she'd heard good things about me. I guess she figured I was harmless enough, but I sensed that there was some other reason for being chosen. Anyway, I went back to town and got my traveling things all packed up in my guitar case. The waitress's sister picked me up at the Heritage, bright and early the next morning. She looked like her younger sister, full figured in the right places, only dressed like a lawyer. We drove up to LA, where she had an apartment with a round hanging bed.

She had to pick up some clothes, but we ended up spending the night. It was all rather strange, especially when her boyfriend started banging on the door. She held her finger to her mouth and let him knock and pound for a long time. I began to worry that he might get in and come at me in his rage, but after awhile he just stopped and left.

I got to sleep in the round bed, and next morning I was still asleep when I heard her talking to someone in the living room. I went in, and there she was with some middle-aged furniture salesman, selling all her expensive furnishings for almost nothing. She even sold the round bed, which cost her $500., for $80! She said she was selling her furniture because it was Sunday, and the banks were closed, and she needed money to go with me to San Francisco! Her logic completely eluded me; it didn't make any sense to me at all; why go to these extremes to drive me to Frisco?

For an escrow expert, she hadn't planned this trip very well! She packed up a small bag and leaving an empty apartment with 300 dollars, we drove up the coast highway. When it got dark, and we were tired, we pulled over and parked on the side of the road, where we could go down to the beach. I made a campfire and pulled out the guitar, and we feasted on chips and cheese and coke, and I played for awhile. Back in the car, we tried to get some sleep, but she seemed motivated to get me to become romantically involved with her. I could feel that she had some ulterior motive for all this odd behavior: It was odd because it didn't seem to be motivated by any attraction to me, either physically or emotionally, but by something else that I couldn't figure out. Kinda-like the ambitious actress on the producer's couch vibe; I had something she wanted.

THE DESPERATE PROPOSAL

When we got to San Francisco, I played at a few of the folk clubs and coffee houses there and over in Berkeley. My strange

benefactor and travel companion tried to manage my appearances at the clubs, and I had to make it clear to her that
the only money involved in the Hootenanny, and open mike
scene, was what we could get by passing the hat. After one or
two nights in motels, she was down to enough money for the
gas to get home to LA. It was on that last day that she finally
made clear what she had been up to for the previous five
days. First, she asked me if I would marry her, and when I just
laughed and said "really! you've only known me for five days
and I'm about to get out of the Navy and live the life of a starving musician...why on earth would you want to marry me?"

At this point, she looked down in desperation and said: "well,
I'm pregnant; do you know any safe way to have a miscarriage?" A miscarriage? You mean if I don't marry you, your
only alternative is a miscarriage? I guess she thought she was
such a prize that I would be delighted with her proposal; remember, in those days the only way to get an abortion was
to go down to Tijuana and seek out some shady butcher in a
back-ally who would most likely leave you with an infection
that you may not live through. I thought to ask why she hadn't
presented the situation to her boyfriend but decided not to
when I remembered her reaction to his desperate attempts to
break her door down. So, I tried to think of some folk alternative - like some Native American root that they would take
for this purpose - but all I could do was tell her she should go
home and figure it out.

We walked to her car, and she tried to smile as she waved
goodbye, and that was the last time "ever I saw her face." She
probably thought I'd have a hard time getting around or finding a place to stay, but she knew nothing of the music scene
in those days. In reality, I'm sure she had only been thinking
of herself for months, and you can't blame her for that, considering her predicament. Anyway, now that I was on my own
it was just a matter of showing up at a folk club and playing a
set, passing the hat, and there would always be someone who

would invite me to "crash at their pad.â€�

CHARLY'S RAINBOW

A big Hoot was going on at the Jabberwocky folk club in Berkeley, and I signed up to sing. I sang a few songs and then decided to do one I had picked up from a grizzled bard in a Beatnik dive in Greenwich Village. The song was called "Charley's Rainbow," and it's about a little girl, probably the old bard's daughter. I sang the song, and it went over really well; as the clapping ended a college girl stood up and said: "my name is Charley." The crowd made a pleasant sound of romantic appreciation, and I felt like maybe I'll have a place to sleep tonight.

When Charley came up to me, after my set, she seemed genuinely pleased that someone had written a song about a girl named Charley. She asked if I had a place to stay, and of course, I said no; at this point however her big brother stepped up and looked me over. He seemed a bit tentative about allowing me to stay the night, but after awhile he drove us to their apartment. Charley was quite taken with the song, but not really into strange folk musicians like myself, and so I was given the sofa for the night.

The next day big brother saw me off, Charley was already in class. So it was back to the streets and the folk clubs. I hitched a ride across the Golden Gate Bridge and was walking into a club in San Francisco, when I ran into Peggy, an old roommate of Sherry's (the blond, beauty) from San Diego. Peggy had told me that I wasn't responsible for Sherry's pregnancy - that it was the guy before me - and she even pointed someone out to me as she walked me to the place where she was crashing.

SAN FRANCISCO

There was a dark haired dude on the other side of the street, and she said "that's the guy," and waved her hand at him. He saw us and ran like hell down an alleyway, a block or two up the hill. His reaction to seeing Peggy seemed like proof that she was telling the truth - that this guy was worried we were after him for bailing on Sherry. He probably thought I was her brother. But all this must have been a coincidence; I mean, he may have believed that Sherry was pregnant by him and maybe she had been and had a miscarriage or an abortion?

However, as I mentioned earlier, I recently found out that I actually am the biological father of the boy, and now he's "Born Again" and fifty+, with a family of his own. The "Real Christians" say "I'm born again," and I say, It's a shame that almost all mention of reincarnation was removed from the Bible over the millennia. It has led to the creation of a cult of mood-making - a special status with Jesus - merely by saying that you are born again because you have accepted Jesus as your personal savior.

What is really meant by the words in John 3.3 (Jesus replied, tell you the truth, unless you are born again, you cannot see the Kingdom of God) is obviously not on the level of an intellectual or emotional decision...one has to be born many times, again and again, to evolve to the level of entering the "Kingdom of Heaven" or permanent God Consciousness. You can't just make an emotional display in front of the congregation and expect to walk and talk with Jesus in Christ Consciousness! It's called Reincarnation folks, get used to it, you've been doing it, and will be doing it for a long time if you still haven't figured out the real nature of Evolution. That's my story, and I'm sticking to it!

Peggy took me to an upstairs apartment where a friend of hers lived with her folk singer husband. The wife was very welcoming when Peggy told her I was a musician from Boston, and I sang a few songs for them in the kitchen as the kids were laid to rest. The wife asked if I would like to share the big mattress with them; it was on the floor in the open living room, kids and all. I could tell by the way she smiled when she asked, that I was going to have to do more than sleep next to these two happy folksy ladies, so I said: "naw, that's all right I'm fine on the floor here in the kitchen." She said, "are you sure?" I said "oh ya!" I made this seemingly uncharacteristic decision, for a 60's musician/sailor, for three reasons: 1. I couldn't imagine having sex with the mother of a baby and a toddler all sharing the same bed; 2. I could imagine having sex with two girls, I've seen videos, but it kind of scared me then and still does, as it's never happened; 3. I didn't want to be found like that by her husband, no matter how "free love" he was. I don't like to be embarrassed!

HITCHIN TO BOSTON WITH PEGGY

The husband never came home that night - he was most likely sleeping with some other folk singer's wife. In the morning, his brother arrived and gave Peggy and me directions and a map so that we could start our journey hitching across the US on 80. I don't think I told you that one of the reasons Peggy had teamed up with me was because she was looking for a traveling companion to hitchhike to Boston. We hitched and got a ride from a guy with the radio blasting the new Stone's release "Satisfaction." It was so cool, we all sang the chorus to-gether as we sped along on our adventure.

I hadn't had more than an hour of sleep in San Francisco, and when I finally woke up, we were half-way across the country and were dropped off by a roundabout, just off the highway. It was rush hour, and we ran across to the middle of the circle and plopped down in the long grass. We both tried to scrunch into my sleeping bag. It was a tight fit, but we managed to get a few hours of sleep until the sun came up.

We were crossing the Rocky Mountains on route 80 going East, with our thumbs out and the guitar in clear view. The guitar helped us to get rides as much as Peggy being a girl did, even though she wasn't a pretty girl. A lone guy hitching has too many scary movies associated with it. A guy with any girl is better, but a guy with a guitar and a girl is about as good as you can get for getting rides unless, of course, your a lone girl; but that's crazy dangerous. The thought would haunt me every so often when I remembered that I was AWOL, (Absent Without Leave) and if the Navy had put out my description to the police, I could get arrested and shipped back to the Marine Brig in San Diego.

I was thinking about this when along came a highway patrol car and parked in front of us; he looked over our driver's licenses and asked a few questions concerning Peggy's voluntary association with me, and of course her age. He wasn't one of those San Diego Nazi's, who act like jailers in charge of the prisoners of the street, and he smiled and wished us well. When we arrived in Boston in the cab of a big semi, we took the trolley to Beacon Hill, Peggy's destination. We hadn't been the best of friends during the crossing; she complained a lot, and I felt burdened. So it was free at last, a free at last parting with no regrets.

THE NEWPORT FOLK FESTIVAL

The 1965 Newport Folk Festival was in full swing, so I hitched down from Grammy's in North Weymouth and saw Son House, one of my favorite blues slide guitar players. There was also Lightning Hopkins, who I used to see at the Golden Vanity, and recently saw in a San Francisco folk club; he was always hitting on the college girls. Mississippi John Hurt was there as well, and it was great to see him again, after opening for him in Bainbridge Maryland. Dylan was there, but I missed his performance, and caught him later with his new band, "The Band," in Boston. I did see Donovan Leitch with his little Dylan hat. I think he was quite self-conscious when Dylan was around, because in those days he pretty much styled himself, the Dylan of the British Isles, with the hat and harmonica holder all around his head.

Jim Kweskin Jug Band

To be fair, Donovan had a unique style of writing and singing, but my favorable opinion of him went south when he came out with his "commercial" album, Mellow Yellow. I saw Jim Kweskin and the jug band; he was one of my high school heroes. I used to see him at the old "Golden Vanity" folk club, which was close to where I lived in Brookline, and at the old 47 Mt. Auburn Street club in Cambridge. When he put the jug band together with Maria Muldaur, Fritz Richmond, Bill Keith, Bob Siggins, Bruno Wolf, Geoff Muldaur, and Mel Lyman, the Mystic harmonica player, they were a fun experience.

Dharma was screaming at me through Dylan and The Byrds, and I had no choice other than to get free. I only had six months left in my enlistment, but that seemed like an eternity to me at the time, since it would have been spent back in Vietnam. So, I asked Ted to turn me into the Navy recruiting office where they soon delivered me to the Marine Brig in Boston. The Brig would have been a straight path to Leavenworth Prison, so I managed to convince them to send me to the Naval Hospital in Newport, which had a mental ward and a comfortable padded cell which they put me in along with three other "Head Cases."

We were all trussed up in straight jackets; two of the guys

had cut their wrists, which were all stitched up with thick black thread. I asked them why they had tried to get out of the Navy by hurting themselves, and they said it was the only way they knew. The problem was that it was common knowledge among the old Salts that wrist cutting would only get you long-term jail or padded cell time, but these two seemed genuinely depressed and worthy of psychological attention.

After two months in the ward my young Harvard Psychiatrist had managed to get me a music practice room and my folk singer outfit: 1 pair of Levis, 1 pair of black Mexican riding boots, 1 Native American shirt with fringe and an Irish tweed cap, all of which I would don for my daily practice with my Gibson guitar. Occasionally, my shrink would sit and listen; he seemed quite positive about my chances for discharge, and even asked where I would be performing once I got out. One day he told me to meet him in the practice room where he gave me a heads up that the board of shrinks would be considering my case later that day.

A half hour later the head shrink (Colonel Zanity) interviewed me in his office, and I heard him click on the tape recorder with his foot. He asked what I would do if I were sent back to duty on my ship; my answer was Top Secret, so I'm unable to reveal it to you in this public disclosure. Just kidding! I told him I would kill myself, of course, and when that didn't seem to impress him, I said to him that all the men on my ship were gorillas and that I would kill them as well. I noticed that he clicked the foot pedal to his tape recorder and my interview was over.

The next day I was informed that I would be getting my Honorable Discharge and that for the next few weeks I would be checked out by the doctors and dentists, getting fillings if I needed them, and all the medical exams that the docs might feel were necessary for a clean bill of health. This only happened before they let you out into the "real world," probably based on some libel-legalese in our recruitment contract? Anyway, I was in a state of Euphoria! I could not believe that my psych interview for the Board had ended up with such a wonderful outcome. I had thought that my earnest sincerity had carried the day, even though I would never kill myself or anyone else; I had believed that for a half-century until recently. Just a few years ago Sherry told me that her father had come to my Hospital ward and talked with the shrinks. Her father was a Navy Admiral, and thinking that I had gone into a deep depression as a result of his daughter breaking off with me after she had become pregnant with our child, she says he came to help me out if possible. If it wasn't my young Harvard Shrink, who was rooting for me, or the recorded interview for the Board, then it had to be Sherry's dad. It was probably all three that set me free.

HONORABLY DISCHARGED

Well, by October 15th I was given an Honorable Discharge, and walked through the Navy gate with a salute and a "good morning sir" from the shore patrol gate guard, thinking I must be an officer. I was in civvies so he had to "sir" me since enlisted men and non-commissioned-officers have to change into their street clothes off base and that felt kinda cool, an officer and a gentleman after all! I found a cafeteria just a few blocks from the base and celebrated my freedom with bacon and eggs, hash browns and orange juice, and of course, coffee. About halfway through my happy meal, the jukebox came alive with "Like a Rolling Stone," Bob Dylan's new release:

"How does it feel, how does it feel?

To be without a home

Like a complete unknown, like a rolling stone."

The chorus of this song was speaking directly to me sitting there during that moment in time; free from the Navy, free to go and live the life I had dreamed of my whole life, just when the music I loved was the most popular music in the country. It was almost too much; if I thought I felt good before, with my comfort meal of freedom, this last touch from heaven put me into pure, blissful, optimistic, supercharged ecstasy.

I felt as if all of Nature had just given me a personal theme-song to go out and fulfill my deepest and dearest desires; really! I felt like I finally knew true freedom. Everyone was singing about freedom and talking about freedom, but until this moment, on this day, it had just been a vague word, used by just about everyone under thirty in those days. Of course, there were a few thirtysomethings as well, Pete Seeger for sure!

ON THE ROAD AGAIN

I was more than anxious to get back to California and the music, but I felt I had to take the science course I flunked my senior year in Germany to get my diploma. Where in Cambridge would you take a science class? Why MIT of course! Albeit, MIT night school. After a few months of night school and a full-time job at a Harvard Square bookstore, I was ready for California. I had been sharing an apartment with my brother Ted and a college girl whom I had met in Cambridge. When she moved into our Beacon Hill apartment, I told her that I had a girlfriend out west and that I'd be leaving in a few months to be with her.

I guess she never really believed me as she was quite upset the night before I left, packing up my change of clothes in my guitar case. She didn't know that my girlfriend out west wasn't a girl, but my headlong, win-or-lose dive into the world of music for a career as a singer/songwriter, signed to Columbia Records just like Bob Dylan. That was my ambition, my ultimate goal at the time.

GREEWICH VILLAGE 1965

Dyan, Suze and Dave Van Ronk

When I got to the "Village," it was evening, and the folk clubs and coffee houses were beginning to come alive. I walked into one that I remembered from weekend liberty I'd taken when I was in Radioman 'A' school, down in Maryland. I signed up to perform and then walked around the Village checking out all the clubs and street people for a familiar face. When I got back to the club to play, they were packed, and I was supposed to be up next. The place was full of tourists and college kids and a few folkies; some used to call us folkies as opposed to Beatniks or Bohemians; Hippies hadn't earned their name yet, they were still in high school.

There was a wash-tub bass player in the house, and when he saw me going on, he came up and asked if I wanted backup. I said sure, but listen to a song or two first and then if you feel you can add something, come on up. He came up after one song, and when I heard what he was doing, I switched to some blues and songs with more potential for him to shine. After our set, a waitress came up and said the owner wanted us to come back every night, for two weeks, at the same time every day. He said all he could pay was what we got in the hat, but he would have two waitresses covering the whole house.

That's the way it was in all the folk clubs in the Village - except the big name clubs where you would get paid by the management. At the end of my set, the waitress came up and asked if I had a place to stay. I said no, and she offered to help find me one; it turned out that she didn't have a place either. She had been kicked out of a flamenco guitarist's apartment - the guy who owned Cafe Flamenco - probably for a new love interest. He was one of the old guard who was there when the Beats still haunted the place. They could tolerate Flamenco, with its almost jazz-like spontaneity based in very particular rhythms and chords, sort of like Indian ragas. I was supposed to meet her back at the club before it closed, in a few hours. The streets were thinning out, and I walked down into a basement dive, where I heard someone singing, and sat in the back.

A kid was playing his guitar with a stub on the end of his wrist, and it was bleeding, but he didn't seem to notice. He was deep into his song, singing his heart out while we all just stared at his bleeding stub where a hand should have been. There were quite a few other musicians in the front of the room, and they were there to support the lad. I tried to think of a way that he could fix a pick onto his wrist somehow, so the stub wouldn't be his only picking tool, but couldn't quite come up with anything on the spot.

When he finished, we all gave him a standing ovation for his brave ambition. He was emulating Bob Dylan, like most of us who had adopted the harmonica holder. Most of those that copied Dylan couldn't sing and figured that Dylan couldn't either, so they had a chance. In reality, Dylan had an uncanny sense of phrasing and timing, and, of course, his lyrics. His fake farmer voice was perfect for the songs he wrote, and his non-verbal stage presence helped his aura of mystery and genius. He never let us know who he was, so we naturally imagined him bigger than life. His silence spoke volumes to his admiring audience. He spoke entirely through his song lyrics and wailing voice and those acerbic interviews, always turning the question back on the interviewer; refusing to play the old games. How did he know to do this? To act like an ancient Guru, whose every word expressed wisdom in his cute little hat and sheepskin folk-jacket! I mean, he looked like he was barely 20 years old, and out would come the crusty voice of an old timer, world-weary and wise, and we fell for it because he, more than anyone else, was speaking our language, the language of our time.

The waitress's name was Jesse, and she was still waiting at the club for me when I got back. She got her coat, and I followed her to a decent apartment near the Village. The living room was half-full of people, some on the couch and chairs, and the rest on the floor. They seemed to be in a quiet mood and were passing a pipe around. I was wondering what they were smoking - it didn't smell like pot - when a girl came over and handed me the pipe. I don't think I asked what it was, but it didn't seem like I had the option to pass on it if I wanted someplace to stay that night; my hair was still Navy and they would probably suspect that I was a narc if I refused. It wasn't long after my few puffs on the pipe that I felt to lay down and stare up at the ceiling. There was a big yellow light above, in the center of the room, and one moment I was staring up at it and the next I was staring down from it, looking at everyone from the ceiling. Opium, if it was indeed Opium, seemed to be an astral travel, waking dream drug; at least it was for me. I mean, floating around the ceiling, looking down at my body and everyone else, in an apparent, waking - state of consciousness; It was like everything I've read about astral travel and soon passed into sleep. The brightness and warmth of the sun woke me up, lying in the same spot on the floor.

The next night, I took Jesse to the 12'x12' dorm room of a friend of mine I had run into, walking the streets near Columbia University. He was the first cousin of my old best friend from Brookline, Johnny Oliphant, and we slept on his rock - hard linoleum floor. I think Jesse had slept on a lot of floors, but she had a lot of soft curves that protected her bones from stiffness and chill. I wasn't sleeping very well, being mostly skin and bone, hips and shoulders cutting into the floor.

ON THE ROAD AGAIN - AGAIN

When the two weeks of performing at the club were over, the owner asked me if I wanted to continue, but I'd had enough of the Village and wanted to get out to California. I came up with the name Troll for my washtub bass player. It may sound insensitive but it fit him perfectly, and he liked it! He wanted to go out west as well, and he told me he had a friend in St. Louis Missouri who would put us up for a night or two. I said goodbye to Jesse, and she looked like she had been in this situation a few times before; she was ready for me to leave and had been since we met. She just said "bye" without a glance, without a trace of emotion, and walked off with a friend of hers. For me, the sailor who had been without a girlfriend, for years at sea, well, I thought she could have been a bit more choked up, but then again, I wasn't all that emotionally attached either. I guess sometimes the, "If you can't be with the one you love, love the one your with" anthem rang true; but it wasn't really "love the one your with" it should have been "enjoy the one your with" or "have fun with the one your with."

So, Troll and I found our way to the freeway entrance; him with his washtub containing his few articles of clothing, and me with my guitar case filled with a change of pants and shirts and socks, folded to fit in with my Gibson guitar. Troll? I didn't call him that unless I was introducing him. He looked more like a Troll than anything else, and he was Troll-fearless! Let me tell you his story: Troll was once married, and he was a salesman with a mortgage in the suburbs. His wife was always pressuring him to come up with all the things that give one social status - the old keeping up with the Jones's syndrome, one of the banes of modern life.

Troll had heard a lecture by Timothy Leary, and he managed to find some LSD. After much inner turmoil and emotional trauma, his "trip" led him to hang himself in the living room of his highly mortgaged home. After almost thirty minutes of hanging there, his wife arrived and cut him down with a kitchen knife, screaming all the while. She carried on, over his lifeless body, until he felt maybe he should get back into it. She was sure he was dead, and he told me that he was, in fact, deceased and had been for some time.

He said he had left his body and floated about the room, trying to get his balance, apparently a hard thing to do when you don't weigh anything at all. Troll had seen the reality of our situation, that we don't die, that there is no death; we merely pass on in our subtle body, to wherever God or Nature or the laws of Nature have determined we should spend some time digesting the lessons we have learned from our recent physical incarnation. More to the point, he had realized that he couldn't die, and that made all the difference to him. And so the amazing Troll just popped back into his body and woke up to his wife's lamentations. She didn't understand that he was trying to escape from what he saw as a life of meaningless work and worry, all for the appearance of being successful, when in a matter of a few decades he and she would die and all their hard work would be for nothing, and their possessions would go to someone else.

ME & TROLL

He understood from his action that the soul survives death, but he had no understanding of the purpose of being alive, that there is a very well organized structure to the whole of creation. Like so many who have had near-death experiences, his whole perspective on life changed. He left his wife - didn't have kids - and ended up in Greenwich Village. He wasn't a poet and didn't have time to figure out how to play guitar, but the simple one string washtub base was do-able, and he was pretty good at it. Now, you must realize that the man no longer had any fear of anything or anyone, because he figured "what's the worst thing that can happen to me? I could die, but I can't!" and this attitude, based on his realization, would come very close to ending my life in this body as well as his.

ST LOUIS

We spent the first night in the basement laundry room of a motel just off the freeway and didn't get disturbed until one of the cleaning ladies woke us up by banging on the top of the dryer with a broom handle. She was big and black and wasn't afraid of either of us. She said she was calling the cops on us, and we made for the stairway, dragging our respective instruments and coats out into the brisk morning air. I think we stood at the freeway entrance for two hours before getting a ride, but when we did, it took us all the way to St. Louis, Missouri.

After looking up Troll's friend, who begrudgingly offered his sofa and floor for the night, I asked him if there was anywhere we could play and pass the hat. He quickly came up with a possibility, and with a more friendly attitude took us to a lounge - a big one - with families eating and lots of folks drinking and talking. It was the Sunday dinner family rendezvous.

We went up to the owner who was curious about us, looking the Troll and me over - especially Troll - with his washtub and broom handle with a thick metal base string attached to it. He said "are you having dinner?" and I said "sure, we will entertain your customers for a meal." He looked incredulous, and I told him we just came down from Boston and New York City, where we played professionally and were passing through on our way to LA. When I mentioned that we played family-oriented folk music like the Kingston Trio, his face lit up, and he said: "OK, give us a song, and if they like it you can play till they don't."

We started with some hits that were on the radio, like Michael Row the Boat Ashore and Sloop John B, by the Kingston Trio. When I sang Michael Row, I got everyone to join in, and we seemed to be a rousing success. The owner gave us two large plates full of good food and a ten dollar bill. We were near starving, not having eaten a meal since we left the Village and our host (Troll's "friend") seemed to be happy to take us home and serve us hot tea before we all sacked out.

PHOENIX

The next morning our crash-pad host had already gone to work when we woke up. He left a note saying we were welcome to crash anytime we came through St. Louis. Our next eventful stop was Phoenix, Arizona, where Sherry was staying at a clinic for pregnant women and girls. The girls live there for the duration of their pregnancy, while the officials sort through prospective adoptive parents. Back then it was a major sin to be unmarried and pregnant, and families would send their girls off to places like this to hide them until they had placed their babies in married couples' homes.

The main reason I headed for Phoenix, rather than going the northern route to LA, was a letter I had received from Sherry when I was staying with Ted in Boston. She informed me about where she was living, waiting out her pregnancy and ultimately having the child adopted. There didn't seem to be any question that I was the father in her letter; still, I couldn't understand what Peggy could have to gain by lying to me about the other guy being the father, that guy who ran from us in San Francisco! So, I had decided to visit her in Phoenix on my way to California, just in case.

Troll and I found a crappy hotel on the derelict side of town to sleep in, but we didn't even spend one night there, as we lucked out playing in a bar and got invited to crash at a Go-Go dancer's apartment. I'll tell the story as it happened: after leaving our things at the hotel, we went for breakfast at a local diner. Our waitress noticed my guitar case and said that we could probably play at a bar she knew in Phoenix. She said that musicians sometimes got up and sang country songs or covers there and that we could pass the hat like the Go-Go girls did. What she didn't tell us was that it was the hang out of Hell's Angels and Apache Indians, a tough crowd. That evening we walked the streets of downtown Phoenix until we found the place and walked in. The first thing that caught my eye was the Go-Go dancer moving around in one spot to the loud music. When her break came, Troll, being fearless, went up to her and asked if we could play a set, and she directed us to the manager. He said "are you any good?" and Troll bragged-on about me and all the clubs I'd played in the big cities back east.

The manager nodded his head and said go on after the next girl finishes, and we waited for around an hour or so until the first girl we talked to, signaled us to take the stage. When the girl came down, and we went up, the crowd started to boo for obvious reasons, I mean they were all men. We began with a folk-blues song, and they quieted down a bit, but after a few ballads, they started getting rowdy and calling for the girls. I asked "what do you want me to sing about, ca'mon anything" and someone shouted out "get off the stage," and so I began:

"I was singing in a bar

when a cowboy in a rage,

started yell-in really loud

for me to get off of the stage,

I told him he was rude

and he threw some of his food, when I saw
that it was chicken,

I picked it up for lick-in,

Ya that finger lick-in chicken

makes me stop my finger pick-in,

every-time I starts to lick-in

I can't do no finger pick-in,

so if your ever in a rage

cause some dude's up on the stage,

just throw some crispy chicken

and that dude will stop his pick-in,

stop his pick-in, stop his pick-in, cause that
chicken's just too finger lick-in good."

Well, it was something like that, probably better! I think I made up the songs in a mostly 12 bar blues format, which allows for repetition, giving you time to figure out the next verse. They loved it and started shouting more phrases and even body parts like, "my broken leg" or "sing about an ugly girl, or your skinny ass." Stuff like that! So, we went on like that for a good 45 minutes, the time the Go-Go girls have to fill, and ended with a good one, leaving some of them calling for more and others calling for the girls.

When we went over to the bar, the barman gave us free beers and said we could have as much as we wanted that evening. I was standing alone, nursing my lousy tasting American beer when a tipsy Apache came up to me and stared into my eyes. He said "I don't like you," and in my usual attempt to cancel a challenge to fight I responded with "why." He was too drunk to care about why or anything else, and so my usual ability to diffuse attackers was not working. This guy was about 5'8" and almost as wide, all solid Chiricahua Apache muscle, so I moved down the bar a bit, but he followed and said that he hated me. I think I asked if he wanted a beer on me, and that I was a great admirer of Cochise and Geronimo, that I felt the Apache Indians were the toughest Indians in the west. My cowardly ploy must have worked because that ended his interest in fighting me, and he wandered into the restroom.

When the last Go Go girl came down from the stage, Troll went up to her and asked if she knew of a place we could crash. At first, she thought he meant just him, and she started to shake her head, but then Troll pointed in my direction, and she smiled and said "sure, you can stay at my place." I would never have dared to ask these girls for a place to crash, they would have had to ask me, and that only happens with pretty boys. It turned out her boyfriend was out of town and that I could sleep in her bed and that was good, it's just that she had rock hard breasts, those old kinds of solid silicone implants like Carol Doda, the San Francisco burlesque queen had.

Troll wasn't satisfied with just a place to stay while we were in Phoenix, he wanted what I had, a girl. He asked the Go-Go girl, Carol, if she had a friend she could introduce him to, and she hesitated, because the Troll was butt ugly, but then said, "yes, I'll talk to her." As it happened, Carol's friend was very cute and slept with the Troll at least for one night. Later, after we left Phoenix, he started having symptoms of the clap, and we had to get him to a clinic for shots. Even if the Troll was ugly and pushy, it still seems nasty to knowingly give him that gross disease.

Anyway, we stayed in Phoenix for several days, and I visited

Sherry at her birthing clinic. It was an enjoyable afternoon because when I arrived for the visit, I looked up and saw four or five smiling girls peering at me through the window on the door to the inner chambers of the place. Then out came Sherry, all sweetness, and light. She was delighted that I had come all that way to see her, and she used it to impress all the other girls that, unlike their impregnators, hers was still devoted to her, pregnant or not, keeping the baby or not. Of course, as I have said, I didn't believe the baby was mine as a result of Peggy's lies. Sherry greeted me with "Hi Baby," which she had done back in San Diego, but it always sounded strange coming out of such a young thing. She was 20 by now, but "Hi baby" still sounded like some coquettish vamp in a 50's movie when her boyfriend, the mob guy, walks into the bar scene.

TROLL & THE HELL'S ANGELS

We played a few more of the bars that our Go-Go girls opened up for us, and were planning to leave for LA in a day or so. After the last gig, we all went to dinner at a place that the girl's friends frequented. That evening it was filled with Hell's Angels, with their black leather jackets, patches, colors, and tough-looking "old ladies." I was about to turn around and retreat through the door I came in when Carol started introducing Troll and me to all of them. They seemed normal enough in the restaurant atmosphere; in fact, one of them invited all of us to a party later that night at the house of the President of the Phoenix Chapter of the Hell's Angels. The Pres's name was Johnny, and he was getting out of prison that night after doing seven years for manslaughter!!

Troll was very interested in going to the party, but I was apprehensive; I knew that a Hell's Angel in a family restaurant with his "wife" is one thing. The same guy two or three hours into a party, with hard liquor and drugs and all his mates to impress, could be yet another. But Troll was going, and I knew I had to keep him out of trouble. So, we went, and after a few hours, I remember sitting on the thick rug in the living room of this somewhat upscale home, which didn't reflect one's idea of a Hell's Angel's pad at all. Next to me was a guy who was taking mass quantities of hormones so that he could become a girl. His voice was cracking octaves like a 14-year-old boy, and he was going on about the operation he was going to have. He was making me feel a bit queasy with all the beer I had consumed out of boredom. I don't remember seeing many of the Angels at the party, but I think they were off picking up Johnny, their leader, and might arrive at any moment.

I guess I must have slept on the floor there because it was morning, and Troll was pushing my shoulder and saying "Rick, get up, get up, we got to go." his tone and attitude woke me up faster than his pushing. We were on our way out the door when he told me that he had gone into the bedroom, Johnny's wife's bedroom. I said "Johnny! the President of the Hell's Angels - who was getting out of prison this very day after seven years for having man-slaughtered someone?" Troll said "ya, he came into the room last night and saw us in bed together. He left a note on the door that I have to be out of town by high noon or he is going to shoot and kill me." "Then we better get our stuff and get on the road," I said, and Troll calmly explained that he wasn't going to run away: "That wouldn't be an honorable thing to do to my new lady."

HIGH NOON

Troll was going to meet Johnny at the bar at noon and face him man to man. I said, "then you will be killed; Johnny won't back down in front of all his fellow Angels." Troll insisted on his insane plan of "honor." He said that he was honoring the wife of Johnny by doing this; he thought she would choose him, over her husband! It was the day we were leaving, but first, we had to go to the bar where Troll was going to face Johnny and his Hell's Angels, and I hadn't realized yet that I was in as much danger as Troll. We came in the front door, and immediately an Angel,"Rebel" came over and grabbed me. He took me to a quiet corner of the bar and said that Johnny would be there at 12, another ten minutes, and that when Troll faced him, "Blood," and another Big Angel would grab Johnny's gun-arm and wrestle him down; Johnny wasn't a big guy, but he was totally insane and wiry.

Rebel wanted me to have a taxi out front, ready to take Troll and me out of town. Rebel and I were supposed to grab Troll and carry him out to the cab and get the hell out of there before Johnny could shoot us. They didn't want Johnny to kill anyone in public; he would have to go back to jail and this time for good.

Out on the curb, I signaled a taxi to come up to the front of the bar, and I told him to wait for a few minutes. Our instruments were out at Carol's place, and we would have to go there first thing. Well, there was a lot of bustling about as Johnny came in the back door of the bar with Hell's Angels all around him. He had his hand in his pocket, just like Rebel had told me, and he strode up to the middle of the bar where Troll was waiting and demanded to know if he was leaving "dead or alive;" Troll responded, "No, Johnny I don't feel it would be honorable." Without another word, Johnny lunged at Troll, pulling a gun out of his pocket; a shot was fired into the ceiling when the two Angels grabbed Johnny's arm. They got him down on the ground, and Rebel ran over to Troll and picked him up by the back of his jacket, forcing him toward the door. This was my cue as well, and together we carried him out to the taxi, shoved him in, and Rebel told the driver to get us the hell out of there.

THE GREAT ESCAPE

The taxi driver must have known who the Angel was because

he didn't seem to need much encouragement in getting us out of there fast. We drove out to Carol's place and ran in as the taxi took off. I was putting my clothes into my guitar case when I saw a car pull up out in front of the house. I grabbed Troll and pulled him down on the floor, behind the couch, against his will. I said, "man they're out in front looking for us, and if they see us, we are dead."

He said "I don't care! I want to face Johnny." "If they see you, they will kill you, and they will have to kill me so that there are no witnesses, you asshole. I have things I want to do; I don't want to die for the honor of you sleeping with his wife." I had to grab him and hold onto him with all my strength, or I really would be dead. These guys didn't mind Johnny killing Troll or me at all; it was doing it in public that they didn't like because their long-suffering leader would have to go back to prison. They drove back and forth to get a better view of the inside of the house, and thank God they didn't want to come in; they were more worried that we might be getting away in the other direction. After about five minutes of peering into the house for movement they took off, and I grabbed my guitar and was out on the street before Troll could get his tub. I started hitching west, after walking down the road a hundred yards or so. I kept looking out for Johnny and his gang, and at last, Troll ambled down the road, without a care in the world, carrying his washtub.

A big rig was coming around the corner, and we held our thumbs up high and smiled big smiles, and thank God he stopped and picked us up. We were about half a mile down that road when I saw that same car pull up in front of Carol's house again. I could see it in the truck's passenger side mirror and two big guys running up the front steps. I thought I saw them come out as we were driving onto the highway, and I could make out the car spitting up dust and gravel as it drove off in the other direction.

There is a vivid memory in my mind's eye of sundown from the back of a Semi-trailer bed the kind that transports big machinery like bulldozers and harvesters. I'm lying down in the middle of it, with my head on my guitar case as we sail along at 70mph through the cactus-studded Arizona desert. I'm in the open dry air as it whips my face with fine sand and diesel exhaust from the round steel chimney sticking up the side of the cab. I don't see Troll in this picture, but I think he was up in the cab with the trucker. I'm staring at the blue eastern horizon as the sun sets behind me, and I feel that bliss of freedom again, the kind that is alive with the joy of the present and the adventure of the future.

The White Mountains are off to the north - the only mountains anywhere out here - and I picture the Apache Indians of old crossing the desert to summer in the cool pine forests, filled with deer and antelope. Recently, I flew over Arizona, and the White Mountains look like they just popped out of the desert in one small, round group, kind of like Uluru or Ayers Rock in Australia, only with snow covered peaks. Both are sacred to the original peoples of these areas, just as the Black Hills of South Dakota are to the Sioux. The trucker took us all the way to LA, where Troll and I parted. He had friends to look up, and I was bound for San Diego and the Heritage out on Mission Beach.

THE HERITAGE

The main reason I went back down to San Diego was that I knew I could play at the Heritage for enough money to pay for food, and I was hungry. There were also lots of places I could stay: Zoya's beach house if she were in town, or Bonnie, Ann & Sherry's place; remember Bonnie - the singer who could take the roof off with her powerful voice? Well, when I got to the Heritage, it was late afternoon and Bill Nunn, the owner, wasn't there yet. There was a pretty blond waitress, a new girl, that came up to me when she saw that I was friends with some of the staff and said that there was a party tonight and anyone with a guitar could go. She and her boyfriend were going, and she invited me to join them, so I did. When we got to the "party," I was a little-taken a-back because the room was dimly lit and quiet. No one was playing guitar or singing, just a lot of joint passing and staring into space. I didn't recognize anyone and got a few paranoid, "short hair, he's a narc" glances when suddenly someone grabbed my arm, and I pulled away and turned to see buxom Bonnie, the school teacher, and folk singer.

BONNIE & THE DEVIL

She seemed glad to see me, but pulled me toward the door and whispered in my ear that some of the people didn't know me and that I was "freaking them out." It seems that this was an LSD party, and being a stranger with short hair was "bad tripping" some of them. Bonnie was the "guide" for all the newbies and politely asked if I wouldn't mind leaving. She saw me out the door and asked if I had a place to stay. "Not yet," I said, and she said she still lived in the place she used to share with Ann and Sherry, and that I was welcome to crash there.

The Blond waitress and her boyfriend hadn't expected this kind of party either and offered to take me to Bonnie's house. When I got there, I crashed on her couch and didn't wake up till the sun was filling up the room. Bonnie didn't get home till dawn, and I didn't hear her come in. After I had fried up the .48 cent can of corned beef hash that I brought with me, and heated up a cup of Bonnie's leftover coffee, I hitched out to Mission Beach to see if I could set up a weekend gig at the Heritage. Fortunately, Bill Nunn was there, and he wanted me to open for someone next week and unfortunately, maybe in a month or so I could do my own show.

That wasn't good enough, opening for whoever wasn't going to pay for food and guitar strings so I figured I'd head out for LA. About this time Bonnie showed up and did some talking with Bill. I waited, sipping some cider until she sat down next to me. She looked into my eyes with the seriousness of a school teacher who is about to discipline the problem student, and asked if I had ever taken LSD; if I hadn't, she could guide me on my first trip. I had been asked this question about five times before and had been resolute in not taking this drug. However, Bonnie seemed convinced that LSD could open one's consciousness to the immensity of one's higher Self and the infinite nature of the universe around us. It looked like she was on a crusade to get me enlightened to the insights possible through the proper guidance of an LSD "trip." Somehow I trusted her experience and conviction, and after offering many of my fears, I reluctantly agreed to the guided tour. Bonnie called her surfboard-making, drug supplier and arranged for him to pick us up at the Heritage. He showed up in a two-seat - pickup truck and told me I could sit in the back with my guitar. I had an immediate disliking for this guy; I didn't know why just then, but I soon would.

When we got to Bonnie's house, I checked him out more closely; he was about thirty-five and gave off the nasty aura of a pimp or pusher, and he was clearly lusting for Bonnie. I could tell he had already had sex with her from the way she would allow his advances, even though it was apparent she wasn't welcoming them. I'll call him Scab, the pusher! It sounds about right! Scab gave Bonnie the LSD in sugar cube form and said she could pay him later, with a twinkle in his eye. Bonnie and I popped the cubes in our mouths, and Scab sat opposite me as if he thought he was going to be my guide. He started to ramble on about relaxing, blah, blah, blah and after about fifteen minutes I looked up, and Scab had turned into the devil - I mean he had the red face and pointy red ears and nasty yellow eyes with a leering look in them, like he couldn't wait to mess up my mind in front of Bonnie. I yelled "Jesus Christ he's the Devil!" and I was about to jump to my feet and get the hell out of there, when Bonnie took my hand and told Scab to "Go, go, go now, your giving him a bad trip."

My want to be acid guru was pissed off. I think he thought I was trying to get rid of him so I could be with Bonnie. He reluctantly left and told her that if she needed him later to give a call and he looked at me with a sneer and that devil face. Bonnie tried to calm me down by putting on a Dylan album, and I was fine until I forgot who we were listening to and said: "who is that ridiculous farmer singing, he sounds like a kid talking like an old farmer." Bonnie laughed and said, "that's Bob Dylan." I was mind-blown; I mean we all knew that Dylan put on a Woody Guthrie or maybe even an "Okie" accent, but to really hear it from the level of Dylan's "acting persona" was like hearing a rank amateur folk singer pretending to be Bob Dylan; it was that obvious and seemed ridiculous. Why was he pretending to be someone else, I thought?

We were up all night sitting there, and I can't remember anything other than the Dylan revelation. Next day we went to a market and walked up and down the aisles. I was still seeing things in a new way and would occasionally comment on them, like "whoa, the cans are so perfectly lined up." Bonnie would shush me; she was afraid that what I was saying would be noticed as drug-induced, and we would get busted. I don't know why? We didn't have any drugs on us, and besides, LSD was legal then, and it was in us, not on us. She bought some food, and we went back to her place.

Bonnie made a yummy dinner and served it to me like a mom. I was starved and gobbled up everything on the plate; I didn't seem to feel the need to restrict my slurps and belches. She was an attentive hostess, and the time was approaching that Bonnie had included in her considerate version of hospitality. She put a massage table in the living room beside the couch and put a sheet on it. I was wondering what the hell all this was about! She went into her bedroom and came back in a bathrobe then after laying down on the table she invited me to get on top of her. Looking at her lying there I realized for the first time that she wasn't chubby at all. I had always thought she was fat! She was skinny with enormous boobs that she would hide by tethering them down to look like a large tummy.

I couldn't help but stare; she was self-conscious about them, and I wasn't helping. Still, after the LSD I wasn't really in the mood for sex, and though I made a feeble attempt, I'm sure she must have been disappointed, I hope she didn't blame it on her boobs freaking me out. I think that her old roommates had overstated my sexual prowess. I mean, when I was with Ann, she had been dumped by her boyfriend, and I had just come back to San Diego from eight months of celibacy at sea, and I couldn't get enough, all night until daylight. With Sherry, it was short but sweet, and she said she came for the first time in her life and was more than impressed, but I chalked that up to Dylan and the joint. Anyway, The next morning I told Bonnie I was heading for LA and thanked her for everything, and she wished me well.

CRASHING IN VENICE

My ride dropped me in Venice Beach where I ate a few tacos down on the boardwalk. My guitar always attracted the kind of people who could help me find a place to stay, and it wasn't long before a young Canadian couple came up and asked that very question. I followed them to one of those small stucco, one story houses from the 20's or 30's, with the full-length porches and low-slanting roofs. We went in, and they introduced me to an older guy who had told everyone that he had been a decorated Green Beret in Vietnam.

His name was Leon, and he was lying in the only bed in the place. He looked like a junky or a wino and didn't have much to say, except that I had to be in by eleven pm and there would be no screwing unless he got some of it too. There must have been ten or twelve places marked with sleeping bags or blankets; it wasn't easy to find a spot on the hardwood floor, but

I pushed some of the bedding closer together and put my guitar and sleeping bag down in the spot I hoped to save. When I got back that night, the place was full of young people, and my guitar had been propped up against the wall with my bag under it. A loud blond girl, about 25 with an Australian accent, ordered some of the crowd to move together so that I could fit in; the junky wasn't there, and I figured she was in charge when he was gone. She asked where I was from, and if I was playing anywhere; she was a dancer and had been auditioning for six months with no luck.

At about two in the morning, someone came crashing in the door, falling about and cursing. This had to be Leon, he tripped over some of us and landed close to my head; he stunk of booze and puke and finally crawled to his bed. I could hear the sound of heavy breathing and Leon yelled out "No fucking unless I get some too!" Most of us enjoyed the couple's embarrassment as they were keeping us awake, and we had a good laugh.

A funny thing happened the next day. The Canadian couple and I were walking down the beach, and I started acting like an eight-year-old, climbing up a telephone pole wire like a monkey and imitating one as I clambered down. I was walking like Long John Silver with his limp and doing my best Robert Newton impression: "Arr Jim me boy, it were the black spot says I." All because the Canadian girl was watching me with an approving smile on her face and I loved to entertain. I had no intention of going after her; I thought the two were very cute as a couple and wouldn't like to see them break up. Anyway, that night when we were all tucked in, and Leon was still out, Joni, the Canadian girl, tiptoed over to me and kneeled down by me. She indicated she wanted to get into my sleeping bag with me, and I looked over at her, who had turned his back and was feigning sleep.

When she was all cozied up to me, I put my arms around her and held her butt and then put my hands on her boobs, and she immediately got out of my bag and went back to her boy-friend. I guess she figured I would act like an eight-year-old in bed as well as on the beach. I think I did the premature feeling-up to send her home to the poor shit lying over there. His so-called girl-friend was doing whatever the hell she felt like right in front of him, whether it hurt him or not. Since then, I've been made the cuckold several times, and I always remembered the Canadians whenever it happened.

HOOT-NIGHT AT THE TROUBADOUR

That was my last night at Leon's house. The next day I took my guitar and sleeping bag with me, hoping I would find a better place to stay. I walked from Venice to the pier on Santa Monica beach, sat in the shade and practiced for a couple of hours, stopped for a Jack in the Box burger and fries and found my way to the Troubadour as the sun was going down. Tonight was going to be a hoot night; I knew I had better sign up to play before all the slots were filled, so I asked the girl in the ticket booth where the list was. In the past, you had to track down whoever had it. When you found him, if he didn't know you, he would look you over and decide whether you looked the part or not. The ticket girl told me just to put my name on the paper she pushed forward, and to put down what I do:

folksinger, comedian, juggler, etc. She said that Tim, the host, would decide when and if I would go on. She said that means you pretty much have to be in the audience the whole night because when he calls you up, you better be ready. I didn't know if Tim would remember me by name from the last time I played here about a year ago, so I found a seat in the balcony and left it to fate.

These were the days when the future superstars of folk rock and pop music shared the same stage with me, and many others who just as likely as not might have been destined for wealth and fame. There was Linda Ronstadt and the Stone Ponies, Steven Stills, most of the members of the Monkeys, the Association, Neil Young, Crosby, the Doors, and so many of the true folk singers who became legends like Taj Mahal, Joni Mitchel and the great guitarist, Ry Cooder. I heard: "Rick Stanley" called about half-way through the show - the best time to get noticed by industry, A&R guys and other musicians. I got up there and did a ballad or two, and then I did my version of "Hero Blues" that I got from John Hammond Jr. The crowd gave me great applause and a lot of hooting which was the perfect response for a funky blues that got them wanting to dance.

THE LEAVES

I went outside for some air, and a couple of high school guys came up to me and said they dug my guitar playing. They had a band called "The Leaves" and a number #1 hit single on the LA charts called "Hey Joe." I had heard it on a car radio and loved it. They wanted me to meet them the next day, and we would all go to the music store, and they'd rent me a couple of electric guitars; a Rickenbacker 12 and a Fender Telecaster. Then we'd go to their studio, and I would learn all their songs very fast since they had a US tour scheduled in two weeks.

The next morning I met the boys, and they were just boys. We rented the guitars, went to their practice studio which was the family garage, and I tried to learn their songs. The trouble was, they had expected me to read their charts, read all the notes from sheets of music. They didn't realize that most folk musicians back then never bothered with learning to read if they had an ear. Most of us could hear a song and pick up the guitar and figure out the chords to the song, then transpose the chords to fit our vocal ranges, all by ear.

When I tried to learn their songs, there was so much going on with bass, drums, keyboard, rhythm guitar and four harmony voices - all going at once - that it was almost impossible to figure out the basic melody to match my chords too. I must also mention that I had never played an electric guitar, and it was a whole different beast; the strings never seemed to be in tune and the action was impossible to hammer-on or do most of my usual finger-picking styles of playing. When they saw that I wasn't adapting fast enough, they pushed the sheet music in front of me, and I said: "I don't read."

They hadn't expected any of this and figured they were going to have to give their old lead guitar player what he wanted after all. It turned out he had left the group when they were arguing over how much each of them would be paid out of the lump-sum being offered by Pat Boone's management company. I was glad to get out of this gig - I was six years older than most of them, and I was only 22. Of course, that sounds silly to me now at 74, a difference of six years, but so much changes so quickly during those critical growing years.

ANOTHER UN-INTENSIONAL AUDITION

When they dropped me off in front of the Troubadour that afternoon, I ran into Zoya's brother. I hadn't seen him for a year and asked how Zoya was doing. "Oh, Rick you should come to her birthday party tonight, Pam Polland will be there and lots of her other music and artist friends." I had no way to get out to Zoya's house, in the middle of the desert, so I asked if he was going out later. Lucky for me he was, and he loaded me in, guitar, sleeping bag and all. Such a fortunate happen-stance! I was on my way to meet Pamela Polland, the great songwriter, who performed regularly at the Troubadour with Ry Cooder, the greatest folk guitar player in the country.

This was the most important turn of events that could have happened for me in my quest to be a Columbia Recording Art-ist. When I got there, Zoya was delighted because she had al-ways wanted me to meet Pamela; she thought we could make beautiful harmony together. Pamela was singing and playing a big Martin D-28 Dreadnought guitar, and everyone was pay-ing attention, especially me. When she finished the song, she said "You must be Rick! ca'mon play along on the next song." I listened to the first verse and came in on the second. I put my capo way up the neck on my guitar so that I could play harpsi-chord-like picking around her chords. She looked over when I started and smiled; that was a good sign because she was used to Ry Cooder's guitar creations. When we finished, she asked if I could sing harmony on a song we both knew and I said, "I'll sing the melody, and you sing the harmony if that's ok." She nodded, and we began; at the end of this song everyone clapped and shouted approval. I didn't know it at the time, but Pamela was looking for a male singing partner on the rec-ommendation of the great Columbia Records Producer, Terry Melcher. Terry loved Pamela's songs but felt her voice wasn't strong enough as a single vocalist.

He wanted to sign her as a Columbia Recording Artist, and do what he had done with "The Byrds" and "Paul Revere and the Raiders" make a lot of chart-topping hits, and a lot of money and respect working with musicians and material he believed in. When the song was over, Pamela looked very pleased and asked me if I was playing and performing with anyone. She wanted to meet with me and make a demo to give to Terry; she said that if he liked it, we would be signed to Columbia Records. She asked where I was staying, and offered to put me up in her spare room while we practiced and recorded the demo. All of this seemed like outrageously good fortune: I'd only been in LA for a week, and I was being offered the possibility of a recording contract with the very company I had prayed to be with for years.

I decided, however, not to "put all my eggs in this one basket," even if it was the most desirable one I could imagine. So, while living and working at Pamela's apartment, I followed up on a few other options that had opened to me while playing the hoots at the Troubadour. One of them was an offer by Eli Lilly (the paper cup guy), who had a recording studio in his LA home. He loved music and art, and he enjoyed playing engineer for musicians he liked. I recorded some of the songs I was performing, which was great as I was getting a free demo of myself that I could use to get gigs and interviews with the A&R people of record companies.

There were a few other potential situations, like Randy Spark's "The New Christy Minstrels," with Doug Dillard, the great banjo player. I went for the audition, but I didn't like the music - it was like the "Lovely Lennon Sisters" from Lawrence Welk, meets korny - pop "folk music" a' la Hullabaloo or Shindig. I just walked out when they had finished doing one of the songs they were practicing. It seems Randy needed a new guitarist to replace one that had just left the group.

PRIMAL SCREAM!

Then there was "The Primal Scream," by Arthur Janov. No, I wasn't going to play guitar while he screamed, but he did hire me to teach his twelve-year-old daughter how to play the guitar. He told me he hired me because Doug Weston, owner of the Troubadour, told him Ry Cooder, Kenny Edwards, and Rick Stanley were the best guitarists that he knew of who might be available. Ry was too busy, and he couldn't find Kenny. I could have told him Steve Mann should have been number two on that list, but Steve wouldn't have done it anyway.

Of course, I took the job; I needed the money, and it was only two hours a week. After several lessons, Janov took me in with him and his pubescent pop-star wannabe, to see if the recording company executive at Columbia would sign her to the label. I don't think it ever happened, but he continued to pay me to give the little lass lessons. He even had a limousine drive me out to Palm Springs to stay over in his big house, Good food! When John Lennon started raving about the "primal scream" technique, it seemed kinda silly to me after watching the family dynamics of the author and never hearing anyone scream or even mildly complain: they corked all their anxiety up like Perrier bottles and remained very quiet at meals. I think the dad had a rule that when guests were around, they were to act like the perfect family so that his books would keep selling, and they could continue to live like rock stars. A lot of this observation was picked up from his daughter, who held a tight lip but expressed volumes in her body language and moods.

THE BUFFALO SPRINGFIELD

One night I crashed at a place just off the Sunset Strip, and in the morning I met a fellow crasher, Hoyt Axton, who didn't have much to say, but when he did, it was like the rumble of my uncle Clem's deep-chested growl, and you just had to listen. It worked out well that I crashed where I did because I had an appointment to meet Steven Stills in his basement apartment on Sunset Blvd. that morning.

I met him at the Troubadour the night before, and he wanted me to come and audition for his new group, which turned out to be "The Buffalo Springfield." He asked me to join in with harmony and guitar once I got the gist of the song, and he started picking and singing. I did OK - I can come up with very original guitar and harmony parts under pressure.

Neil Young came in just after me, along with a few others that day. He and Steven had already joined forces. Steven had approached him after seeing his group perform in Canada. Steven told me that whoever else he picked would get to go to Phoenix for a big concert. He said that the last time he played there his group was a big hit; also mentioning a possible record contract deal with some music backing corporation, which didn't excite me. Not long after my audition with Stills, Terry contacted Pamela and was raving about the two of us. He wanted to get us in the studio as soon as possible; to

make a demo

The Buffalo Springfield

for the Columbia Record Execs.

RILEY WYLDFLOWER

Some time passed before Terry had time to get us into the studio. Pamela had already started to recruit other musicians to back us up, and I ended up in the Valley staying in a rented house with two of the potential band members: Riley "Wyldflower" Cummings and a drummer from Riley's Beatles-clone group. They had toured the southwest, and one of the groupies (Candy) latched on to them in Tulsa by offering the money she received from an insurance claim for her broken leg so that the drummer could buy a new set of drums. Riley wrote his songs in the vein of the early Beatles, like "Love Me Do" and "Twist and Shout," which didn't interest me at all; it had been done more than once and couldn't possibly attract a record company or get us on the radio.

Riley was six-foot-five with wild, light-brown, curly hair and was almost always stoned. He was a likable, Irish-American, son of a car dealership-owner in the hills of Calabasas. He played decent rhythm guitar in the typical pop band genre. But Pamela and I were acoustic folk musicians, and I couldn't understand why she wanted a pop guitar player who couldn't sing well enough to add a harmony. I think she just liked him, and so she would come over, and we would practice her songs and a few others in preparation for the Columbia demo with Terry. Meanwhile, we were trying to come up with a name for our group which is always more fun than practicing.

One night Riley had "scored" a kilo of grass with Candy's money, and he proceeded to lay back on his bed and blow pot smoke into the face of his cat, who just lay there on his chest looking up at him and throwing cat kisses with his eyes. Riley said "He's such a gentle soul," and I jumped on this and said "That's the name for our group, 'The Gentle Soul,' " and so it was! Riley must have thought that marijuana was a universal balm for all creatures great and small and that it couldn't possibly do any harm.

Lots of hippies thought that, feeding it to their kids in brownies and cookies. It turns out to be detrimental to kids and cats as well. The next day the cat was acting like he'd eaten fifty pounds of catnip, running, flipping and jumping in a spastic frenzy; seeing something invisible and lunging for it only to flop upside down on his back. He got up and dashed headlong into the patio window and lay there unconscious for a while. I guess the poor guy managed to get out of the house, and we never saw him again.

(below) I'm being sarcastically stoned for the camera, that's me on the right.

Bobby & Riley were totally stoned!

Early Gentle Soul with Bobby The Bass Player

Later Gentle Soul With Sandy The Drummer

THE GENTLE SOUL

The Gentle Soul Album Cover

JIM MORRISON CRASHES IN THE ATTIC

After a few months in the Valley, we all moved into an old house on Venice Beach that Pamela and Candy managed to lease. Each of us had a room, and I rigged up some bamboo curtains on the walls all around my little abode and slept on an old mattress with a new cotton cover that I found in a thrift store. Pamela still had her own place and would come over to practice. Candy and the drummer had the choice room downstairs, and Riley and I had our little rooms upstairs.

I was beginning to feel like this wasn't going anywhere, the drummer didn't know how to drum, and Riley's primary focus was getting high. Anyway, Nature doesn't allow a vacuum to persist, and Candy brought a stranger to the house. He arrived when the drummer was away for some reason, and he pro-

153

ceeded to seduce Candy without much effort. After four days of being serviced by the stranger, her previous lover returned, the inadequate drummer. Candy pretended that nothing had happened and offered the attic as her new lover's bedroom. The loft/attic was where we practiced, and this didn't suit lover boy at all. He never spoke a word to any of us; only Candy was privy to his profound thoughts. He would sit and stew when we were up there, making all kinds of bored and inconvenienced expressions, with his little poet-pad in full view and his pencil sticking out from behind one ear. I didn't like his attitude at all. He didn't contribute anything for rent and expected us to feed him as well; all for the price of sex with Candy when the drummer wasn't around. You won't be surprised to know who this guy was since his name is in the chapter heading. I have more to say about him later on.

The whole thing finally came to a head when the drummer discovered Morrison and his true love Candy going at it in his bed. He flew into a rage but ended up begging her to stay with him. It was clear that she finally understood why he wanted her; the bloody drums and the rest of her insurance money to live on, of course! Candy made her choice, and that day the little drummer-boy packed up his drums and left the house. Morrison didn't hang around much longer either, and by this time Riley and I had found an excellent stand-up bass player named Bobby. He was a jazz player, but he adapted very well, and we would let him do some impromptu jazz riffing during a break in a song now and then.

LONG-ASS GIG AT THE GOLDEN BEAR

After a few successful weeks performing at the Troubadour, the owner of another big folk club offered us a gig down at the Golden Bear, in Huntington Beach. We went over well as the opening act for Jose Feliciano and other big-name acts, and they kept signing us up for three weeks at a time, sometimes as the main event. We were developing a Golden Bear following.

I hadn't mentioned a musician friend who put me up in Hollywood for a month or so after we left the house in Venice, and before we moved into the Chateau Marmont. She was a lover of all men who could play guitar better than she could, and who might show her a picking style or a song. She introduced me to Steve Mann, a serious picker. I'm sure she doesn't remember my name! She was a friend of Pamela; and wrote the big hit song Windy. We were just two passing ships on the sea of artistic ambition, to get all purple - prose. Her name was Ruth-Ann.

NEIL YOUNG'S ZEN MASTER PLOY

Ruth-Ann came down to Huntington Beach to test me; dependent upon my answer, I was about to be replaced by a new prospective boyfriend named Neil Young who was apparently into Zen Buddhism. She took me for a walk on the beach and asked if I knew what Zen was; when I said "no," she looked troubled and said that she knew a guy who was telling her all about it and that he was a good guitarist as well. She said that she probably wouldn't be seeing me much when I got back to LA, and I said "Ok!" She walked up the beach acting all sorrowful. What if I had said, "Oh yes, I studied with a Zen master in Japan until I became an adept?" Remember, this was before the "Buffalo Springfield" existed and I was probably better known than Neil in LA. After all, I was about to be signed to Columbia Records with the best producer in LA, and he was just another Canadian singer-songwriter looking for work. I know, sour grapes. Ruth-Ann had been very thoughtful even to come and tell me about her change of heart. I had already assumed that after two months of living and performing in Huntington Beach without a word of communication between us, that my time with Ruth-Ann had expired, and I was pleasantly surprised even to see her that day. It was never a very serious relationship after all, but I thought it was worth mentioning since it involves two very successful and well-known songwriters and little old me-

Neil Young At Gordon's House

of course.

Actually, I remember meeting Neil about six months later at a friend's small apartment. He was a silent witness like Morrison; he never said a word, just sat there the whole evening. You got the feeling that he was looking down on all of us, like Morrison did. That was the night I first saw Maharishi's Poster on the wall; I looked closely at the picture of Maharishi, and knew he was what I was looking for in all my recent searching for a guru, an enlightened master. It was that very lecture, given by Jerry Jarvis, that I attended a few months later that got me to start TM, Transcendental Meditation.

DYLAN'S DRUMMER

While we were at the Golden Bear, Terry Melcher came down to check out our live performance, and he brought Bob Dylan's tour drummer with him. He was a little, pale Jewish guy named Sandy Konikoff, and he looked incredibly cool. Terry wanted us to bring him into the group, but at the time we had four group members, and we were entirely acoustic. Pamela and I would exchange harmony parts and lead vocals while I played fingerpicking guitar and Riley played solid chords behind us. He supported us with rhythm guitar, chunking to Bobby's swinging base beat that was always just ahead or just behind the beat in a good way; their synchronicity gave us a very funky backbeat without drums. It was nice while it lasted, but Bobby missed the jazz world, and when we went back to LA Sandy joined us, and we all moved into the Chateau Marmont on Terry's dime.

LIVING WITH LEVON AT CHATEAU MARMONT

Chateau Marmont

Sandy, Riley and I shared a huge room in this "Musician's Hotel" with its soundproof walls. There was a tiny room (a closet) with a locked door that we were curious about. When Sandy had set up his drums, he started practicing, and no sooner had he begun than the locked door swung open and out popped Levon Helm, the drummer for "The Band." He had a big smile on his face when he saw that the drummer was an old "Hawks" band-mate, and came over and hugged Sandy. The Band was formed by Levon Helm when he was with Ronnie Hawkins of the Hawks from Toronto. Levon came from a musical family down in Arkansas, and he took his music and southern culture very seriously. When Dylan took The Band on the road with him, Sandy replaced Levon as the drummer. Like Ry Cooder, Levon Helm would spend entire days and nights in his room studying the songs and tunes on old 78 rpm records, and playing mandolin, guitar and his drums to them. his walls were stacked to the ceiling with his record collection.

COLUMBIA RECORDS

At last, Terry gave us our first Recording session in studio 'A' at Columbia in Hollywood. The demo came out great, especially the vocal harmony and Pamela's songs. Terry took it to A&R, and they pounced on it. Later that week we were asked to attend a meeting where we were expected to sign over the next three years of our creative lives to the Company. We all went up the elevator to the top floor, passed ogling secretaries and young execs to meet the big shots. They were all business, as usual, and we were just another contract that they could put money behind, or not, depending on a million different karmic manipulations. Once we signed up, Terry rented a Mexican style hacienda for us, just across from the Château Marmont, on Sunset Strip. It was the house of a famous Opera singer who was in Europe, where they love their opera. He had no idea his beloved Steinway Grand Piano - when not being used to create music - was often the receptacle for half-smoked joints and wet glasses of wine. So many party people made their way into the house and treated it like they were rock-stars. Well, some of them were rock-stars.

THE GENTLE SOUL HOUSE

We ran around the house to see which room we wanted, and Riley made a firm stand for a big bedroom downstairs next to the kitchen. I didn't argue; I wanted a particularly cozy room upstairs with windows that opened sideways onto trees with Rose of Sharon or Mother Divine flowers growing all over the reaching branches. Sandy wanted the room just above Riley's, which was just as huge. Pamela chose the room across the hall-way from mine, it was north-facing, and windows lined the north wall looking out on the ascending hills of Hollywood.

A few days later a Columbia representative arrived with several large catalogs of Fender guitar supplies. We could choose anything we needed or wanted out of them, and we did. I ordered a Fender Jaguar electric guitar, not because I wanted it but because it was the most expensive. I planned to trade it in for a Gretsch Tennessean at McCabe's Guitar Shop down in Santa Monica. I also ordered a behemoth piggy-back amplifier that I never used. Riley ordered a Fender Stratocaster and a Fender Base guitar; he also ordered one of those piggy-back amps that were even bigger than he was. Sandy wanted a custom set of Ludwig drums with natural wood finish, and Columbia agreed to pay for them. After the first session, Terry decided that Sandy was a great road drummer but not so strong in the studio; he wasn't a session-veteran like Hal Blaine. Hal was the session drummer who Terry used on the Byrd's albums and all our studio work. He also did the Beach Boys' drumming, The Monkeys', the Mamas' & Pappas,' Elvis,' etc. etc

SESSIONS WITH GLEN CAMPBELL & PAUL HORN

Glen Campbell

Paul Horn

A few remembrances of recording at Columbia with Terry: One evening or early morning we were going over the same song over and over because one of the session men kept blowing the take for everyone. I was amazed as I watched Glen Campbell dozing off to sleep with his head down, almost touching his guitar. Then as if by magic when his part came, he would wake up on queue, his head would pop up, and he would go full throttle, perfect playing every time. It wasn't Glen who was blowing it; it was some other musician who had insisted on getting a pot break and hadn't come back for half an hour. When he came back, he couldn't play. It was this same dude who told me that my song was musically wrong! "theoretically & technically" it doesn't work. He kept telling me I had to change my chord sequence or melody for him to play it.

He kept belittling me as a songwriter and costing me more and more time in the studio, which I am supposed to pay out of album sales. Fortunately, the session leader was the great Paul Horn, who stepped up and said "what's the problem!" to the guitar player. The player said, "the song is theoretically flawed, and until he changes it, I can't play on it." Paul said, "I'm sorry I thought you were one of the session musicians, I didn't know that you were the Columbia Recording Artist?" "If you are not the Artist then you can either play or leave; I have two university degrees in music theory; the song is original and creative which is why Rick is signed to Columbia, and you're not." After that, he played his part quite effortlessly.

DAVID CROSBY WANTS TO JOIN THE GENTLE SOUL!

Once, Pamela and I were standing in the lobby at Columbia, during a session break and Terry came up to us with David Crosby in tow. Terry had played some of our tracks for him, and he was excited about our harmonies. David was there recording some of the last songs the Byrds would record, and he was looking for another group to join. He seemed interested in getting together with us and trying out a three-part harmony--probably like his work with The Byrds. But Pamela and I couldn't help notice that David was very high. We had given up drugs for meditation and didn't want to get back into working with anyone who wasn't all there all the time. So, we passed on the great Crosby. Probably another step back from success and fame, but two steps forward to Self-Realization. Well, maybe? Soon after, there was "Crosby, Stills, Nash, and Young," the voices of the 60's.

RY COODER

Terry was great in the studio, but I didn't like his idea to have Ry Cooder playing slide mandolin on "Younger man Blue;" somehow it sounded wrong to me, so I kept telling him that I didn't like it until it. Terry played it back, with all the instrumental and vocal parts, and I was astounded: I let out a big "Shit, that's incredible," and Terry smiled. I don't think I ever doubted his musical genius again until we were recording the vocal parts on the single "Tell Me, Love." Terry said over the intercom "try singing with a yo- and a yo-ho-ho on that break, you know a sort of pirate thing, it sounds like a sea shanty to me." I said, "Oh God No!" I hated it. "Tell Me Love" was a song I wrote from my experience of God Consciousness, and he was trivializing it with pirate crap for commercial reasons. I have never forgiven myself for allowing it to remain on the recording when I could have just refused to sing that.

CBS TV SPECIALS

There isn't much to say about recording songs, except maybe to mention well-known musicians, and I think the reviews I've included - in the appendix of the 2nd book - do all the name dropping that The Gentle Soul ever needed to be taken seriously. There are, however, some notable names-droppings that can be shared when talking about "The Gentle Soul House." During the time that we lived in that Hacienda-like paradise just up from the Sunset Strip, we were visited by lots of famous people, street hippies and Television Crews, like INSIDE POP: THE ROCK REVOLUTION - CBS-TV specials that looked at the pop music world of 1967. Brian Wilson and members of The Gentle Soul were among the interviewees. There were two of these shows. I was there for the first one; the second one found me on a spiritual retreat in the wastes of Malibu Canyon, living in a small tent and meditating most of the day and night, with breaks for a few hours of sleep and brown rice with Jasmine tea.

BRIAN WILSON SHOWS UP & THE LEFT BANKE LEAVE!

Brian Wilson

Riley and I were sitting on the rug in the enormous ground floor music room that had a 10' by 15' foot window at the north end; it looked down across the garden and onto the Sunset Strip. We were listening to Ravi Shankar, (the Sitar Master) with our backs against the south wall, with its long drapes hanging around the windows. From the patio entrance, a tall man appeared and stared at us from the door. He seemed confused and didn't quite know whether to come in or go back out. I recognized him as Brian Wilson, but refusing to appear impressed with famous people, I just stared back until he finally went the way he came.

Terry liked to tell people about us, especially his friends, actors, and musicians. The group "The Left Banke" were about to do the same thing; their hit "Just Walk Away Renee" was climbing the charts, and either the folks at Columbia or Terry recommended they come and meet us as some of our music had

Baroque influences with cello, viola, violin, and harpsichord, like their hit. Walking out the front door and down the garden steps toward the strip, I ran into them as they were about to walk up our street. I said "Just Walk Away" as a light-hearted gesture, but they just stared at me as if I were some insane groupie after an autograph. They turned and got back in their car and left, and I continued with my amble down to the Chinese restaurant for something to eat.

PAUL REVERE AND THE RAIDERS VISIT

Jim "Harpo" Valley, the lead guitarist, and Phil "Fang" Volk, the bass player for the Raiders, used to come over quite often and jam with us. One evening they wanted to go out to the north side of the Valley and "score." Of course, Riley was ready for that, and I enjoyed their company, so we joined them. When we arrived, we walked up the steep steps to a small house perched on a hill in a residential neighborhood. Fang, Harpo, and Riley did what they came for, all in the attitude of visiting friends, and we were on our way again. Harpo handed me a small pill, and I asked what it was, "acid" he said, and I popped it down; this was before we started TM. We drove about four blocks when someone noticed that a police car was following us.

Later I found out they had that house staked out and were stopping and searching anyone who came out of it. They kept on following until we were out of the neighborhood and in a desert area. Suddenly, the lights and siren went on, and we pulled over. Two young cops came up and searched us all asking for the usual licenses or ids. I didn't know where our Raider friends had hidden the drugs and figured that this would probably soon be revealed.

The pill I had popped was beginning to wake me up with an increased awareness of the subtleties of our interaction with the cops. Riley was talking to the police like a cop himself; having sold cars for his father he could be best buddies with anyone, and they were enjoying him. He showed no fear, something that could save us all from things going bad. Riley told the cops that these two guys were members of Paul Revere and the Raiders, which was a favorite group at the time with number-one hits and a top-rated TV show. They were very impressed and somewhat delighted they had met the boys, being fans of the show, but they were about to take one last look for drugs, just in case and started to open the trunk.

I was feeling entirely guileless at this point, something that happened when I was on LSD. It was innocence, like a blissful child with no fear, no guilt, and the awareness of being altogether my Real Self, standing in the power and protection of Nature. I looked at Riley and noticed he was starting to get paranoid. I stood in front of Riley and engaged the police with an immediacy that captured their attention, sort of like "These aren't the Droids you're looking for," I told them we needed to get the Raiders back for their TV show before they missed their performance. To the surprise of Fang and Harpo, who had been extremely nervous and agitated, the Cops slammed the trunk closed without looking inside and said "alright you guys, the show must go on, what time does it start? we don't want to miss it either!

MOBI GRAPE & IRON BUTTERFLY

Skip Spence, the rhythm guitar showman for "Moby Grape,"

dropped by once, and I was glad because I liked his perform-ance when I saw them play at the Monterey Pop Festival. He was just as frenetic in our kitchen as he had been on stage, al-ways moving and jerking and laughing. He had either been on speed both times that I saw him, or that was the real Skip? In either case, he was entertaining. Ry Cooder came over every day for a couple of weeks, and we worked on our guitar parts, getting the songs ready for recording with Terry. Once we were in the studio, Danny Weiss of the "Iron Butterfly" joined the group for a short time and came in for a few sessions. Terry asked me to produce one of my songs with Danny. I went crazy, he could play just like Jimmy Hendrix (or anyone else), and I spent the whole session getting down a myriad of his very funky guitar parts, none of which were used; probably for the best.

Skip Spence of Mobi Grape

Danny Weiss of "Iron Butterfly"

Terry knew we had a unique sound and didn't want it to turn into the "Iron Gentle Soul." Bob Norby of the Kingsmen (Louie Louie) joined us as well, and at this point, we had Bob, Sandy, Danny, Riley, Pamela and me. We were trying to get all these musicians to meld with our Gentle Soul sound, and we were only going further and further away from it. Talking about musicians who took a turn at being members of the Gentle Soul, Jackson Browne filled in for me while I was on my month long meditation retreat. He and Pamela had been hoping to work together since he was a lad of seventeen. But by the time I had returned from my retreat, Jackson was gone. I think his lack of experience singing harmony, and playing the guitar had been the reasons for his departure. One would think his greatness as a songwriter would have been enough for him to stay?

For some reason, we weren't getting enough food. Terry was providing for our food, but the kitchen was never really stocked with much more than brown rice. There was the occasional feast which was not enough, and we kept losing weight, at least Riley, and I did. I think I weighed around 145 pounds at the time at 5'11." Poor Riley was six foot five, and I don't think he weighed more than 155 -160 pounds. He spent more of his time smoking than practicing which should have made him ravenous.

Most of my weekends had been spent searching for a Master who could initiate me into an authentic sadhana, or practice of meditation. Most of the books I was reading indicated that one must receive one's training from a realized master, preferably from an ancient lineage. Enlightenment or self-realization was the supreme ideal and the ultimate goal of all life. But this lofty aspiration was only attainable through natural evolution or the blessings of a master. "The Gospel of Sri Ramakrishna" and Yogananda's "Autobiography of a Yogi," were two of my sources for understanding this new (to me) and ageless world of man's intimate connection to God and Nature.

PSYCHOLOGICAL HEALER

The Gentle Soul House started getting a name for itself. Pamela was like the Earth Mother, of the Sunset Strip, and I was some strange Spiritual Guru who could do magic with LSD. One morning a tall girl came into the house and said she wanted to speak with Rick. I was standing behind the kitchen counter, looking out into the dining room area. I said "That's me," and she said that she was Gina and asked if she could speak with me alone. "Sure," I said and took her into the kitchen.

She said that she had ovarian cancer and that she was supposed to go into have the tumors surgically removed the next day, and that there was a fifty-fifty chance of success. She wanted me to perform some mojo-magic on her. At this point, I began to remember who she was. I had seen her before when I opened the door to Riley's room several months earlier, and she was lying, naked, on her back with two guys kneeling on either side of her. They were feeling her up and messing with her privates, and when I looked at her face, I saw that she hated what was happening and most of all she hated men. I had told them to get the hell out of the house and slammed the door. Riley would have thrown them out as well, had he been there. Now, I could understand why she might have problems with her lady parts. So, I felt that if I guided her with just a small dose of acid, she would see me when we were on it. When I was on LSD, I was like a child, sweet innocence; it was as if my lower chakras would close and my higher ones would open wide.

Aside from that, I felt absolutely no attraction to this girl, which was the prerequisite for her to have an epiphany that her warped conviction that all men are sexual predators - lusting for her was a projection of her own heart and mind. When all this had flashed through my mind, I told her to come back that evening, and we would try something. I had never bought drugs from anyone, except that one ridiculous Tijuana run, and had to ask around the house where I could get a couple of 250 microgram doses of very pure LSD. I can't remember by whom, but I was given the necessary medicine of revelation in time to try my experiment. Gina arrived and walked into the music room looking nervous and impatient. I noticed her and asked her to follow me up to my room.

I could already see that she was sure I was going to try and seduce her or work my hedonistic magic out on her in some sleazy way. We entered my room, which was almost entirely taken up by my King sized mattress sitting on a box spring on the floor. I had a beautiful blue-green bedspread, all cotton with subtle gold designs all over it. At the other end of the 15'x12' room was my alter with a photo of Sri Ramakrishna in the center and Yogananda to one side. There was a picture of Jesus and Krishna and a few others, I can't recall. I told her to sit on the floor next to the bed, and I put a pillow down for her. She seemed a bit perplexed by this, especially when I sat up on the bed above her but about six feet away, cross-legged.

EPIPHANY

"So, we are going to take a little LSD and just sit here and pray for God to give you insight into your illness which will allow you to heal yourself." I washed my pill down and handed her the glass of water, and she paused and said "are you sure this will help? I've never taken LSD before." "Just close your eyes for awhile and put your attention on the place of your disease and pray for healing." After about an hour I could see she was moving about a little and looking around as if in fear of something and I said: "just relax and put your attention on your sick area." She calmed down, and it must have been another hour or so when I felt her looking at me, and I slowly opened my eyes and looked into hers. She stared into my face expecting to see a leering sex-fiend lusting for her, and instead, she saw my inner child, all innocence, and sweetness. She screamed in agony "it's me, it's me, it's me," shame-faced, and inconsolable she grabbed my hand and sobbed, "I'm so sorry." I told her to sleep if she could, and left the room.

PAYMENT BY MARRIAGE!

When I got back in the house, Gina had gone to her appointment for surgery, but that afternoon she came smiling into the kitchen. She was ecstatic and wanted me to know about it. "My doctor did a preoperative check on my tumors and didn't find a trace of them. He couldn't believe that they had disappeared overnight and did an MRI and still couldn't find them. He wants to know what I did, but I didn't think it would be wise to tell him. Anyway, I want to give you something, but all I have is myself. Would you like to marry me? I'll marry you if you like." I laughed and said, "No, that's fine you don't owe me anything, you healed yourself." She kept insisting that there must be some way she could repay me, and I thought that if I could get her to believe in God and Angels and the Joy of getting in touch with our inner Selves, and banish all fears, that at this moment she was primed for realization.

So, we drove up to Mulholland Drive to a dirt road that led out onto a large field which dropped off like a cliff at its end. I had once come to this place with a girl who was living at the Gentle Soul House with her mother, and we had seen a silent single-engine Cessna gliding down over this field, and just as it was over us the girl dropped to the ground prostrate, with her hands in the Indian Namaste salute, stretched out above her head. I was amazed at the time, and she told me that the craft, a UFO in disguise, had held a Venusian Master who had just acknowledged us, and his light and power was so blinding that she had to fall at his feet. This girl was only fifteen years old and was able to see everything around her, material, astral and celestial, which was the reason we welcomed her and her mom to live in our house when they couldn't pay their rent.

Gina's Angel

Just as Gina and I got out of the car, I saw way above us, probably over a hundred feet and about fifty yards out over the field, the light, or ethereal-form of an Angel about fifteen feet tall with her flowing robes and long hair trailing behind as she headed out over the cliff toward the sea. I pointed her out to Gina, who cried out "Oh my God, an Angel." I didn't plan all this out: thoughts of what to do next just came one after the other in an entirely natural way. I think Gina was unusually blessed. Months later, I abruptly left the Gentle Soul House and stayed for a day or two on Gina's couch while I organized a meditation retreat for myself in Malibu Canyon. Gina was a fashion model, but I have never seen or heard from her again.

Earlier, when I was going on about Neil Young being a silent witness at Gordon's house, and about seeing the large poster of Maharishi on the wall advertising a TM lecture; that was when

I made a mental note that I had to go to this talk on TM. About two months later there was another lecture about to be given by Jerry Jarvis, the SIMS' (students international meditation society) leader. I think most of us at the Gentle Soul house attended the talk. I was disappointed that it was a guy in a suit with a comb-over and not Maharishi, but I put all my attention on him.

Being used to staring at things and into people's eyes for long periods of time without blinking (a form of Trataka yoga), I stared into Jerry's eyes and body language for two hours and didn't see anything - no pretense, just a guy who was speaking from a place as solid as a stone foundation. He was Himself. When I approached him after the lecture, I walked up and asked him something - I don't know what - but his response almost knocked me off my feet. The light on his face and the quiet repose of his smile shattered my unnatural projection of baseless power; my ego deflated like a balloon, and I was sold.

Riley, Pamela and I went to the second lecture, where we signed up to be initiated on the following weekend at 1015 Gayley Avenue in Westwood, by UCLA. Knowing that I wouldn't be taking any drugs after my initiation, I decided to give LSD one last go for attaining Self-realization. I had read that Julian Huxley had taken vast amounts of the drug trying to do the same thing. The amount I took was ridiculous, so much so, that all I did the whole night was sit, motionless in a chair with my mind spinning like a slot machine, spinning every thought or picture I had ever seen, round and around in my minds eye; it was not in the least enlightening or enjoyable.

This last acid "trip" was at Ned Wynn's house, the son of Keenan Wynn and grandson of Ed Wynn, the comedian. I think he lived in Benedict Canyon at the time; he liked to hang around Terry's house and the musicians Terry was producing or friends with, like John and Michelle Phillips, etc. He was a familiar sight at the Gentle Soul House, a very entertaining guy; he could, perhaps, have been a great comedian but in my humble opinion he seems to have devolved into a spoiled brat of the Hollywood-Elite variety.

INITIATION

Believe it or not, it was the very next day after an entire night of non-stop visual mental activity via LSD (like a video fast-forwarding for six hours) that I went in to be initiated. The line was very long, maybe fifty students, and when I got to the desk, a college girl accepting payment said: "35 dollars please." I poked around in my pockets, having forgotten that this would cost, and all I came up with was two dollars. I said "I only have these two dollars," and she said, "that's ok, whatever you can afford - the money is for your benefit, a traditional offering, you can pay later if you like."

Sitting in the center waiting room, I was still burning from the effects of the drug: brain burn and face burn, and Jerry Jarvis looked over at me and said: "has everyone been off drugs for two weeks?" Everyone said yes! or nodded their heads, and he said directly to me "and you?" I said "sure!" Jerry said, "I won't initiate you, if you can get someone else, fine." At that moment, Rikard Fleur (Jensen), the New York Met. opera singer/TM Teacher, came out of one of the rooms and asked if I was next, and I said "sure." When we went into the initiation room, I immediately bowed down to his feet, and he laughed and pulled me up and sat me down. He said "we only do that with Maharishi," and proceeded to instruct me in the TM technique.

The moment I received my mantra I transcended - I was deep in my Self, and it was clear and unbounded. After initiation, I skipped and danced and ran down the street - this was what I had been looking for - this is what the books were pointing to, and it was mine and real and it was in me, and I could do this twice a day, every day! So very cool (Of course I don't recommend drugs, especially soon before or ever, after being initiated into TM, I was fortunate to have transcended).

WE TRANSCEND MID-JAM

Riley couldn't keep up his practice of TM twice a day and lapsed back into smoking his weed. It wasn't easy for him with Wendy and Sandy around. Wendy would prance around the house leaving joints on everyone's bed or table, and I had to tell him to stay out of my room. Riley couldn't refuse and soon stopped meditating altogether. Sandy was into cocaine; I imagine he felt it helped with his drumming, but it made him especially paranoid.

One afternoon we were jamming in my little room, Sandy, Riley and I when we reached a sudden spontaneous point where we all became as if one unbounded entity. There was a blinding flash of light that filled the room like soundless lightning, and Sandy screamed and jumped out of his seat, throwing his practice-pad down and running for the door. I jumped up and ran after him. I chased him all the way out of the back door and down the street. He was screaming the whole way to the Sunset Strip, and I imitated his scream with my own.

Sandy seemed to be frightened of anything spiritual or supernatural; probably one of the reasons he never took LSD or started meditating. For some reason, his abject fear unleashed by our collective transcendence through music inspired me to chase after him. Do I have any idea why? Maybe I wanted to show him how silly he was being by imitating him, hoping he would wake up and realize there was nothing to be afraid of. We never talked about it, and I don't know if the others saw what I saw, but I know they felt it.

THE CRASHERS ARE BUSTED & OUSTED

Wandering hippies and musicians were always knocking on our door or just walking in off the strip, having heard that they might be able to crash for a night or longer. At first, we would let them sleep out on the patio, on the floor in the big music room or even out in the gardener's house in back. One early morning I heard loud voices downstairs, and I peeked out Pamela's window and saw two or three police officers escorting all our "guests" out the back way and into their cars. I was worried some of them might have had drugs and that we would get busted right along with them, but wealth and in our case, the appearance of wealth, has its privileges.

It turned out that a "Whiskey A Go-Go" party girl who had been caught with a boyfriend in her sugar-daddy's, Bel Aire, rendezvous apartment by said sugar-daddy, was thrown out onto the street. She had come by and asked me if she could stay the night in the gardener's house and I had told her it was OK. Big mistake! She had a late visitor who parked his stolen car in our carport. Not only a stolen car but he was also the junky boyfriend of our junky Whiskey girl with junk on him and in him. Poor Riley was grabbed up by the cops along with everyone else crashing in the outside patio. It seems he had been romancing the daughter of one of our "guests," a very underage girl. He was lucky the mother was a total hippy, free-love-addicted earth momma who "didn't see a thing." I think she might have been party to the intended debauchery! After this close call, we decided to keep the house closed to all but our closest and mutually agreed-upon friends.

Even old Troll came by one day, hoping he could crash for a few days but I had to tell him the house was no longer open for guests, that all the members of the group had to agree on any exceptions. So, we talked for awhile, and he told me about ladies who had taken care of him; he seemed to be quite good at getting mature, self-sufficient women to support him even though he looked like a Troll.

Sherry had been visiting me every once in awhile, starting with the first place I stayed at with Pamela before we were The Gentle Soul. Sherry had arrived by bus from San Diego and didn't realize that I was living in Pamela's apartment. Feeling understandably uncomfortable with the living situation, she opted to take the next bus back home, even though Pamela and I were connected musically, never romantically.

KERRY THE NYMPH

Kerry was a beautiful red-headed nympho (no opinion or judgment from me!) who used to like to bed down with entire groups of musicians (male or female) and was a close friend of Pamela's. She was the embodiment of the "Free Love" crowd. One evening she came over and asked Pamela if I was sleeping with her; Pam said: "no, why don't you go in and see if he is attracted to you?" I had been practicing guitar in another room, and Kerry called out to me "Rick, come here and get in with me." She had climbed into my bed.

I just said "no thanks," but she kept taunting me to hop in. Knowing her history, I was afraid she might have some dark disease of the privates. I think Pamela was both happy with my refusal and unhappy at the same time. The fact that I didn't feel a physical attraction to Pamela was based, mainly, on my professional musical/career - attraction to her. Physical relationships don't last, especially if they are emotional and professional at the same time. Professional associations sometimes have a better chance if they remain professional.

RILEY THE BODYGUARD

Riley sometimes acted as my bodyguard and relationship mentor. Ever since Sherry had returned from Phoenix, she would come and visit for a day or so, wherever I was living. Perhaps to keep the relationship going even though she was seeing other guys at the time. I thought she was continuing to act out the story that I was the father of the baby she had given up for adoption and using it to feel absolved of the loss by sharing it with me.

Little did I know that it was all authentic; she was sharing it with me as it was mine to share! Occasionally, I would find out about her being with some guy and Riley, and I would find her. One time she was living in a trailer with a girlfriend, and we knocked on the door, and the girl let us in. She was sitting with a guy outside of a closed bedroom door, waiting for Sherry to finish. Apparently, the girlfriend wasn't into the partner of the guy with Sherry. I told the girl to "tell Sherry, Rick is here" and she knocked on the door and yelled it out. I heard the guy swearing and banging around, and then the door abruptly opened, and a red-faced, unslaked, muscular dude thrust his half-naked torso in my direction. He caught a quick glance of Riley towering behind me and realized he had better let out his horny anger some other way. So he smacked open the trailer door and let out a few more swears as he tromped off, blue-balled and frustrated, trying to get his arms in his shirt.

SHERRY & THE PAPA

Another time, I was at a party that I was led to expect Sherry would attend. She had agreed we would meet there and sort out whatever there was to sort. After about an hour of waiting for her someone came in and said that she wasn't coming and we commenced to interrogate the messenger until he told us exactly where to find her. Riley and I got in the car and found the roadside apartment. We banged on the door, no one came, banged harder and I could hear someone inside say "just a minute."

The moment we heard the voice we opened the door, which wasn't locked, and there on a bed was Sherry and Denny Doherty of the Mamas & Papas. They quickly got up, and she approached me, holding a sheet over her and said: "what are you doing here?" I said, "you were supposed to come to the party to talk with me." Doherty at first hung back, not knowing what we might do, having found him in bed with my girlfriend. When he saw that Sherry had it under control, he came forward and stood behind her. She made it clear that she didn't want to see me again. I was really hurt this time, having seen them in action, but also because I had been led to believe that she and I were going to be talking things out. I had grown attached to our mutual mythology, even though I thought it to be based in a lie. This was the last time I tried to hold on to Sherry and the emotional turmoil that had been suffered by both of us. I guess I must have known subconsciously that we had a son together; it kept me hanging on to her and she onto me.

WAITING FOR TERRY

The group was doing just about everything but performing. After the Golden Bear we really didn't play anywhere; we were probably expected to be ambitious, practicing and writing and creating a super group. Columbia would send us to media parties where ten to twenty photographers would snap pictures of everything we and the other groups did. I remember seeing several of these teenybopper magazines with Riley, Pamela, Sandy and me, lolling about by a pool looking like real Pop stars, sneering at the cameras and basically laughing at the whole scene. They would send us out with big-time professional photographers who told us to run over there, grab Pamela, run with Pamela, run away from the groupie, lie down in the grass on top of each other and all the fun-time Pop music group crap. We would hop around town visiting other groups and musicians like the Monkeys, Eric Burton, and the Animals and Tim Buckley down in Venice. Tim was an exceptionally sensitive and intelligent guy; I liked him the moment I met him.

Tim Buckley

RAVI SHANKAR

I had a Sitar, one of those cheap imports that Sara bought with her credit card at an Indian imports store in the Valley. Somehow, I managed to get it in tune, even all the sympathetic strings, which were numerous. Ravi Shankar had his studio in Hollywood, and when I told Terry about it, he said I should go and take lessons with him, that Columbia would pay. So, I did! of course, Ravi didn't give personal lessons unless you were famous or rich, but his disciple teachers were very good, and Ravi himself would come out of his back room and give us all a group lesson at the end of each day.

Terry asked us if we wanted to perform at the Monterey Pop Festival which he was organizing. We really had no idea how important it was to be a part of this festival. Now it is considered 2nd only to Woodstock in its representation of the Love Generation's musical culture. We declined the invitation to perform and possibly become an immortalized part of our magic decade but we decided to go up and enjoy the show anyway. Terry told me that he had saved me a seat in the large sound booth where the performers could watch the show in relative privacy. I was enjoying Jimi Hendrix's legendary performance when I noticed a very excited Indian man next to me yelling bravo, bravo. I turned and realized that I was sitting next to my sitar master, Ravi Shankar. He said oh, he is very, very good! Who is he?

I also had a great seat outside, in the 4th row up front, and barely sat down during Janice Joplin's set. I noticed that Mama Cass and company were flipping out with appreciation for Janice who was swaying about on stage with a half-empty bottle of Jack Daniels whiskey in her little hand. Before and after Janice's set, she was attracting a lot of audience attention with her loud, drunken behavior, waving her bottle in the air in her first-row seat. She was so different than the cute eighteen-

Ravi Shankar

year-old blues singer

I saw at a Big Sur concert a few years earlier.

As I explored the festival grounds, I saw Brian Jones walking nearby and was amazed to find myself concerned for him. He was ambling along like a man with a lot on his mind; as if being one of the Rolling Stones was more of a curse than a blessing. I suppose he was high or low on drugs at the time, but it wasn't long after the festival that they found him dead in his pool in England. There wasn't even an attempt to make it look like suicide but of course to the mainstream media almost all celebrity deaths are suicides.

GEORGE HARRISON

One day, George Harrison came for his private sitar lesson with Ravi Shankar and introduced himself to me: "Hello, I'm George Harrison" he said. He shook my hand, and I said: "hi, I'm Rick Stanley." My wife, Claudine, treasures the hand that shook George's holy hand, as did my daughter Gwen years ago when she was into the Beatles. My study of the Sitar turned out to be of use when Maharishi was making a music video for the King of Nepal, which featured music and song written and performed by Renie, Donna, and Myself. Of course under the guidance, and completely choreographed by Maharishi. Maharishi asked if I could make the guitar sound like a sitar, and I told him I had a sitar and could play a little. He told me to go and get it, and when I had tuned up and played for him, He said: "You play a good little Sitar."

THE LOVE IN

One of the first big "Love-Ins" was held in Griffith Park in LA. I was just a guy who aspired to know the truth about Life, a seeker of Self-Realization, and a folk musician with relatively short hair â€" not a Hippie. The long-haired Hippies were mostly the high school, and street kids who were basing their lifestyles and outward appearance on the 60's rock and pop group members like the Stones, the Beatles, and pretty much everyone who let their freak-flag-fly, with flower-power art-covered albums and posters, bell bottom jeans, etc. etc. Almost everyone who smoked pot and dropped acid ended up as part of the Love culture whether they looked the part or not. LA wasn't quite as freaky as San Francisco and Haight-Ashbury. The Northern California hippies had the longest hair and most colorful freak outfits, but neither of the communities had very many serious spiritual seekers. They spent most of their time looking for drugs and sex, being cool-man.

The Love-In at Griffith Park, LA

But as I walked about that Love-In, I came upon one guy I could relate to. Looking into his eyes as we passed, I saw the humility of a fellow lover of God. On the rare occasion of fellow seekers and finders of Divine Truth finding each other, recognition and acknowledgment of one another with a smile of appreciation and a slight bow of the head, maybe even a namaste with folded hands would be the spontaneous response. I'm talking about those of us who had experienced something of our Higher Selves, our Sons-of-God awareness.

The sun was sinking, and I was sitting in the grass investigating the crowd when I noticed several Hell's Angels wearing their colors, the black leather jackets with all the club insignia's. They were young guys and were playing king of the mountain on a small hill like children. Suddenly, I heard crashing and thudding and screaming over by the entrance to the park. I stood up and saw a line of cops with their night stick-batons, flailing and beating down the people, and screaming through a megaphone that everyone had to leave the park, that it was an illegal assembly. The Hell's Angels caught wind of what was going on and raced through the crowd to get to the front line where the action was. A teenage girl had been beaten and bloodied by the helmet-headed barbarians, and as they trampled her underfoot, the Angels charged the cop who was standing over her and knocked him on his fat-ass. Two of them grabbed the girl and carried her off to safety and hopefully the hospital. I ran into Riley as I headed in the opposite direction of the oncoming hoard of baton swingers who had taken an oath to serve and protect, and I wondered who exactly they were serving; it sure wasn't anyone at the love-in.

TERRY'S HOUSE

People mostly took LSD to get "high" or "trip;" "I'm tripping man" was a cliche that I couldn't stand, and also, "I'm seeing colors man." To experience the real benefits of Acid, you had to be fearless and trust in the Divine or Nature to be your guide and protector. You had to set up a situation where you would be entirely alone, with nothing in your heart or mind but the desire to find God, (whether in the form of Krishna, Jesus, Buddha or as Love itself, within oneself, without and both together). If something were to happen, like say an astral entity should come a knocking at your door, you only had to ignore it and put your mind on God - think of God, or pray for God, and the entity would disappear along with the fear. (However, I don't recommend LSD. Start TM).

Once, I was sitting by the pool at Terry Melcher's house in Benedict Canyon, and I had taken a little LSD. I just sat there staring at a tree, which gradually showed me the CO_2 coming out of its leaves; Like red smoke, it rose, luminescent, into the sky. I saw the same thing one evening at the Gentle Soul house. The eucalyptus trees were swaying and emanating the red colored gas, into the dark atmosphere (as most trees do at night, but you usually can't see it).

THE MAGIC CHRISTIAN

Meanwhile, Terry Melcher began showing more interest in me. He sent word via the Daywin Music offices, his mother's (Doris Day) publishing company. The secretary called and asked if I would come down to Terry's Beverly Hills office at Daywin publishing. When I arrived he was sitting behind his massive desk; it seemed a bit too large for such a young man. He smiled and was somewhat embarrassed by the subject he wanted to discuss with me. After getting comfortable by initiating small talk - like are you happy with the house and how the recording is going, etc. etc. - he got to the point. "Well, Rick you know that I can make you a wealthy man, all you have to do is work with me. I'd like to make you a music producer, you would work for Daywin Music, and you would receive a very comfortable salary plus a sizable commission on record sales and publishing. At the same time, I would like to pursue your career as a recording artist. How does this sound to you?

I said "it sounds like more than I could handle. I am more into following my spiritual goals and my music." Before this meeting, Terry had displayed his garage full of Jaguars, Mercedes, and BMW's and had taken me on a suicidal late-night race in his XKE from one end of Mulholland Drive to the other, going seventy miles an hour, most of the time. It was obvious he had been priming me for his Guy Grand test of my seeming indifference to material wealth. He asked if I had ever read the book "The Magic Christian," which was just released as a movie, starring Peter Sellers as a Billionaire and Ringo Star as the only person who couldn't be bought. I said "No," and he went on, "you remind me of Ringo Star's character in the movie, and I wanted to understand your thinking and attitudes a little better as the subject is intriguing to me."

You see, in the movie Guy Grand is an eccentric billionaire who spends most of his time playing elaborate practical jokes on people. A big spender, he does not mind losing large sums of money to complete strangers if he can have a good laugh. All his practical jokes are designed to prove his theory that everyone has their price it just depends on the amount one is prepared to pay them. Terry was most interested in Ringo Star's character, who was the one person who couldn't be bought by Grand. By the end of our meeting, I don't know what conclusions he came to about me, but he did invite me to have dinner at his place with his live-in girlfriend, Candice Bergen. With candlelight, white linen tablecloth, fine wine and a vegetarian meal. Candice and Terry treated me as more than an equal as if I were a respected psychic or guru.

The purpose of my invitation, I soon realized, was to validate their attempts to pay humanity back for their relative good fortune. Terry said, "we drive down to the poor part of town, and if we see a homeless person or a wino or junky, we give them sometimes five hundred dollars even a thousand to help them out." They seemed to think that this was the best way to give back something, but it struck me as a rather superficial gesture; just throwing money at the problem! I said "that's a nice gesture, but it will probably be short-lived as in most cases they will use the money to go on an ultimate bender that may lead to an even worse situation than they were in when you gave them the money. To create an environment where they could have a place to stay, to eat, to live and to be helped to change their lives for good would be a more practical approach in my humble opinion!"

My reaction wasn't what they had wanted to hear. Terry and Candice wanted me to praise their efforts and make them feel good about themselves, but I have always been brutally honest, especially in those days before Maharishi taught me to "speak the sweet truth." However, they must have done something right because just a short time after they moved from that house, Sharon Tate had moved in and she and several others had been murdered there. Sharon was ripped open by the pool where I had, several months before, seen the tree releasing its oxygen into the air. I saw the story in an English newspaper while I was on my Teacher Training Course in India and wondered if Terry and Candice were alright. I could picture every room, patio, and pool as I read about the placement of the bodies when they were found; such a close call we all had. Manson might have sent those brainwashed killers at any time before Terry's moving since he had the address - having sent Terry a demo tape of his songs - and was probably upset that the great producer had never responded.

However, the landlord (Rudi Altobelli) said later that Manson had shown up at the guest house where Rudy lived, just fifty feet from Terry's home, and asked him where Terry had moved to; fortunately for Terry and Candice, Rudi told him he didn't know. Rudi Altobelli bought the big house and guest house for $86,000 in the early 1960s and often rented it out. Residents included Cary Grant and Dyan Cannon (it was their honeymoon nest in 1965), Henry Fonda, George Chakiris, Mark Lindsay, Paul Revere & The Raiders, Samantha Eggar and Olivia Hussey. Terry and Candice split in early 1969, with Melcher relocating to Malibu.(Wikipedia)

One of the things that deflated any ambition I might have had to be a famous person was being present at Terry's house when the lead singer for the Raiders was living there. One mid-morning, he was sitting in front of his Hollywood mirror with all the light bulbs surrounding it; he was fixated on his face like a movie starlet. He was putting on makeup, base, blusher, lipstick, eyeliner, eyebrow pencil, eyelash darkener, a few splashes of Gucci cologne and a pretty red ribbon for his ponytail. I thought, oh well, he must be getting ready for his TV show or a photographer. But no! He was getting ready to ravish the three or four pubescent groupies who were waiting outside the gate, like Elvis and his cousin used to do at Graceland.

Terry seemed to enjoy the show, but it totally neutralized any respect I had, for rock n' roll prime-donnas or for that matter any person who uses their fan's false, idealized impressions of their stage persona for sexual and ego gratification, especially when they use and abuse vulnerable kids, often under 16 years old. As I left Terry's and was going out the front gate, I took a look at the fans, half-grown little girls, all wildly excited that they would be meeting their great hero. Of course, this was the common thread that made young guys want to become rock stars - the young girls throwing themselves at you. I'm not talking about full grown girls, of course, that's another thing altogether. The groupies who are still offering themselves to strangers with guitars at 18 or older, usually started very young and became some of the hardest people I've ever met. I guess this attitude makes me a Yankee puritan like my father, oh well!

I remember some of the girls like this who came to the Gentle Soul house looking for rock or pop stars. We had an open-door policy for awhile and seemed to attract the whole gamut of street hippies and groupies who would, on occasion, proudly list all the famous musicians they had sex with; the status prize went to the girl who had been with Mick Jagger. This is what the Music Business looked like from the inside, and is one of the motivations that moved me to find a more honorable and responsible way to live. There is too much temptation when everyone around you is using drugs, alcohol, and girls, all the time. It's not conducive to Self-realization, especially if you start believing you really are the character you portray on stage or in the movies. Karma is real: you do reap what you sow. And so began my departure from the life of a big-company-professional-musician to the life of a spiritual seeker.

HOT LIPS

I remember Rudi when he lived in the guest house in back of the property he rented to Terry. He told a friend of his, who was also a movie/actor talent manager (can't remember his name) about me having potential as a guitar-picking cowboy actor. I guess I looked the part? When I left Terry and Columbia, I signed with Rudi's friend, and he tried to get me into the Hollywood Movie scene by introducing me to a few top directors and producers who were looking to cast a leading man for their movies. They were perceptive men and could tell that I had no ambition for fame or fortune, and without that desire and motivation they're not going to make money off you; like a racehorse with no sense of competition. My new agent also managed Fred Astaire, "Hot Lips" Sally Kellerman (from MASH) Christopher Jones, and several other actors.

He used to hook me up with some of these people; he had my wife (Sara), and I escort Sally K. to an intro-lecture on TM by Jerry Jarvis. Jerry was known for his two-hour lectures, even longer when you included the questions and answers. I was a bit worried after an hour or so that Sally would want to leave, but she hung in there and seemed quite interested in TM. After the lecture, we took her to 31 flavors and sat outside at a roundtable. Hot Lips had a devious way of playing footsy with me while she talked earnestly with my wife. I wasn't responding in any way to her clandestine groping. I was

so shy then that I just acted as if nothing was happening as she gently rubbed her bare foot up and down my leg, under the table.

Anyway, after the Sally Kellerman date, my new manager wanted me to give guitar lessons to his up and coming leading man, Christopher Jones, who was supposed to play the US President and the guitar in his next movie, "Wild In The Streets" With Shelley Winters and Hal Holbrook. This guy was very talented; he had painted the walls in his apartment with Greek gods portraying the mythology of the pantheon. He also had an enormous little man complex, and if my wife were around he would constantly challenge me physically saying "c'mon man lets box, c'mon you chicken or what." He would hit me a few times on the shoulder and dance his little sparring dance to let me know that he

Sally Kellerman

was a contender. He had a James Dean complex as well; he not only looked like Dean, he acted like him, depression and all.

Sara would respond to his flirtation, but that was her nature. She was always on the lookout for someone who had money, looks, station in life, and who was attracted to her. I was my theatrical manager's only musician other than Sally Keller-man. I didn't want to sign up for an acting career, all I wanted to do was get a few thousand dollars so Sara and I could go to teacher training in India. Finally, my publisher, at Doris Day's publishing house, told me I should go to ASCAP and ask for an advance on my publishing rights with Daywin Music. I did, and they happily handed me a check for twenty-five hundred dollars. Now I could go to India and get on with the business of permanent Self-Realization. We all thought it would only take about five years to become Realized or Cosmically Conscious practicing TM; of course, it takes a hell of a lot longer, and you may not make it in this life. As long as you are

Doris Day, over 40 and cute as a button

rested and regular in your TM, life becomes worth living for "Almost everyone!'

Before I go to India and leave Hollywood behind, I should finish my tales of Terry's house and my times there. Some time after my dinner with Terry and Candice, Terry asked Pamela if we would come to his house for dinner and he would like it if we would sing a few songs for his guests. When we got there, the first person I noticed was a smiling lady sitting over by the baby grand piano. I wondered who she was until Terry introduced us: "Rick and Pamela this is my mother Doris Day." She was quite flirty, something I found to be common among most of the over 35 actresses that I met. She would look over with an "I'm gonna get you" sort of teasing smile, and those innocent, big blue "bedroom eyes." It certainly wasn't my good looks or charisma, although I was kinda cute I suppose, looking at photos taken back then; but I think it was something they did when they passed their prime of being beauties with endless male attention, to see if they were still attractive to younger men.

THE MAMAS & PAPAS

I looked around the room and saw a couple sitting opposite Pamela and I. They were quite recognizable, John and Michelle Phillips of the Mamas and Papas. When Terry introduced us they seemed aloof, they barely acknowledged us, but after we sang at the end of the meal they're attitudes toward us appeared to have changed from superior to competitive, which I preferred as it was a compliment. Another time, Terry invited us to hear Bob Dylan's newest album "Blonde on Blonde" with "Sad-Eyed Lady of the Lowlands" on it. Sandy and I climbed up the ladder to the loft, which was situated above and facing the huge stereo speakers downstairs. Terry put on the LP, and we went into a trance for the whole album. I was mesmerized by Sad-Eyed Lady, the pictures Dylan painted with his exquisite lyrics and the haunting repetition of the long verses; then the mind-blowing chorus: "My warehouse eyes, my Arabian drums, should I put them by your gate or sad-eyed lady should I wait." I will never forget the inspiration it gave me, and at the same time, the depressing feeling that I would never be this good.

LEARY, METZNER & ALPERT

Another time I was sitting on Terry's guest room toilet (we used to call them John's in Boston), when I saw all this movement coming in the window and flowing around my legs and about the room like a spirit swirling. It really had no color and is usually invisible to our normal eyes, but I could see it as clearly as I could see the floor. Outside you could see the wind on a larger scale, in the same way, like water flowing in eddies, waves, and circles in the sky.

Dr. Ralph Metzner used to make the rounds of all the serious seekers who were sincerely, and religiously, taking LSD for reasons other than party-tripping. He was very interested in my experiences, and his Graduate student-assistant would write down everything I said. After I started TM, he came by and wanted to know if I had any breakthroughs. I told him "Yes, I finally found a Master with a deep meditation technique that does everything and more for my quest for permanent Self and God Realization. LSD can never give you permanent realization." He looked extremely disappointed and packed up his notes and said to his assistant "we're done here,

Dr. Ralph Metzner

let me know if you start using again."

After I started TM, he came by and wanted to know if I had any breakthroughs. I told him "Yes, I finally found a Master with a deep meditation technique that does everything and more for my quest for permanent Self and God Realization. LSD can never give you permanent realization." He looked extremely disappointed and packed up his notes and said to his assistant "we're done here, let me know if you start using again."

Dr. Tim Leary

Dr. Timothy Leary came to LA and asked for all the professional musicians and artists to come to a talk he was giving at
some monastery, can't remember exactly where. We sat for
over two hours waiting for him, and when he finally showed
up, he was too high to communicate and went upstairs to lie
down. I saw him again at the Santa Monica Civic Auditorium, where he gave his famous "Turn On, Tune In, Drop Out"
lecture. The Leary "LSD-guru lectures" were happening at the
same time the US Government was distributing free Sandoz
Labs, LSD in San Francisco and LA. The plan was to get the
Viet Nam student protesters out of the way, let them join Timothy's crowd and drop out of society altogether. I don't know
if Timothy knew about the Government agenda, but it probably backfired anyway.

Most of the kids who took Tim up on his LSD advice took it
in party-mode along with booze and pot. Opening yourself
in this way would hardly tune you Into the subtler levels of
awareness or awaken in you the desire to leave society and

school to find God. As it turned out, many of those who used it as a tool for glimpsing into the more profound nature of things, with caution, reverence, and sincerity, ended up dropping by the local TM center instead of out in the woods. Of course, there were those few who chose the communal lifestyle but not for very long. Few remained in the commune and fewer still with an affinity for the recluse way of life, ended up in the monastery.

I think it was Dr. Richard Alpert who was involved in the original LSD experiments at Harvard with Timothy Leary. He ended up taking on the role of a guru of Indian philosophy, name and all. Last I heard, he was living the life of a beach-boy in Hawaii, enjoying as much beach-girl attention as he can attract with that big enlightened smile and those bliss-soaked eyes.

A few years later, I was sitting in the lecture hall at Rishikesh Ashram, Maharishi's home in India, where the Beatles, Donovan, Mia Farrow and the Beach Boys had made a showy attempt at gaining wisdom and a Guru a few months earlier. They were not there to become teachers like the rest of the people on that course who had been meditating for years before attending. In fact, they were far from ready for long-rounding and prolonged meditation. With the constant pressure of Yoko, the Beatle's manager, and "Magic Alex;" John Lennon, in an impressionable, mental and emotional state from the release of stress and impurities from extended meditation, managed to find reasons for insulting Maharishi and leaving the course prematurely. It took quite a few years before the Beatles realized that they had behaved irrationally and made a formal apology to Maharishi.

Having left Columbia Records, Terry Melcher, and the LA music scene to become a Teacher of Transcendental Meditation, I was at Maharishi's Ashram for four months of extended meditation and the first-hand knowledge and experience of gaining Self-realization and God-realization. One of the course participants asked Maharishi what LSD was, and if we had taken it, would it hinder our aspirations for enlightenment? Maharishi thought for awhile and said, "You have heard of Soma, the plant used in Vedic ceremonies in ancient times? It was also used by Masters to give their disciples experience of higher states of consciousness so that they would have the faith to continue their meditations for many years until they had purified themselves enough to gain permanent Realization.

He said this drug (LSD) similarly affects the nervous system, but more abrasively. Although it can give experiences similar to Soma, it roughens the subtle nervous system, necessitating long rounding, long meditation and courses like this one to purify the nervous system enough to gain higher states of consciousness. He said that this course would purify all of us of any of these impurities. That was good news for many of us.

Before going to India, a friend of mine and I would go and see Indian Swamis at the SRF, Self Realization Fellowship and the Ramakrishna temple in Hollywood. Even after finding our true Master and Meditation, we still enjoyed going to see "Holy Men." One time we were sitting at the feet of a Hindu Swami of the SRF who looked down at us and said: "Oh, you are two of those foolish young men who fancy themselves disciples but spend all your time taking drugs." I looked into his eyes and said: "No Swamiji, we are disciples of His Holiness Maharishi Mahesh Yogi of the Shankaracharya tradition of masters, we no longer use drugs." He looked astonished and tried to compose himself. He had received a shock to his system, and at the end of the talk he approached us and in sweet humility said he was sorry he had been so rude.

Gene Spiegel, a friend of mine, said he knew of a cave that was situated about a mile from the ocean, on a small canyon-creek. After hearing about my month-long retreat in Malibu

Canyon, he wanted to camp out and meditate in the cave with his girlfriend Patty and me as retreat guide. We parked on a dirt road where the creek ran down into the ocean, and the path leading up into the long wooded park began. We only had enough food for a couple of days, and I also wondered if the park rangers might be a problem. By the time we reached the massive boulder with a small cave inside of it, the sun had gone down, and we lit candles inside and tried to level the rough rocky ground enough for three sleeping bags.

About three in the morning, I woke to the sound of, "squeak squeak squeak" and the familiar feeling of something running over me, back and forth. I sat up and lit a candle and saw a whole family of rats lined up along a rock ledge just above our heads on the inner wall of the cave. By this time Gene poked his head out of his bag and said: "what's all the noise?" I said, "look at the real owners of the cave; they don't seem too happy with us sharing their home." Patty sat up and screamed, frightening some of the Rats who jumped at us while the rest made a retreat for their nests. We all ran out of the cave, and after calming down a bit, got our bags and spent the rest of the night out by the creek.

The early morning was cold, and I started a fire and made some Jasmin tea, and we did our morning meditation all wrapped up in our sleeping bags. We weren't going to spend another night in the cave, but at least we could meditate a bit longer and leave before sunset. Well, after a meager breakfast and another hour or so of meditation I heard someone tromping up the path toward us. I got up on the boulder and caught a glimpse of a uniformed police officer. I said to Gene, "don't tell him I'm here, I'm going to hide." I don't know why I thought this would be better than the cop finding two guys and a girl together, but remembering how it all worked out, it did make a difference; I think it was the appearance of a romantic couple that diffused any potential drug or kidnapped girl suspicion. Meanwhile, I had climbed to the side of the boulder and closed my eyes and just melted myself into feeling that I was a part of it. At first, Gene, Patty, and the cop were on the other side of the boulder talking, but gradually they moved around to the side I was lying on, almost vertically, like a rock lizard that can change color. At one point the cop was looking directly at me and couldn't see me.

When this was happening I was psychically melting myself into the rock - I felt as though I were actually inside the boulder. They were only eight or ten feet away from me and my perch, and I kept expecting to hear the cop exclaim "who the hell is this?" but he never saw me. Before he left, he wished Gene and Patty a good day and reminded them to "make sure you leave before sunset."

When I was sure the cop was gone, I jumped down in front of them, and they were astonished that they hadn't seen me right in front of them all that time. Thank God the cop hadn't seen me hiding like that, what would he have thought or done? I don't know? But it was a great experience being able to be invisible, and I have managed to do it successfully several times since. It's just a matter of concentrating one's awareness on the whole body and shifting or melting that into one's environment - like feeling one with the boulder until you are the boulder!

The only other part of it is that as you become a part of the background, whether it's a wall, a boulder or a sofa - you keep your face averted, and your eyes closed and cut yourself off from the awareness of others by cutting them off from your awareness. Separate or hide by excluding everything else except your oneness with the boulder. It's like freezing in place when you see a deer; if you become like a tree, you become invisible to deer as long as they can't smell you. I've had deer come up to me as if to see if I had any tasty leaves hanging off, but deer are much easier to fool than people.

BILLY JAMES

Remember I was talking about Jim Morrison and the Doors? Well, to continue my connection with them we have to introduce another of the outstanding players of the 60's music world, Billy James. Billy was a great friend of Pamela's, and she would take me along to visit with him. He was a publicist and a talent scout, and as the publicist for Columbia, Billy became Bob Dylan's emissary at the label and was reportedly one of the only "suits" Dylan trusted. Pamela wrote a song for his son Markus, which endeared Billy to her all the more; It was a great song, and we recorded it on the Gentle Soul album. After Pamela and I had worked up some songs, we played them for him, and he seemed quite supportive and offered to be our manager.

I'm pretty sure we never signed anything with Billy, but we were contracted to Columbia, and it wasn't long before Terry wanted us to sign with him as manager. Just before we moved on to Terry, Billy asked Riley and me to go to the London Fog and see what we thought about Jim Morrison and his band the Doors. We sat down in the back of the small Sunset Strip club and watched Jim gyrate around the stage and groan on the microphone. He was soused, and both of us thought he seemed like a Wino who had just got up from the audience to do his best drunken Elvis impression.

The band was just below average for the Strip, but we thought they would do a lot better with someone who could sing and wasn't a drunken boor with delusions of being a sex god. Later we found out his illusions were communicable. Please understand, this was before Morrison had any recordings or much experience singing. We informed Billy of our opinions about "The Doors" and that was that. Not too long after, Billy came up to me at the Troubadour and gave me a good dressing down for screwing up his chance of discovering the great Jim Morrison and the Doors and signing them to Columbia. He has resented me ever since. He should have understood that he sent a folk singer to evaluate a pop/rock singer who couldn't sing at the time.

Of course, he couldn't have known that I might have a hard time taking a drunken, sexually charged, prime-donna seriously. Even Riley thought the guy was a blow-hard. Looking back, I should admit that he had the balls, the ego, and the self-assurance, albeit drug-induced - to take on the challenge of being a "Rock Star." He even had an original sound and song-writing ability, although I have never enjoyed his music.

When Pamela and I settled into our regular meditations with no drugs, the house became divided. There were Riley and Sandy on one side and Pamela and I on the other. Wendy was still close to Pamela and continued to run about the house with his joints, and there was a bald black girl, who fancied herself a Buddhist Nun, who would come over to visit Pamela as well. She painted nice Yantras and Mandalas and gave one to me. I wondered why she chose that particular one for me; probably just one that was laying around. She had to be a lesbian and Wendy was gay but what else was new or unusual in Hollywood?

Pamela had lost her ambition with the group, and so had I. One day, without telling anyone, I put a change of clothes into my guitar case and headed for Gina's house (the model). She said I could sleep in her bed, still feeling in debt for the cancer cure, but I opted for the couch in my celibate-monk frame of mind. A friend I called Little Sue came by and told me that Riley had told her where I was. Little Sue was what you would call a groupie, she was only 16 and used to come by my room in the G. Soul house.

I was too afraid of getting her pregnant to have sex with her. We were friends, and she would give me the news about the other music group houses she frequented on a regular basis. I told her I was going out to the woods in Malibu Canyon to meditate; I had no idea for how long. Sue had her mother's car and drove me out to a hippie trailer which was hanging perilously on the edge of a cliff in Malibu Canyon. She left me there with a junky named Willie who had stayed in the G.S. house for a short time under the guise of being a TM meditator.

I wasn't there long before a car pulled up and out came Joe Ellen Shattuck and her sister Linda. Joe Ellen was married to Jim Yester of "The Association" at the time. They were in the mood to party, but when Joe Ellen saw me, I imagine she saw a party-pooper, considering our past in San Diego. I asked her if she and I could take a ride, thinking we should let Willy and Linda be alone since I wasn't going to party. After all, I was all about meditating and being celibate for the next year or so; a recluse Brahmachari, like Maharishi, I fancied.

Once we were in the car I told Jo Ellen that I was going to live in a small tent in the Canyon and meditate all the time; all the while ignorant of the fact that my spiritual adventures might not be of interest to her. Jo Ellen tried to look interested but was probably feeling bummed out that her evening was being hijacked. After an hour of bending her ear, we returned to Willy and Linda. Without her sister sharing the party, Linda's mood had completely vanished, and both she and Willy had just sat there staring at the walls. Joe Ellen was a great girl, very kind and patient with my off-the-charts spiritual ambitions.

HERMIT FOR A MONTH

The next day I got a ride to Malibu Canyon where I planned to live as an ascetic. Somehow, I managed to find the little prospector's shack of a friend on a small dirt road in the Canyon. No one was there so I walked in search of anyone who could give me permission to camp on the wild canyon land adjoining their property. There was a rather large, natural timber barn-made-into-a-home not far from the shack of the people I knew. I knocked on the door with my guitar in hand and an older guy, early forties, opened up and asked who I was.

I told him, and he said he had heard good things about our group. He was a well known LA radio personality. He played some old LP's that he especially liked and gave me something to drink and went on about political stuff I didn't care about. Finally, he asked why I was wandering around the back roads of Malibu. I told him what I wanted to do and that I just needed permission to camp for a while in the Canyon. I told him I wanted to meditate and work on songs for our album. He said that he didn't own that land and that I didn't need his permission but that I could come and get water from his outside hose. So, I thanked him, and with my guitar and rolled-up tent, I made my way back past the shack and down a path that led deep into the Canyon.

I was about a mile from the shack when I came across a spot that was just under an over-hanging cliff wall that faced the south. It wouldn't block the hot sun, but it might cut down on a cold night's wind. The tent was set up, and I had a fire going to cook my brown rice and boil my Jasmin tea. I began meditating longer than the prescribed twenty minutes, twice a day which was against the instructions I was given, but I had heard that on the courses with Maharishi they would meditate as long as they could - all day if possible, and some even went most of the night. I didn't realize that this was prescribed only when under the guidance of Maharishi.

I just went by what I'd read in the books - about recluse yogis doing long meditations every day for years and becoming jnanis and sidhas and saints. That's what I wanted! I established a routine of a few hours of morning meditation, then songwriting for a few hours, then evening meditation for another few hours, and then I'd cook up my rice and tea. I'd sleep for around four hours and then sit up and meditate for a couple and go back to sleep for two or three more.

I went on like this for about three weeks. I wondered why I wasn't having any flashy experiences and would find myself staring at the cliffs all around until they would appear like a movie scene, one - dimensional and faint. I realized that I saw the material world as it is, as Maya the illusion. But it was a very flat experience just seeing the surface, the illusory reality of the material world. It looked like a one-dimensional hologram. I wanted to feel bliss and unboundedness and see God. Almost thirty days and nights had passed, and I realized that I owed a karmic debt to Terry Melcher, to Columbia, and to Pamela. These thoughts and feelings haunted me for several days, and I was determined to make it right once I finished my retreat.

CHEESE IT THE COPS!

On a Saturday evening, I heard a helicopter coming my way as I was cooking my rice. The copter went directly over me and circled a time or two, then went on its way west. I could see that it was a Sheriff's helicopter and it was obvious to me that he would be investigating my presence there. At the time I didn't know that it was against the law to build fires in the Canyon, but I felt an impending danger if I remained at my campsite.

I packed up everything on Sunday afternoon and headed up the path to the old shack. The guys were playing Frisbee with friends and family, and I must have been a sight trudging out of the bush with my guitar in hand and my tent hanging off my back. They remembered me and said they had no idea I was camping out back all this time. They said I should have come and had dinner with them or used their hose for water.

I washed off my face and hands with the garden hose and thanked them, and started down the road when Jimmy, a meditator from the TM center in Westwood, called out "Rick, where are you going, need a ride? I'm leaving soon for UCLA, have to get back for school." Of course, I took him up on the ride, and he let me off at the Ramakrishna Temple where I had decided to meditate before I ventured back to the Gentle Soul house, only a few blocks down the Strip.

UNBOUNDED AWARENESS

Inside Vedanta Temple Hollywood

Outside Vedanta Temple

The temple was quiet and empty, the smell of sandalwood incense wafted over me from the shrine, in the front of the room. I sat down in the back and began to meditate, after about twenty minutes I found myself coming out of profound, vast silence, much of which came out with me. I noticed activity up front around the shrine and opened my eyes to see two or three people dressed in silk robes making offerings to the pictures of Ramakrishna and others. I was still in this unbounded awareness and soft, warm, bliss that had accompanied me out of the silence. Eyes open or closed it embraced me as the sweet smell of incense and the soft sounds of sutras caressed my soul. It seemed like a gift that I received for both purifying myself with the retreat and for coming back to fulfill my karmic debt to Columbia, Terry, Pam and myself.

I understood that the lesson in this was that my dharma was activity in the world for the upliftment of myself and others, not the life of a recluse whose sole desire is for his realization. The moment that I left the temple, what appeared as a large helicopter flew down over my head, shocking my awareness back to the mundane. But It was obvious to me that this wasn't a helicopter; it first appeared over me with all the roaring but went completely silent as it flew back up into the sky only a few hundred yards distant. This had happened to me before, several months after I started TM, and, I knew who it was. (I'll explain later in "God C." chapter)

THE DIVINE PLAY & ILLUSION OF MAYA

During my last days in Malibu Canyon, the vision (literally) that everything about me was an illusion and that I couldn't see beyond the self-projected rock cliffs and trees frustrated me, it all looked so unreal! However, when I came back from my Canyon retreat and had the beautiful experience of Unbounded Awareness at the Vedanta Society temple in Hollywood, I realized that my time of meditation and fasting had been the very basis for my Temple experience. The fact that the experience of samadhi was given after returning to face my unresolved responsibilities in the world inspired the realization that I didn't have to be a recluse and live in a cave to gain enlightenment. The first thing that happened when I left the "cave" (i.e., my tent in the mountains) was an experience of my unbounded Self as verification of this.

I walked out of the Temple and down the street to the Gentle Soul house not even thinking that I might not be welcomed back, that things might have changed completely. After all, I had left the group with no warning or reason for going - but somehow I wasn't in the least worried about that - I felt like I was being guided spontaneously by an unerring intelligence with absolute knowledge of every move I was making. I walked in the back door, and the kitchen was empty, walked around into the living/music room and up the broad staircase to Pamela's room. Fortunately, she was there and was somewhat surprised to see me. I had no idea, at the time, that she had asked Jackson Browne to join the group in place of me and that he hadn't worked out. I don't know if it was Terry who was disappointed with the replacement or if it was Pamela? It's true that in 1967 Jackson wasn't the great singer or guitar player he was to become.

Anyway, Pamela told me that the rest of the group was practicing at Columbia and that they were working on songs with a new member, someone who was a friend of Riley's from the Troubadour. She said I should check them out and see if I still wanted to be in the group. Perhaps she intended to do harmony with the new guy - he could sing well and played good guitar - but he was more into folk rock than a Gentle Soul sound. I walked into the practice room at Columbia Studios, and Riley and Sandy looked as if I was intruding. When I was a significant part of the group, Pamela and I called all the shots, did all the singing and wrote all the songs. Now, there appeared to be a power play going on with the new guy and the others that would join the three of them and Pamela together. In reality, the new guy and his songs would be replacing me and my songs. He would be singing with Pamela as well, returning the balance to a duo with two backup musicians.

However, it was clear that Riley and Sandy assumed that they would now be as important as the new guy since they had offered him the job. I listened and didn't care for what they were doing at all and went back to the GS house. If they had their way, the Gentle Soul would become just another rock and roll group, shouting instead of singing this new guy's songs. Pamela and I talked, and I told her that we didn't need any of the guys that were presently in the group. We didn't need a bloody group! After all, none of them were of session musician caliber to record with us, and we never played live anywhere anymore, and probably wouldn't until we had a single on the radio. Then we could hire any of the great musicians in LA to back us up on tour.

She agreed with me, and the next time we were recording at Columbia studio B with Terry we told him that we had decided to go it alone, that we didn't need Sandy, Riley or the new guy at all. I mean, did the Everly Brothers need anyone else? Chad and Jeremy? Simon and Garfunkel? Peter and Gordon? Sonny and Cher? No! He agreed, and we continued to record several singles and the songs for the album as well, including one of Jackson Brown's songs that he had written about Pamela called "Flying Thing." I fulfilled my contract to record an album and some singles for Columbia Records, but most importantly, I completed my part of our creative effort to do something beautiful. Whether it was released or not, we had created our art, like a painting, there it was for us and everyone, to enjoy.

Two of the Gentle Soul singles came out before the album when we were still signed to Columbia. When "Tell Me Love" came out on the radio and could be found on every Jukebox Box in LA - a friend told me about it and took me down to a local dance club on the strip. I entered the dark lounge to hear my voice filling the place with the powerful dirge-like - Celtic chant that I wrote just after my experience of the Divine on Lompoc beach. (see the "God" chapter) The club was filled, and everyone was dancing to "Tell Me Love;" it was so cool, I'll never forget how good it made me feel! I think two of our singles made the charts, one was in the top 40 and the other around 70; not too shabby when you consider there was absolutely no publicity behind us.

As I mentioned, the reason that Columbia/Epic released the album but didn't push it was because Pamela and I went our separate ways just before the record was released. In hindsight, perhaps we could have had it all. However, I was only interested in Self-Realization, and Pamela was interested in going to Greece with Greg. So, I asked a big-time music lawyer to get me out of my contract with Columbia, and he managed it with a single one-minute phone call. I was free to go to India and study with his Holiness Maharishi Mahesh Yogi and write songs and record albums of pure knowledge. Still it was nice to see "Billboard Magazine's" review; in short, they said, "The Gentle Soul,"..." the most beautiful...album of the year." (1968)

SERRA RETREAT

I had been meditating for a couple of years after starting in 1966, and during that time I had become involved in the SIMS activities of checking peoples meditations, getting them on the right track if they were having trouble remembering the effortlessness of the technique. My SIMS center compadres and I were also traveling to all the universities and colleges in LA, and the outlying areas, giving introductory TM lectures. The first Residence Course (for advanced talks and more meditation) was held at the Serra Retreat, in the Malibu hills overlooking the vast Pacific, and I spent most of my time meditating in my room instead of following the course schedule. This is not something I would recommend at all. The evening lectures with Jerry were great, and one night he gave a talk on the three gunas, which would become quite meaningful soon after we broke for milk and cookies on the outside patio.

I was standing, looking out over the dark open ocean from a large hillock at the top of which the Serra Retreat dominated the valley below. Serra hill was only a bump on the side of the high bluffs which ringed the Malibu coast. The smell of the eucalyptus and salt air and the wonderfully relaxed and restful feeling of the course was filling us all. A brilliant light broke the black night with a flash, straight out over the sea, or so it seemed from where we stood. It was like a Hollywood sized spotlight floating far above the ocean where it hovered without a sound. I thought it must be some radio tower-light coming on with the darkness, but that would mean there was a tower I hadn't seen between Serra and the beach.

At first, there were only two of us who noticed it, and then the second light about a hundred feet to the right of the first flashed on, and we yelled for everyone to come and see the light show. Now there were at least twenty of us watching and wondering what would happen next. Were these lights UFOs, angels or what? After another five or ten minutes of dramatic expectation, a third light lit up the darkness and they glowed like three twenty-foot full moons. The white transformed to yellow and orange and then red, and we were all transfixed and wondering if their next move would be to come down and take us all away - at least that's what I was thinking. Just as unexpectedly as the first light went on, it went off; then the second and then the third, and we all waited to see if there would be more. But only silence remained; the silence and the dark night that had been there all along. I suddenly realized that the meaning of the lights might be found in the evening's talk on the three gunas - that the lights had been celebrating Maharishi's gift of Vedic knowledge to the world; who knows? The three lights may have been on one vehicle and not three separate ships as it seemed to appear; it was too dark to see anything but the lights.

ASILOMAR

There were at least two SIMS residence courses after the Serra Retreat at Asilomar in California. I attended two of them and performed at the talent show both times, once with Pamela. The talent finale became a tradition for ending courses in the TM movement. The attendees were a mix of hippies - many of whom still took occasional acid trips and smoked pot - SIMS college types, twenty-somethings who followed Maharishi's recommendations almost 100%, a few of the older folks from the SRM and a few parents of the twenty-somethings. I think it was the second course that Pamela and I performed at and we went over well with a standing ovation. Two of the group members of the "Doors" were at one of the Asilomar courses, and there was one other course participant who was a professional musician with "The Loading Zone," a San Francisco rhythm and blues group who played at the Filmore. One of the lead singers was Susie Levin, who is now a "Rajesharee,"(a Queen in the TM movement hierarchy) and later, Linda Tillary. The guy at the course was a keyboard player and "soul" singer named Paul Fauerso. He had his best friend with him, Michael Ritter, the group's sound man. They seemed a bit put out by our popularity, or maybe they just didn't like ballads? I don't remember Paul playing at either of the talent shows. A few years later I ran into him in Majorca Spain, and he seemed quite interested in playing for the course and Maharishi, but that's a story for later.

SIMS

Once Pamela and I had started practicing TM, we began having visitors from the TM community who mostly lived in Santa Monica and Westwood, near the Students International Meditation Society (SIMS) center by UCLA. Pamela's cousin, Gene Spiegel, became a regular out in the walled courtyard where most of our "guests" entertained themselves. He was a school teacher and started a Montessori school for tots with his Artist girlfriend, who was quite a good teacher herself; she even had an art studio in Venice CA. It was Gene who introduced himself to Sara, and then Sara introduced herself to me. She would become my first wife. She was a friend of most of the SIMS crowd, who were mostly college "did you take psyche 101 with Hawthorne?" types. Keith Wallace, a Doctoral student at UCLA, was the younger of two brothers who had pretty much started SIMS with Jerry Jarvis. He used to come to see Pamela; he was intrigued with girls who stood out from the crowd – musicians, models, actresses, etc. He is also a great man, one of the first scientists responsible for bringing TM into the world of scientific research and proving the enormous value that Transcendental Meditation has had for millions of people all over the world in almost every area of human life. Keith's brother Peter came by the Gentle Soul House and taught us some Hindu Bhajans (chants) that he had learned in India. He was a bold spiritual seeker and went all the way to India and the greatest lady Saint, Anandamayi Ma to find his Master. For all his travels, she directed him to Maharishi, and we ended up on the same TM (TTC) Teacher Training Course, together in 1968-9 at Maharishi's Ashram in Rishikesh India.

CHARLIE LUTZ

Before SIMS, the SRM, the first organization that Maharishi

established all over the world, had been the only place you could go to begin the technique of TM and attend lectures and courses for more experience and knowledge. Charlie Lutz, a one time FBI agent and steel salesman, used to give talks at the SRM building owned by Geordie Hormel, of the Hormel meatpacking family, who had an office there. Charlie used to lecture about most anything he had read about UFOs, Angels and metaphysics, whatever he was interested in was part of his spiritual worldview and lectures. It was entertaining, but sometimes you could tell if you had any intuitive discrimination, that he hadn't really experienced directly much of what he talked about. Still, many of the SIMS student meditators who had been going to see him even before SIMS began would go to his talks and take him at his word as to the veracity of his stories.

I went along with them two or three times and could immediately tell that he was telling stories for our entertainment mixed with his experiences with Maharishi. Charlie was loved by many and with his gruff exterior, his G-man shell, he seemed all the more lovable. I've heard rumors that in later years he was giving his opinion about some of Maharishi's courses and techniques that he felt were only there to make money for the movement. I'm sure the courses and techniques were worth whatever was charged for them! Maharishi had a world to enlighten and billions of souls to expose to the knowledge of Self-Realization; how can he be faulted for sharing the path to enlightenment and accepting the means to spread and organize a movement to do so? Check out the internet for some of Charlie's stories of traveling with Maharishi. During the early days of the Movement, Maharishi would sometimes make use of his "Short Cuts" when necessary.

LEON THE CON

A story with a lesson involved an old acquaintance of mine: remember Leon the "Green Beret"-junky who reigned over the

Venice beach crash-pad? Well, several of the meditators and I had become checkers of meditation; we would come in the afternoon to the Westwood SIMS center and check the meditations of the students who may be having some difficulty with their TM. I came into the center one afternoon and immediately wondered where everyone was because the place was empty. The girl at the welcome desk said she thought they were out taking a break in the little park in back of the center. So, I went out to see what was going on and there they all were in a neat little half-circle around some guy with an odd looking red hat.

I walked up and stood to listen for a moment and heard this guy saying, with a phony Tibetan accent, that he was a Red Hat Lama from Tibet; the TM-checker from Latin America broke in saying "Jampa is staying with me at my apartment while he is here in LA!" After "Jampa" had given his little Buddhist talk and started to answer questions in halting English, I said "Jampa, don't you live in a crash pad down in Venice?" The others were horrified by my apparent insult and got all indignant, how dare I? At this point, I took Keith aside and told him that "this guy is an impostor; he is a junky-con-artist from Venice, and I used to crash in his junky-pad by the beach." I told the Winquist brothers as well; everyone wanted to believe that we had a real live enlightened Lama from Tibet right there behind the center, sitting in the grass.

Leon wasn't stupid, he had done his research and knew exactly where he was; he was a pretty good con-man, and they trusted him more than me when it came to discerning a con-man from a jnani. Finally, people needed their meditation checked, and they pulled themselves, reluctantly away from the grace of Leon the con. I was amazed at how blind these people were; they had almost no powers of discernment whatever. And these were the cream of the newly initiated crop; the ones who had benefited most from their meditation. I have been sadly aware of this inability of many of my fellow seekers of Self-realization to discern the real from the illusion over all these years since 1966. Dubious gurus, healers, self-proclaimed replacements of Maharishi, like the girly-man "Sri, Sri, Sri, etc.," who Maharishi proclaimed a speaker of "sweet poison," have attracted the constantly seeking, clueless worshipers of the mere appearance of Enlightenment. They go from one promise of realization to the next without a clue as to what they are looking for. It's sad really! To have never experienced even a glimpse of the reality; they must wander blind, hoping they will bump into God, when all along they were given the keys to his Soul by Maharishi. "Give not that which is Holy unto the dogs, neither cast ye your pearls before swine, lest they trample them under their feet, and turn again and rend you." – KJV, Matthew 7:6 (a' la the TM-exers).

DIVINE AWARENESS

So, who am I to have opinions? Well, I'm just a Cantankerous, 74-year-old fart who doesn't care who you think I am; I don't even care who I Am. So, let me tell you some of the more unusual stories of my evolutionary path to Cantankerous, Old-Fart - Consciousness: First of all, you should understand that the experience of one's external "God" is the reflected experience of the Divine Being that is within you, your deepest most cherished Love. Your inner and outer realization of Him/Her/It might include any or all of the senses. You might see Jesus or Krishna or the overwhelming presence of infinite, unbounded awareness. You may not see anyone, but you find yourself in the loving embrace of everything, the whole creation, and the immensity of a Divine personality is loving you so unbelievably tenderly, saying, in your intuitive mind, that you are His Son and He is your Father. We are all Sons and Daughters of God, some have realized this and all will, eventually.

After about six months of meditating regularly with no drugs at all, I took a day trip to the beach at Lompoc CA. with two cars full of friends. The muscular drummer, Alfonse, wanted

217

to make a bonfire, and he and his mates spent a few hours gathering driftwood while I decided to take a hike down the beach. After about a half hour the combination of sun, cool salt air and the toasty warmth of the sand under my feet gradually soothed me into what seemed like a walking meditation. I saw my legs walking and the environment moving outside, while inside it was like watching a movie from an unmovable mountain of Me. I closed my eyes with the wind waving my shirt and hair like a caress.

Then it happened suddenly: My awareness drew me within to witness my mind collapsing down into, a point. My consciousness, my perception black-holed itself down into a focal point, an infinitely dynamic black hole with no actual time for remembrance of awareness, then exploded like a consciousness-volcano and I was suddenly Me! My Natural State of Awareness. My limited obscured consciousness had lifted like a veil, and I could "see." My mental horizon had expanded beyond my body limitations, out and out, I couldn't feel any limits to it. Looking ahead of me I could see all these beautiful flowers growing in the sand along the beach that I hadn't even noticed before; I heard my voice respond and it sounded so sweet, like a baby cooing. The more I walked along, the more I became permeated with a warm bliss until I transcended in an instant into pure joy, I was pure-blissful-joy, And there, was God! The invisible Divine Father above me, "You are Pure blissful joy... I am your son!" (my open-heart, my Being, cried in ecstasy).

In this Realization of my divine connection with God, I danced around in a circle making sounds I've never made; I ran up a sand-hill in ecstatic-bliss like a beautiful warrior hero. The loose sleeves of my Native American shirt and my long hair were blowing in the brisk wind as I stretched out my arms to the sky: "you are my son, my beautiful son," He said, and I was! Running down the beach, I had to thank you for this gift, My Lord! I grabbed two handfuls of flowers and ran to the water, threw them in, and fell to my face prostrate in the wet sand at the feet of Thee My Love. I walked a short way, and You washed the flowers up with Your wave - hands; one single finger of your ocean made its way to me and placed the flowers there, just at my feet. I cried out, "Love!"

Heading back down the beach, I realized that what I had lost was all fear, and what I had gained was our very Nature when fear has gone. This was the ecstasy of pure-freedom, real freedom, Blissful-Being!

Beach Flowers

Then, You were there, over the ocean,

You were there watching me,

hiding from my roughness that was very gradually returning.

You wanted to show me your face, but I was not ready.

Still, You peeked at me

and shot rays of Your Love at me that pierced my heart

with the most exquisite ecstasy of Love and Purity;

like a small child playing hide and seek,

we played as the sun was sinking into You,

with a rainbow of colors, I had never seen on this earth before.

My divine connection remained, but its intensity was slowly melting, and as I walked back toward the others I passed Alphonse struggling with a log and making all sorts of animal noises directed at me. He was about forty yards from me, enveloped in what looked like a translucent cocoon, outside of which was the world, as I was seeing it. An older guy was trudging down the beach, moving like a stiff robot in his more opaque cocoon. He passed me about twenty yards away. The cocoons were the auric-boundaries of the individual awareness, almost like little worlds within infinite, unbounded consciousness; they were the limitations of the small, egocentric self.

I could see Gordon's wife watching me, and as I approached her, her face began to light up and flush with color. When I came up to her, she embraced me and invited me to sit with the others around the huge bonfire. Alphonse arrived hauling the massive log that I had seen him with, and he was still directing his animal-sounding profanities at me. He was upset that I had spent hours wandering down the beach while he and his friends were hard at work gathering wood. However, I was immune to him, hiding in his cocoon. I sat close to the fire as the sun went down and darkness spread around us.

Alphonse deliberately piled the big log on the pyre and stood back to watch as I would, hopefully, cry out in pain. But I didn't feel any pain; It seemed somehow natural, like the compassion of God, that the fire felt cool on my face; in fact, I snuggled a bit closer as the flames rose higher and I passed my hand through them. It was like moving your hand through a living spirit; I said "the fire is cool," and noticed how sweet my voice sounded, my first spoken words to them. Everyone else had moved back about six feet, and Alphonse looked like he had seen a ghost.

THE LIGHT-SHIP

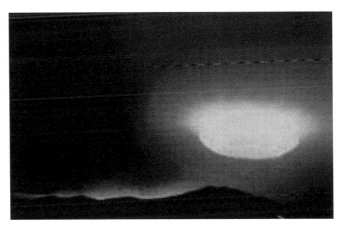

There was a big star moving toward us over the ocean, and when I saw that it was slowly coming down, I said: "look, a light-ship." No one looked up, but they started to gather their things and head up the small cliff toward the cars. I remained by the fire, looking at the ball of light as it descended toward the beach. Soon, it was just a hundred feet above me, and my subtle awareness had become gross enough to allow fear of the unknown to play with my mind.

I hadn't yet made the connection between the light-ship and my ongoing encounter with the Divine. I turned and walked up the hill as the craft came down to around fifty feet in altitude. As I climbed the cliff-top, there were some old 19th-century train tracks just ahead, all rusty and unused. But there! Thirty feet down the tracks was a man with a kerosene lantern, waving it back and forth as he walked toward me. After all that I had experienced that day, I wasn't shocked to see a man in a 19th-century conductor's uniform with his lantern coming my way. I was keeping my eye on the light-ship, and when the "conductor" said "what are you looking at?" I just stared at him and said "the star," and immediately turned to catch up to the others. Was this guy an old railroad re-enactor? All alone in the dark?

The Railroad Conductor

It was all happening faster than I could make sense of it, but I remember him smiling with a twinkle in his eye when he asked me what I was looking at as if he was there to make light of the situation somehow and lessen my fear. Now I know he was someone from the light-ship - an angel, a master or a guide of some kind. By the time I had reached the cars I had seen the light-ship turn into a helicopter; it had gone from silently cruising overhead looking like a big round light to the sudden raucous whining of a noisy machine. The helicopter was hovering overhead, and the cars were waiting for me. Alphonse jumped out of one of the cars and ran up to me screaming to get into a car, "let's get the hell out of here!"

I looked at him and lost my fear; I grabbed his arm and pulled him up on top of a dirt hill and shouted to him that they were just love, "just love." He threw my arm off and ran for his car as I stood on the hill, and the helicopter hovered for a moment and then flew off west toward the ocean; when it got about a hundred yards away, it suddenly changed back into a ball of light noiselessly gliding out to sea. One car was waiting, and I opened the door and slid in. Gordon, his wife, and Gene Spiegel were in the car, and we headed south along the Pacific Coast highway toward LA.

Things were almost normal aside from the stone silence of the others in the car. They were all staring straight ahead as if afraid to look at me, or in some trance. We were climbing a long hill when, just as we got half way up, a huge - I mean a Giant - brilliant orb lifted itself over the crest of the hill. It took up the entire horizon and continued to rise as we ascended the grade. I was astonished and said "Oh my God look at the huge. . " and then I realized it was the full Moon, but so much larger than I had ever seen it before. Yes, my senses were still working with celestial subtlety, I was seeing through the celestial level of awareness. Almost everything else looked as it does in ignorant, cocoon-enveloped consciousness: the cars, the people in my car, the ocean, everything! But when we got over the hill and were coming down close to the ocean, there it was again!

The light-ship was hovering over the water about a hundred yards out. I could now see its shape, more like the flying saucers that you see photos of, only made of light. The ship was dropping something into the ocean, or it was pulling something into itself from the sea, I don't know. Whatever it was, it was shiny, shimmering in the light that the ship emanated. The ship was going along the coast with us. It was, as if, following us, and I kept trying to get the others to look out their windows to see this incredible sight. They wouldn't move their heads; it was like they were frozen in time.

Now, the cars slowed down and we found ourselves in a traffic jam. The Light-Ship stopped with us, and I noticed that something was coming out of it. Whatever it was, it was shaped like a giant charcoal briquette and glowed from the inside just like a glowing piece of charcoal only it was about twelve feet from top to bottom and somewhat less in width. The color was saffron, from dark, almost black, to a beautiful glowing and radiant saffron/orange. At the time I thought the more shaded areas must be someone in it, that it must be a small light vehicle for personal transport, but I have since come to a different conclusion. Like souls who take on a different form in the astral plane, orb-shaped or just a human-shaped form of light; beings on higher planes of consciousness can be in the form of a ball of light, an Angel a railroad conductor, whatever! They are, after all, made of light.

Anyway, first one came out and flew directly over the traffic ahead of us and then flitted over the cars, somewhat playfully, until it came to our car, went over us and then out to the big Light-Ship again. Now, two were flitting over the cars and then three. I'll tell you something else; when the last mini ship or being was about to go over us, I grabbed Gene's head and forced him to look out the back window of the car so he could see the orange briquette as it swooped over us and out to sea. He yelled "shit, what the hell is that?" or an equivalent expression of shock and awe. Before I forced his gaze, I kept telling everyone to look but no one could or would. Part of that was because they couldn't see what I was seeing, like the Moon; they just saw the cocoon consciousness-sized Moon and thought I was "seeing things." The difference came when I put my hands on his head, and suddenly he could see what I was seeing.

Once the road had gone inland from the shore, I lost sight of the Ship for a while. We were going through a small town and were passing by a police car on the other side of the street; we were going south, and they were going north. I saw a thought form shoot out of Gordon's eyes and land on the head of the driver of the patrol car. It was a fear thought and immediately attracted the cop's attention. He did a big U-turn behind us and followed for a while.

Meanwhile, Gordon was emptying his pockets of rolled joints and frantically handing them out to everyone; he said: "eat em fast, just swallow them." I hadn't had any drugs in half a year and didn't intend to do that now! Gene saw that I wasn't eating and grabbed the two joints out of my hand and seemed to have a hard time getting them down with the lack of saliva left in his mouth from the ones he had already managed to chew up.

When the Cop approached our car, Gordon was whining "gosh officer why did you stop us? We don't do drugs, and we haven't done anything wrong." His inner voice screamed, "I'm a drug user, and I'm scared of you, I'll say anything to get you to leave me alone." I knew that the cops could hear the fear in his voice and it kept them looking for drugs. They made Gordon and his wife get out of the car. It would be harder to get Gene and I out since this was a two-door, so one of them thrust his arm through the open window and demanded our I D's.

Then the other cop stuck his head over the front seat and looked me over. I just stared into his eyes, and with impatience and even anger, I said: "I don't have an ID with me, I keep it at home since I'm not driving and no law says I have to have it on me all the time." Somehow, I spoke to his soul; my tone was fearless and honest, and at the same time I could feel the power in each word - a deep silent power - and the cop just backed out and said, "These guys are alright" to his partner, who was now standing beside our car with his hand on his gun.

"Go ahead folks, have a nice evening." In other words, what I said, for the second time in this memoir, was, "These Droids are not the ones you're looking for," yet again. That's how it worked out anyway. Once we were on our way, Gordon asked, "how did you do that? They were about to search the whole car, and they probably would have found the lid I have tucked under the seat cover." I responded, "you heard the conversation!" I felt some anger for him as well; he had asked the cops to harass us with his paranoia.

When we got back in sight of the ocean again, the light-ship was waiting for us, hovering and dropping or retrieving the shiny stuff. As we drove along the highway, I started to have thoughts about this strange craft that wasn't visible to anyone else in the car. I began to wonder what they wanted of me, were they after me? Just as I started to entertain the slightest worry, a voice in my head, so distinctly not my own, said: "We are Love, just Love, Brahmananda Saraswati Maharaj." I felt a wave of joy filling my heart, and I said out loud, "They are Love, just Love, they just told me that they are Love." Of course, Gordon, Gene and Gordon's wife ignored me and my ravings, but I didn't care at all. Now I knew this was all the continuation of my close encounter of the highest kind on Lompoc beach. Sometime after this telepathic communication with the light-ship, I came to know who had been talking to me. His name was Brahmananda Saraswati Maharaj Jagad Guru Bhagavan Shankaracharya of Jyotir Math, and he was my Master's Master, the one in the picture on the puja table. I discovered this when I bought "The Science of Being and Art of Living" by Maharishi; there on one of the first pages of the book was "Guru Dev" with his name just under his picture. Many more were to see this light-ship when it appeared in Mallorca Spain on one of the TTC courses.

POST LOMPOC

Having returned from Lompoc Beach, Gordon dropped me off at the Gentle Soul house, and I went into the Music/Living room and sat down. There was an LP with a picture of Maharishi on it and the title "Love & God," which I immediately put on the stereo. As I sat back and listened in the quiet darkness of the empty house, the pictures that Maharishi was painting in my mind and heart were the very realities that I had just experienced in my own life on the beach at Lompoc.

I began to relive the divine love emanating from the sky above the ocean and piercing my heart with ecstasy and peace. By the time the record ended, it seemed as if Maharishi had recorded his experience to validate the experience of others, like me for one. This was the experience of one's personal God that he had talked about, I had no doubts about that; I had just met him, and my master had described my meeting from his own experience. By the next evening, my divine consciousness and perception had been replaced by the longing for its return. It was strange how it imperceptibly drew back inside of me without notice.

I stood in the courtyard and looked to the skyline of the Hollywood Hills just north of us, and there it was again! My Light-Ship was hanging there above the hills, and I called everyone who was there and told them to look. Everyone could see it, I could see it! I'm sure Guru Dev could turn our seeing off and on at will, of course! The ship returned to the same spot every night for almost two months, and the word got out among the TM center folks that Rick was going on about UFO's coming to visit him every night. Robert, One of my fellow TM checkers, seemed to find this a perfect time to ridicule something he had never experienced. Every time I ran into him he would look skyward and point with his finger, arm extended, shading his eyes with the other hand and his face mocking me with expressions of astonishment. He's a fun guy if you don't mind being the brunt of his cynical sense of humor.

In 2013 he and his brother visited my harp shop in Fairfield. I hadn't seen him in thirty years, and still, he couldn't wait to do his UFO routine, the whole ridiculous put-down, all in fun of course, but disrespectful as hell. Only now he understandably figured I would laugh along with him because, of course, he expected it had all been mood-making on my part, that he had been right all the time! Of course, in his mind, there had never been a Light-Ship. But there had, and it wasn't a UFO it was more than he could imagine, and I quietly said "yes, that was more profound than I could have realized back then." He didn't hear me, he was invested in his need to relate to me as the 60's hippy mood-maker, or maybe he was probing to see if it had been real. I'm really glad that I never told anyone all that I am telling you now; I probably would have been haunted by many more irritating skeptics from 1967 to the present (2017).

2ND COMING OF THE LIGHT-SHIP

Two or three years later, I was with Maharishi in Mallorca Spain on a (TTC) teacher training course. I had already become a TM Teacher in 1969 and had been asked by Maharishi to come to this course to be with him and to write and perform songs for the participants. Maharishi took a seven-day silence every year when he would retire to his room, and fast the whole time. I had been taking this yearly silence ever since my TTC in India. The evening of the sixth day Maharishi would come out and give a short talk about his plans for the coming year; he would always have some new direction that he wanted to concentrate on for enlightening the world.

On this particular evening, Maharishi had John Bright (aka Black) drive him to the tip of a peninsula viewable from our hotels. He told John to park, and then closed his eyes and appeared to be meditating. Soon, a brilliant light-ship appeared just over the sea in front of the car. The ship was spilling or extracting the same light material from the ocean that I had witnessed at Lompoc. It floated in the air for some time as if

229

communing with Maharishi and finally flew out over the sea. When it had gone, Maharishi slowly opened his eyes and told John to drive back to the hotel. When they arrived, Maharishi went to his room, and John joined us in our breaking the fast with roasted almonds and Mallorcan grape juice.

Many of us had witnessed the Light-Ship and Maharishi's car just sitting there, and I asked John "did the ship drop shiny stuff out of it or suck it up from the water?" and he said "yes." It was obvious to me that Maharishi had been communicating with Guru Dev, just as I had a few years earlier, only I'm sure that for Maharishi it wasn't out of the ordinary. The following evening, several of the course participants asked Maharishi what that UFO was doing out over the peninsula, and Maharishi just said: "how many saw this?" When they raised their hands, he said "Very good."

To those of you who are unfamiliar with the world beyond the mainstream media, the movies, TV, and the Internet, much of this first phase of my life may seem like a fiction, but to those who have spent their lives cultivating the discernment of reality from illusion, my life is a rather ordinary one. The next book covers my seven years spent living and traveling with His Holiness Maharishi Mahesh Yogi 1968-75. From our first meeting on the Four Star Productions set of Rod Sterling's movie documentary of Maharishi to India and beyond. My teacher training was just after the Beatles and movie stars had left the ashram.

I was thankful for having avoided the super-star TTC course in India since I probably wouldn't have been given the opportunity to become Maharishi's songwriter and troubadour with the Beatles and Donovan and Mia Farrow requiring all of Maharishi's attention.

However, the rich and famous had already been contracted by major recording companies, like I had, to write hit songs, not songs of the truth of life, which Maharishi would have appreciated. Having gotten out of my Columbia contract through a top Hollywood music lawyer before attending my TTC in India, I was free to write and record for Maharishi which I did, starting right at the end of my TTC in Kashmir India.

There are a lot of untold, candidly revealed, stories from my years with Maharishi. There is even some insight into living and learning from a Divine Master, mostly from making mistakes, which I find is the best way to learn the lessons lived. See you in book two.

Jai Guru Dev

Rick Stanley

My Song Of Life
Book II

THE MAHARISHI YEARS

DEDICATED

to my wife and true friend

-Claudine-

She has unselfishly supported me through 25 years of my creative work, both musical and literary.

And to my son Brendan, who tirelessly edited this book, never sparing my ego for the "sweet truth"

To my sweet daughter

Gwendolyn Rose Stanley

&

My Good Friend Henry Eckstein

*Please forgive the quality of photos in this book, most are ancient-amateur pics that I included because sometimes a picture is worth, maybe not a thousand words, but...Aw shucks, let's face it, I don't care about the quality, I just like pictures in books!

Cover photo by Alan Waite

Memories 1968-1975

INTRODUCTION

This 2nd book is an honest and straight from the heart telling of my time with Maharish Mahesh Yogi. Although it's mostly about me and my life around him, there is a lot of candid insight into what it's really like to be a western disciple doing his best to attune to the lofty consciousness of an Enlightened man. I make many mistakes and misunderstandings but still I manage to fulfill his intentions for the only thing I could offer him, my music.

Maharishi inspired me to write songs infused with his knowledge and he even gave me his teaching in poetic form that I put to lyrics & music for the first album "Song Of Life" and the 2nd "Something Good Is Happening" with Paul Fauerso.

"The truth of Life is eternal and the same everywhere,

the Light of Life is eternal and the same everywhere,

what is here is everywhere,

what is not here is nowhere at all,

now begin from where you are,

to find who you are."

The "Song Of Life" Album Cover

THE GOLDEN TOUCH OF LOVE

One day when Maharishi was in LA for the Four Star movie production of Himself, directed by Rod Sterling of "The Twilight Zone" fame, I was called by Jerry Jarvis to come to Malibu Lake to meet Maharishi. When I arrived, Rod Sterling was about to take a lunch break in his Rolls Royce. And there was Maharishi sitting in the grass with several of my SIMS friends in a semi-circle around Him. There was a beautiful grove of eucalyptus trees and the lake just behind Him.

Jerry approached me and asked where my guitar was. I hadn't brought it, and so we set about trying to find one for me. Someone had a cottage nearby, and she had a nylon string or classical guitar which I wasn't used to at all. She didn't have a capo either, and I needed one to sing in a key that would suit my arrangement of a song I'd recently written about Maharishi. Finally, after transposing the song into another key, I walked over to Maharishi and the SIMS group. Jerry got up and said "Maharishi, this is Rick Stanley, he is with Columbia Records and has written a song to you that is on his new album. I got down on my knees and bowed before Maharishi and then picked up the guitar and started to sing:

"I would have been unhappy if you hadn't come my way,

I could have been a night bird if I hadn't seen the day,

everything was waiting for me to come to you,

in the fullness of your presence is there something I can do,

and everywhere I look I see the golden touch of love."

There is more of the song, and you can hear it on the "Gentle Soul" album. The song is about Maharishi and me and when I finished singing there arose a strong wind as if singing through the eucalyptus trees and it went on for about two minutes. Maharishi, held up his hand as if pointing to the trees and said:

"The Nature Responds." It did seem to be true, that Nature itself rallied behind the sentiment of the song in praise of Maharishi, her blessed Son.

THE LAKE LOUISE COURSE

I heard about a building that the SRM had rented to have a lecture hall for Maharishi to give a "private" talk to SRM members-only when he was in LA. Some of us relative-newbies stood outside the door while a select few of the original SIMS students got to be inside. When Maharishi came out, he wondered why we were all refused admission by Charlie's oldies. He wanted as many meditators as he could get to come up to a course he was going to give at the Château on Lake Louise in Alberta Canada. Leona Bach, was our mentor, our Mother Divine, and even though the SRM had told the SIMS leaders that no student TMr's would be accepted on the course, she told us to "just go, follow the Master and ignore the small minds." We made ready and filled the little blue Simca up with gas, got a few maps and headed for Canada.

Sara was driving through the dark rural landscape while it was my turn to meditate and get a little sleep. After an hour or so I woke to the car making a noise like a cracked cylinder and vibrating like a paint mixer with a low powerful hum. I looked out the window and up in the sky and saw what looked like a UFO going along beside us, no blinking lights. Sara said that she had been watching it in the rear view mirror for some time. Now, it was coming over us and the hum and vibration were increasing, it almost seemed as if the thing was intent on keeping us from getting to Maharishi. Maybe it was Charlie Lutes in his own private SRM lightship trying to deter the SIMS kids from sharing Maharishi?

Sara stopped the car and I took over the driving so that she could do her evening meditation. Several hours later the UFO was gone and we made it to Lake Louise late that night. Surprisingly, the Canadian SRM welcomed us with open arms. I think Leona had called and given us a glowing recommendation; after all, Leona was Canadian SRM and loved by all. I was also surprised to see so many SIMS meditators, but they were mostly the people who had been SRM before SIMS started; Tom and Robert Winquist, Keith and Peter Wallace, Nini White and Casey Coleman, I think, and others I can't remember?

We were very impressed with the hotel; the dining room was elegant in the extreme, Victorian English aristocracy, linen napkins and tablecloth, crystal glasses and silver everything. The waiters were in tails and there was an unbelievable view of the glacier and the lake and the stone cliffs above them, easily seen through the huge windows which lined the high walls. Our first encounter with the ancient elevator, or "lift," at the hotel was when Sara and I were going up to our room. The old Victorian elevator came Klunketing down and landed on the main floor in front of us, we got in with guitar and luggage taking up most of the floor. The elevator operator deftly handled the controls, a set of joysticks, with the fingers of his left hand, aligning the cab dead-on level at each landing. With his gloved right, he pulled open the folding gate, followed by the door, allowing us to exit. "fourth floor, watch your step getting off." He reversed the process to close the door, then the gate, before continuing his journey.

Our first encounter with Maharishi at Lake Louise happened when we were standing in front of the elevator waiting to go up. The bell rang, the gate creaked open, the sliding door slammed, and out came a whole arm full of flowers held by our little Indian Guru in a white silk dhoti. He had long black hair and a grey and white beard. I was more than surprised and just stood transfixed in front of him as he smiled and said: "Jai guru dev, very good, you've come!" Jerry, who was just behind him smiled and said "Rick, could you move please?" Realizing that I was holding them all hostage in the elevator, I too-quickly tried to get out of their way and backed up into and onto several equally transfixed Canadians. I was feeling blessed that I had the good fortune to bump into Maharishi literally and noticed for the first time that I had a beautiful, fresh, red rose in my hand. I was quite amazed that he seemed so happy to see me; little did I know that I was to play my part in the World Plan.

This was the course that the CBC was filming and is probably one of the best professional government documentaries of Maharishi and His message ever made. The Chateau at Lake Louise has an in-chateau harpist who wears the full flowing dress of a queen and plays one of those huge golden orchestral harps with cherubs and carvings all over it. She also plays an Irish hand-carved harp that I made for her several years ago. I wonder who the harpist was that was playing throughout the CBC documentary in 1968? I don't think they had a harpist back then, so it was probably added on after the TV show was filmed.

("The Harp Angel"of Lake Louise with the Celtic Harp
I made for her several years ago)

I can't remember much about the daily experience of the course, it was the usual extra meditation and advanced lectures given by Maharishi. Although, I remember one meeting near the end of the course when Maharishi asked how many would be going to India to attend the Teacher Training Course in Rishikesh in December 1968. I raised my hand and was looking off to my left at, I don't know what, when he said something that I didn't hear. I suddenly felt Robert Winquist's elbow in my ribs and looked up to see everyone staring at me. I asked Robert what he had said, and he told me that after he asked us how many were going to TTC and we raised our hands, he looked in our direction and said "Very good, Rick is coming!"

That was the first time of several that Maharishi would say something about me, or to me in a group situation and I would never hear what he said. It became apparent to me that this was intentional on Maharishi's part because if I had heard him complimenting me or saying something nice about me it would go straight to my head and I would probably have become an unbearable egotist in short order. After the final evening lecture of the course, we were all standing in the hallway with flowers ready to offer to him as he passed each of us on the way to his room. He was taking them and saying the usual "Jai Guru Dev" to each of us.

When he came around a corner in the hallway where I was waiting, he stopped and took my flower and as he was taking it he took my hand in his and held it as he looked me in the eyes and said "very good, Rick, very good;" then he handed me a flower and said "Jai Guru Dev." This was the end of the course, and we had to leave our room the next day, but since Maharishi was staying on for another day, we were offered a room opposite the advanced techniques room where Maharishi was initiating people all night long with the door open. We left our door open as well too, hopefully, share some of the good vibes. But the vibes were so intense that neither of us could sleep, and when morning came, I had finally nodded off for an hour or so.

I sat up and meditated and then became aware of someone moving about in Maharishi's room across the narrow hallway. I tip-toed over to the half-open door and peeked in. There he was, packing his little suitcase with the few items he owned, extra dhotis an extra pair of sandals, a shawl and that was about it. He looked up and saw me and said "you are still here?" and I responded, "yes, luckily enough our car broke down, and we got to stay one more day." Maharishi looked surprised and happy; pleased with my response, he repeated what I had said in the middle of his laughter "luckily enough my car broke down, luckily enough," he said. And then in the middle of laughing, he asked: "and it can be repaired." I was laughing now, and said: "Oh yes, it will be fine." "Luckily enough, your car broke down...hee hee," you know, he was laughing!

Maharishi and his close followers from Canada as well as Jerry and Debby Jarvis and several other Americans went on to Calgary that morning, and when we finally were able to get our car fixed the following morning, we headed that way too. By the time we arrived in Calgary, it was the early afternoon of the next day, and everyone was gone. Jerry had left word that Sara and I could stay the night in the room Maharishi had occupied the whole previous night giving out advanced techniques. I thought, "well another chance to soak up Maharishi's wonderful consciousness, I'll sleep right here on the very bed he sat on all night giving out techniques." Sometimes, too much of a good thing can be a bad thing. Between sleeping across a three-foot hallway from him the previous night, feeling like I was vibrating with awareness all night, to sleeping all night in the very bed, he had sat on all the next night was too much of a good thing and I woke up the next day sick as a dog. It's called purification or release of stress if you like.

After a good releasing purge we packed up and headed for home. However, our car had, even more, purging to do before we would ever make it to LA. The first flat tire occurred before we made it out of Canada, but that was easily remedied with the spare I had in the back. The second flat tire blew us off the road a few hundred miles after the first, and we found ourselves stranded on a small street off the highway at dusk with no spare. Some angelic dude in a truck came to our rescue and took us and our two flat tires to a local station after it was closed and somehow got the guy to repair both our tires and then he took us back to our stressed out little Simca. You may think that our car had released enough stress to get us home safely now. But no! after another few hundred miles we had another flat, three flats in all. Fortunately, we had the spare, and we limped all the rest of the way to LA on our half-sized little spare tire; a whole lot of karmic debt paid for in time, trouble and tires.

SQUAW VALLEY

After the course, the word got around that Maharishi wouldn't be traveling out of India again. He had already gone around the world ten times over a ten year period and had established centers in many countries but, considering the world's population, a relatively small number of people had shown interest in the technique and the teaching. He had done his best to enlighten humanity, at least that's what it seemed like until Jerry Jarvis made a deal with Maharishi that if he could get at least 300 students to attend just one more course then Maharishi would come, especially if a good number of them would go to India to attend Teacher Training. Jerry pulled it off, and there were at least 300 of us that came to be with Maharishi at Squaw Valley, many of whom had already decided to go on to India for TTC with Maharishi in January.

SHORTCUTS

An interesting phenomenon occurred at the end of the course when Maharishi was interviewing the prospective India course applicants. At first, we would hand him our application, and he would ask a few questions, but after awhile it was clear that there wasn't enough time for interviews. I didn't really notice it myself, it was Robert Winquist who sidled over to me and said "Rick, watch what Maharishi does with the course applications. I watched and noticed that he was just taking the application from the student and putting it in either of two piles; one pile was for the Nays and one for the

Yeas. The line to sign up was so long, at least two hundred, that there wasn't time to interview everyone who wanted to attend the course, so Maharishi had to use his strong intuitive abilities to evaluate the remaining applicants. I noticed that he wouldn't even look at the person as they placed the form down on the table in front of him, he would simply put his hand on top of it, for just a moment, pick it up and put it into one of the piles. I looked at Robert and said, "wow! he's evaluating them with his superpowers." It was funny that no one else noticed that this was happening, only Robert, and that would have been it if he hadn't told me. During the seven years that I lived with and traveled with Maharishi, there were many instances of his using his "shortcuts" to get things done or even to instruct.

ME & KENNY

Back in LA, I was trying to make a living by performing around with Kenny Edwards, Linda Ronstadt's partner in the "Stone Pony's." My goal was to try and get enough money to attend the TTC in India in January 1969. Kenny and I worked up our songs with harmonies and guitar parts and started playing at the coffee houses, birthdays, bar-mitzvahs. When Linda Ronstadt had gone, solo Kenny ended up in the same situation that I had put myself in, without a Record Company or manager or agent to get us work.

LINDA RONSTADT & KENNY EDWARDS

Although I was still managed by the big time movie star manager, he wasn't any good at getting us music gigs. Anyway, we both had good reputations, and somehow, word got around, and we found ourselves busy on the weekends.

Paul Horn, the flutist, jazz great of the Paul Horn Quintet had worked with Pamela and me leading some of the sessions at Columbia as I mentioned earlier. He was a TM initiator, and I would run into him at the Gayley center and at Columbia often enough for him to take a business interest in Kenny and me when he heard that both of us were free of company contracts. He offered to be our manager and take us to Epic Records to see if he could get a recording contract as a duo. This may sound kinda crazy since I had just managed to get out of my Columbia/Epic contract but at this point, I was still looking for money to go to India, and I figured I could get an advance from Epic if I signed with them again, nuts!. Paul took us around to the office of an A&R man, a friend of his, to audition and we sang a few of our songs for him. His response was typical of the small minded execs who ran the companies in those days; he said: "can you guys sing like Seals and Crofts?" We laughed and walked out.

Kenny had started TM, and he even brought Linda Ronstadt to a party we were having at the SIMS center in Westwood. I knew her pretty well as she used to come over to the Gentle Soul house to see if Pamela had any new songs that she could record. She even asked me if I had anything a girl could sing but my songs were philosophically typecast for the Gentle Soul or me and she had to pass. "Different Drum," Linda's massive hit single, had a B side with one of Pamela's songs on it. Pam was collecting royalty checks, I peeked at the amount, and it was juicy! A month-long pre -TTC course was being held at Humboldt State College in northern California, and Maharishi was going to be there, so Sara and I drove up, and Kenny and Pamela were both there as well.

HUMBOLDT- ONE

When the course was winding down, I asked Kenny if he would like to go to India and become a teacher of TM. He didn't think he'd be able to being a relative beginner in his practice of TM. I said: "let's ask Maharishi," and I did just that, as he was leaving for his car to the airport. I said: "Maharishi, would it be alright if Kenny came to India with me? he would like to become an initiator, and we play music together." Maharishi replied, "yes, yes, come." I think Kenny was a bit mind-blown that he was really going to India, a place he had been intrigued with for years. He actually played a little sitar and had been study-ing Indian philosophy. Somehow, we both managed to come up with the money for the course and travel expenses just in time to make it to India that January.

Earlier I mentioned that Terry and his mother Doris Day owned the publishing house that The Gentle Soul was signed to, Daywin Publishing. It was the manager of Daywin who I went to see about an advance on publishing royalties. He said that I should go to ASCAP (American Society of Composers, Artists, and Publishers) and that they would very likely give me an advance. Yes, I have already mentioned this, and they did give me $2,500 which was just enough to get to India and back and pay for the four months that we were there, plus buy a beautiful harmonium from Riki Ram in Delhi. Of course, there were several saris for Sara and a few pajamas for me.

Before it was time to fly to Delhi, Sara and I camped out at Tom Winquist's apartment, and we met Karen Blasedale, a one-time girlfriend of Elvis Presley, and longtime meditator. He used to fly her up to Las Vegas and put her in the seat reserved for the most honored guest, right in front of center stage. She said they would sit up all night talking about meditation and spirituality, and one assumes they probably did a little more than that, but she never said they had. Both are long gone now, but she was one of the most classically beautiful girls I've ever seen.

THE APSARASA

One early morning I had a waking dream, which means I felt totally awake. I was floating in the Astral/Dreamworld, floating through the air when a beautiful Apsarasa (celestial dancing girl) floated up across from me. She was so ravishingly gorgeous that I immediately felt an overwhelming attraction and she appeared to have the same reaction. We were about four feet away from each other, lying on a 45-degree aspect in space. (the angle you see taken by 1940's film vamps, lying seductively on their couches with one arm supporting the head and the other holding a martini or a long cigarette holder) She moved her hips, just a slight thrust, which made both of us erupt in a blissful sensual climax which woke me up. Thankfully, it hadn't translated to my physical body but I was still in a state of satiated sensual fulfillment when I rolled over and told Sara that I had just had sex with an angel and that we didn't actually touch or lose energy, we gained energy and bliss as well.

This could mean that if you "ran" into someone in the subtle planes who you were attracted to, and they to you, you might just partake of this beautiful, sensual sharing that would leave you both in a sensually fulfilled, blissful state, without even touching, and then just float on your merry way! This was a revelation for me in that it explained the difference in the laws of Nature for sex in the subtle, astral and celestial worlds vs. the physical world. Sara was less than happy for me and was actually jealous! I realized on thinking about it, that if it had been my wife who woke me up to share the sensual dream experience she just had with an angel, a demon or even Elvis Presley, it would be a bummer, especially if it was a very real, waking dream. Oh well! Just thought you might be interested.

RIKARD FLEUR

My TM initiator was an opera singer for the New York Metropolitan Opera Company and on our way to TTC in India we stayed at his apartment in Manhattan which was also the local TM center. Rikard Fleur was his stage name and Rikard Jensen his real name. He told me that he had taken vocal lessons for twenty years and could control all the muscles from his throat down to his diaphragm which allowed him to be able to sing low or high just by flexing the muscles that would best do the job. He said he could hit notes spot on from any other note or octave. "But you're not singing Opera so all you need to do is one thing and it won't take you long to master it." I said "what thing," and he said, "Just sing on the level of the meaning of the words and you will spontaneously take the right amount of breath and sing with true emotion." It took awhile to get the hang of it but after four months of singing the Holy Tradition for full moon boat rides and for TTC, I began to sing effortlessly, and it only got better until after a year or two when someone asked Maharishi what angels sound like when they sing he said "Have you heard Rick?" That actually happened in Mallorca a year or two after I had become an Initiator, teacher of TM.

DEUTSCHLAND

Well, first we flew to Germany via Icelandic airlines with its Rolls Royce prop engines for $150. Each, one way. My mother was pleased to see me and to meet Sara whom she immediately loved; my mother was very fond of intelligent women and wondered out loud how on earth I managed to marry one. Maybe you will remember that according to my parents I'm supposed to be mildly retarded despite the genius IQ! Only my father has finally, at the age of 94, having received the gift of my 8th CD and being influenced by my brother as they listened to it, actually told me on the phone yesterday that I'm really, "We all think your really Great...an extremely creative and talented man...we all know that." He said that just after I told him that arthritis in my shoulders has curtailed my ability to perform on the harp or build and carve the Celtic Harps that has been my livelihood for the last 20 years. He felt sad about that and let down his Bostonian stiff upper man-lip and admitted how he really felt for the first time in my life.

We stayed with "Ma" for several days, and I performed at a German version of a Boston coffee house, one of those Jazz Caves in Heidelberg. Somehow, they had heard of me and introduced me as "The great Columbia Recording Artist, Rick Stanley of The Gentle Soul." I was a bit shocked that the owner of the Cave had heard of me, but I played along and made the most of it. Next, we took a train down to Tubingen near Munich. This was a town with a population of great Opera singers and classical musicians, and there was a really friendly TM initiator who had invited Sara and me to stay at their home until it was time to take our flight to India.

The family we stayed with consisted of two brothers about my age, one was a TM teacher/scholar at the university, and the other was a Flamenco guitarist. Their mother was a retired opera singer, a local Diva who had about fifteen students. She wanted me to sing and play for her students, and I felt really unsure about what their reaction would be to hear a cross between Dylan and Donovan breaking all the vocal rules they were so diligently mastering. I was more than right to be worried; when I had finished one song, they just sat there looking like they had smelled something horrible and it was clear that the Diva would use my performance as a lesson on all the things not to do when singing opera. They were all very confused, having heard the spiel about my being a Columbia Recording Artist; this was the Germany that still had Umpa Oktoberfest music on the top hits radio stations. Folk Rock was still a few years down the road, especially in this part of

Deutschland.

INDIA

We caught our flight for Delhi India in Frankfurt Germany, and as we came in for the landing I was looking out the window, even before I could see the smoke, I could smell it. Down on the ground, there was a vast cloud of smoke that extended as far as I could see. On the outskirts of the city the morning fires sparkled in the midst of the smoke and as we flew over the dense clouds of wood and dung fires the smell became pungent and even spicy with a flavor that is only found in India. We got off the plane, got our bags and headed for the taxis. There were quite a few westerners, and it wasn't hard to tell the meditators from the others as they were looking all around for each other with wide open smiles.

The cab we got in was halfway down the line of cabs. The only reason we got in his cab was that the cabby had approached us in the terminal and grabbed our bags. Then he quickly led us out and put them in his trunk. A couple of other obvious TM-rs saw us and asked if they could share the cab with us, and we were okay with that. However, when the cabby at the head of the line saw what was happening, he ran down to our cab and knocked on the driver's window. Our cabby opened it and started to have a very violent argument with this guy until a fist came through the window and knocked our cabby into the girl in the front seat. We were yelling at him to drive away fast since the other cabby was still trying to punch him through the open window. With his body halfway in the girl's lap, and his left foot barely touching the clutch, he managed to screech out of the line of cabs raising a cloud of dust and a Hearty Hi-yo Silver, Away down the hard dirt, airport road.

We knew the name of the hotel we were supposed to go to for the initial few days of the course, it was called the Ranjit, definitely not a four-star paradise but adequate for twenty-somethings. I was a bit taken aback when we were introduced to our room by the bellhop. It was all concrete block walls with a thin covering of very off-white paint, and the furniture, lamps, and drapes looked like a yard sale in Iowa. But what really caught my eye was the bathroom. The toilet was a large, long, tarnished aluminum stall where you would stand and do number 1 or squat and do number 2, depending, of course, on your sex. The sink was like a shop sink in the USA, the kind you use for getting stains out of shirts or for cleaning paint brushes. There was no mirror, just a dirty piece of stainless steel that probably hadn't been reflective for years.

Our first meal smelled delicious and looked great, but when I took my first mouthful, I had to cover my mouth and drop it back on the plate. Hot, beyond hot, beyond any hot I have ever tasted! It would be impossible to eat if all the meals were this hot so I asked one of the waiters if they could get the cook to make our food with just a little spice, just a hint. They brought us a freshly cooked version of the food we had tried to eat, with hopefully, much less spice involved. Again, I took my first mouthful and just had to spit it out; it was precisely the same as the food they had served before. They swore that it didn't have any spice in it and I just ate some fruit and drank some scary water and went to bed. The next day we talked to someone who handled the course participants complaints and requests, and they said they would take care of the food situation. As I can't remember not eating, either they managed to cool off the curry, or I just got used to it. I think I got used to drinking at least two or three glasses of water with every mouthful of food.

I'm not sure how many days it was until we saw Maharishi, but when we did, it was in his ground floor hotel room, and there were around twenty of us. The final number of course members was 150, but at this point we were it. The meeting was called so that Maharishi could get our input on what we wanted for food. He told us that the Puris (adobe cabins) and lecture hall weren't ready yet and that it would be a week or two before we would be able to bus up to Rishikesh. California avocados, tofu, salad or burgers and fries, so many picky people all wanting what they thought was the only food they should or wanted to eat, and poor Maharishi in his homeland, the ultimate host. It was as if we were guests in his house, he did everything to give us whatever we could possibly want, but in India, in 1968-9 there was little chance of finding California health food or Big Mac's & Fries.

After two weeks of very hot curries and wandering around Delhi buying clothing for the course at the Government Store, Maharishi scheduled one-on-one appointments for all of us. When it was my time, I gently knocked on his door and went into a dark room. I could just see him sitting cross-legged on his deerskin on the couch. There was just enough light, candlelight as I remember; so that when I sat in the chair opposite him, I could make out his outline and the light shone off his silver Dhoti. He asked a few questions to make the meeting a bit less unusual than it really was, and then he asked me to close my eyes. I did, but after a few minutes I pecked and saw him staring at me, and he first concentrated at the top of my head, then at my face, then my throat, chest and when he got to my navel and lower waist he stopped and looked as if he needed to take a second look. Then he closed his eyes and did something inside, and I could feel some sensations in my second chakra area.

It became quite obvious during the course that Maharishi had closed my second chakra because I had absolutely no sexual feelings during the entire four months of rounding (meditation/asanas/pranayama/meditation etc.). My wife hadn't had the same treatment, and I'm afraid she became quite frustrated with me, although she only made a few unsuccessful advances, my abstinence and probably her unstressing, forced her to divert her attention elsewhere. There was a wealthy, white South African with diamond mines and an eloquent speaking voice who picked up on her glances and invited her to share the luxurious houseboat that he was living in all alone. He wasn't entirely without manners, as an after-thought, he invited me as well. My wife made it clear that she was going to move to his place with or without me and I fig-ured that if she was unstressing, I could at least keep an eye on her. However, the conversations were constant and animated between them, and I felt like her brother. When it was time to go to shore, he would escort her into the shikara and then sit next to her. My only choice was to sit next to him. It felt ter-rible being cuckolded.

The brown monkeys and the crows at the Academy in Rishikesh were quite a nuisance. The dogs, who were just try-ing to do their job keeping the monkeys at bay, were blamed for all the racket, and at the demand of some of the older folks, Maharishi had to have the dogs gathered up and trucked sev-eral miles away and abandoned. Soon, the monkeys did take over and attacked some women sunbathing on top of their puri. They ran and screamed as the monkeys chased them off the roof. I was sitting and eating lunch in the dining hall that had no glass in the windows, just a roof overhead. The Brown monkeys were in the trees all around the dining hall and one of them, probably the male leader, kept threatening to jump down on us. I made a face and said "get out of here," and he immediately jumped down right in front of me and grabbed something off my plate, then jumped right back into the tree. This infuriated Al Bruns, a good friend, who jumped down out of the windowless window of the hall onto the ground and was picking up a stick when it looked like the big brown monkey was preparing to jump on his back as he bent over. I shouted at Al to "stand up, watch out, he's gonna jump on you." Just in time Al ran back around the hall and came in the door pissed-off and scared all at the same time.

It got so bad that the very people who had demanded that the dogs be sent away asked that they be brought back, but there was no way the Brahmacharies could find them. Eventually, they found their own way back, and the monkeys kept their distance. Another monkey story that happened on the course just before ours concerned the famous actress Mia Farrow. She was doing her meditation with the door open to her puri when a menacing brown monkey shocked her out of her silence as he shook the end of her bed frame violently. She screamed and screamed until a passing Brahmachari (an Indian monk/disciple of Maharishi) came to her rescue and scared the monkey off. However, Mia was so freaked out that she attacked her rescuer and tore his dhoti almost entirely off.

"Viggie" or Virginia, a long time meditator and daughter of an English Lord, was on the TTC course in Rishikesh that the Beatles Joined. She had stayed on for the next TTC as well. Viggie told me that Maharishi looked so sad and concerned when he asked John Lennon why are you leaving? and Lennon replied, "if your so cosmic you tell us!" John had been told by Magic Alex some gossip that Maharishi had held Mia's hand which was probably true! Only, Alex implied some sinister motives, and John was dark enough to accept his disinformation as fact.

Viggie said, you could feel the karmic reaction to John's words, and Maharishi's heart, as if stabbed with the violation of his sincere and loving hospitality. Maharishi would hold the hand of many of us, (see the back album cover photo of Donovan's album with a picture of him sitting with Maharishi holding his hand) usually when we would hand him a flower and were leaving or just arriving. It was a beautiful thing and felt like something you wish your father had done. Mia never claimed any sexual advances by Maharishi, and the Beatles later retracted the story; however, it had served its purpose to get the Beatles away from Maharishi. Yoko and the group's management were also afraid of losing their cash cow if the Boys decided to spend any more time in India.

Dr. Deepak Chopra gave another insight into the Beatles & Maharishi saga: Chopra said that in his meeting with Harrison and Maharishi he asked Maharishi why the Beatles left India, saying that, Maharishi turned to Harrison and said,Tell him. George said, It's because we were taking drugs. The actress who claimed Maharishi propositioned her was not Mia Farrow. It was another actress from Los Angeles who had been hired to make the false claims. This is well known by now. The allegation is that a Beatle associate named Magic Alex thought he was losing his influence on the Beatles and did this to get his previous influence back. He had a financial motive as well; his plan to sell John a Greek island was being sidetracked by the Beatles fascination with Maharishi.

Maharishi's House

Above, is the house that Devendra built for Maharishi in 1966 or so. This is what it looked like in 2013. When I was there it was quite a nice place, only a few years old, but the forest reclaims everything into itself.

Sivaratri ceremony in the lecture hall at the Rishikesh Academy

On this special Sivaratri night, I received an advanced technique from Maharishi and watched the sky on the horizon light up with forked lightning. I had never seen the whole atmosphere like a spider web of brilliant flashes of light before. As we watched from our perch about a hundred yards above the Ganges, standing just outside of the hall, I saw a bolt of lightning as wide as the power plant it hit come down from the dark clouds as if consuming the huge building. The intention of Maharishi and the pundits to communicate with Lord Shiva, to offer him praise and petition his blessings was definitely having a dramatic response from Nature.

"RICK! YOU'RE JUST UNSTRESSING"

A few days later I was sitting in Maharishi's house waiting to complain about the advanced technique He had given me. By the time I was told to enter his little cave of a room 8'x10', it was dusk, and the only light was a small candle on a table in front of him. The walls and ceiling were all of bamboo, and it seemed like some tiny forest-dwelling that a hermit might live in. Maharishi was lying on his side on his single bed with his head held up by his rather massive forearm and muscular hand. He looked as if he would like to take a nap but I was all

257

about myself, and he said "Jai Guru Dev," and we said the same and handed him our flowers. He said "you are doing well?" and I said "actually, Maharishi I am having trouble with the technique," in a Whiny sort of way, and just as I finished my sentence Maharishi said "Rick! you are just unstressing."

The moment He said "Rick" I found myself separate from the little complaining mindset I had been in. I was looking at my little self from Maharishi's mind which had awakened my own higher-Self mind. It was as if what I had said had come out of someone else's mouth and I could still hear it from my own higher Self. At the time I knew I was hearing what Maharishi was hearing and we laughed out loud at my own little whiny self. I said, "thank you Maharishi, Jai Guru Dev." He said the same and "then, go and rest."

NEAR DEATH

Most westerners who go to India and don't stay at the hotels that only foreigners could afford (I'm talking 1969) get sick with amoebic dysentery. I have always envied those few who can even eat from the street stalls or the restaurants, wherever they happen to travel. Every time I have gone and been careful not to get sick, I get deathly ill. It happened the first time in Rishikesh at the academy where they were avoiding unpurified water and not even stirring the food with their hands, which was the traditional way you stir a big pot of whatever. Still, I was confined to my puri, and during an evening lecture by Maharishi I was beyond feeling uncomfortable and weak, having lost twenty pounds or so in a matter of days; I was actually rising out of my body, and it felt good to be free of it.

Suddenly, Maharishi somehow became aware of my situation, and he asked my wife where I was. She said, "back at the puri, he's sick Maharishi." He immediately looked over to where the English Doctor was sitting and said: "Go, go, quickly." I don't know if my wife showed her where our puri was but I can only remember the doctor coming in and by this time I was hovering above my body and I felt something still attaching me to it. Then, Bam! I popped back into my shell and felt the nasty pain in my intestines and my general sickness. I immediately fell in love with this lady doctor who had saved my life. She had given me a shot of something that snapped me back from my pleasant death. Whenever I saw that lady again, I would smile and feel a sweet love for her.

While I was recovering from my latest bout of dysentery Maharishi helped by inviting me to sit with him on his sunny rooftop every day as he worked with Carol Hanby, a Canadian Initiator who was acting as his secretary. The cook would bring us all fresh squeezed orange juice, and I would bask in Maharishi's radiance. It didn't take long, a week maybe, and I was back to rounding and going to lectures. After we had been rounding (meditation-asanas-pranayama = 1 round) intensely all day for a couple of months, we began coming down in the number of rounds we would do in a day. During the height of rounding, we would have one lecture a day in the evening where we would discuss our experiences. As we came down in rounds, we would have an afternoon lecture and an evening lecture and then a morning lecture as well. Much of our time after the rounding was spent in teacher training, lecturing, checking meditation and learning the process of initiation.

TAT WALI BABA

ANANDAMAYI MA

To make life more fun during the learning process, Maharishi would invite special guests for our enjoyment. Tat Wali Baba was the most beautiful looking Saint in Rishikesh. He looked like an American Indian warrior. He almost rivaled Anandamayi ma (above) in physical beauty. The picture (directly below) shows him being escorted to the lecture hall where we were to witness the most entertaining event of our course and which has become legendary in the TM movement.

Tat Wali Baba being escorted to lecture hall

It happened that we had an elderly aristocratic English Lady who was attending the course and sitting up front in the audience just down from Tat Wali Baba. Maharishi had been acting as interpreter for the great Saint and doing a lot of laughing at the same time. Having two enlightened men playing with a room full of totally ignorant seekers seemed to be quite entertaining to both sides of the Self/ self-interaction. The questions we would ask would inspire a very playful response from Tat Wali Baba, and Maharishi could barely contain himself with mischievous delight. The reason was understandable, Maharishi would do his best to make everything spiritually-palatable to our lowest common denominator, those of us overly brainwashed with a pragmatic, western, scientific, materialistic worldview. Tat Wali Baba would do no such thing; a perfect example of this was his response to the British Lady's question, "Mr. Wali Baba (imagine a thick upper-crust, pompous British accent) have you ever been to London?" Tat Wali B. immediately responded in perfect English "Madam, I am London!" This actually caused Maharishi to fall over on his dais with high pitched laughter.

REMNANT OF THE BRITISH RAJ

Maharishi had always coddled people like this remnant of the British Raj by explaining everything that she couldn't handle with kid gloves, but Tat Wali's flat out expression of his living and expounding Unity Consciousness by telling it like it is was just what Maharishi had probably been patiently holding himself back from doing. The Lady went red in the face and blustered out with "what do you mean you are London? Of course, you are not London sir, you have probably never even been there." Meanwhile, Maharishi had to control his joyful laughter and catch his breath. The woman was by now irate with Maharishi as the Hall was resonating with the hilarity of our laughter and she supposed it was all at her expense, of course, it was! Finally, Maharishi explained to her that what Tat Wali Baba meant was that in his unbounded awareness he encompassed everything, not just his human body, but every-thing in creation, he is the Self of everything that is. She didn't seem to be mollified by Maharishi's explanations since by now she had become emotionally attached to her own dig-nity, the grand majesty of the British Empire had been made a laughing stock.

At the end of our enjoyable meeting with Tat Wali Baba, everyone had gone to lunch, and the Saint had moved off the stage and was sitting in a chair waiting for his Disciple to come back from lunch and take him on the long walk back up the hill- trail to his cave. I had remained in the hall just because he did and I noticed that he was looking in my direction, but his eyes didn't seem to focus on mine, only my location. He smiled and nodded, and I could see that he really couldn't see my face. Later, I found out that he was entirely blind from the constant smoke in his cave, but at the time I just said "Jai Guru Dev," and I walked by him and off to lunch.

THE TWO GERMANS

Two German course participants erroneously thought that because Maharishi had described Tat Wali Baba as being in the highest state of consciousness attainable, "Supreme Knowledge or Unity" that He, Maharishi, must somehow be in a lesser state. Most of us believed that Maharishi never talked about or described a higher state of consciousness unless He had actually attained that state. When you go over the early lectures and see that as the years went by M. went from describing Cosmic Consciousness as the ultimate to God Consciousness some years later, then Unity Consciousness, and finally Brahman Consciousness. Jerry Jarvis once confided that at the end of Maharishi's annual silence in the late 60's he came out of his room with white in his beard and started talking about Unity C. for the first time. Of course, Tat Wali Baba had the look of some great and ancient Ascetic, with his hair that touched the ground and his loincloth held together with a thick ringed golden chain. People tend to judge by appearances. Both of these great men were living the fulfillment of life's ultimate goal in Unity Consciousness, but Maharishi had the extra adornment of being a World Teacher, a Maharishi.

The German lads decided that they would pay a visit to Tat Wali Baba and promise their undying devotion as disciples at his lotus feet. They left Maharishi's academy and walked up the steep hill through the thick forest until they arrived at Tat Wali's cave. The great Master was sitting, and the two crawled into the cave and bowed low to his feet. "What do you want," Tat Wali said in broken English. "We want to be your disciples master." When Tat Wali heard this, he said: "but you are Maharishi's disciples!" And he pointed at them like Indra flashing a lightning bolt and something entered them that made them take flight, and they jumped up and ran down the hill as fast as they could, screaming in agony the whole way until they fell on their faces in front of Maharishi. They cried "Maharishi, please help us, we are in horrible pain." Maharishi must have done something, for their cries of agony turned into sobs and tears, and I don't know what happened to them after that, maybe someone knows the rest of the story?

MOTHER OLSON

There are some fascinating stories associated with Helena

"Mother Olson," the great lady who along with her husband Roland, invited Maharishi to stay at their home whenever he came to LA which he did more than ten times over ten years of circling the globe. She shared a few of her memories with me, and I don't see any good reason to keep them secret. One of these mini-TM legends took place in Rishikesh at the academy. Helena was taking a brief afternoon walk by Maharishi's house when she heard a hissing sound and looked up through the open doors and saw, to her amazement, Maharishi, Tat Wali Baba and Guru Dev sitting around a giant King Cobra. They seemed to be communicating with the Serpent, and it would make a hissing, whispering sound in return. Becoming aware of her presence, Maharishi motioned for her to leave.

She said that later when she asked Maharishi what it was all about and who was that giant snake? Maharishi replied that the snake was the Deva king of the snakes and that they were requesting him to keep the poisonous snakes away from the academy with all the westerners about. The great Naga complied, and there were no participants bitten by snakes on her course or on ours. This was interesting to me since I saw a two-step viper just behind Maharishi's house and the moment he became aware of me he darted down a hole in the ground. I thought that if I had walked there in the dark or had stepped on him, I would have been dead; but perhaps he was obeying the great King Cobra and would never have bitten me, whatever I had done? Meanwhile, one of the Brahmacharies told me that many a monk was bitten and died in the local caves every year and that he and one of his brother Brahmacharies had just found a man killed by snake bite in a cave not half a mile away.

LESLEY JAMES

The conversation with the King Cobra had probably kept some of us safe from the snakes but not from the scorpions. Near the end of our time at the Academy, a friend of mine, Leslie James, was on his way back from the evening lecture and he passed by my wife and I. He took a left toward Maharishi's house in the pitch dark. I think I must have felt some apprehension as he didn't have sandals on and couldn't see anything on the ground if it was there, and we had been warned by the Brahmacharies to watch out for scorpions, especially in the dark. Leslie was skipping along the path in front of M.'s house and singing some song, he seemed so joyful even though his new wife in LA had filed for divorce. Suddenly, he was cursing, and crying out:

"Oww..oh.Owww..Oh.God..shit..Jesus...help...help....scorpion, scorpion, I'm bit, Owwwww.

He came hopping on one foot all the way over to us, in great pain and we got on either side of him and helped him back to his puri. I managed to find one of the course participants who was a doctor; he was an inexperienced German about 26, but he knew which shot to give poor Leslie, just not how much. We sat with Lesley for several hours and his leg got worse and worse, his leg was throbbing and changing color and spreading up to his thigh. I asked one of the Brahmacharies if there was an Indian doctor nearby who could help and he said: "Yes, yes, he is called the snake healer, just across the river; I will go and get him." It took about two hours for the "Snake Healer Doctor" to arrive but when he did he asked the German Doc. how much of the pain medication he had injected and when the German told him the Indian Doc. laughed and immediately filled up a large horse syringe full of the stuff and stabbed it into Lesley's leg.

He stuck the needle in vertically and then began moving it around in a 360-degree circle pushing the handle down as he went. He did this several times in different places on the leg, while the German doctor looked on in horror. At first, the German Doc. argued with the Snake Healer, saying that this was too dangerous an amount but the Indian Doc. said: "you may know medicine in Germany, but you are ignorant of what

265

is necessary with Indian Scorpion bites." Immediately, after the very painful injections given by the Snake Healer, during which Leslie screamed bloody murder, our poor Irishman, Leslie James, began to smile and say that the pain had gone. Sara stayed with him until the sun came up, nursing his Scorpion bite and his broken heart, both of which had come on the same day.

DOWN TO THE GANGES

The forest was thick all around three sides of the Academy, although the south side was thickly forested it was really a cliff that dropped precipitously. "Located in the holy "Valley of the Saints," the International Academy of Meditation, also called the Chaurasi Kutia ashram, was a 14-acre compound. It stood across the River Ganges from Rishikesh, the "yoga capital of the world" and home to many ashrams in the foothills of the Himalayas, 150 feet (46 m) above the river. Maharishi's facility was built in 1963 with a $100,000 gift from American heiress Doris Duke, on land leased from the Uttar Pradesh Forest Department." (Wikipedia) One afternoon a friend asked if I would like to go down a secret path that led from the scary "jungle" on the eastern side of the academy down a steep incline all the way to the Ganges. I was hesitant as I looked from the edge of the compound into the dark jungle, or forest, as it's called in India. The dense trees and undergrowth began only ten feet from where I was standing, and I could hear some of the creatures that populated this place.

I was most worried about the tribes of those fierce brown monkeys who had no fear of attacking white people, and of course, Tigers were an ever-present danger. All it took for me to lose my apprehension was the vision of Turid, the German girl in her tiny bikini passing by me, heading fearlessly down the path. I walked and slid down the dirt path in my buffalo sandals which have a tendency to slip off your feet going uphill but going down they rip into the space between your big toe and pinch the skin. There were two other guys, and they made it down and onto the stone covered beach on the shores of the Ganges before me. Across the river, you could see ascetics and holy men washing their dhotis in the sun on rocks that had been used for this purpose for many thousands of years.

TURID AND THE HOLY MEN

Turid was a beautiful blond German girl, all tanned and made up like a Playboy Penthouse Model. She stood enjoying the sun and being admired by all, posing this way and that and tripping along the rocky shore toward the water. The ascetics on the opposite shore were horrified! In all the years of their celibacy, they had never encountered a more challenging visual memory that they would have to try and burn from their inner vision than Turid. I saw at least two of them run from their washing for the safety of anywhere but the Ganges. Turid waded into the river and swam across to the other side through the powerful current which took her about thirty yards down river before she made it to shore.

I waded out into the river up to my waist where it was too powerful to walk and dove forward into the fast-moving stream. The current was so strong I fought to get as far as Turid did but lost my pace when what felt like a human body slammed into me and I spun around trying to get away from it. Once I started making headway again I felt a couple of large fish hit my legs; they were big fish, maybe ten to fifteen-pounders. With all that, I managed to get out of the current far enough to wade up the shore. I was a good fifty yards further down from where I started on the other side, and I noticed that all the Holy men, monks and ascetics that had been on this side of the river were gone. Turid was a little saddened by this, and when an angry Indian man came up to her and waved his finger at her, saying that she should go in English, I think she realized how inappropriate her bikini was in the midst of a group of men who were desperately trying to kill all thoughts of sex and desire. What was kind of cute was her seeming innocence; she thought all the holy men would be like children, she would be like the naked Saints she had read about. After all, she had just seen an almost totally naked Tat Wali Baba visiting with little more about his loins than her bikini bottom.

Maharishi & Turid

Most of us didn't realize that there were so many dangerous creatures all around the Academy. Tigers, Leopards, King Cobras, Two-step Vipers, Scorpions, Vicious Brown Monkeys and worst of all, Amoebic Dysentery. One night we were all awake to the sound of a huge Tiger going from door to door looking for a juicy human morsel. He made that unmistakably resonant Tiger groan that you may have heard at the zoo, and the Brahmacharies were running about making sure all of our doors were locked tight. These guys were fearless and tireless and were all raised with the timeless Indian law of hospitality; the guest is God. Maharishi exacted this universal precept to the letter, among all his Indian disciples, and we were taken care of night and day. Another night, we heard what sounded like a big cat in a desperate struggle with another animal.

We were afraid it was a human that it was tearing apart, but the next day we were told that it had been a Leopard being attacked by a couple of the Academy dogs who were killed driving the big cat off the Academy grounds.

WE VISIT A FRIEND OF MAHARISHI'S

Near the end of our time in Rishikesh, there were several excursions and pilgrimages. Some of them were not with Maharishi, and I didn't want to spend any time that I could be with Maharishi, away from him. It seemed ridiculous not to take full advantage of this rare time with a fully realized Master, especially when he was our own. Now, there are so many who would give anything to have been with him in those days. Anyway, I went with him to Haridwar, most of us did. He wanted to expose us to as many realized saints as possible, and so he took us all to see a great saint who had a large Ashram and many disciples. They welcomed us and sat us down in a cozy alcove where several pundits serenaded us with the Sama Veda while the saint's brahmacharis served us hot Chai in little clay cups that they had made for our visit. When you finished your tea, you could just crumble the cup in your hand and throw it on the ground as it was clay after all.

The saint sat in a humble looking seat with the paintings and photos of the Masters of his lineage on the wall behind him. Maharishi sat next to him, and they held hands as Maharishi often did with fellow God-realized saints. We were given a talk by this Master, and Maharishi would translate from the Hindi to English. This guy seemed to be kind of tickled by the fact that Maharishi had so many westerners as his disciples and would often make subtle jokes that would crack Maharishi up as he was translating. When M. laughed and tilted over in his seat, it would become infectious, and everyone including the saint's followers couldn't help but join us in a room full of laughter and happiness. Maharishi had told us that when the saint had finished his talk, we were to come up single file and offer him a dollar or a rupee, not sure which? A rupee would be almost nothing! There were eight of them in a dollar at the time. When it was my turn to kneel before the saint I first knelt in front of Maharishi and touched his knee with my folded hands, then I rose and knelt before the saint and put my dollar in the pot at his feet.

When I bowed to Maharishi first, something that no one else had done, Maharishi smiled and looked at the saint who looked back at him and made an approving sound as he nodded his head and smiled at me. I felt that it was only proper to first acknowledge your own master before acknowledging another and didn't care what anyone else thought about it.

That turned out to be an excellent intuitive decision; to me, it was as if I was getting my master's permission to bow to another master even though it was quite obvious that Maharishi wanted us to make an offering to the saint for his hospitality, it felt great!

THE BULL ELEPHANT

When it gets hot in India most of the people, who can, travel to the "hill stations" to ride out the Monsoon and the intense heat. We packed up our few belongings and headed out on the forest road behind the Academy. This road was built long ago for the local Maharajah as a hunting access big enough for his elephants and entourage. This was long before the English invaded but it's still there and is often used by wild elephants living in the forest. We were all in a line of cars and a few buses. Maharishi was in the car in front of us, and the road was really rough and bumpy. We were trying to sing some bhajans with one of the Brahmacharies leading us as we tipped and bounced all over each other; there was a lot of laughing and car sickness as we trundled down the long dirt road.

About a mile down, we saw Maharishi's car pulled over, and he was waving us past with his arm out his window as he peered

into the forest across the road. I looked where he was looking and saw the trees thrashing left and right until, suddenly,
I saw a colossal Bull Elephant smash through an opening in
the trees. Maharishi began waving more aggressively as the
wild and angry Titan charged into the road. We raced passed
Maharishi's car, the last vehicle in the procession, but the
beast chased after Maharishi's car which was now just behind
us. Later we were told that we had been very fortunate to
get passed that Bull Elephant when we did as it was in rut and
would have smashed our car and us if it had caught us.

We came out of the forest road and crossed the Ganges on
the old steel bridge which had been built by the English in
the 19th century. I remember getting on a train that took us
to the foothills of the Himalayas where, at a small airport in
Jammu, Maharishi sat up on the counter-top on his skin. It was
kinda cool to see him perched up there just as natural as a bird
in a tree, while the airport employees gave him space and did
their work, respectfully, around him. It seemed as if a Guru
perched on a counter-top, was something like a visiting digni-
tary or Movie Star; that's how they treated him. We waited for
the weather to change for several hours and were finally told
that the plane was ready but that the crosswinds were going to
be rough, especially as we passed through a particular gap in
the highest peaks of the Himalayas that led down to Srinagar
airport.

CRAZY FLIGHT TO KASHMIR

It was a small two engine airplane, and there were only about five or six of us on board with Maharishi, the rest of the course had gone on a larger plane. They hadn't exaggerated about the winds, and if Maharishi hadn't been there, I would have got my self-ready for a crash landing on the side of a 20,000-foot mountain. I was so concerned that I stood behind the pilot and stared out at the mountain peaks towering above us and we were like a little boat on a rough sea being blown left then right then down and up again. I could tell that the pilot was worried that we wouldn't make it through the mountain pass, that we might be blown to one side or the other or swept into a dive. He was actually considering turning around, but the co-pilot told him there wasn't enough gas to get back to an airstrip and so he stepped on the gas to get as much altitude as possible.

Obviously, we made it through the mountains even with the harrowing crosswinds, blowing us about. Srinagar in 1969, with its endless, wall to wall, two-story, wooden store-fronts, was a change from Delhi's one story, ramshackle, open fronted, lean twos. We walked down the paved main-street to the cabs, and there were parks with tall trees sparsely spaced, and the ground looked kind of scrubby with clumps of grass every few feet. Then we drove several miles to the shores of Lake Dal which is populated with a mix of Indo/Aryans called Kashmiris who have light skin and many look like northern Europeans only with dark hair. I was told that the Aryans came through Kashmir on their way north.

The Hanjis are the boat people of Kashmir, and they say that they are descended from Noah; how can you argue with that? The shikara men are not high on the social status scale as they only have their little canoe-like boats and are the taxi drivers of the lakes. I remember them waiting for us late into the night as we listened to the evening talks by Maharishi. They sat in their little shikara or squatted on the land in front of it with a bowl of embers hidden in their lap. They wore large body covering blankets like the Mexican Serape with the ember bowl inside and it would keep them nice and warm all night long if it were required of them.

SHIKARA "TAXI" ON LAKE DAL KASHMIR

HANJI INSULTS MY WIFE

The big House Boat owners and town merchants are pretty high on the status level and are extremely touchy about their boats and rugs, respectively. I sat back in a chair in the house-boat I was staying in, and one of the chair legs broke under my prodigious 145lbs. The average Hanji weighs-in at around 125lbs. I sneakily stuck the leg back on and exchanged the chair for another which was against the wall. Weeks later as we were about to leave, the owner came up and said: "you must pay extra, you have broken my chair." The thing was, I didn't have any more money at all, but of course, they don't believe you, after all, I was a stereotypical wealthy American oozing with cash.

Kashmiri Houseboats

When he finally believed that I had no money he started pointing his finger in my face and almost roaring like a little lion; he actually said: "how can you be poor with a whore like that." Now, he was pointing at my wife with her shiny, silver, silk sari looking like a Maharajah's favorite wife. This was way too much, and I started after him, and he ran around the big table, trying to get away. Fortunately, a friend was there and said "Rick, don't you have something you could give him to pay for the chair." The Boatman said, "yes, yes, you have some nice shirts, I will trade for shirt." I was sure he meant my nice cotton shirts, but he turned up his nose when I offered him one of those. He said, "no, no the shiny one, the shiny one." He wanted a shirt that I detested as it always clung to my back and arms with static electricity and this deflated my anger into smiles from both of us, as he grabbed it as if it were pure gold. It seems they didn't have plastic shirts in Kashmir yet, and to him, he got the better deal by far.

THE FUMES

Maharishi loves to go boating, especially when it's full moon. One afternoon Maharishi organized a daytime, full moon event comprised of over a hundred course members and just about all the shikaras on Lake Dal. We were all roped to a motorboat that dragged us around the lake like a mother duck and her ducklings following behind. I was in the shikara just behind the motorboat, and M. was in a shikara about four down from us. Sometimes when the carbon monoxide spewing tugboat would make a small circle, our Shikara would come somewhat close to the back of her and I could smell the fumes in the air. Just as we were about to do another circle, Maharishi waved, and one of the guys in his boat yelled out to me "Maharishi wants you to get in another Shikara away from the motorboat fumes. This was transmitted via waving and shouting until the lead boat pulled us all to shore.

I got out and walked to Maharishi's shikara, and he said: "get in one of the boats behind me, out of the way of the exhaust." Then we resumed our boat ride for an hour or so more. I had always wondered why Maharishi singled me out from among the three other course attendees in my boat. Years later, after I left Switzerland and Maharishi, I found myself working in a silkscreen factory, standing over a vat of lacquer thinner cleaning silkscreens all day with the overpowering fumes killing innumerable brain cells. After that, I painted houses in Fairfield for many years, breathing in oil-based trim paint fumes all day long, sometimes in closets where I would find myself on the ground having fainted from the toxic fumes. Upon reflection, it is quite understandable why Maharishi wanted to make his point with me on the boat ride; I was the one who was going to end up breathing in poison for a living.

THE KRISHNA TREE

A few of us accompanied Maharishi on an outing not far from Srinagar. It was kind of mysterious, and I'm not too sure what the significance of the Holy Place was other than it was famous for a five-thousand-year-old Tree that was growing in the middle of a tiny pool of water surrounded by a round brick fence about a foot tall. There were some colorful silk clothes on the tree, blue and gold and a golden crown on top. There were pundits and Sanyasis, all around the place and they appeared to be in a mood of deep reverence as some of them chanted from open book scriptures and others stared at us as if our presence was defiling the place. As soon as Maharishi appeared, the atmosphere improved from a hostile vibe toward a group of foul western tourists to pride in their own tradition that would attract westerners to follow one of their own saints and recognize their holy places. It turned out that this was a tree that Krishna himself used to sit under in meditation, much like the Buddhist tradition of the Bodhi tree two thousand years later.

SWAMI LAKSMANJOO

Another Great saint who was loved by Maharishi was Swami Laksmanjoo who had an ashram at the end of Dal Lake on the side of a precipitous Himalayan foothill. Maharishi told us that Laksmanjoo was in the state of "God Consciousness," having realized God in the form of Lord Shiva and cognizing the knowledge of the Shiva Sutras, 112 ways of transcending thought and experiencing the source of thought, pure consciousness, one's own intimate Being, Atman. He was a very sweet man, and when Maharishi and the Swami were together there was constant laughter and smiles, and they would sit and hold hands with the innocence of children.

MAHARISH & LAKSMANJOO

LAKSMANJOO'S BIRTHDAY SONG

It was almost time for Laksmanjoo's birthday and Maharishi wanted someone to write and sing a birthday song for him when we attended his party. There were two professional singer/songwriters among us, myself and Kenny Edwards of the "Stone Pony's." Ned Wynn was mentioned as a songwriter and he could sing and play guitar a little. He had written the lyrics to a song or two, one of them was recorded on a "Mommas & Pappas" album called "Nothing's Too Good for My Little Girl" (Ned Wynn). I asked him if he wanted to audition with Kenny and I, and his response was "maybe."

So, in the end, Kenny backed out, I think because he was very shy around Maharishi and figured that since I had already written songs to Maharishi on my Columbia album "The Gentle Soul" and had a close relationship with him, that I would be more at home with the job. To tell you the truth, Kenny was still un-stressing from all the long meditations and was a bit too sensitive to be put on the spot creatively. Actually, I think there were one or two others who were not really professional but auditioned all the same. The audition went something like this:

The musician walked into Maharishi's room and sat down just opposite him. He then asked a few questions and said "we are writing a birthday song for Laksmanjoo, I will say a few words and you see if you can sing them with an original melody while playing your guitar. The few musicians before me came out with rather sullen faces and this seemed like an unusual thing, usually anyone who has just come from being with Maharishi is in a state of blissful enthusiasm; "Yikes" I thought "I wonder if he auditioned the Beatles or Donovan on the last course, and if they failed; Maybe that's one of the reasons they left?" No! they were too bogged down with overbearing wives, managers, publicists and contracts to create any music that wasn't agreeable with their owner's sense of what would sell. Still, I think they could have come closer to singing the song of life than "Jai Guru Deva, Om." Om is never used with the expression Jai Guru Dev; they could at least have got that right!

When my turn came, I walked in and Maharishi said "Rick, sit, sit." He gave me the above instructions and I started to pick a little to warm up, finding the chords I would be able to sing to best. Then he just began with a phrase that didn't rhyme and wasn't about Laksmanjoo, like "when we do our TM we are free from stress and doubt." This was easy to sing and to put a melody to, so I sang it with a spontaneous melody that lent itself to the rhythmical phrasing of the words and put in a minor chord or two just to make it less sing-songy and more serious. Maharishi said "very good, very good I think you will do very well." He didn't wait to declare a winner but started right in with the birthday song. I wish I could remember it! it was probably recorded but I have no idea who might have it! We finished it in about a half hour and Maharishi asked if I would learn it so that I could sing it at the birthday party at Laksmanjoo's Ashram. As I vaguely remember, Ned Wynn stepped up and sang a harmony with me on the song for Laksmanjoo; I think we practiced for a few minutes just before we sang. You have to realize all this happened almost half a century ago!

MAHARISHI LOOKS THIS WAY AND THAT WAY FOR RICK WHO
IS SINGING LAKSMANJOO'S BIRTHDAY SONG.

Pretty girl below, who, with her husband, became
an initiator and a devotee of both Maharishi and
Laksmanjoo. The guy with the beard? I think he's a
Canadian, I thought he was very cool.

As we sang the birthday song, all of Laksmanjoo's disciples and
our hundred and fifty course members joined in on the chorus
something like:

"Happy Birthday to you, our dear Laksmanjoo,
happy CC,
happy GC,
happy Unity to you."

Maharishi had mentioned that the Swami was in God consciousness and didn't recognize any need to move on to Unity or Brahman Consciousness, the ultimate state of consciousness attainable by man. So, Maharishi purposely included Unity consciousness in the lyrics to remind Laksmanjoo that he could attain an even higher state of awareness if he desired to, but it's hard to wish for anything more when you already have achieved God-realization. The Swami's disciples were a friendly lot, and they welcomed us all with hospitality, bringing sweets and tea around to each of us, smiling and curious about all these westerners studying Vedic knowledge and doing long sadhanas with meditation, yoga, and pranayama.

I SING A SAD LOVE SONG FOR MONKS!

Before we left Laksmanjoo's ashram, Maharishi went for a walk with the saint and had me come along with my guitar. I walked behind them as they sauntered hand in hand and finally sat down beside a small brook. Maharishi said, "Rick, sing a song." When he gave me the choice of what to sing, I couldn't help but choose whatever new song I had recently written, and this was one of those times. Instead of understanding that I was singing for Holy Monks, I sang a love song of personal joy and sadness. Oh ya, it was beautiful with sweet sacrifice and gorgeous melody, but it was the essence of attachment and Kali Yuga Maya all wrapped up in a golden-throated warble. Of course, Maharishi put up his hand and stopped me. He had hoped I had learned to sing devotional songs for Realized saints or the puja, but I had to take this test a few more times before I learned my lesson.

When Maharishi left Laksmanjoo's ashram and drove down the lake to the Governor's Mansion, I was in one of the last cars to leave, and I saw him walking in the middle of the road looking for something or someone. I stopped the car and rolled down my window, and Laksmanjoo walked up and said very quietly "has Maharishi gone?" I couldn't hear him and asked: "sorry, what did you say?" He repeated himself and smiled so sweetly; I said: "yes he has gone to the Governor's Mansion where he will be staying for awhile." He just smiled and looked in the direction that Maharishi had gone, lowered his eyes and waved goodbye. That was the last time I ever saw him. He loved his friend Maharishi.

WALKING THE MASTER

After we parted from Laksmanjoo, Maharishi wanted to visit the site of Laksmanjoo's God Realization and Cognition of the Shiva Sutras. Several of us drove to the site with Maharishi and walked into a canyon of sloping, rolling, green hillside with huge, half-buried boulders that had fallen from the towering mountain cliffs above us. You could see that some of the rocks had recently fallen and it made you wonder if one just might come down at any moment. But as usual in potentially hazardous situations, when we were with Maharishi we figured he would sense any danger before it could come. He wanted to walk up the steep side of the mountain a bit, and as he began I felt compelled to take his hand and help him since his sandals were not made for slippery slopes, and his Dhoti was getting caught underfoot.

We walked on until he found a flat rock to sit down on above us. I crouched down in front of him and angled my camera so that I could take a shot from underneath, looking up. He didn't approve of my odd angled attempt and put his hand, palm out in front of my camera to make it clear that I shouldn't take such an undignified portrait. I realized I was getting a little too familiar, taking advantage of his blessing me by letting me hold his hand and help him up the rugged hillside, which made me feel like a warrior protector of my Great King. It really did feel like that even though I knew he could have floated up the hill at any time.

SWAMI LAKSMANJOO-MAHARISHI-RICK

A TRUE DEVOTEE

After we came back down the hill Maharishi sat again in a shaded grove of trees, open on one side. We were standing in a semi circle around him when some of us noticed a little man crawling on the ground. We moved out of the way so that he could pass. He started his obeisance about forty feet from Maharishi and crawled on his stomach all the way, chanting as he came, until he could reach up and touch Maharishi's feet. Maharishi smiled and almost purred with love as he put his hand on the little man's head. It was extremely sweet to see how humble and reverential the Indian disciple could be and I'm sure that some of us felt humiliated to be standing there in the presence of God in man after seeing a true devotee.

When it finally came time to graduate and become Initi-ators we all waited our turn outside of Maharishi's building that was on a small earthen peninsula in the middle of Dal Lake. Since we all lived in the houseboats we had to travel by Shikara to Maharishi. There was a large tent in front of the building where we would sit for lectures and meetings as the course wound down to its completion. Some of the course participants were not made initiators and others were made teachers of certain age groups but most of us made it through successfully and when it came to my turn to go into Maharishi's dark room, I was only slightly apprehensive.

I BECOME AN INITIATOR

I knocked on the door and heard "come." I went in and couldn't see anything as it was sunny outside and pitch dark inside. Soon, I could see Maharishi and chairs and puja table by the candlelight. Maharishi asked me to do puja and upon its completion he gave me instruction. We had already learned and become proficient at checking meditation experience, and in the Initiation procedure; this was the final instruction. After instruction, he sat down and told me to sit. It reminded me of that time in the Ranjit Hotel when Maharishi sat in the dark looking me over for possible problems he might be able to resolve before the long meditations started, waking my sleeping elephants (dormant stresses).

This time however, he sat with his eyes closed for a long time, maybe ten minutes. At the end of that time he opened his eyes and said "You will be Realized, very good." I rose and went down on my knees and bowed and touched his knee with my folded hands and said "Jai Guru Dev" and he said "Jai Guru Dev." Then I turned and opened the door and went out into the sunlight. Someone said "how come you took so long? it's supposed to take only ten minutes at most." I laughed out loud and skipped down the old concrete steps. I once saw a photo taken just after this momentous day in my life, and I had on a cowboy shirt and looked like a sixteen your old with a smile and eyes as pure as a joyful toddler in the midst of a laughing fit.

THE SONG OF LIFE

It was the end of our Teacher Training and most of us were headed home to fill the growing demand from thousands of college and high school kids for TM, the technique that the Beatles, the Beach Boys and Donovan had made "Cool" by going to India to be with Maharishi. We had planned to go to Germany where my mother was still living and teach the GI's but Maharishi wanted me to stay and work with him creating an album of songs that we would write together. It would be an introductory lecture in song and just before each song he would write prose that I would speak on the Album and during my intro. lecture Concerts. The prose would introduce the knowledge contained in the song. He wanted us to stay in a particular houseboat that he had picked out and he had a Brahmachari take us to see it. The plan was that he would live in the Governor's house that was rented for the purpose and I would come every morning and meet him in the garden where he would give me the seed phrase of a song and I would spend the rest of the day writing music and as many verses as I could. Then I would meet him in the late afternoon, and we would go over what I had written and begin the prose clarification of the song.

BIG MISTAKE!

This was all very wonderful, another month or two with Maharishi One on one. There was just one problem; on my way back from checking out the houseboat that Maharishi had rented for us, Jerry Jarvis ran into us as we came ashore and said he had been looking for us. He wanted Sara and I to go and stay at the new "TM Academy" building site on the side of the mountain at the end of Lake Dal where there were four or five partially finished houses and a kitchen in the middle of construction. He said he wanted us to keep an eye on a couple who were going to stay there; the wife had already had an affair with a god-like Indian Adonis, a Hatha Yogi who had visited the course in Rishikesh when the local saints had come. Jerry was very intent on us policing the place even though I told him that Maharishi had already told us where we should stay. But I was used to following Jerry's authoritative suggestions and when he said that it really didn't matter where we stayed, and that it would be helpful, I agreed, and that was a big mistake.

We managed to slock our way through the ankle deep mud a couple of hundred yards up the side of the mountain to the "New Academy." Huge fallen rocks were all around the barren houses and the Brahmachari who was cooking for us said that a few of them had come down during the night close to his house. These houses were basically walls and a roof with bare drywall and a block of cold cement for a floor. There was a king sized mattress on the floor with no cover or sheets or any heat source. We covered ourselves with our coats and there might have been a thin plastic blanket.

It was cold and wet, it was hard to get down and harder to get back up the slippery dirt path and through the fifty foot barrier of mud. I felt really bad for Sara in her silver and white, silk sari, slocking through the mud and rain to catch our ride every morning. It was a quarter mile down the hill to the lake road and then a couple of miles to Maharishi. We would both be covered with wet mud when we arrived at the Governor's house and Sara would have to go to the bathroom and try to wash the bottom of her sari. I'd take off my shoes and my socks would be soaked and caked with mud, so I went barefoot. When it rained, or was cold, or both, I would meet with Maharishi in his room.

THE INHERITANCE AND THE PRISON RUG

The sunny days were really beautiful in the garden by the mansion with Maharishi, and the songs poured out with ease. Some days he would be involved with other projects and I would work on the songs with performance in mind. One of the course graduates had inherited a large portion of IBM stock, enough to make him rich beyond belief. He kept going to Srinagar to buy presents for Maharishi, star sapphires, rubies, diamonds and costly Persian rugs. Maharishi would never accept his gifts but the more he refused them the more Allen would try to find something that the master would accept. One day he arrived with a rug that was considered a treasure by the rug merchants and it certainly was unusual and beautiful. When he unrolled it, Maharishi threw up his hands and said take it away, take it away! Poor Allen was shocked and said "but Maharishi, that little rug cost twenty thousand dollars, it was a Maharajah's treasured possession.

Allen reluctantly rolled up his purchase, probably a little worried that the rug merchant wouldn't take it back and left the room. We found out later that Maharishi told Allen that the rug had a very bad past and had been made by prisoners. He said that no one should have it in their home, that it would bring only sorrow. That reminds me of another day at the Governor's Mansion when I wasn't working with Maharishi and he was talking in the living room about the future of the TM Movement. The subject of Jyotish came up and the thought that it would be good to consult a reliable Jyotishee. One of the persons involved in the discussion volunteered his opinion, that the "I ching" should be consulted, that he had good results throwing the coins and interpreting the Chinese symbols for fortelling the future and he took out his book and was about to hand it to Maharishi.

CHING CHONG CHINA

Maharishi burst out with "we don't need any ching, chong China magic." He was obviously upset that anyone would think we were without our own traditional Vedic knowledge for this purpose. The guy's suggestion reminded me of the kind of conversations and discussions that were common among people planning the religious and philosophical practices of a Hippy commune. I must admit that years later when I threw the I Ching, trying to win the Iowa lottery, I did get two numbers out of the six which was better than I ever had before.

The prose writing was coming along beautifully and Maharishi asked Allen if he would like to join us in the creative writing process. I wondered why Maharishi wanted him to sit in on our sessions, just because he had a boatload of money or what? It turned out that Allen was a poet, a good poet, and he had lived a normal life, public schools, college loans and dirt cheap dorm rooms when suddenly upon becoming an Initiator he was blessed with an unexpected, massive inheritance. What I'm saying is, that he wasn't your typical spoiled rich kid with an attitude. So, he sat humbly by and Maharishi said that he should listen and if he thought of some poetic word or phrase that might improve on what we were writing to speak it out.

To my surprise and delight, he even improved on a few of Maharishi's phrases as we wrote and composed, edited and improved upon the material. I have a tendency to create different melodies for the same chord structures and lyrics from one day to the next until I stick with one melody that seems to remain in my long term memory bank. Melody, seems to change with emotion; even when I have a relatively fixed melody for a song, depending on how I feel, that tune might change its feel entirely, slow down or speed up, become sad or melancholy or even beautiful if I'm at my best. My best is when I am witnessing, when I'm not doing it at all and it's clear someone else is doing everything, either the real Me or some Devi Muse.

SICK AGAIN

The songs and prose were complete but Maharishi wanted us to stay, remain with him in Kashmir and then go back to the Academy in Rishikesh in the fall. By this time I had been sleeping on the cold stone floor and getting wet so often that I came down with bronchitis. Sick as I was, we still went to the Governor's house every day for the heat and the incredible food. I would sit in one of the big plush chairs in an alcove by the living room and medi-sleep, the kind of meditation that usually accompanies sickness. When the master-chef and his assistants would stock the big dining room table with delicacies, I might amble over and partake of the buffet. One day Shiitake mushrooms were being avoided by all the Indians and the westerners took full advantage, they were so delicious, especially the way this chef seasoned them.

After two weeks with no improvement in my health, I felt I should leave India and hoped that West Germany and my mother's house might make a difference. Maharishi, seemed sad that we were going and wanted us to wait longer and live in the mansion with him and it seemed that I would surely improve. We stayed for another two weeks in the Mansion but I felt I was a drain on everyone there, with my coughing and flu-like symptoms I may be endangering others with contagion. So, we packed up and left for Srinagar and the airport; it really felt as if we were leaving our whole world and heading into empty space. We looked out the airplane window and watched that magical land of saints disappear as if it had never been there.

TEACHING TM IN WEST GERMANY

We landed in Frankfurt (hot dog!) and my mother picked us up and brought us to her apartment near Heidelberg in Schwetzingen. The first thing we did was to call Graf und Grafen Blucher (Count and Countess) leaders of the SRM organization of the TM movement in Germany. We wanted to let them know we were fresh from Teacher Training and ready to start teaching American soldiers in the area. They invited us to dinner and we discussed how to go about it. Sara and I were quite experienced in the advertising and postering end of setting up Introductory lectures, having done it for two years at the Westwood SIMS center in LA. We were also pretty good at giving the lectures which we had also done all over the Los Angeles area.

But now I was to give my part of the Intro. via song and poetry, everything I had created with Maharishi in Kashmir. Sara was an excellent lecturer with a sweet smile and a clear, intelligent mind and she would give the talk we had trained for in TTC. At the end of my musical intro. Sara would explain the technique and how and what it could do for health, world peace, fulfillment and enlightenment. Then we would both entertain questions and answers, usually the most entertaining part of the presentation. According to our natures, I would play the comedian and she would play the straight-man. Jerry Lewis and Dean Martin, sort of, if Dean were an attractive girl.

By the time I finished singing the names of the masters of the Holy Tradition almost everyone in the audience had become severely relaxed-and-open for Sara's talk, she would charm the GI's and the question and answer period would end with a large percentage of guys wanting to start TM. After our success in a concert hall in downtown Heidelberg we asked Count Blucher if he would like to give the 2nd Intro. or preparatory lecture for the hall full of GI's who had showed interest in starting TM. About 45 minutes into the count's speech, the soldiers began leaving, and after over an hour of deep philosophical brilliance much of the room had emptied out. This was the reaction to the old philosophical style of presenting TM and why the youth hadn't embraced it, all over the world. However, it was a wonderful speech, full of the truths of life, just not enough about the actual technique and the practical results expected from practicing it. Much too profound for our young soldiers to be expected to find interesting. However, despite the negative reaction we still signed up about forty GI's to start TM, our first initiates.

Just before we left India Jerry had a talk with us; he wanted us to go directly back to the US and start teaching. I told him we were to go to Germany first to visit my mother and teach the GI's. He was hesitant to agree but how could he refuse to let me visit my mother, probably the only chance I would get for years. So, compassionate Jerry gave us enough money to rent a place to use as home and as a TM center and said "teach there only as long as you are successful, in the states there are thousands of students wanting to start right now." He was totally right and we managed to start only forty GI's in the Heidelberg area over a two month time period. Then, the well went dry and our rent and food money ran out so we headed for the USA.

THE TINY HAUNTED HOUSE

A few interesting things that happened while we were in Germany. When we could no longer afford the rent for the first apartment, we found a place in downtown Mannheim. It was a tiny house built in the middle of a quadrangle of large apartment buildings that had been resurrected from the bombings of WWII. The little house belonged to a family who had survived the bombing and had rebuilt the house after it had been destroyed with their grandmother in it. Oma was still earthbound on the Astral plane in her little house, and when we would try to sleep in her old bed we would be so cold we'd have to make do with the couch and one of the large chairs. Why were we cold? Well, most of you know that dead people seem to take the warmth out of a room and perhaps, from the bodies of the living in the room; I have had the experience several times. Once, I was sitting in the big chair doing my morning meditation and I could feel her moving in front of me, she was moving about the room in a huff because I had moved the chair to face the East and she hated that; it was her house after all.

We had to go through the family apartment to get outside to the street and that morning I was passing through and the man of the house, Oma's grandson said "you shouldn't move the furniture about please." I said "yes, I have come to that conclusion as well, someone doesn't like it very much." He looked at me with a curious grin and said "yes, my grandmother died in the war in that house." It was obvious that he was well aware that Granny was still hanging around in that place. He must have had other tenants complain or just leave before their lease was up.

THE GHOST OF OMA

The next day one of the GI's I had initiated came to get checked to see if he was doing the technique correctly. I heard a knocking at the door and when I opened it and said "come in" the poor guy took one step up and fell back from what seemed like a powerful rushing wind that pushed him forcefully out of the doorway and he was sent sprawling onto the hard brick walkway. I had seen some color and what looked like a blurry movement swish in front of me. The GI couldn't figure out what happened; his only conclusion was the obvious one, I must have pushed him out the door onto his ass. But somehow he knew that I was standing back too far to have done it. He looked at me questioningly and I said, "sorry, this place is haunted and the old lady must be deathly afraid of the American Army uniform since she was bombed to death here years ago. Funnily enough, he accepted my explanation and we made an appointment for checking somewhere else. We couldn't sleep in the house and we couldn't initiate or check meditation there either, so we packed up and spent a few days at my mothers, then flew off to Boston. I do think that the old lady must have liked us, we probably warmed her up a bit and as long as I didn't move her furniture, I think she enjoyed the meditation; she was quite at ease when I was meditating.

HAAVAD SQUARE

When we first arrived in Boston, we took over running the Cambridge TM center, well, Sara did and I helped. The center was in a very old colonial house that was once the meeting

place of the New England "Transcendentalists." "Henry David Thoreau, Frederick Henry Hedge, Ralph Waldo Emerson, George Ripley, and George Putnam (1807–1878; the Unitarian minister in Roxbury) met in Cambridge, Massachusetts on September 8, 1836, to discuss the formation of a new club.";
(wikipedia)

We lived and worked there, and there was an interesting older, psychic lady who helped out and it was she who told us at lunch in the kitchen that some of our own TM teachers who had been the first to live and teach in this house had actually been members of the Transcendentalist Club of the early 1800's. She said that Jerry Jarvis and Joe Clark had been notable members but didn't tell us who they might have been. There was a ring of truth in her story and she was always so deadpan and spoke so quietly and without emotion, that when she said anything, you felt that she really didn't care if you believed her or not. She only told us because a few of the others convinced her to. Of course it doesn't matter a bit, we were all somebody else many hundreds of times but it's fun to imagine Jerry and Joe as Emerson or Thoreau.

The administration of a center and teaching TM is almost the same as any other instructional school or organization. Advertising, lectures, instruction in the technique, checking for proper understanding and advanced knowledge based on direct experience of the daily practice of the technique. The difference between school learning and Maharishi's teaching is that the knowledge is based on direct experience through the practice of TM and that makes all the difference.

JOE CLARK

While we were living and working in Cambridge Massachusetts we would be asked to help with potentially large, out of town, courses where they would need several Initiators to be able to instruct everyone on just one weekend. Joe Clark was one of the strongest (most effective) Initiators and organizers on the east coast and he asked if I would help him do a course at Yale University. We went down and I did my introductory concert and he did the lecture part. It looked like most of the packed audience were going to come back for the second lecture preparatory to initiation. About halfway through the second lecture, two students about ten rows back, started to get up in the middle of Joe's talk and he said, "Hey! you two sit back down I'm not finished yet." I was shocked, no one ever talked so boldly before or since, but they sat back down and they actually started TM and at the end of the three days of checking they came up to Joe and said "thank you for being so forceful when we were leaving, we were put off by something you said but it turns out you had been telling it like it is; we would never have started if you hadn't been who you are." How did Joe know that these two needed him to be so strong? All I can say is that I was impressed.

JONI MITCHEL & HENRY LEWY

RECORDING THE "SONG OF LIFE"

AT "A & M RECORDS, LA

We didn't stay in Cambridge for very long. Jerry managed to set up recording time at A&M Records with the great Engineer/Producer, Henry Lewy to record "The Song of Life" album that Maharishi and I had created in Kashmir. Henry Lewy was the genius behind most of Joni Mitchell's albums; all the best ones. She was actually finishing up "Court and Spark" with Henry when we were there. I wasn't destined to meet her, she would always have just left the studio when I arrived but Henry would play some of her best takes for me. Many musicians owed Henry musical favors and he called them all in for "The Song of Life" because he loved Maharishi and his meditation and his sweet wife who was one of the early TM Teachers.

Some of the great musicians who added their instrument to the album were: Jazz great Charles Lloyd, Paul Horn, the great Canadian flute player who also played on my "Gentle Soul" album produced by Terry Melcher for Columbia Records, and Emil Richards, the premier percussionist in LA. Paul Horn was one of the early TM teachers as well, and Emil and Charles had started TM way back when. Jerry Jarvis and the A&M Records art department took care of the art work with a beautiful album cover. The TM movement, most probably the SIMS center under Jerry's command, and later MIU press, paid for the manufacture and distribution of the album. As a result, most of the meditators who came to the TTC courses already knew most of the puja (on the album) which is one of the more time consuming parts of learning to become an Initiator (TM Teacher).

POLAND SPRINGS COURSE

In 1970, Jerry told us that Maharishi was holding a TM teacher- training preparatory course at a Victorian hotel located in Poland Springs, Maine with 1,200 participants and needed Initiators to come and help with instruction. We arrived and it looked as though the entire street population of Haight Ashbury was there to greet us. They were swimming nude in the local pond and pairing up, it was like a Love In! When Maharishi was lecturing and we were teaching the process of checking meditation, most of the participants were involved and active in the learning process but when it was time to study on their own or rest, many would be down at the swimming hole or getting to know each other more intimately in their rooms. I wanted to round, to do more meditation and I did. The problem was that the atmosphere was thick with sex, the unmarried couple next door were making so much noise getting to know each other that I found myself trying not to listen, it became intolerable and it was just then that Maharishi called for me to entertain the troops. I tuned my guitar and practiced my latest love song and went down to the meeting.

Maharishi said, "Sit, sit here, and sing." I started singing and playing the new love song that I felt very deeply and I was about half way through when Maharishi started talking. He managed to begin at exactly the moment when it sounded as if I had finished the song. I was shocked again, just like the last time it happened in Kashmir with Laksmanjoo. I hadn't learned my lesson! When Maharishi asks me to sing, He wants a song about TM or some aspect of the knowledge or "The Holy Tradition" or "Love & God," the poem he wrote that I put to music. I just sat there feeling really spaced out, the long meditations I was doing (off the program) in that bordello atmosphere had done a number on me and so I went back to helping with the course, something I should have been doing all along.

Someone on the course wanted Maharishi to hear the Beatles new song "Across The Universe" that had the lyrics "Jai Guru Deva, Om" as a chorus. They put it on and everyone started to sing along with the chorus "Jai Guru Deva, Om" and Maharishi looked as if he was not enjoying the song at all. It was obvious that he was angry with the group and the rude ignorance that John Lennon had displayed when they left the ashram and Maharishi's loving hospitality. Also, "Om" is a recluse mantra for monks only. The song was turned off before it finished, someone with some sense had realized Maharishi wasn't pleased and turned it off. A few hippies booed and yelled "put it back on" and of course that didn't happen.

The late night, private meetings with Maharishi where just a few of us sat with him and acted as sounding boards for concerns and ideas and feedback on how everything was going, were memorable. One night I couldn't focus on a thing he was saying because there was a mosquito humming about his head. It kept trying to land and have a Holy feast but Maharishi would wave his hand gracefully, just at the right moment and the insect would retreat and make another circumference around him and come back again several minutes later. It was obvious that Maharishi didn't kill insects or anything else for that matter but I remembered he had told us that house holders could kill insects and vermin. Another time I asked if I could add the head stand to my yoga asana routine and he said "let me see." I did a pretty good balancing act on my head protected by my cupped hands but when I came down he said "it is not safe, you can paralyze your body if you put too much pressure on the top of your head."

DRIVING MISS NINI, SARA & THE TWIT

I don't remember much about the Poland Springs course. Later that year Maharishi held a similar four-week course at Humboldt State U. in Arcata, California. About 1,500 people attended and it was described as a "sort of a crash program to train TM teachers." We packed up and headed out west for Arcata California. We got a ride from Cullen, one of those very eccentric, educated Englishmen Monty Python satirized as "Twits." Nini White, the daughter of a once famous actress and good friend also came with us. We shared the driving and the gas money with Cullen and he remained silent for much of the three thousand mile trip; although he would often become silently perturbed with our American way of speaking rudely to each other when we were tired or frustrated. I could tell he was interested in Sara and it was clear she wasn't interested in me. However, Nini seemed quite interested in me as we sloshed through a shaded creek to cool off and she somehow managed to soak her tee shirt, enhancing the vision of her sensuality, bouncing and smiling and giggling until we both went red. But I was Mr. true to his word, true to his vows and have never been able to shake that moral credo from my last incarnation "Keep Tryst," meaning keep your word, be faithful and true which I've done through three marriages.

HUMBOLDT II

The University was haunted by a self righteous Bible Thumper and his two or three "saved" minions who hung around the campus waylaying students with memorized mistranslations of the Bible. They shared an old student rental house off campus. The simple minds who follow guys like this believe that if the prophet has memorized the parts of the Bible that fit his agenda and he can quote chapter and verse, he must be a true man of God; especially if he acts like the Jesus in the movies. They seem to love feeling self righteous and browbeating others by playing on any guilt the poor lost Christian might feel especially if they had been indoctrinated with Christian fundamentalism when they were young.

Anyway, this guy came to Maharishi's introductory lecture which was open to the public. He had a worn out bible in his hand with a myriad of book markers hanging out of it. He had dirty unkempt hair with a patchy, scraggly, almost beard. During the lecture the Thumper thrust his bible in the air and shouted out at Maharishi "you are the anti-Christ, you are a false prophet." Then when the Thumper ran out of nasty things to say, Maharishi waited until there was a general silence, as everyone wanted to hear his response.

Maharishi straightened his back, got close to the microphone and said in a pained voice of pity and anger "you wouldn't even come to see him (Jesus) if he came to your airport." his thinly veiled remark meant so much to anyone who knew the truth made obvious in Mother Olson's remembrance of a time when Maharishi was staying in her house and she went upstairs to his room and questioned him. She said "Maharishi, I feel very strongly that I was your mother at some time in the past, who were you then?" He didn't respond and she left the room. She persisted the next day and still there was just a smile. Finally on her third try she said "Maharishi, please tell me who you were when I was your mother." He was silent for a few minutes and then said "you know that picture downstairs in the hallway?" And Mother Olson put her hand to her mouth and cried "Oh, Maharishi did it hurt?" He responded like a child speaking to his mother, with his head down he shyly said "yes."

JESUS & JOHN – GURU DEV & MAHARISHI

Who was the person in the picture in the hallway downstairs? It was a painting of John the Baptist. (Guru Dev) his Divinity Swami Brahmananda Saraswati Maharaj Jagat Guru Bhagavan Shankaracharya of Jyotir Math was Maharishi's master in our time. Using logic and my intuition, magnified by my proximity to Maharishi, I believe that two thousand years ago Christ was John The Baptist's master, Swami Brahmananda Saraswati was none other than Jesus Christ in his previous incarnation and Maharishi was John the Baptist. They have both incarnated together, master and Disciple many times out of compassion for humanity.

What of the second coming of Jesus? It is highly probable that he was born in India in 1870, having achieved the highest level of consciousness possible in a human body and having fulfilled his life's work culminating in the creation of a Maharishi to enlighten the world, he ascended in Mahasamadhi in 1953. He wasn't blond and blue eyed and he wasn't Jewish, he tried that more than once and was tortured to death along with his disciple John the Baptist. I can truly understand why Guru Dev spent most of his life (70 years) in caves deep in the Jungles of India, communing with the Divine, far from Men. Finally, He had to come out of his seclusion and share his Enlightenment and the truths of life with the millions of India, and through his disciple Maharishi Mahesh Yogi, the entire world.

Anyway, forget about the bible thumper, he ranted on a few more times and I noticed when I was walking to and from the dining hall or lectures, that some of the course members seemed interested in him and a few of them even left the course to be part of his little cult. I don't feel sorry for them, they most likely left him for someone else, on and on until they remembered the way they felt when they used to do TM twice a day. I think it was at the end of one of these courses that Jerry asked Sara and I to go down South and teach; he wanted us to start a center in Atlanta and use it as a base for teaching throughout the South. We ended up finding our greatest interest for TM at the Colleges and Universities in Georgia, North Carolina, Tennessee, Louisiana and Florida.

So, off we went to Atlanta where we rented a house that had a large attic with a floor. I think there were three bedrooms so we used two of them for Initiation and checking. The attic was for lectures, and we rented around fifty chairs for the purpose. If you sat on either side of the row of chairs your head would bump against the ceiling with only five or six chairs side by side. There were ten rows of chairs and occasionally they would be full. Usually, we would get ten to twenty people signing up to start.

Sometimes we would hold TM courses at small colleges in remote parts of Georgia and Tennessee. Somewhere down there I was giving instruction to a small group of new TMr's when someone knocked at the door. I opened it to see a man standing there with the head of a gorilla. He began to talk to me and all I could hear were my own thoughts "this guy has the head of a gorilla." I could see his human face behind the Ape face and without considering his reaction I jumped back and said "whoa! you're a gorilla." He smiled nervously, obviously embarrassed and I said "I mean, I just saw a gorilla head on you; maybe I was seeing a past life?" Five minutes later there was another pounding on the door and I opened it to see the local Sheriff with his hands on his hips and a big cigar in the corner of his mouth. He told me that they didn't like weirdo hippies like me around there and that I better pack up and get out of his town by sundown. Fortunately, the new TMr's had finished their three days of checking and all was well, so I packed up and left for Atlanta.

NEGROES IN THE HOUSE!

Our neighbors wondered what was going on in our house since we would have so many visitors, especially on weekends when we were initiating. College kids were coming and going with little bags full of fruit and handkerchiefs and some of them were actually black, you know Negroes, and this was Atlanta! The lady across the street was red with anger as she stormed up our lawn and asked who was it that actually lived here? I said, "my wife Sara and I, why?" She said "what are you running here, you selling dope or is this a cat-house? How dare you have them Nigaas coming here! we got a clean neighborhood heeya and the cops gonna know bout this." We hadn't experienced the real South until this moment and it was kinda scary.

The cops did come by and warned us that we couldn't be teaching or holding public meetings in that neighborhood, that they had received complaints from the neighbors. We just kept on holding our courses there and teaching out of town as well; Athens Georgia, Knoxville Tennessee, Miami Fla., Baton Rouge La., New Orleans La., Palm Beach Fla. etc. etc. Sometimes we would teach in separate places, me in Miami and she in Knoxville or somewhere else. We had a few part time helpers and another Initiator, Peter Muldavin who was helping us run the center. We held a course in Knoxville that was memorable in that our contact there was a weight lifter with arms the size of his thighs. He and Sara would talk and such for hours after I thought we had all gone to bed. I could hear them laughing downstairs and wondered!

THE WEIGHT LIFTER

When we got back to Atlanta, Sara packed up and headed back to Knoxville without really saying much of anything. At this time Maharishi was holding a TTC in Estes Park Colorado and I received word that I should come and sing for the graduating teachers. When I arrived someone told me that Sara was sharing a room with the weight lifter and I went to the dining hall for something to eat. The place was packed with people I knew and many who were becoming teachers. I could feel their eyes on me as I walked through the hall and I was soon to find out why. There, sitting at one of the long tables was Muscle Man and I could tell by his sideways glance that he was checking me out to see if I was going to attack him from behind. Just about everyone was watching me by this time and it was clear that the rumors were rampant.

Of course I had no thoughts of confrontation; I was well aware by this time that Sara made her own decisions. I made no physical signs that I was anything but happy to be on the course for a few days to sing and see Maharishi. Next morning I met with Maharishi and he asked "do you still love Sara?" and I said "yes, Maharishi" then he said "I will ask her if she still loves you and we will see." Later, Maharishi told me that she didn't want to be with me any longer and he told me I should come and be with him in Mallorca after leaving Estes Park. That night I sang a song I had just written about Guru Dev called "Raja Ram." Just after the song, Maharishi whispered to me "how do you know that name for Guru Dev." He seemed slightly upset that I had used the childhood name for his master; he thought only a few people knew about it and I guess it was too personal, too close to his heart. I told him "Maharishi, the whole story about Guru Dev's life is in the book you put out "Love & God." I found it there!" He asked me not to use it again and that was the last time I sang that song.

MAHARISHI & DONOVAN

There is a picture on the back cover of one of Donovan's albums that really got me motivated to be as close to Maharishi as Donovan seemed to be in this picture. There is Maharishi and Donovan sitting across from each other, holding hands. It reminded me of all the times I had seen Maharishi holding hands with his saint friends like Tat Wali Baba and Laksmanjoo. I thought, if Donovan was able to be as close to Maharishi as the greatest saints, why couldn't I? I became determined to hold hands with him the next time I met with him in private. After all, I had been meditating for years before Donovan or the Beatles started! Well, I didn't mention this before when I was relating my meeting with Maharishi in Estes Park concerning Sara, but when we were talking about her I took Maharishi's hand and held it for what seemed like an hour. It was probably only five minutes, but as I was holding his hand I looked into his eyes and realized that he knew very well why I was holding his hand, I was envious of Donovan and that became embarrassing enough for me to take my hand away. When I did, Maharishi made a little sound, almost a laugh and very subtly rolled his eyes.

"DON'T LET YOUR HEART GET HARD" (MMY)

Before I could go to Mallorca I had one last course to teach in Knoxville Tennessee. I gave my introductory lecture and went to a health food store to get something. Walking down the aisle I ran into a girl who worked there whom I had initiated a few months earlier. I remembered that Maharishi told me to not let my heart get hard before I left Estes Park, and when he said it, he was also telling me to be open to love and relationships. He was saying it all in those few words, "don't let your heart get hard." Anyway, when this girl turned around, her face lit up like she had just run into her long lost true love. I was blown away by her full flowing heart, full of sweet love coming at me like a tornado. I immediately recognized that I had Initiated her some months before and my heart opened up and embraced her. She asked if I would come for dinner and I said "sure!"

Whenever Maharishi put his mind to my love life, one or even two girls would suddenly manifest an almost unnatural fascination for me. This wasn't the only time that Maharishi played Cupid in my love life; a few years later he was doing his best to set me up with several different girls, one after the other, over a three year period. I say girls because we were all just kids back then, in our twenties. I'll tell you all about my other failed attempts at accepting Maharishi's choices of a proper mate for me when I get to that part of the story.

With a softened heart I flew to Boston and it was coming on Christmas. Keith Wallace offered to put me up for a few nights until the charter flight to Mallorca Spain was scheduled to fly out of Logan airport. I stayed one night at Keith's apartment and the girl who babysat for him or cooked and cleaned or both, ran into me in the kitchen and I smiled and she smiled and Maharishi's magic took over. She invited me to stay the next night at the apartment of an MIT math professor's family she was house sitting for. We watched TV but couldn't find an interesting channel after over an hour of trying.

We ended up in a large closet where she had a small futon, no major hanky-panky, just some heart softening touchy feely, kissy-facing. When I awoke, she was gone and I appeared from the closet at around ten the next morning to a living room full of family. They were as shocked as I was; I think the professor thought I was a burglar at first, he looked so freaked out. I said "oh, sorry! Judy let me crash in the closet last night, I didn't have a place to stay." This probably didn't look good for the poor Nanny but you have to remember this was the 60's. Anyway, the family wasn't supposed to return for another day or two. Finally, they recognized me after staring at me in fear for a few minutes; they probably figured I was cheating on my wife. I was just keeping my heart from getting hard, right? Right!

MALLORCA SPAIN

Then it was off to Mallorca Spain and Maharishi. When our bus came within ten miles of Maharishi I suddenly felt his presence, the very edge of his aura I guess? At least that was my experience. I had a lot of experience being aware of the powerful emanation of his serenity; like moving into a deep meditation while you are speeding down a two lane road. It wasn't long after this that Maharishi became aware that he needed to hold-in his vibe as it was too much for some people. It was too intense for me on the Lake Louise course, when I chose to be in too close proximity to him all night with my door open as he gave out advanced techniques. I got sick the next day and I've told you the story about my car, how it had three flats on the way home; even my car was un-stressing from too intense a shot of purification.

This was the first of two TTC courses in Mallorca and Maharishi would often have me sing for the course. Sometimes when he was late for a lecture, completely absorbed in a brainstorming session with his PhD's and needed entertainment for the crowd, he would say "have Rick sing." Many times he would have me sing before the evening lecture to settle things down, especially during long rounding when the rounders had excess energy that needed calming. Back then, music was the language and religion of the young, and like I said before we looked to our musicians for lyrics that expressed the optimism of our little 60's "Golden Age" 5000 years into Kali Yuga. All this performing kept me very busy writing new songs; I could sing the same song a few times but then it was time for a new one.

I wasn't a course participant in Mallorca, I did my TTC in India and now I was Maharishi's Troubadour; on call to perform for the courses and for visiting dignitaries, scientists and professors that he liked to entertain in his meeting room with a song or two. During Mallorca II, Maharishi established a special group of Initiators he called the 108; to be in the group you had to be self-sufficient and able to pay your room and board and any travel expenses that might arise in accompanying Maharishi for at least six months, preferably a year. The 108 were put in charge of keeping their respective areas of the globe and the TM organization's National leaders of those areas, informed and in communication with Maharishi and his latest projects for getting the population meditating. I was quietly given the status of a 108 even though I didn't have to take on the responsibility of acting as liaison for a particular country. There were two other categories of people around Maharishi, course participants and International Staff.

Even though I was an impoverished musician I was sponsored by Maharishi because I had written and recorded an album of music, "Song of Life" that served as an introduction to TM as well as a tutorial for learning the puja that had helped the Movement financially. I hadn't received any payment for this until I was asked to stay, free room and board in all the five star hotels Maharishi stayed at; all travel expenses flying around the world with Maharishi were covered, as well as a bank account monitored by the 108 banker, Michael Dimmick, that is, until I proved unable to take money seriously and lost a pocket full of cash ($200.) in London that Dimmick had given me for a new suit. When Maharishi heard about this he smiled, I think because as a monk he kind of appreciated my lack of attachment, but all the same he cut off my supply line with Michael D. down to necessities unless I really needed more.

Mallorca 1 was the course where Maharishi discovered that westerners had far more stress to release than he had imagined before the long meditation un-stressing of the India courses so he introduced the rounding sadhana (the practice of breaking up the long meditations with physical counterparts which included pranayama and asanas). It was the rule that illegal drugs were taboo at least two weeks before starting TM and by the time you were eligible to attend TTC you should have been drug free for at least six months. However, there were lots of folks who were taking prescribed drugs for depression and other mental problems who, I believe, were not supposed to have been accepted for TTC. However, several participants either lied on their forms or their drug use was overlooked and they ended up requiring extra assistance even though they were "rounding." Rounding had worked very well to ease the release of stress, so that as the old tensions and poisons left the body, their potential overshadowing influence on the mind and emotions didn't take over.

"M" BOYS TO THE RESCUE

These people needed more than rounding, they required hands- on aggressive massage by a special group of young men who were trained to neutralize the unbalanced stress release of these special cases. We had a special name for them which I can't remember now. There was Ned Wynn, Casey Coleman, Rob McCutcheon and one or two others in this group. These guys were also members of "M" group, Monk group! Several initiators around Maharishi were part of this group and took vows of celibacy, although I believe Ned changed his mind about the vows at the very last minute. Purportedly, they were given the same technique that the Indian Brahmacharies received when they took their vows. At the time Maharishi had no idea how fickle westerners were about self-discipline.

It didn't take long for him to realize that they didn't have any discipline at all! In fact, the way these guys behaved shortly after they had taken their vows, seemed as if becoming monks actually catapulted them into doing as much to break their vows as was humanly possible. In La Antilla Spain two TTC courses after Mallorca, I would see them drinking in the local flamenco bar almost every afternoon. One of them ran off with the wife of an initiator and most of them stopped meditating altogether. Maharishi was extremely disappointed and until he started the Purusha group many years later, he never trusted westerners to take the vows of a Brahmachari.

Then again, to be fair, during their time as medics to the over-the- top unstressors, they did a great job; nothing short of heroic. I remember hearing that a guy got up one morning and walked into the ocean; I don't think he was ever found? Another lady, a couple of floors up and several down from me had threatened to jump off her balcony; she had stopped taking her Valium in the middle of rounding and that was that. The massage crew were running about all day and into the evening taking care of these drug unstressors. You can be sure that the next Mallorca had very strict rules about not allowing people on prescription drugs, who were patients of Psychiatrists or Psychologists to attend TTC or other rounding courses.

One of Maharishi's most memorable talks was in answer to the question: "Maharishi, because the people on this course are obviously the most fortunate and evolved people in the world, what wonderful things did we do to deserve to be here with you? Maharishi's response was so cool! "You were responsible for losing the teaching in the past and are here because it is your responsibility to bring it out again." Many of us immediately thought of Jesus Christ and how different it would, perhaps, have been if the crowd had called for Jesus to be released that day 2000 years ago instead of Barabbas the thief. Maybe he was referring to that very event when the crowd chose ignorance over enlightenment. During my seven years around him, Maharishi made many leading comments that when taken together clearly point to the time of John and Jesus.

SARA RETURNS? *NOT!*

Sitting in the dining hall, finishing up my lunch, I remember Sara sitting down across from me with a smile on her face. I figured she must have left the weight-lifter in Knoxville to be with Maharishi and maybe, since I was still her husband, she might act the part of wife again. Funnily enough, the nanny I had shared the "kissy-face" closet with back in Boston came up with a big smile and seemed to have the same plan as Sara. Of course the poor nanny had to defer when she realized that the girl sitting across from me was my missing wife. Some complicated facial signatures ensued and without much more said, she took on the part of a passing friend, which is really what she was, and walked away. I'm sure she had imagined that when she came to the course we would take the friendship a step further and even though she was very sweet and good natured, once I was with Maharishi in those days, I was all about being a monk. This was a recurring problem for the wives and husbands of many couples on courses with Maharishi. The wife would aspire to celibacy or the husband would, but rare was the couple that came to that decision together.

Many of us were already teachers of TM and were there to either round, or work on International staff. The staff were initiators and meditators who helped run the course. When Maharishi didn't need me to be his troubadour at the height of long rounding, I went into silence, and one of the hotel kitchen workers brought up my dinner every day for a month and left it inside my first of two doors. Initially, as I was increasing in rounds per day I would read course literature that was supposed to earn me college credits like "Malcolm X" and other books, mostly biographies of famous black people for a professor friend of Sara's who had agreed to my taking his literature course long distance. After a week of this my mind was doing whatever it wanted; when I tried to read I would find myself staring at a page for thirty minutes during my break time. You get so used to the deeper awareness that the surface of the mind and senses become completely transcended. Sometimes I would open my eyes to see if the twenty minute meditation time had passed and my watch would tell me that two hours of unaccounted for transcendence had taken me for a deep dip in it's silent pool.

There was a guy across the hall from me who had barricaded himself in his room. One evening when I peeked out to see if my food was coming I noticed his outer door was open and the inside one was reinforced with a queen sized mattress and a box spring covering it. "How did he get his food" I wondered?

This very dedicated monk remained in silent rounding for the full three months, he was an initiator and very experienced at remaining deep in the silence of the Self for extended periods of time. He later became an "M" group member and ultimately a leader of the "Purusha" group, which is really like a monastic order where celibacy and sadhana are the order of the day and night. John Bright aka (Black) has been a member of this group for the last 30+ years as well; remember? he's the one who drove Maharishi out on the peninsula to visit with the light-ship (Guru Dev) in Mallorca.

I won't go into the inner life of my silence during that month but I will tell you about what happened when I came out. When you finish a long silence and rounding time you are extremely sensitive, heightened awareness to the max. I walked out of my room for the first time in thirty days and down the staircase toward the dining room, at least my body did! That silent awareness (Me) just sort of noticed the wall going by and the dizzying downward movement as my legs and feet did their job without my help, they moved on the basis of my inner intentions but seemed totally separate from Me. Just as I was about to reach the swinging steel door someone came through it from the other side. I looked up and my gaze met theirs and they said "Hi" and when I returned the greeting, I didn't return the greeting, but I heard my voice and felt my mouth move and the air in my chest move. My voice sounded a little distant and was exceedingly sweet, like some beautiful soul inside my body was speaking for Me; like the time at Lompoc when I heard my voice around the campfire sounding so innocent, sweetness itself. They call it witnessing, an experience of Cosmic Consciousness in action, I suppose!

RACE CAR DRIVER

There was a "professional" race car driver on the 108 and he was supposed to pick someone up at the Palma airport. He asked me if I'd like to take a drive with him in his red-hot sports car. I thought "well this might be fun for an afternoon's diversion" and I got in. As we pulled out of the hotel driveway, he stepped on the gas, took a sharp right, and we went sideways around the entire corner squealing all the way. I realized that this was going to be a life or death ride on a narrow road that barely fits two cars in it's two little lanes. Once we were out of town and flying through the air over small hillocks and down onto the other side at over 100 miles an hour, I couldn't talk, I was afraid I would distract him, as even a small part of a second could make the difference. Being a race driver he would go from one side of the road to the other and the road was looking like an unraveling black ribbon that we were racing up and down, more in the air than on the pavement.

You must imagine, this guy had only one hand on the wheel and he was totally relaxed, sitting back in his seat with a little smile on his face, as if we were on a Sunday drive in the country, a leisurely afternoon cruise. During the ten mile race I was sure that he had a death wish, I thought that he was going to intentionally drive us into another car coming the other way. I had no idea that a car could be driven this fast on a small, curvy county road with no clue as to who might be coming the other way, over the next hill, or if a cow or some sheep might be right in the middle of the road just over that hill..."Shit! I thought, he's going to kill us." We arrived safely in Palma and I realized that there was always just a little more to what could be achieved or done than what I thought was possible. I mean, I had been driving since I was 16 and thought I had mastered the driving of a car around corners without tipping over and I was really good at driving on snow or ice, but what John Mortinson could do without even trying was very impressive. I thought, "if he could o that fast on that road, what could he do on a big old race track." Ahhh the rich and their hobbies!

PAUL OF THE "ZONE"

Remember the big guy I mentioned earlier when I was talking about the Asilomar residence course, where Pamela and I performed and this musician and his sound engineer were making faces during our performance and while everyone was applauding. They had a group in San Francisco called "The Loading Zone" that was the house band at the Fillmore. They were basically a Rythem & Blues band and Paul Fauerso was the keyboard player. He tried to sing like a black dude but his falsetto, that so many try for, was kinda thin, so they had a curvaceous grad. Student, Susie Levin singing lead until Linda Tillary joined the group. Anyway, that guy and his wife Josie showed up on the course, I guess for their Teacher Training. Someone asked me if I had ever heard the guy, I hadn't, but I made a point of checking him out.

I was exiting the dining hall when I heard someone playing the piano and I went over and listened. It was Paul, the guy from the Loading Zone, and he was a good keyboard player. I asked him if he wrote any songs; he said "yes" and began playing and singing and I thought "this guy is too good not to perform for the course; maybe I should tell Maharishi." I think I asked Paul if he would like to play for the course participants and he must have said yes because the next time I was alone with Maharishi I said, "there is a musician who plays and sings his own songs, maybe he could sing for the course." Maharishi said, "are you sure you want to do this?" The look on his face and the understated meaning of his question was, "are you sure you want to give up your position as the exclusive Troubadour for me and the Movement?" At the time I intuited his meaning but felt that I would be selfish not to share my status with other musicians who were deserving.

Little did I know then, how a few years later this musician and his wife would treat me and my homeless and destitute little family when we had no place to live and no money for food in LA, CA. Anyway, at the time it seemed like the right thing to do and Paul and I started writing together and performing for the two or three thousand people on the course. Josie, Paul's wife, seemed to have the mind of a business woman or maybe it was the fact that she was rich and stood to inherit a fortune, that Maharishi found her useful, and she spent a great deal of time going over his ideas and plans for spreading TM with him. It was actually hard to get in to see him after Josie took over his time. I know that Paul was starting to feel neglected. To fill the void Josie left, he sometimes enjoyed the flattering company of aesthetically-sensitive young men who, in turn, enjoyed counseling him on how to spend his money, especially when it came to fine food and clothing and Rome.

"THE NATURAL TENDENCY" IS BORN!

Once Maharishi had video taped ten or so (SCI) Science of Creative Intelligence lessons for an introductory course for (MIU) Maharishi International university, Paul and I were summoned to Maharishi's room where he explained his wish to have all the SCI lessons put to song. He wanted a song for every lesson, I think there were 33 or 34 lessons and we were to write all that music together. As he had done with me in India, Maharishi said that he would write down the most important points of each lesson. He gave us the points for four or five of the lessons to begin with, and we were off and running. We would perform the songs almost as soon as we wrote them, sometimes too soon after we wrote them. Writing a song is one thing and performing it in a professional way is something entirely above and beyond. We had to work out perfect harmonies, perfect guitar and harmonium accompaniment all without cliched riffs, and with interesting changes, original music and lyrics that didn't sound like TM advertisements or SCI instruction manuals.

One of the songs was a list of the goals of the World Plan. There were so many and they made no sense at all as a song. Each goal had it's own natural meter which we found impossible to weave into one or two or even three melodic and rhythmic structures. We tried for two or three days to put the list of goals to music and just couldn't do it in the same way that we were writing music for the other SCI course lessons. Finally, I came up with an idea; we would write music for each separate goal and tie them together with linking segues that sounded like a natural flow of one music into another. We tried out my theory and after linking two or three of the goals together we experienced a creative epiphany and laughed and cheered ourselves. We actually managed to make each goal build from the preceding one the way composers change keys, going up the scale to intensify a song with a growing, ever higher and more intense immediacy. It made the goals of the World Plan come alive.

It was a feat comparable to putting a thesaurus or a dictionary to music. It may have been my idea but Paul had the music theory smarts and deserves major credit for his masterful segue and melody contributions. Paul and Josie became 108's and we traveled with Maharishi from course to course and country to country. Mallorca I, where I welcomed Paul aboard; Mallorca II, Fiuggi Fonte and La Antilla Spain, where we wrote most of the SCI songs for the "Natural Tendency" Album, "Somthing Good Is Happening." Then Lake Tahoe where Maharishi was finishing video taping the SCI lessons which by this time had become somewhat boring as science often does to a man who thrives on spontaneous creativity. We musically soothed the master's tedium from all those many weeks and hours of translating Vedic Science into The Science of Creative Intelligence.

As Keith Wallace, Paul and I sat around him in his room, Maharishi said, "Oh, science is so boring, so boring, sing a song; play some music." Keith, the scientist, looked a bit put out by Maharishi's remark and Paul sang "Master of My Heart." When Paul finished Maharishi said "This is not appropriate, not good to put the tender feelings of the heart into the harsh atmosphere." Then he looked at me and said sing "Holy Tradition!" and lying on his side with his head supported by his propped arm and hand, he closed his eyes.

It hasn't surprised me that Paul continues to sing the song Maharishi had told him was "not appropriate" since he always gets great approval from his audiences when he sings it. After all, I shouldn't have been the only "Natural Tendency member" who had devotional songs like "Love & God" and the "Holy Tradition" when performing for Movement functions. Maharishi had given me the authority and personal training to sing portions of "The Holy Tradition" in public when giving my introductory lecture & "song of life" presentation as well as his poem "Love & God," the ultimate devotional song, which I put to music. Paul's "Master Of My Heart" and "Cosmic Consciousness" are great devotional songs and I would love to take credit for any small part I played in inspiring Paul's competitive nature in their creation.

LAKE TAHOE

(below) is the very house, or should I say compound, that Maharishi was staying at in Tahoe. It was the one they used in the movie "Godfather II." Remember the scene where Fredo was taken out on the lake and snuffed? That was the house where Maharishi filmed the last of the SCI course videos. The place underwent a major purification.

DEAR HENRALS

It was after the second Humboldt U. course in Arcata California that Paul and Josie joined Sara and I doing the singing introductory lecture all around northern California; Paul would accompany me on the "Song of Life" songs, and Josie would do the lecture part with Sara, then at the end we would all answer questions. There was a young Manhattanite 108, Henry Eckstein, who became our roadie. He would haul our sound gear and instruments, a very strong lad who had swum the English Channel. He could play Reverend Gary Davis guitar an extremely complex finger-picking style.

One day Henry and I were passing through Big Sur and we decided to camp down in the Redwood forest for the night. It was kind of cold sleeping on the ground with just our coats over us even though we had spread the oriental rug we used for concerts on the ground. It must have been around four or five in the morning when Henry let out a scream that sent me a few inches into the air. I jerked myself up and said "what? what's going on? He just pointed out in front of him, there was nothing there! He said "He was standing right there, didn't you see him? I hadn't and said "who was there, a bear? "No, it was a huge guy with a Smokey the bear hat on, a forest ranger hat. But the guy was eight feet tall or more just looking down at me." He said that "it was so real, he must still be around in the woods." We got up and looked around for awhile but there wasn't anyone there. Henry said the guy had a very large axe which startled him and then the Ranger or Paul Bunyan said "you can't camp here on an oriental rug, get out." We were sleeping on Henry's rug that we used for performing onstage. I figure it was the ghost of some 19th century lumber jack or trapper, a very large one.

THE SPY?

Out in the hills of Calabasas California not far from Topanga

Canyon, Sara and I rented a room in the house of a beautiful lady who had been on our TTC in India, Samantha for now. She didn't know, and neither did I for sure until later, that her live-in boy friend (Ken) was actually a spy for some government agency, infiltrating the TM movement. There was always something fishy about him with his hair implants and rangy six foot five frame of Navy Seal Steel, cat-like moves across the floor. He was older than us all by about ten years and when he was in the company of women or girls, he emanated an Alpha dog vibe as if in competition with any man in the room; he'd flirt and smile mischievously with all pretty women. Sometimes I unintentionally surprised him in the living room with Samantha's fifteen year old daughter cuddled up in his arms on the sofa. He would have a big, Cheshire Cat grin on his face implying that he was innocently filling in for her absentee father but then there would be that strange vibe.

Years later, in the Kulm Hotel in Switzerland, Maharishi held a special meeting where he told us that there was a spy in our midst and that he better tell the truth about what he was observing to his superiors. I looked over at Ken and knew that it was him. I mean how was he paying to be a 108 by simply selling his rug shampooing business which consisted of an old white van and a single shampooing machine? That was his explanation when asked. I started watching him and noticed that he could speak fluent German as he chatted up one of the attractive ladies with that twinkle in his eyes, a real James Bond. A few years later I ran into him when Maharishi was visiting the Video studio in LA where he was working. I do hope he told the truth to whatever government agency he worked for about Maharishi's good intentions and the scientific proof of the positive results of TM. He was very friendly to me, especially in the later years. In truth, I think he was using his government spy position to pay to be a 108 because he really loved and believed in Maharishi and the TM movement. That's my impression anyway, kinda cool!

HARI KRISHNA

The time between Mallorca I and II was spent teaching TM in California, Washington State and the Mid West. It was probably Jerry who asked us to go to Madison Wisconsin to give the Song of Life concert lecture. The concert hall was filled with students and professors; I remember four hundred signing up to start, at least half of the entire audience. We initiated about two hundred people that weekend and Walter Koch with several other initiators were coming the next weekend to start the remaining two hundred. At another introductory concert in Cincinnati we were harangued by Hari Krishnas who enjoyed raising their voices so loud that the audience actually yelled them down; there were many there who really wanted to hear what we had to say. During the question and answer period the loudest Hari K. became quite belligerent and said that we were selling spirituality in the guise of science. I said, "this teaching is free in India and for Native Americans in this country, most other people don't value what they get for free, especially in the USA." Then I asked "what is it that you people are asking for when you do your song and dance at the airports?" I was smiling when I said this and the audience began laughing until the lead Hari shook his fist at me and they walked out.

I remember when we were in Cambridge Mass. the Hari's used to chant in Harvard Square and tear down our Introductory lecture posters as soon as we put them up. They sure had good food though! I knew a few initiators who liked to go to their dinners even though they had to listen to the shaved heads proselytize. The Hari's had imitated all the outer trappings of an Indian sadhu with no concept of the inner life of a true seeker or finder of liberation, at least this was my overwhelming impression based on their behavior. Bhajans, shaved heads, saris, Dhotis, sandals, 3rd eye bindus, incense, pictures of Gods and saints and Swami Prabhupada their Guru, and lots of curry dinners. They made a lot of noise and danced a lot and ate a lot. Oh yes, they spent most of their time panhandling for the Swami which accounts for the lavish temples he built.

His translation of the Bhagavadgita looks like it was intended for children with it's cartoon depictions of Lord Krishna, Arjuna, the Kurus and Pandavas. Judging from the born-again types that he attracted it is probably fair to say that he was spot on in his assessment of their intellectual and spiritual capabilities when it came to understanding Vedic knowledge. Please forgive me if I have misjudged your followers my dear Swami...after all, you did get a lot of kids into the streets and airports and exposed them to Indian culture and cuisine and taught them how the pros beg in India; hand us something with a smile, as if it were free, then open your palm for payment. But reducing your followers to the status of untouchable Indian beggars seems a rather undignified strategy for gaining money and spirituality. Then again, the materialistic nature of many westerners could probably do with a little taste of the life of a beggar chanting for God.

THE PSYCHIC

I think it was also in the New England area that I was giving the second or Preparatory lecture to starting TM, during the question and answer period; when a man stood up and said "are you psychic? does TM increase your psychic abilities?" I said "we are all capable of what you call psychic abilities, they are a latent part of our full potential. We are using only five to ten percent of our potential, by diving into the full reservoir of our consciousness twice a day in deep meditation we gradually begin using more and more of our total potential; greater sensitivity through all the five senses, clearer perception and intuition, realizing the unlimited power and bliss of the human mind and consciousness. Psychic abilities are just the beginning of realizing our full potential.

After the lecture and sign up he came up to me and said "I'm psychic you know! and I can tell you your grandmother's name and what she is doing right now." I said "that's good and TM will balance your abilities with the rest of your life, your mind and emotions, your fulfillment in life. When he saw that I wasn't outwardly impressed he gave me the name of my Grandmother and what she was doing at the time. I said "yes, that's good but I can call my Grandmother on the phone and find out what she is doing at any time." I didn't want him to think that being psychic was the goal of TM; it was just one of the possible results that could be had through regular meditation. Anyway, that was the way he took it, he said "you mean the rest of my life could become more balanced by doing TM? that's what I need! My personal life is a mess and being psychic only makes it more complicated." I said "yes!"

MALLORCA II

Maharishi was giving out "special techniques" for people with problems like obesity and such; I didn't have a weight problem so Maharishi asked me why I wanted to get the technique. I told him that I was gaining too much weight and found it hard to stop stuffing myself. I was really getting any technique that I could get just to have them. This was probably a habit, developed in the mad race to get all the advanced techniques and rounding courses that were offered; we were all in a race to get enlightened and we wanted to be the first to win the prize.

Sara was waiting in line with me and when we got to Maharishi, just before we got the technique, I asked him if Sara and I could become a celibate couple. I had heard that Jerry and Debby were; I just wanted to do everything I could to get enlightened fast. When I asked this question I noticed that Sara had a look on her face that said "what! you didn't ask if I wanted to do this, and your asking Maharishi?" I'm sure that he noticed and besides that he also knew very well that I wasn't really capable of being a monk, and Sara? forget about it. He didn't respond to my question but went ahead and gave us the technique which worked very well after the first and last time I did it. I went in to eat lunch and the food looked and smelled, really "off putting," I couldn't eat more than a few bites. This was a powerful tool, I thought, if I ever needed it in the future.

After this, Sara became distant and Paul and I were constantly writing, practicing and performing so I didn't see much of her at all. She even got herself a separate room down the hall from Paul, Josie and me. When Maharishi went into silence that year I went in as well. I did this every year for the week long duration of fasting, drinking only juice and water or just honey water some years. Near the end of silence I heard music playing through my window out over the ocean. When I closed my eyes I could see the Ghandarvas (celestial musicians) playing instruments, about four or five of them floating over the waves. They played for several hours until it was time to come out of silence that evening and I had to leave my room. Several of us were standing around outside Maharishi's room waiting for him to come out. Paul and I were eating too many roasted almonds after our fast. He said "were you playing music awhile ago?" I said "No! were you?" I said "I heard this beautiful music playing outside my window over the ocean and Paul said "yes, that's what I heard, like Indian instruments playing for a few hours."

Sometimes, someone would hear voices coming from Maharishi's room where he was supposed to be in silence. There were a few who said they saw men who looked like Rishis or Monks dressed in the traditional manner when they looked from the window of a room across from Maharishi's during silence.

ERROL FLYNN & SARA BURNHEART

I think it was during this time, after I came out of silence, that I saw Sara sitting with a guy who looked sorta-like Errol Flynn, having breakfast in the dining hall. I recognized him from previous courses, a rich kid raised in a broken home like many of us, only his home was a mansion with thoroughbred horses.

When I was rounding In Mallorca, I could actually hear my wife and her paramour in the room above me at night. When they moved in, two doors down from me in Fiuggi, I was really hurting, something that Sara probably couldn't imagine possible, thinking that I was so intent on being a monk that I didn't care about her; maybe she thought that? Really, I thought of her as my best friend and wife. Finally, they left for the States to legalize our divorce and their marriage.

THE WITCHES OF IBIZA

Before the Errol and Sara story began, Maharishi sent him to the island of Ibiza southwest of Mallorca. I think he was supposed to either check out hotels or teaching opportunities, not sure? Anyway, he came back pretty quick, supposedly the island has a large population of witches both male and female. Apparently, our boy was being watched and followed by them; they even stood outside the place he was staying. The word was that they were threatening and he high-tailed it out a-there.

Not long after his return it was like the dark forces gathered and created a fierce ocean storm with lightening, thunder and gale force winds. All the power went out of our hotel and Maharishi was forced to climb the six or seven flights of stairs to his room. But, instead of making it seem like a problem, Maharishi made it one of the most special nights in my time around him. He had the staff hand out candles to each of us and when he ascended the first staircase to the second floor he sat down and gathered us all around him and told us an ancient story from the puranas. By the time we reached the third floor, we were all captivated and had to know what happened next. As we were going up the stairs the thunder and the lightening got louder and more threatening with every step. When we made it up to Maharishi's floor there was only the final interpretation of the lesson to be learned from the tale, and standing there, glowing in our candlelight, he smiled and raised his hands with a "Jai Guru Dev" and all the hotel lights went on as he turned toward his room.

THE LESSON OF THE STORM

"It may be that the clouds are gathered. Let them come and go. They go as they come. Take no notice of their coming. You go your way, make your way through the clouds, if they lie on the way. Do not try to dispel them, do not be held by them, they will go the way they have come. They are never found stationary. But, if you would like to pause to see them wither away, wait for a while...the wind is blowing anyway. It is to clear the clouds from your way. Just wait to see the clouds

325

*wither away, and the sun, the same old sun of love will shine
again in fullness of its glory. When night comes, all appears
to be dark, but darkness does not last. The light of the dawn
comes on and spreads the love and charm of life. So we shall
not mind if the darkness of the night sets in for a while. For
the light of love can, for certain, not be gone forever."*

That very night at about four in the morning I turned onto my
left side and intuitively half-opened my eyes. There was a lady
in what looked like a silk dress. She was just standing there
looking down at me and glowing in a subdued, diaphanous
sort of shimmering aura that was like looking at a life sized
hologram of an astral lady. She said "Obewan, Obewan, you
are our only hope" Nah, Just kidding! couldn't resist. Anyway,
there was no negative feeling about her, no fear or elation, or
even the cold that would accompany a ghost. It was funny at
the time because I saw her and looked at her for a few moments and then just turned onto my back. When it was happening I was in a state of innocence having just woken up from
deep sleep and it meant no more to me than having seen the
wall or my shoes. But after lying there for several minutes
my ego fully manifested and the thought "I just saw a ghost or
a witch or maybe my guardian angel standing there, I guess I
should make note of it since it would be impressive to people
to talk about tomorrow."

I wondered if this glowing lady might be connected with the
island witches? Maybe she was one! These were my thoughts
at the time, since just after the return of Errol Flynn from Ibiza
the intense storm followed and seemed like some evil force
was battling with the devas just above our hotel. It was like
the eternal battle between good and evil, sattva and tamas,
yin and yang. Later, I realized that this beautiful being was
definitely not a witch or a ghost because I have awoken to
a fear filled room and seen an evil Native American Shaman
floating above me, trying to get at me, and I have awoken

to the scary, evil presence of a dead banker who haunted the basement of the late 19th century mansion my family lived in, in Fairfield Iowa, and that was a whole different experience.

KINGS AND QUEENS

There is a caste system in the TM Movement much like the one in the general society; it's based on people who have money or Movement status and those who don't. The two go hand in hand, and have for the last forty years or so, ever since the establishment of the 108. Before that in the early days of SIMS, wealth and fame took a backseat to how many courses you had been on, how long you had been meditating, if you were an initiator and how nice you were, how selfless and compassionate and how much attention you got from Maharishi.

Once the Beatles, the Beach Boys, Donovan and Merv Griffen revealed how TM could become popular with the masses virtually overnight, paying attention to famous people in entertainment, music and even science was the obvious way to accomplish Maharishi's goal of bringing humanity into a golden age of enlightenment through individual meditation. Maharishi felt he had to make the rich and the famous feel especially welcome by raising them to the highest status in the movement. This status gave them greater access to his presence and special seats at all functions. Honorific gestures, like making you a King or Queen for a million dollars, even designing special Golden Crowns and suits for you to parade yourself from your stretch-limo to the Golden Dome and onto the stage where your special padded seat awaited your arrival. And there you were, looking down on the groundlings who sat admiring the spectacle.

This was all well and good since Self-Sufficient people who aren't still obsessed with becoming even more wealthy, have the time and money to help run the world movement. People like Raja Luis, a major influence for TM in South America, have been miraculous in their ability to further the fulfillment of Maharishi's lofty goals for humanity, World Peace and Enlightenment. Of course, Maharaja Adhiraj Rajaraam, Dr. Tony Nader, MD, PhD, the present spiritual leader of the TM movement is another story. Whenever I have been present at one of his talks I can feel the presence of Maharishi. I know what Maharishi's presence feels like after seven years of basking in it, living in it and traveling in it. No doubt, Tony's got it!

Of course there are the folks who have been with Maharishi for almost fifty years who do much of the real organizing, like Bobby Roth, our beloved celebrity-schmoozer who has a way with the rich and famous, and is truly one of the most valuable assets the TM movement has ever had. Then again, he himself may not be rich but he is famous among the celebrities. The point behind all this is that while Maharishi may have impressed upon us the importance of becoming materialistically successful (self-sufficient) at the same time as he was creating innumerable costly courses, techniques and health programs that one would have to be wealthy or on international staff to actually take part in; he was also saying "it's harder for a rich man to get into heaven than it is for a camel to get through the eye of a needle.

Of course, this is the New Testament quote that the Bible says Christ made, indicating that with the increase of wealth comes an increase in a serious responsibility not to let it overshadow your humanity, to use it to help others less fortunate and thus be blessed by it. (see the King Janaka story in the Ramayana). What I'm saying, in essence, is that money really doesn't bring spiritual enlightenment. It may raise your social status in the TM movement, and in the world, in it's present materialistic state. But in reality Maharishi was just trying to get our money-crazy world to respect and to start TM. Meditate and Enjoy doing what you like. A simple and uncomplicated life is less stressful. Don't work yourself into the grave just so you can show us on Facebook how much fun you are having in Mexico, sipping umbrella drinks! "Take it easy, take it as it comes."

MAHARISHI – MAHARISHI – MAHARISHI MAHESH YOGI

One of the songs that Paul wrote was "Maharishi." It's a song you would expect to hear in a first grade classroom with it's chanting of "Maharishi, Maharishi, Maharishi Ma-hesh-Yo-gi." One late afternoon in Mallorca Maharishi wanted us to sit up in front of the lecture hall singing this song with everyone standing and joining in on the chorus like a chant. The only problem with this was that he wanted us to perform this song as he slowly walked into the hall holding two armfuls of flowers with the hostile BBC filming it. I didn't want to do it because the guys on the British film crew were serious skeptics with that superior English attitude toward "Indian Gurus" and especially toward the mindless "followers" that we appeared to be in our apparent zealous worship.

It was clear that they were there to put a phony Guru, brainwashed desciple's spin on the whole scene! I could tell by the shit-eating grins on their faces as we practiced singing with the group before Maharishi made his entrance. Later, we saw what they had managed to turn this innocent love of Maharishi into, on English TV. Maharishi and all of us were upset and I realized that perhaps I should have been bold enough to say something to him when it may have made a difference. However, it is highly unlikely that my negative prediction would have prevailed. In the vast stretch of time, who knows how many will see this video in the distant future and won't even recognize the superficial sarcasm, they might only see the great master being respected and revered.

RINDY SWARTZ

The Maharishi song was included on the Natural Tendency album, "Something Good is Happening" that we recorded with Henry Lewy at A&M Records. The kids from the first Maharishi School in LA were invited to come and sing at the studio with Paul and I on the chorus and it turned out very sweet and innocent. We stayed at the house of Rindy Swartz the daughter of a respected Psychiatrist or Psychologist. Rindy used to go out with my old music partner Kenny Edwards, she was a musician herself and treated Paul and I with great respect because we were close to Maharishi and because she loved music filled with his knowledge. She invited us to stay at her beautiful home on a cliff in the wooded hills somewhere north of Bel Aire.

Waking up and looking out over the beautiful eucalyptus trees and down the steep hills into the valley below was such a sweet way to begin our days of recording down in the city. Rindy would cook us a wonderful breakfast and then she'd be off to school at UCLA. Maharishi told her to finish her BA degree before she could come and be with him. After she got her BA he told her to get her PhD which she did. It was hard for her; not because she wasn't brilliant, but because all she wanted to do was be with her master and become Realized. She finally arrived in Seelisberg in 1975 just as I was about to leave for the New York Academy to record another album with Paul; we called it "The TM Album," after the popularity of "The TM Book" but even though it was quite beautiful, it wasn't meant to be! The time for using western music as a carrier wave for spoon feeding our hippy generation the seeds of Natural Law was over by 1975, and the actual sounds of the divine creative, the Gandharva Ved, Sama and Rig Veda became the music of the TM movement.

It was 1972 when we were staying at Rindy's and recording the best of the songs based on the SCI lessons that Maharishi had created, he called the album "Something Good is Happening." To me, it's not very interesting to go on about the recording process; it was just very fulfilling to work with the master of the recording studio, Henry Lewy and Paul wasn't too shabby either. Henry called in his list of favors owed and came up with some great LA musicians who added their creativity to our songs. Doug Dillard the great banjo player for "The Dillards" gave the song "Rest Is The Basis of Activity" a real Bluegrass flavor.

Here is the list of players and instruments
that are on the album:
(Words and music, composed and arranged by Rick
Stanley and Paul Fauerso).

"The Natural Tendency"

Production & Sound by Henry Lewy

Rick Stanley — vocals & guitar

Paul Fauerso — vocals, piano, organ

Emil Richards — vibraphone, percussion

Tom Scott — woodwinds

Cielle Kollander — vocals

Doug Dillard – banjo

Produced at A&M Studio 1972

RICK STANLEY & PAUL FAUERSO

THE NATURAL TENDENCY

Here's the song list

"Progress and Happiness"
"Knowledge is Structured in Consciousness"
"Rest is the Basis of Activity"
"The Science of Creative Intelligence"
"The Artist and the Scientist"
"Infinity"
"Water the Root to Enjoy the Fruit"
"Natural Tendency"
"200%"
"Cosmic Consciousness"
"Maharishi"
"The Seven Goals of the World Plan"

"I LOST MY HEART IN FIUGGI FONTE"

It was near the end of the course in Italy that Sara and her lover Errol flew off to the hallowed shores of Connecticut and the rare air of his families "Kennedy lifestyle." Meanwhile, Paul and I were walking across a lawn in Fiuggi Fonte when I felt a sudden painful sensation in my heart. It truly felt as if I had only half of my heart left, and I fell to the ground and said to Paul "Oh my God! my heart." He said "what? are you having a heart attack?" "I don't think so; it just feels as if my heart has been torn in two." Then I said "Sara just took her vows of marriage with Errol." Not long after this experience Paul told me that Sara and Errol were married at exactly the time that I had the heart rending.

From that moment on I felt like I was half alive, half conscious, half-hearted. I lost all desire to do anything and Maharishi told me to just take it easy and to round as much as I wished. Alone in my room I began writing a song that just appeared out of my wounded soul. As I wrote it I thought I was writing a love song about Sara but soon I realized it was about me and my capacity for loving.

"THE WAY I LOVE YOU"

"Yes, I love the way I love you, and I know you'll understand,
can you feel the soft surrender, you are love my closest friend,
no one feels sad, nothing is lost love is found,
I feel so glad....oh..oh..oh..ohohoh...love is found.
can you see now where my heart is in the moments that I sing,
can you feel the soft surrender, love I have and love I bring,
no one feels sad, nothing is lost, love is found,
I feel so glad....oh..oh..ohohoh love is found."

These are a few of the lines that I can remember, not really in the original order and most is missing but they convey the epiphany that I experienced when I wrote the song. I realized (physically, emotionally and mentally) that my love for another was actually within me...the other person could come or go but that love was mine, not theirs to take away. This realization was a total revelation for me; the fact that my love for another was mine and it was still there, even though it felt like half of my heart was gone. Just after I finished this song Maharishi called for me to sing for the course and he was sitting up on a rather high stage on his dais surrounded with beautiful flowers. He said "sing" and I started singing the new song "I love the way I love you" but Maharishi thought I was singing a broken-hearted love song, he was hoping for a knowledge song but he knew I was in the throws of healing a broken heart and thought that I could only sing about that. So, once again the song was cut short but I got a hearty applause and I believe the reason why, was because this was a knowledge song for me and quite a few people in the audience; a very subtle and real song of the Self Realization of love's true location.

The next day a girl I had been attracted to, but felt intimidated by, *(she was too educated for me, I thought)* came up and asked if she could talk to me for a moment. I said sure, and we went to my room just around the corner of the hallway. I told her I had just finished writing a new song and would she like to hear it; she said yes. I sang the song and she said "Oh, you are still upset about Sara." I said "well actually the song has healed a lot of that, it's a revelation that all this feeling is my capacity to love and it is within me and is mine; Sara didn't take it with her."

"I see," she said "now I don't know if it's appropriate to ask my question or not." I said "go ahead." She said "Well, I have been wondering if you would like to marry me?" "Wow!" I said "I wish you would ask that question in a few more months when I'm more myself." She didn't wait for anymore excuses; I'm sure underneath all that self-confidence there was a rejection defense mechanism that went off with a hair trigger. She left the room saying she was sorry and was probably embarrassed, but she had no idea how often I had thought of her and her great voice and personality; I won't mention her body, whoops! I did. We could have been a super duo; she could sing fantastic harmony and she looked so good; bad timing, terrible timing!

Anyway, when I wasn't rounding, writing and eating at great Italian restaurants I moped around Fiuggi for most of the time we were there. I like to watch people. I like to use logic, intuition and observation to figure them out, what their up to. Until I became a performing folk musician I had always felt alone, a witness to other peoples lives; even as a kid I would climb the highest tree in a park and watch others come and go, picnic, make out, whatever. This was my way of being an Indian Scout; it made me feel like I was in an adventure.

I remember seeing Errol go off to a hippy girl's room for an afternoon delight. I thought, he's so straight looking and that girl is the ultimate hippy queen; she must like his Errol Flynn face, hip or not. They came out of her room about an hour later, just as I was returning from wherever I was going an hour before when I saw them go in. Of course, our dear Errol wasn't the only rude-boy in town, several others, that I mentioned before, aspired even higher. They desired the spiritual status of Brahmacharya by taking monk's vows of celibacy with Maharishi. Only a few westerners were given this privilege at the time, only to run off with other men's wives or frequent the local flamenco bar while everyone else was doing their meditation. These "Skin Boys" were more or less man-servants to Maharishi in spite of their close physical proximity, they were far from being his closest disciples.

NED WYNN

I used to think I knew "Hollywood Ned," the "life of the party Ned," but In fact, I didn't. He had another side, that came out one day as we were sitting around a dining room table in Mallorca. There were a few other guys there and Ned was entertaining us with his witty sarcasm and brilliant comedic timing. I had just taken a mouthful of milk when Ned looked right into my eyes and delivered a punch line so powerful and hilarious that I lost my physical ability to hold the milk in. I spewed it all over Ned's beautiful cream suit. I tried to stop it with my outstretched hands but it blew all over him, his face and shirt and jacket and pants. I really believe he was trying to get me to spew that mouthful of milk by directing the climax of his joke right at me, in mid-gulp. I guess It didn't occur to him that he might be in the way of the blast!

He looked down and swore his best swears and in a fit of anger he left the table, and from that moment on he made it clear that he hated my guts. I don't remember ever talking with him again. It was pretty bogus of me to blow a mouthful of milk on his favorite cream suit...I'm sorry, I lost control! Comedian's can do that to you, and he would have made a great stand-up comedian.

THE FIUGGI GHOST

Talking about Fiuggi, Paul and Josie and I were assigned rooms in the upper city or old Fiuggi, which is located 2500 feet above sea level. The natives call it "Fiuggi Citta". Fiuggi Citta is a medieval walled and fortified village, which was around even before Roman times. Our three room apartment in the ancient house was haunted by an old lady who enjoyed waking us up at night. Our first night there, at around eleven or twelve, Josie woke us all up with a frightful scream. "EEK! there's an old woman in my bed, get out, get out." Josie jumped in bed with Paul and about an hour later he gave a loud yell.."get the F. . outa here" and he jumped out of bed and looked around the room and said "someone's touching me in my sleep, was that you Rick?" "No!" I said and went back to sleep.

It must have been about three in the morning when I felt my ear being flicked. I rolled over and sank back into sleep when my other ear was flicked. I turned my head up in an angry and abrupt movement and stared directly into the misty face of this old lady and shouted in my loudest and strongest voice "get the hell outa here." She moved so fast that all I could see was a shiny white streak that went all the way through the door to Paul and Josie's room. Paul called out "hey Rick, did she just give you a visit?" I said "Ya" and fell back to sleep till morning. When I got up Josie said that she couldn't sleep the rest of the night and Paul didn't get much rest either. We decided that we had to get out of this place that very day; I think that they got a nice hotel room at their own additional expense. I had to convince the guy with the cowboy hat who ran the course housing to find me another room and that took all day. My new building didn't have any heat or electricity as it was still under construction and the nights were getting really cold.

THE GROTTO

Earlier I mentioned eating at great restaurants. There was a real large cave that housed the best pizza place in the world. All they had was one small oven, not a professional pizza oven, just one of those half-sized little white jobs that you might see in a one bedroom flat. That's all they needed! They had a special way of making their pizza. First they flattened the dough to a thickness of about five pieces of paper. Then they baked a few of them at one time till they were just getting crisp. Then they would take them out of the oven and put all the toppings on with plenty of olive oil to soak into the shell. When the cheese was melted all over the toppings they would take them out of the oven and serve. The crust was crispy, wonderful pizza! A family had been making pizza there for at least a hundred years and according to the boy who served us the place had been an eatery for four hundred years

Now, if that wasn't cool enough, the boy who served us was ten years old and he could memorize every particular topping that eight of us had individually requested. He never wrote a thing down, you simply told him the three, four, five or even six toppings that you wanted on your pizza and he wouldn't even repeat them back to you, he would just show up fifteen or twenty minutes later with all the pizzas and every one of them had exactly the right toppings on. He even remembered who got what pizza with what toppings. He was the son who would someday inherit the Grotto and pass it down to his son or daughter. Remember that! "The Grotto" in Fiuggi Fonte if you want an experience you will never forget. Who was it that created the myth that pizza was invented in the US?

MONK - SO HORNY

There is a funny story about Paul and Josie and me when we drove up into the hills near Subiaco, Italy to find the Sacro Speco, the sacred cave where St. Benedict lived for many years. During the time that Benedict lived in this small cave tucked in the side of some very steep hills, the only way he could get food was by way of a friend who would drop a bucket on a long rope over the side of the cliffs above the cave. The bucket would contain enough food for a week but there were times when his friend couldn't come and Benedict would have to fast and live on water alone. There were times when he was tempted by visions of beautiful women and delicious foods, tempted to leave his meditations and his search for God. There was a rose bush just in front of his cave that he would jump into, thorns and all, when he was particularly overcome with sensual desires. It was St. Francis who had given Benedict the rose bush cutting when he first came to meet him. We were told all of this by the monk who was giving us a tour of the cave and the adjoining monastery.

The funny part of the story comes next. Our tour guide at St. Benedict's Monastery was a very horny middle-aged monk who, like the stereotypical Italian man, well they like to pinch women's butts. Now Josie was standing in front of his holiness as he was pointing out the frescoes above us and in his broken English, he sounded quite knowledgeable. Just as all of us were admiring the art work Josie let out a squeal and jumped a foot in the air. Paul said "what happened Josie?" and she said in a very quiet voice "he pinched my butt!" I heard her and I looked at the guy who had a sweet smile on his face, and I looked at Paul. He took Josie's hand and they walked very quickly toward the entrance with the monk trailing after shouting "No! bellissima, wait-a, wait-a, der ees mooch mor-a to see, bellissima! bellissima! Wait-a."

ST. BENEDICT MONASTERY

When we got to the car I said, "what happened, did he pinch you?" She said "not just once, he kept bumping up against me from behind. I thought it was by accident and I would move away, but he persisted and I tried to shoo him off with my hand...but he kept coming closer again and that last time he pinched my butt really hard..so I screamed."

THE BIG SPENDER

Paul was going to Rome to buy some suits and he asked me if I'd like to go. I guess his usual fashion-friends weren't around at the time. There were a couple of aesthetically-inclined young men who enjoyed Paul's company and the chance to help him spend his money. I suppose Paul just recognized the actual talent these guys had for fashion and the finer things. Anyway, I figured that since I didn't have any money, going shopping with a guy who intended to have a couple of fine Italian suits hand tailored would leave me bored stiff in a sitting room. Paul remedied the situation by offering to let me pick out something for myself, so off we went

When we arrived I imagined that I would be standing there with Paul and we would both have a little Italian man fussing around the hems of our suit pants and measuring our arms and chests for the jackets. Well, Paul was all set to do just that, at least for himself, he was picking out the material for his two suits when he noticed that I was standing there wondering what the deal was. He came over and said "Oh, Rick do you want to pick out a tie for yourself?" I said, "Oh, ok!" and that was my reward for tagging along. I actually thought he might be getting us similar suits to wear when we performed as a duo, something that would have added a professional touch of class to our performances; instead of him impeccably dressed, and me in my ten year old, ugly sport jacket.

On another trip to Rome we went with Josie and ate at two of the best specialty restaurants in the old city. One of the places was famous for their eggplant Parmesan which was outrageously good. Fresh melted mozzarella an inch deep over a small, steaming, soup bowl full of crispy Parmesan encrusted eggplant in a spicy marinara sauce; It was the best I've ever had. The other place had extremely good spinach fettuccine Alfredo, yum! Still, the Fauerso's really had a hard time with generosity to others who weren't able to afford their rich taste in everything. Maharishi had tied Paul and I together with his music projects and I found myself having to accompany my music partner to expensive restaurants that I couldn't afford. I've never held it against anyone if they were generous, only if they weren't.

Even though I had no problem with people sharing their money karma with me, Paul and Josie had experienced the negative side of giving freely of their nouveau-riche status when Josie first inherited her trust fund. Paul's group, "The Loading Zone" were probably the first to find out that their keyboard player was no longer lacking in funds to buy whatever he needed. They soon started hitting-up Paul and Josie for big ticket items, usually in the form of a loan which they would never pay back. I'm sure it became a drag when everywhere they went all the group members would expect the Fauerso's to cover the expenses, restaurants, gas, etc. Finally, after many thousands of dollars of Josie's money had been lent and spent by the boys in the band; the Fauersos cut them all off.

What interested me was that the money wasn't cut off because of the outrageous demands by the freeloaders but because these old friends began to resent the fact that they owed the Fauersos so much money that they opted out of their friendship rather than pay back what they owed. The generosity of the Fauersos caused the resentment and jealousy of their friends and group members. Understandably, much like most people with money, the Fauersos seem to socialize mostly with other people with money, and pretend their money is all tied up in investments if they are waylaid by hungry meditators with get-rich-quick-schemes. I guess it was easier to just make a rule to go by and stick to it. I don't know, never had that problem! Years later, in the late 1970's, Josie's monthly allotment dwindled quite a bit, at least that's what Paul told me, and that seemed to put the fear of poverty into their hearts; only for a few years though, until the mother-load inheritance. I guess the moral of this tale is: "you can't have poor friends when your rich unless you're willing to just treat-em-all like your kids."

SPONTANEOUS BACKGROUND MUSIC

The final days of the Fiuggi TTC found Paul and I sitting on a stage in what looked like a large, dark, dance hall with a low ceiling and all the course participants performing the puja for experienced Initiators in order to fulfill the teaching requirements. We were there to play background music to cover the whispered transmission of mantras from Maharishi to each of His students as they finished their puja performance and stepped up to the dais to receive their mantras, one by one. My guitar was in an open tuning so that I could play raga-like drones and improvisational melodies. Paul was also droning and chording on his harmonium and I think he played the flute for awhile as well. We kept playing and playing for hours, I think it was a total of six hours a day over a two day period until Maharishi had instructed every new Initiator, and by then we were drunk with blissful fullness in a unity of spontaneous creative expression.

The whole atmosphere in that hall was thick with Awareness that increased by the hour; it was almost like being under water. All of us were so connected, there were no longer individual personalities. We were all joined in one warm, incense filled Being with the soft singing of many pujas and the harmonious music pouring through Paul and I by some unseen master musicians playing us as their instruments. We were brought food and drink and one of us would continue to play while the other ate. When it was all over, Paul and I stood up and found that we couldn't really walk, we were so inebriated with pure consciousness mixed with Bliss that we had to take some time to get acquainted with our bodies abilities to function in ways that had nothing to do with playing music.

TIME IS AN ILLUSION, OR IS IT JUST ME?

All these stories are separate little memory bubbles that have no connection. Unlike fictional stories in which the Moderator can remember every word that was spoken and every action that led to the present and all future dialogue and actions as well. So, forgive me for not remembering the place in time that each of these bubbles occupied and when each one was created. In fact, much like those last moments of life in a body when you see your entire life unfold before your eyes in a matter of seconds, these memories, whether from childhood or from last year, all seem to be from now as I write them down. The only difference is how clear they are, one to the other, and that I feel, is based on how deeply they made an impression on me; emotionally, mentally, physically and even sensually. A smell will open a memory bubble as vibrantly as a visual cue or the sound of a voice or taste of a candy I had as a child.

LA ANTILLA

La Antilla Spain was the next stop on my seven year adventure with Maharishi. The Rig Veda pundits, Brahmarishi Devarat, his son Somashravas who looked like an American Indian and the Sama Veda pundits, Krishnaswami with his great, strong voice and withered left arm and his partner, Subramanyam, the "Loud Snorer," were living in the basement of Maharishi's hotel." This rather skinny pundit was the bane of the basement dwelling Indians. One day I walking down there to meet with krishnaswami about getting me a sitar when he went home to Bombay, when I heard, what sounded like a full grown male lion roaring down the cement walled hallway. Devindra, Maharishi's top Brahmachari, half English, half Indian, very tall and a lawyer as well, came up to me and said "Isn't that awful? it's the middle of the day and he does this all night as well." I said "who?" and he mentioned the name that I can't remember. I think Devindra was embarrassed about the Loud Snorer being an Indian; it was one of the grossest things I've heard in my life, although from what my wife tells me, I might even be able to compete with the little guy.

BRAHMARISHI DEVARAT

BRAHMARISHI DEVARAT, HIS SON & MAHARISHI

Brahmarishi Devarat and the others lived in the basement of our hotel in a series of stark, cement rooms. He lived mostly on Carnation instant milk. I watched as he filled a gallon jug in the bathtub and mixed in the powder for half an hour before it became drinkable. The old guy was supposed to have cognized some sutras of the Veda that hadn't been cognized before. One day he invited us all down to the dining room to watch him dance to the Vedic Hymns. We had never been told that there was actually a traditional dance intimately connected with Vedic recitation that had been passed down, father to son, master to disciple for thousands of years.

Needless to say, most of us were on the edge of our seats to see the old master in his dhoti and bare feet prancing around the hall with his white beard and twinkling eyes. He looked quite happy to be sharing this little known part of the Vedas with us, but suddenly the door swung open and one of the "blue-suits/red-tie gestapo," rudely interrupted the happy occasion declaring that Brahmarishi would have to show us the dance later, that Maharishi requested that the venerable old sage meet with Him. It was all too apparent that Maharishi didn't want the westerners to see Brahmarishi perform the dance. I'm sure that M. thought that some of us would think it was silly or undignified for an old man to show his legs as he pranced about but I knew all the people in attendance, there were only twenty or so, all very respectful and admiring of Brahmarishi. The worst they would have done was to be impressed with his mastery of Vedic Tradition. But of course if he had danced the whole course of two thousand would have wanted to see it and that could have ended up on the evening news as representative of what you do when you start TM. Maharishi always had his pragmatic reasons, almost always based in his one pointed desire to spread TM the world over.

Occasionally, I'd be walking down the hallway on Maharishi's floor and I would pass by the kitchen. There he'd be, Devarat, the old sage cooking up some special sweet treat, fried in ghee. Usually, he would call me in and offer his latest delicacy with a great smile on his face. He would be all covered with chick pea flour and smelling of turmeric and curry. He'd walk down the hallway poking his head into each room and offering his treats to everyone. Maharishi didn't like him to behave in such an "undignified" manner because he knew that westerners and many Indians as well, just don't respect childlike innocence as an enlightened behavior. Of course when they talk about enlightenment, childlike innocence is on the list but when they see it in real life they don't understand it, they see it as weakness, not dignified, not greatness. For me, these two qualities are my favorite behaviors in all creatures, great and small.

SENSUAL THREADS & GOLDEN NEEDLES

There were all sorts of healing modalities going on during the course. Dr. "E" was trying his hand at Chinese acupuncture with golden needles and an attractive nurse who would hold the needle once it was stuck into whatever part of you that seemed appropriate to your problem. The problem was that these two were having a steamy affair after hours and when I was under their care all that steam went from her hand directly into my body and I was trying to be "M group" and celibate. One time they were holding clinic on the beach in the warm sun and I was lying there on the massage table; E stuck a needle in my solar plexus and the nurse moved it about and twirled it. All the while they were exchanging fond glances with licking of lips and adjusting of hips. I could feel her passion pouring through my body and heading straight for my privates. When I got back to my room I had to relieve myself of the sexual pressure that had been transferred through the needles and had taken over my second chakra; the unwelcome gift of two would-be healers. They had obviously not read enough from the books of Chinese Acupuncture to practice the art. I'm sure that the state of physical and mental purity of the healer is a prerequisite to healing others of impurities in traditional theory and practice.

The weird thing is that the next day when Maharishi got back from one of his many trips, he looked me over, took my flower and said "Very good, you have done very well." Maybe the fact that I didn't go out and seduce one of the course girls to solve my 2nd chakra problem was, having done "very well." Or, maybe he thought I did have sex with someone and was looking forward to seeing me get married again since I was never able to prevail for very long over my attraction to feminine grace. It might have been the last choice since he said the same thing to me a couple of years later when I had been intimate with a young lady on staff and he had returned from wherever.

He took my flower and said "Very good, you have done very well."

A year later she did end up convincing me to marry her so she could stay in the USA. But, that doesn't hold water either because he didn't really seem to approve of that marriage! Of course, on his return he hadn't met the girl yet! It's hard to second guess Divine Intelligence. All I know is that after the La Antilla course when we went to live in Switzerland for three years, Seelisberg, Vitznau, Veggis, Hertenstein, Gersau, Brunnen, Engelberg, Mürren and Arosa, Maharishi kept putting me to work with lady musicians and girls he thought might make good wives for me; just one at a time, of course. After all these years of what-if's, it is painfully clear that any of them would have been preferable to the choice I made in a state of total unstressing.

Maharishi had me work together with a few talented ladies, for the wonderfully creative music combined with Maharishi's knowledge that we wrote together, and of course, in hopes that the girls might find a like minded husband and I, a musical wife. This was after Paul had decided to go to music school in Texas; he was feeling unfulfilled with "The little songs" we were writing, as if the size of a musical piece has anything to do with it's depth and emotional power. I'd put "Moon River" or "Eleanor Rigby," maybe "Like A Rolling Stone" or "Penny Lane" up against almost any Classical composition for its ability to move the human heart, well, my heart anyway!

After all, much of traditional "Classical" music was based on folk ballads which are expressions of real human emotions. The mathematically minded composer would make the folk melody the theme of his "masterpiece" and add endless complicated counter-melodies, harmonies and key changes until the original song had lost it's soul, and one would have to be a student of the technical genre to appreciate what the composer had done to it. I'm referring to some of the more arcane technical pieces in which I can find little that moves me. They seem as if created by computers, exercises in just how mathematically complicated can my genius make this. Of course there is classical music that absolutely causes the heart to soar; Oh my God, Pavarotti where are you?

MILEY & MURREN

Moving right along, my first Maharishi inspired musical partnership with a lady was with fellow 108, Miley. She could play a little guitar and keyboard and she had a nice voice, a bit much on the classical vibrato but we managed to meet in the middle between Folk and Opera. I first met Miley when I was teaching TM in the San Francisco area with the Fauersos. She was in the San Francisco Opera Chorus and I thought of her as a rather conservative, straight person, in other words, she didn't dress like a student, an artist or a musician and she was more inhibited or restrained than I was used to. Her sister was just the opposite. Anyway, many of the people who were actively working on projects with Maharishi, and all the 108's went way up into the Alps almost to the top of a mountain to a little Shangrila called Mürren. Mürren is a traditional Walser mountain village in Bernese Oberland, Switzerland, at an elevation of 1,650 m above sea level and unreachable by public road. That's two hundred feet over a mile straight up by cablecar, the only way you can get up there.

A series of four cable cars, known as the Luftseilbahn Stechelberg-Mürren-Schilthorn (LSMS), provides transportation from Mürren downhill to Gimmelwald and Stechelberg, and uphill to the summit of the Schilthorn and the revolving restaurant Piz Gloria. This was a principal filming location for the James Bond movie "On Her Majesty's Secret Service," released in 1969, in which Bond (George Lazenby) made his escape from the headquarters of Ernst Stavro Blofeld (Telly Savalas) and fled four of Blofeld's henchmen in a car driven by his girlfriend Tracy (Diana Rigg). As I was being pulled up that steep grade by a single steel cable, I couldn't help but think what it would be like if the cable got loose way up there. It didn't, but it's a really freaky ride up and a little less riding down.

HALF WAY UP THE MOUNTAIN

PIZ GLORIA THE REVOLVING RESTAURANT

I can't remember many of the songs we were writing at the time but it was one of Maharishi's projects that required over twenty songs, one for each of the "The Sixteen Principles of SCI" and a song for each of "The five Fundamentals of Education." I'm sure that Miley and I didn't write all twenty one songs but it was probably the ideal goal of our project. We wrote quite a few and actually worked up at least five for performance.

I can remember performing with Miley for Maharishi, the 108, and all the staff. We had some nice harmonies and even though the lyrics sounded like Sesame Street lesson-songs they actually expressed real truths of life, a little less on the poetic side than the songs I did with Maharishi for the "Song of Life" album and the "Something Good Is Happening" album with Paul Fauerso.

Back then I was still attracted to girls who emitted pheromones in large quantities and who flirted with me blatantly enough for me to overcome my timidity. For a few days after a performance I would expect a few girls to be interested, but if I hadn't performed I was too frightened of rejection to approach anyone who didn't display overt signs of attraction. I could tell that Miley was interested in me but she was so dignified and even more guarded against rejection than I was, and then, she knew I had no money. She however, has always had money and has continuously expressed an interest in me up to 2012+. Her sister often made a point of letting me know that Miley "Was Willin." Back in Mürren we kind of bumped off each other like two positive poles trying to touch. Not long after Mürren when we were all comfortably situated in Seelisberg, Miley needed a ride to Zurich to catch a jet to her home in San Francisco. She asked if I would drive her to the airport and we got permission to use one of the staff cars.

By the time we got to the Zurich airport I was starving. I hadn't eaten breakfast that morning and I didn't have any money for lunch. Miley wanted me to drop her off at the front entrance. I had expected her to treat me to lunch, or at least ask if I wanted coffee before I made the return drive, you know, as a thank you for driving her what was a total of four hours back then. Now, you can make the drive in just over an hour each way. Anyway, I watched her walk into the airport without the slightest concern for me. She knew I didn't have much money but how can a person who has never been without money imagine what it would be like to have No money and No food all day! I'm sure that if I had told her my situation she might have been more forthcoming, but this one instance gave me an insight into how it would be for no money to marry into money. Of course I had already seen this outcome in the lives of Josie and Paul, he seemed to be under pressure to make his own money. I'm sure one would want to in that situation.

Miley expected to hear from me or perhaps thought I'd write her a letter but I was pissed off and couldn't help resenting her lack of consideration in Zurich. This is how I thought at the time; now I know I had only myself to blame for not making a deal with Miley. I'll be your chauffeur, you buy me lunch. A week or two later a friend of hers told me that she called and wanted to talk to me. The girl gave me her number but I didn't have the money to call San Francisco and she didn't say to call collect. So, what we have here is a failure to communicate, on my part for not waking her up to the possibility that some of us don't have money to do the things that others take for granted. On her part, for a lack of sensitivity, consideration and perhaps even curiosity as to why I lost interest. Anyway, that was Maharishi's first attempt to get me married again or as he used to say, "Settled."

HOTEL GHOSTS

When we first arrived in Mürren we were busy trying to get our rooms livable. What I mean by that is that many of these old European hotels have dead people "living" in them. Or, should I say, have dead people occupying another dimension which exists in the same space as the one we occupy. An example of this is when your trying to sleep in the big old oak bed and you feel really cold no matter how many comforters or wool pajamas you cover yourself with, your freezing! I had one of those rooms, so I took the mattress off the bed and slept on the floor for a few nights which actually solved the problem of sharing the bed with the ghost because his or her astral mattress didn't move to the floor when I moved the physical one. His or her negative, cold space still made the room colder than normal but bearable.

On day three in Mürren, one of the video boys who claimed that he was the reincarnation of Leonardo DaVinci was going around all the rooms in the hotel saying that if you had a problem with ghosts he was the man that could get rid of them for you. He knocked and asked and I said "yes, I have one on the bed." He closed his eyes for five seconds and started for the door. I said, "hey, what did you do?" He said, "I just tell them to go to God." It turned out that this was exactly what Maharishi told us to do in the same situation. It actually took another day before I noticed that the cold had gone and the feeling of someone being there had disappeared. Since then I have helped several souls pass over from the earth plane using this very same telepathic encouragement.

THERESA OLSON & THE "WEE FOLK"

I was walking down the little roadway from the hotel into the tiny town of Mürren when Theresa Olsen came happily by and started to tell me about the "wee folk" who kept her awake half the night. She said she was sleeping soundly and noticed that her cover kept falling off. She pulled it up several times until it became apparent that it wasn't falling; it was being pulled by someone. She peeked over the side of her bed and saw three little people pulling her covers off. She immediately got up and they made their purpose clear. They wanted her to do a puja, so she did one but then they wanted another. After three pujas poor tired Theresa shooed them all away and got in bed but was unable to sleep. She ended up doing her meditation and coming out for a walk. I knew that I would remember her story for the rest of my life, like the one she told me when I ran into her outside of the Kulm hotel in Seelisberg. I saw her looking up above the hotel, way up at cloud level. I said "what are you looking at?" She said "There is a battle going on, a Rakshasa is fighting with a Deva." I asked who was winning and she said she didn't know yet.

THERESA "OLSEN" SORFLATEN

THE PHYSICIST

Somehow, my memory is telling me that it was when we were in Mürren that Larry Domash, the physicist, was working with Maharishi quite a lot and he would treat himself to all the finest things that money could buy at the "movement's" expense, presumably to counter balance being in the master's powerful presence more than he could handle. I saw him in one of the finest hotel restaurants one late afternoon with a smile on his face as he launched into a juicy fillet mignon steak with all the colorful side dishes and a full bottle of very expensive wine. I watched him because he looked so happy grounding himself with food and drink. Larry went on to help Maharishi lay the groundwork for the math courses at MIU and he made the videos for the "Core" courses on physics and SCI. I had seen his appetite for food, red meat and wine (taboo around Maharishi) and his taste and appetite for girls was just as healthy. There was a cute red head that he would bring back to his room which was just down from mine. She would giggle and giggle for most of my meditation and I wondered if he actually still meditated; maybe he was just forgetful with all that cuteness and those big blue eyes to fathom. Ya, sure, I was slightly envious. He seemed to have his cake and was enjoying eating it to! Sorry, that's even too corny for me.

When I was staying on Lake Lucern at the Seeblick Hotel and Maharishi was down the lake a few miles in Hertenstein, the professors and Maharishi were still organizing MIU. I would attend some of these meetings, but for the most part they were extremely boring for me. I decided to write a song about Larry, thinking that Maharishi would like his professors to be honored in this way. So, as I sat listening to Larry go on about one discipline and then put his two cents in about another, not even in his field of expertise, yet seeming to be knowledgeable, without any argument from the PhD's in the subjects he felt impelled to claim for himself, I wrote a little song for him:

> Larry Domashy-he, tells us a story,
> He tells us a story bout Einstein's glory,
> everything he says, it sounds like a thesis,

in Physics and Chemistry, Math and Biology.

That's all I can remember of it! I asked Maharishi if he wanted to hear my new song. He said, "yes, sing, sing." So I did and he looked at me as if he were wondering what had gotten into me. He obviously didn't appreciate the song. I know now that it was something you just didn't do; sing the praises of one of the master's worker bees while the greatest man on earth is sitting there and you are ignoring the amazing things that he is doing to rid the world of suffering. Oh well! Larry loved it. He had always ignored me before I wrote him a song, probably thought that I was full of myself being the darling troubadour of the movement. But when I ran into him on my way to my room, he smiled and said "thank you for the song man, I really appreciated that." The song was never heard by human ears again, but at least it won Larry over to stop ignoring me.

JANE

Maharishi's entourage traveled so often that I'm having a hard time remembering where we went when, but it was 1972 when I see myself on a jet sitting next to Jane, a cute, athletic 108 from a wealthy Connecticut family. I had on headphones and was in a state of ecstasy listening to Eric Clapton's new hit song "Layla." The music was filled with martial intensity, gloriously brave warriors charging headlong into battle on fearless stallions with eyes blazing fire, and steel swords flashing. Of course, that is my own internal music video but I bet there are others who see something similar. Jane seemed to like men, I guess we were men? but as I look back at us we were more boys than men in the 70's. She would have at least two or three that she was spending a little time with each day and as we prepared to land at Queen's University in Kingston, Ontario, she seemed interested in me.

Once I was settled in my room I heard a knock at the door and opened it to see Jane standing there with a coquettish grin. She said she just wanted to make sure she knew where my room was, then she was down the stairs before I could respond. I went to my window that looked out over the entrance to the building and saw her walking up to a handsome young man I hadn't seen before. I figured he must be one of the symposium participants that she knew from before. Jane's flirtation didn't lead anywhere until some time later in La Antilla Spain. I guess she decided to spend her time at the Queen's symposium with that handsome guy.

BOOS & BLISS

That evening Paul and I were told that we were to perform a few songs for the course so we did a quick practice of two of our most popular TM Songs. There were around 1,000 young people from all over the USA and Canada in the Concert Hall. The stage was about 30 feet long and the Rig Veda pundits, Brahmarishi Devarat and his son, were sitting next to Paul and I; Maharishi was sitting on a dais on the other side of them. I can only remember one other time that Maharishi encouraged everyone at an introductory course to improve their appearance by getting haircuts and wearing ties, but he was quite serious about it this time and some of them started booing. However, the majority shut down the rude boys by finding them laughable, and when Maharishi joined in laughing, there was no controlling the crowd.

It was almost like a drinking party of best friends, the Hall was shaking with riotous laughter; almost falling out of your chair laughter for four or five minutes. Suddenly, we heard a loud tapping noise on a microphone. I looked to my right and saw Maharishi hitting his mic with a rose and falling back and forth in his seat, trying to control his high pitched laughter. He took a minute or two to stop laughing every time he tried to begin speaking. The joy that was experienced by just about everyone in the hall was probably the most enlightening part of the course. It was obvious that this little man packed a powerful punch of bliss just sitting there and that was exactly what each and every soul in the room was there for. By the time Paul and I finished singing and ended our set with the Holy Tradition, the feeling level of the crowd had melted into devotion, reverence and a heartfelt smile on every face in the Hall.

JANE etc.

Jane wasn't one of the girls that Maharishi paired me up with to do music or as a potential wife. She seemed to be around just to be in Maharishi's incredible vibe and at the same time she was interested in self-sufficient (wealthy) males. She was interested in me, it seemed, entirely because I was trying so hard to be celibate and "one pointed" as an "M" group member, and of course, I was readily available in my room most of the time, rounding & writing music as a free-to-do as I wished, Troubadour for Maharishi. I think it started in La Antilla when she knocked on my hotel room door and said she wanted to talk to me. She would stare into my eyes with a big blue intensity and those Colgate perfect white teeth pouring out of her interested smile.

In Switzerland she used to make a stop at Michael Dimmick's room before mine and I think John Loyd enjoyed her company for awhile as well, they liked to play tennis together. That was before John and I taught a Teacher Training Course in Engelberg a little way from Seelisberg, where the TM Movement owned a couple of hotels, the Sonnenberg and the Kulm. I'm not saying she would have sex with all of us, but she would certainly tempt me. She was like a delicious meal set in front of a starving man and she seemed to enjoy this kind of flirtation.

We went for a long walk down the beautiful Spanish beach, at least five miles, with a brisk salt wind whipping our hair around. She had on a skimpy bikini, not like those string things they cram into their butts and crotches these days which are less appealing to some of us old-school geezers. The longer we walked the more I wanted to lay down in the warm sand with her but she didn't seem to be interested. I wasn't obvious about it! I just felt that way and could feel nothing from her. On the way back we passed through some high dunes and my craving grew as our privacy increased.

She was strange! When she came to my room she would move about smiling and oozing sexuality but out here in the sun and sand with the cool breeze where I was far more tempted, I was the last thing on her mind. For me it was sort of like the way food tastes so much better outside, the thought of cuddling on a remote, secluded beach seemed to increase my appetite for her. We were almost back to the hotel when she raised her arms and started singing Ra, Ra, Ra, and something else I can't remember, but she was moving across the sand in zigzags and circles singing Ra to the Sun which was setting in the west into the ocean. It seemed that Jane felt the eyes of God were on her out in Nature and that made sense to me considering her mind was almost entirely absorbed in the environment during our long walk.

Maharishi wasn't thrilled with my on again off again flirtations with Jane. One time she and I were waiting for others to show up for a meeting with the master and the three of us were sitting in the same little room for at least a half hour. He would look at me and then at Jane in total silence. She was extroverted and sometimes a little rash and Maharishi could sense our sensual attraction in our behavior. Not long after that I was being interviewed for an advanced technique and Maharishi said "you don't even do your night technique, why get another one?" I'm sure I went all red, and I got mad at the same time because I always did my night technique, Jane and I hardly ever met at night and we really didn't do much as far as sex went. Anyway, I responded with "I always do my night technique" and he acquiesced and instructed me in my next advanced technique.

I'm pretty sure that Maharishi had asked Paul or Josie about Jane and I after we had been in the room together with him, because I can remember Paul knocked on my door one night, a week or so before my advanced technique interview, and when he saw that Jane wasn't in my room he said "Oh, where's Jane?" and I said "I don't know, she is never here at night." He looked at me with a sarcastic little smile and said "Uh-huh!" He actually warned me that I really shouldn't be hanging out with her, that she was bad news and Maharishi was upset that she was causing problems with many of the 108's who were trying to be one pointed and focused on their work for the Movement and the knowledge.

It was all very true but it was also hard to stop a beautiful girl from coming to your room and flirting with you. She told me that she found out some of her past lives and that in the last one she was a dark witch, a seeress who lived by a small pond and performed black magic for those who would come to her and request her help. That seemed plausible to me at the time considering how hard she was making it for me to be celibate, not to mention the others, most of whom I never knew about.

RECORDING THE PANDITS

RIG & SAMA VEDA PANDITS,
TRINIDAD CA 1972

Some of us were lucky enough to be with Maharishi when he brought the Rig and Sama Veda pundits a little way up the coast from Arcata CA, to a house on the ocean cliffs of Trinidad in order to record them on video and audio. We were all over the place in this glass walled rental. Maharishi and the pundits with the video crew took up most of the big room with the rest of us scattered about on the floors and in a few chairs that were there. The place sat a comfortable distance from the wild cliffs which stood a hundred feet above the vast Pacific ocean. Pacific? I've never understood why they named it the Pacific, the waves are huge compared to the Atlantic where I grew up, and the rough and ragged coastline with it's jagged boulders jutting up for the surf to smash and throw cold white water into clouds is everything but pacific. Northern California is more like the west coast of Brittany times 10.

The pundits chanted night and day for about four days straight and we sat as long as we could in what seemed like meditation on sound, the repetitive chanting of the sounds of the Veda. It was intense and expansive, especially the Sama Veda with Krishnaswami and his deep powerful voice playing off the higher raspy voice of his partner. A year or so later I found out what made Sama so powerful. It was Paul who noticed it first, the high pitched drone that sounded like a third voice when the two pundits were chanting. It didn't sound like it was pronouncing the mantras or words of the chant but it was created by the tones that they were singing, a perfect fifth of pure harmonic sound vibration above the pundits.

When Paul asked me if I could hear it, I listened for a moment and said "yes, I wondered what that was." We asked Krishnaswami and he was a little surprised that we could hear it, he said "that is the voice of Mother Divine, the Sama Veda has a scale of seven pure tones or notes that are all capable of intoning the third voice that you hear. The more we are successful in singing those notes in perfect tune, one to the other, the more clearly you can hear the third voice or harmonic, and the more powerful is the affect on the environment." Paul said that the third voice was always a perfect fifth above the pundit's voices and he was right.

I could also hear that voice, the fifth above the notes, in some Celtic melodies especially when sung by the Irish and Scottish Sean-Nos singers, the ancient Celtic style of singing. However, they don't sing all the notes of the Sama Veda scale and as a result you can only hear the third voice every third or fourth note depending on the scale and melody. But still it is there, no wonder Celtic melody moves me like no other.

I can't remember sleeping during those four days. There were around twenty of us and it was just a two bedroom house. I think we just slept off and on; when we couldn't sit any longer we would just lie down on the floor with our coats under our heads. I seem to remember that someone was cooking up food in the kitchen and samosas and paper cups with rice and dahl would be passed around every once in awhile. We were mostly surviving on the celestial atmosphere of pure prana being cooked up by Maharishi and the pundits.

Once Maharishi was satisfied with the taping of both the Sama and Rig Vedas he decided he would like to see the 5000 year old Redwood tree which was just up the coast and inland at the Redwoods State & National Parks. When we got there Maharishi had the pundits do a special puja to the tree that he said was here when Lord Krishna walked the earth. He seemed as delighted to be sitting beside this great ancient tree as I've seen him when he is in the company of his saintly friends Tat Wali Baba or Laksmanjoo.

Above: The first seated row from the left is Brahmarishi Devarat's Son, Somashravas, B. Devarat, Maharishi, Sama Pundit Krishnaswami, Sama Pundit Subramanyam "Loud Snoarer." The next row standing from the left is John Loyd, Never knew the next guy's name, ?,? ,?, Dr. Squires on the end.

THE MIT SYMPOSIUM

MIT, The Massachusetts Institute of Technology was a memorable symposium for me. Maharishi asked Paul and I to sing several songs for the packed lecture hall. My father Norm and his 2nd wife Barbara were there in the front row. This was the first and last time my father would ever see me 'doin ma thang,' if you will! He was of the opinion that guitar playing crooners were just a fad, not real music like his jazz, especially swing. To me his music was great stuff, I grew up hearing it; I was force-fed Benny Goodman, Errol Garner, The Jazz Messengers, The Dorsey's and he even liked Sinatra, because "The Voice" was a jazz band crooner. Whenever he would drive us home from Grammy's, usually every weekend except during the summer, we would be treated to non-stop jazz on the car radio and Dad drumming real good on the steering wheel.

At the end of Maharishi's evening lecture which ended with Paul and I singing around four songs, Maharishi stayed seated on his dais with all those beautiful flowers around him and I brought my father and Barbara up to introduce them and I presented Barbara as my mother. They were very shy but it was kinda sweet. Later Maharishi asked me "was that your mother? I thought the lady I met in Seelisberg was your mother!" He remembered my real mother Jean, as "A very old soul." Of course, then I told him that Barbara was my step mother. At this point I figured he understood the reason I introduced her as my mother but for your edification it was because she had always wanted to be our real mother ever since she had taken our father away from us. Like most step mothers, she hated my real mother, and Jean, in turn, didn't have much love for her. In Maharishi's presence I could only be my most empathetic and compassionate self.

After Dad and Barbara had gone home I was walking through the audience still milling about, and a bright and friendly guy with a big smile approached and said,"Rick, loved the music, my name is Rusty Schweickart." "Hi" I said, not knowing who

Rusty Schweickart was, but like George Harrison, (1st book story) he seemed to be optimistic that everyone he met must know him and had I any interest in the space program I'm sure I would have. When he realized that I was clueless, he said "I'm an astronaut, the Apollo 9 Lunar Mission." I probably said "Wow" or "Cool," musician speak from the 60's that is still part of my non-conformist, artistic self-identity and what I usually say when someone tells me almost anything. Well, the "Cool" is for almost anything and the "Wow" is for something impressive or sarcasm. "Wow, that's really Cool" might be even closer to my response to Rusty's introduction.

RUSTY SCHWIECKART APOLLO ASTRONAUT

Rusty got kind of quiet, and said "let's sit over here, I want to show you something. Have you ever seen a UFO?" I said "yes, I have" and he smiled again and said "then you will appreciate these." He opened a large manila envelope and took out several large black and white photographs and proceeded to show them to me one by one, explaining where and when they were taken. He said that they were constantly being observed by UFO's during the mission and that Commander James A. McDivitt took most of the photographs. The NASA photos below are a selection of McDivitt's and some of the more recent Apollo and Mars missions.

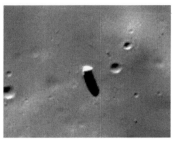

MONOLITH ON MARS MOON 255 FT HIGH

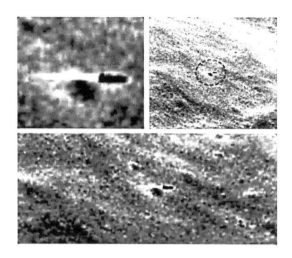

LOOKS LIKE A TORPEDO SHOOTING ACROSS THE MOON,
PROBABLY ONE OF THOSE CIGAR SHAPED SHIPS?

NASA PHOTO

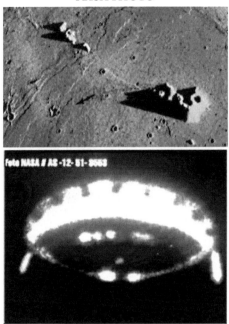

REMAINS OF BUILDINGS?

MOONHENGE?

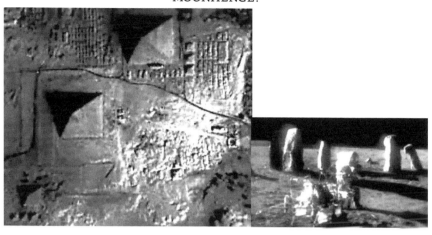

PYRAMIDS!

OBVIOUSLY NOT INHABITED LATELY!

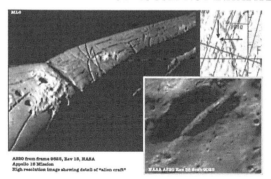

An Ancient Ship on the dark side of the Moon, supposedly over a million years old. Amazingly, it looks very much like one that recently crossed through our solar system. No one had ever seen a comet or space rock that was cigar shaped before, and some scientists believe it's a ship like this one!"

(The above) are NASA pictures of buildings and towers, whole city sized complexes on the Moon. No wonder we don't go there anymore! It's the base of operations for more advanced civilizations to monitor the war-like peoples of the Earth, to make sure we don't destroy our own beautiful planet and everything on it. It's interesting that UFO sightings dramatically increased when we figured out how to manipulate the atomic level of creation; from the late 1940's when we started destroying each other with nuclear weapons. For me, it's a great relief to know that we won't be allowed to destroy Mother Earth. It's far more likely that She will destroy the cancers that inhabit her surface through their own ignorance and greed, those of us who have polluted and ravaged her once pristine body. "If we continue to allow greed to thrive on our planet, if money equals power over our environment and everything else in our lives, we are doomed to our own self-destruction."*(DavidBryant)*

"In September 2013, I (David Bryant) had the privelege of chatting to Apollo 9 Astronaut **Rusty Schweickart** and also of attending a lecture he gave the following day. To my amazement, he was very forthright about the existence of life elsewhere in the cosmos and hinted that its existence has already been accepted within the scientific / intelligence community in the USA."

RUSTY & DAVID BRYANT UFO RESEARCHER

THE EARTH FROM THE MOON

GRAMMY LEAVES WITH TWO ANGELS

Being at MIT with Maharishi at the exact time that my dearest relative "Grammy Stanley" died, was a miracle in my life. I hadn't seen Gram for years and she lived all alone in the house by the beach at Fort Point. My father told me that when she was diagnosed with cancer it was all over her heart, far too advanced to do anything about. They took her to her daughter Dot's house for a short while and finally to the hospital. When I arrived in Boston, Dad took me to see her and she immediately got up out of bed to sit in a chair, I guess she didn't like being visited as an invalid. She said "Oh, Teddy it's so good to see you." My father looked at me as if to say "she doesn't remember names anymore, but I could see the love pouring out of those sweet, caring old eyes; she knew exactly who I was.

The next day my brother Ted told me that Grammy had died soon after my visit with her, and that there would be a funeral in a day or two. I wasn't sad, she was in a lot of pain and had been for years, even when I stayed with her on weekends back when I was a kid she would rock in her rocking chair saying "oh Ricky, my poor old legs." As long as I can remember she had been in pain from severe arthritis and then the cancer all around her heart which I'm sure she manifested from years of worry. She spent her whole life worrying about her son Norm and all his troubles. She had paid her dues and I was glad she was free to be with God whom she truly believed in.

The day of the funeral I was ushered into the viewing room

where Grammy's body was lying in a casket in front of rows of chairs. No one was in the room when I went in; they were all out in the entrance room too scared to go in. I immediately went over by her body and pulled a chair up close. I looked at her lying there and I could see some shimmering light just above her and knew that was her spirit. I closed my eyes and thought the Holy Tradition as if doing a mental puja for her, without the offerings, of course! As I was thinking the Tradition I felt her embracing me and it was like a tingling all over. When I finished I slowly opened my eyes and something shimmering from the far end of the room seemed to be approaching. I could feel that there were two beings which I assumed were Angels coming to take Grammy to God, to Heaven. They stopped about twenty feet away and I could sense Grammy's spirit moving toward them with the grace of a young lady. Then I saw/felt them all ascending through the ceiling where the two had entered the room.

I closed my eyes again and heard someone coming in the door. It was Peter, my first cousin, eldest son of Dotty my father's sister. He had been very close to Grammy as well and when he saw her lying there he broke down sobbing and had to leave the room. Then my father and Ted and the rest of the family shuffled in and slowly walked past Grammy's now spiritless body. They all sat down and the funeral director gave a little speech and everyone looked so sad because Grammy had been like a saint to all of us. We all loved her more than anyone in the family because she was an incarnation of compassion. She had been our connection to God, to the belief that there had to be a Divine creator; otherwise, who could have made our Grammy?

Everyone was miserable standing around the grave site waiting for the coffin. I was in a state of bliss, knowing that my Gram had been escorted to heaven by two Angels of God. What a way to go! your favorite grandson and a Lord of the Universe in town to escort you home. What a Great Lady, a Mother Divine.

CLAUDINE "GRAMMY" STANLEY

From 1969 to 1972 I was teaching TM pretty much all over the US and especially in the South, of course I was also going on all those courses, Mallorca I & II, Humboldt I & II, Poland Springs and the tail end of Estes Park TTC. We ran the Cambridge TM center, the center at Berkeley California and started the main TM center for the south in Atlanta Georgia, and I was happy to see that it was still there in a big Old Southern plantation house; effectively neutralizing all that antebellum past. I guess I must have initiated almost two thousand people into TM by 1972.

When we settled down for awhile in Switzerland, Maharishi had to find something for me to do. I had written the "Song of Life" album with Maharishi and recorded it with Henry Lewy at A&M studios in LA. It was very popular as a musical presentation of TM, sort of an abstract singing lecture and also served as a way to learn the puja before you even attended TTC. "Something Good is Happening," the next album, was inspired by Maharishi's SCI gems of pure knowledge. He asked us to write a song for every one of them ie. "Knowledge is Structured in Consciousness," "Rest is The Basis of Activity" thirty four or so, songs in all.

As I mentioned before, Paul and I dedicated ourselves to the task and recorded twelve of the best of them in Los Angeles at A&M studios with Henry Lewy. Ever since then we were called "The Natural Tendency," the name Jerry Jarvis coined for Paul and I. Soon after the release of our album "Something Good Is Happening," the movement began to incorporate the musical expressions of "Vedic Science" into our daily programs, celebrations and concerts. Maharishi took us back to the very source; the music of the Veda; Ghandharva Ved performed by classically trained Indian musicians, and Sama, Rig, Yajur and Artharva Veda, performed by traditional pundits, all with their own music, rhythm and rhyme.

THE TM ALBUM?

Western style songs were still written and sometimes recorded, actually Paul and I recorded another album of songs at the Livingston Manor Studio around 1975, we were going to call it "The TM Album" since "The TM Book" was so popular, but the movement wasn't interested in manufacturing it at MIU press and Maharishi hadn't requested that we do it. I hadn't learned the lesson of getting the master's approval before taking on a project. I thought "the movement doesn't want to pay for another TM album, that's all it is." So I went out and looked for investors after several years of distilling Maharishi's latest knowledge into another album of songs I called, "In The Golden Dome" written at the Saboba Academy in California and in Fairfield IA 1978-1979.

"IN THE GOLDEN DOME" ALBUM

Still wishing to sing the praises of TM, I managed to raise $30,000. dollars to record "In The Golden Dome." The new album was financed entirely by sincere supporters in Fairfield. Around 1980 I recorded the album in Nashville with the help of Mac Gayden, hired on as co-producer. Mac had been one of the illustrious "Nashville Cats," and was recently inducted into the Country Music Hall of Fame. These "Cats" were and are, very experienced session musicians who played on most of the best recordings that made Nashville the place to go to make a record. Mac called in favors from many of the best players in town. He did his best to make the album something he could be proud of having been a part of, in service to Maharishi. It's a beautiful piece of work that will someday be appreciated. Not many people have actually heard it since I couldn't think of a way to market it other than in the TM Movement, and that became impossible.

My marketing plan was to tour the world singing the song of life, songs from all four TM albums at every center and every venue that local meditators could fill, but just as the new album was delivered to my door, several thousand of them, Maharishi made a rule that no one was to go from center to center or town to town doing advanced TM lectures or TM concerts. There were to be no more "Golden Boys" (a group of very effective TM teacher, lecturers) or movement gypsies (Charlie Lutes & others) going about spreading confusion among the flock, according to Jerry J. Was this a reaction to Charlie's lectures, popular for his take on spirituality and esoteric lore? The one time FBI agent and steel salesman, totally disregarded Maharishi's wish to keep the teaching pure and keep TM from being classified as just another New Age cult fad. Charlie liked to spice up his TM lectures with whatever far out occult story that both he and we were there for. There was always the chance that these were his own real experiences. Some of the impressionable students and seniors, readily took him to be enlightened or psychic. Me? I thought he was a neat combination of G-Man and Teddy Bear, a big heart inside a big man. When Charlie told his stories about his adventures with Maharishi, traveling the world...now that was more than enough to spice up his lectures.

He had great stories of those early days with Maharishi. Many of us who knew Charlie went to a few of his talks for the fun of hearing just how far out he would go...how far from Maharishi's teaching he would wander. Also, there were other Initiators who were very popular speakers, guys who could go deeply into the science, psychology, metaphysics, philosophy and dazzle the audience with their brilliance. They would travel the country giving introductory and advanced lectures gaining followers and some cultivating Guru complexes to the point that they would break away from Maharishi and form their own little group of "Culties." However Jerry Jarvis would spread the word that the purity of the teaching was being diluted by someone's ego, and we would do our best to let everyone know. I imagine this is the main reason that the centers were declared No Trespass Zones.

But now I didn't know what to do! I had thousands of LP's and two thousand cassettes and nowhere to sell them. They ended up in Lynn Durham's basement in Fairfield and sat on the damp, cracked cement floor for twenty years until she asked me to move them. Most were mildewed beyond salvaging and by then no one bought LP's except audiophiles. My investors had believed in me and I had believed that the Movement could still use uplifting music with every song expressing one or more of Maharishi's most recent expressions of pure knowledge. Ya! Ma, I am truly retaaded when it comes to marketing myself. knowing that if the TM movement didn't want me performing my TM music in the centers, there was no other way to sell "In The Golden Dome" back then, there was really no alternative but to write contemporary songs or go back to my roots and sing "My Song of my Life;" original and traditional-Celtic songs that move my heart.

INDIA & MAHARISHI 1980

But before I gave up completely, I thought, "maybe if I went to see Maharishi and offered the new album to him, he might support it?" I brought a few boxes of the finished LP to India with me to present to Maharishi as I had done twice before with "The Song of Life" and "Something Good is Happening" albums. I walked up to him as he sat there on his dais in the Indian Express building in front of 3500 Sidhas and Governors with an album in my hand and kneeled down before him, handing him the record. He pointed to the table, as if to say put it there and asked, "What is this?" I said Maharishi it's my new record album "In The Golden Dome." He said "tell everyone."

I didn't expect this, in the past he had always been the one to introduce my music. What I didn't realize was that even though I had raised the money and done all the creative and manufacturing work intending to lay the finished creation at Maharishi's feet as a gift; the project had never been sanctioned by Maharishi. I had never asked him if I should do it in the first place. As a result he treated it as my own personal enterprise and if I wanted to sell it to meditators I was free to do so, but he really had nothing to do with it, and even invited me to announce it through his microphone.

I was kneeling there offering it to him and there was no way I could possibly start hawking it to his course members as if it were mine. Sounds a bit strange I'm sure, but I was so proud of it and so much wanted him to be pleased with me after leaving him five years before in order to create more TM knowledge music, something I wasn't able to do in Switzerland as there was no recording studio. I wanted to prove that I had left being with him, sitting at the master's feet as his court musician to do another album of TM music as I had promised to do, and there it was sitting on the table. I wanted him to feel that I had been right not to stay as he had wished me to do when he said "why do you wish to go?" and I said "to record songs" and he said "you don't have any songs" and I said "I'll write them in the studio in New York, like the Beatles" and he said "The Beatles!!"

He was so upset with the Beatles at that time that I couldn't have said anything more hurtful to him but I couldn't imagine him being hurt by anything. I had a juvenile sense of what being Enlightened and human at the same time really was, even though I had experienced it on the beach in Lompoc California. He responded "Go then!" but that was in 1975 and this was 1980. Feeling completely destroyed and without purpose, I left the record on the table and said "Jai Guru Dev" and melted back into the crowd. Sitting here, thinking more deeply about that time, I wonder if his response was based in the hurt caused by my flippant remark in 75'? It was almost like John Lennon saying something rude to Maharishi when they were leaving him in India, just using their name as a precedent for anything would have been hurtful. But of course I had no idea what I was doing back in 1975.

KIM TEIRNAN

But as we've seen, the time of the Movement's need for western music-based knowledge songs had become "in house," Music for the Movement's own appreciation like Mother Divine's Emily Levin, who recently released a CD and Kim Tiernan who has written and recorded several albums of songs along with her fellow musicians on Mother Divine; devoted to God and Guru and gaining enlightenment. It must be over forty years since I taught Kim's TTC in Engelberg Switzerland, she was so cute and sincere. I think she must have been inspired by Paul and I to sing the song of life because she is still doing it. I ran into her in Holland on Guru Purnima after Maharishi had ascended. She was painfully thin but still excited about the music. She must have been over sixty, she looked around 38 but I'm sure if she put on a few pounds she wouldn't look a day over 35, inside she was still eighteen.

It would have been fun to play the harp with her but judging from the girl who seemed to be her mother superior, there wasn't going to be any time spent on music or anything else between us even though my wife Claudine was with me. However, I may have been reading too much into facial clues and vocal innuendo? The difference between the music that Emily and Kim create, and what Paul and I did, was that we had just come from the worldly music scene of Columbia & RCA Records as professional recording artists; Paul from "The Loading Zone," the Rhythm & Blues genre, and me, from "The Gentle Soul" Folk & Folk Rock. We were like Donovan and Sam Cooke doing Everly Brother's harmony. Somehow we managed to synthesize our voices and musical styles. We tried to express Maharishi's profound spiritual knowledge in music that the world could relate to. Emily and Kim have always made music that they feel reflects the spiritual quality of their subject, although Emily does come from the Classical Genre and sings in an operatic style, Kim and her fellow Mother Divine's seem to come from a classic, New Age Indian devotional, Sanskrit and English with American accents genre.

NOREEN TART

Noreen Tart, "Renie," was a pretty, dark-haired folk singer back in 1974 when Maharishi was still making use of us to create music, and later, videos to motivate National leaders like the King of Nepal in hopes that his Majesty might be responsive to the offer of free TM instruction in their schools and Military etc. At first Maharishi coupled me up with Renie and after some time of working and performing together she expressed an interest in me that seemed more than musical. You have to understand that she was usually very tough on my ego, right in front of our audiences she would put me down in a way that indicated she thought I was quite fond of myself as a musician; I thought she was just trying to make herself look good by putting me down.

Noreen Tart

One evening after dinner she knocked on my door and stood in the doorway with a flower in one hand and a little gift-wrapped present in the other. She was either interested in forming a more perfect friendship of our two persons or maybe she was just thanking me for working together; I'm not sure? Anyway, that's how I interpreted it. She was beyond sweet to expose herself to the probability of my heartless rejection and I was very flattered, but ignorant of my own nature and need to be with a woman. Looking back, I can't believe the good fortune I might have had. Susie and now perhaps Renie! Maharishi must have put a love mojo on me! I was still fancying myself as a Brahmachari, I was still hoping to be a monk and live the celibate lifestyle.

RICK & RENIE PRACTICING (SEEBLICK HOTEL ON LAKE LUCERN)

Trying to be celibate and singing all day with beautiful women wasn't supposed to be the appropriate path to monk-dom, according to my fellow "M" groupers, Kirby C. and John G. After confronting Maharishi a few times with my wish to secede from my musical union with Renie, I managed to get him to free me of working with her, only to find that a month or so later he wanted me to join Renie, and her new singing partner Donna, to create a music video in praise of the King of Nepal. I very reluctantly obeyed his command and told them that I would just back them up on guitar and help with arrangements and such.

RENIE & DONNA & RICK & PAUL & MAHARISHI

VIDEO FOR THE KING OF NEPAL

When we started working on the video, Maharishi asked "Rick, can you make the guitar sound like a sitar?" I said "I don't have to Maharishi, I have a sitar in my room." He asked me to go and get it, and when I brought it in he said "come, play." I sat down in front of him and started to play and he said "drums?" and Rick Archer ran into the kitchen and came back with a few pots and pans of different sizes; being a good drummer, he made them sound almost like a set of tablas. We played for awhile and Maharishi said "You play good little sitar, play more and record." So, Rick Archer and I played what we thought sounded like Indian music for almost an hour, so that the Video guys would have enough to pick and choose from for the Video soundtrack. When Maharishi said "you play good, little sitar" he didn't mean I was playing a small sitar, but that even though I could only play a little, what I played sounded good enough; after all, I did take sitar lessons from Ravi Shankar along with George Harrison. Ravi was the most famous Indian sitarist in the world back then! (Not the "sweet-poison" dude!)

Maharishi seemed to have endless enthusiasm and delight in this creative production. At one point he had us all sing "Mangalam" over and over with guitar and sitar; we even had a flute in there. Paul "Raja" Potter was our flutist. Once the songs had been recorded and the background music was mixed, a few of us were recruited to pull the petals off of roses and marigolds and then we dropped them like snow over a large picture of the King of Nepal as the music played and our voices chanted "Mangalam, mangalam, mangalam" over and over. I asked what the word meant and Maharishi said "Auspicious, good fortune." When the video was completed and it was time for the trip to Nepal, quite a few people went with Maharishi. As a result of the King's reaction to the video and Maharishi's presence, I'm sure that helped just a little; thousands of Nepalese started TM. It wouldn't have been possible without the help of hundreds of earphones and endless lines of wire. The earphones made it possible to initiate hundreds of people in the time it would normally take to start just one and all instructed by Maharishi himself.

Here is a remembrance of the event from another perspective by Paul Mason:

"Apparently, in 1973 Maharishi sent Hans Bruncken to Calcutta 1973 to teach SCI. But Hans found that the intelligentsia there wanted to support communism and not their own traditional knowledge. In 1974 Hans and Charlotte moved to Katmandu where they again began teaching SCI and came into contact with the government. Whereupon Maharishi then asked the government to allow initiation of all the Nepalese people to which the government agreed. So, every day Hans talked to one of the ministers, and the King was also involved in this. It is claimed that because the king is a descendant from Lord Rama the Nepalese understood Maharishi's idea of making a `Rashta Cavach', an `umbrella for defense', to destroy communism in Asia and wherever. For this reason, MMY wanted to establish a TV station at Swayambunath and distribute TVs in every village and have relay stations in the mountains and to that end he sent a plane filled with technical equipment and engineers."

"The idea of Maharishi was to celebrate the puja on TV with the pundits in the villages, and then Maharishi would tell the people how to meditate, because they all have their family mantras. The only thing was, 'to do it easily like it is done in TM'. But apparently, when the West German government heard about this, they forced the Nepalese government to stop the project. So the Prime Minister himself decided "to open the gates for Maharishi but that the door opener will not be seen!" MMY agreed and went there and during one week initiated 35,000 people in Ratna Park.

At Swayambunath the TV Station had been established and TV sets had been brought to all influential people, so they could see TV 24 hours a day. Nepalese artists stood in queues to present their songs etc. So the influential people were distracted from what was happening in Ratna Park. However, after one week groups came to disturb the whole thing, therefore Maharishi left and departed next day early in the morning with the plane. Maharishi said, "This thing has stopped the communism in Asia."

"I was in Arosa, Switzerland with Maharishi and the gang preparing for that trip. It was one of the most fun and exciting times of my life." (Rick Archer).

RICK STANLEY PLAYING SITAR FOR MAHARISHI

FROM LEFT SEE DONNA & RENIE SUSAN ME RICK ARCHER & SUSIE

MAHA RENIE

ATR AT THE ALEXANDER

The Prachli Hotel in Arosa was situated on the side of the mountain with those beautiful sweet faced cows drinking from the brook and grazing all around. I was often conducting ATR's, (advanced teacher residence courses, eight of them) and one of them was at the Alexander Hotel, a gorgeous walk down the mountain and through the woods. I followed a natural path every day and practiced my Karate and Kung-Fu moves as I fast walked in my bare feet. I had recently seen a Bruce Lee movie and it was the middle of winter with six-inch-deep snow on the ground. The cold and snow only seemed more of a challenge and by the time I got to the Alexander my feet were numb and bleeding and I entered the ATR course hotel looking like I'd had an accident.

I walked into the course room and put on the usual video tape of Maharishi giving one of his talks. I sat down and put on my socks and shoes with half the course participants staring at my mangled feet. When the tape was over I said "any questions?" Of course, I meant about the lecture we had just watched. Just about every arm went up and I nodded and two or three people said what happened to your feet? I was so into Samurai/kendo and martial arts at the time that the question propelled me into a discussion about Arjuna and Krishna and the ancient (Kshatriya) warriors of the Bhagavad Gita. This was normal for me; I have always preferred to talk about whatever I am into at the time. Whatever the discussion or question is, I will find a way to interject my passion of the moment; sorta-like Charlie, only I stick to Vedic texts like the Mahabharata and Siva Purana's.

ANDY KAUFMAN

The comedian Andy Kaufman, "Latka" from "Taxi," was on that winter ATR in Arosa at the Alexander Hotel. He loved to mess with me, and the first time I became aware of him was the second or third day of the course. I walked in the front door of the Alexander with the video tapes under my arm, all dressed up in my sport jacket and tie. As soon as I entered the lobby this guy who was tripping down the stairs from the second floor, loudly called out "Hey, Rick Stanley, oh my God! are you really Rick Stanley the famous musician? Oh my God, can I have your autograph? Can I touch you? Are you really teaching our ATR? Oh my God!" He was so good at it almost anyone would believe he was sincere, in fact the few who were in the room did believe him. It seemed so unnatural to me that I played it cool and said "that's right boy, I'm the Man! I'm the coolest of the cool, hippest of the hip, and I'm here to tell you boy, that you better do better than that if you want my autograph." You must know by now that I fancy myself a deeply discerning perceiver of human and animal thought and motivation.

He was slightly taken a-back with my reaction but kept up his act without missing a beat and when he got down the stairs he bowed down to my feet and touched one of my earth shoes in a pranam. Then I said "where's your tie boy, the dress code is jackets and ties." He said "But I don't have a tie Mr. Stanley, I don't have a tie" and he began to pretend to cry and walk slowly up the stairs crying "I don't have a tie." That was my first experience with Andy Kaufman and it was only after it that I found out who he was. At first I thought I was going to have to send him home, that he was having a mental breakdown but we soon became good friends and he confided that he wanted to continue using me as a sounding board for his comedy which was basically unexpected and inane behavior. I love inane behavior, it's so spontaneous and creative, however, I would never presume to initiate it with him as he would easily make me look ridiculous. I could only respond to his lead, he was fast on his feet and could be much more convincingly crazy than I could.

At the end of the ATR, all the courses in the area, and all the international staff assembled for the usual talent show that would take place the evening before the course was over. However, this show was going to feature Andy and they let it be known that he was going to do a convincing Elvis impression. I think one of the organizers knew more about him than they were telling, but most of us didn't have a clue as he hadn't become famous yet; he hadn't been Latka on Taxi or on Saturday Night Live or on the Tonight Show. The first two rows were taken up by some of the old folks, the Granvilles and other notable SRM types as well as other "leaders" of the movement and people who were supposed to be important to Maharishi. I was sitting about eight rows back and after a few of the amateur acts had performed, the master of ceremonies announced:

"Our next act is a comedian from New York, ladies and gentlemen, Andy Kaufman!"

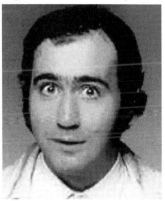

ANDY KAUFMAN

Andy jumped onto the stage, and in his best Eastern European accent said "Howdy doo, howdy doo, I am comedian and tell some funny Joke to you" he began telling totally lame jokes but would omit the beginning and go straight for the punch line, like "Take my wife, no take her!" the Rodney Dangerfield joke, which didn't really make any sense unless you were using the wife as an example to make a point! He continued like this, forgetting jokes in the middle of telling them, and acting like he was very embarrassed, with his face going all red, hemming and hawing until people actually started to boo him. The fact that this was a laid-back, meditating audience made Andy have to work a lot longer to get the audience to hate him than a New York crowd. Mr. Granville even shouted out for everyone to leave him alone, "can't you see your hurting his feelings." But Just when everyone was fed up with him, he began to cry and thump on his conga drum. He would cry "huh huh, huh huh, rub his tears away, then thump on his drum then he would repeat that and pick up the pace until his cry turned into Harry Belafonte's Day-oh, Day-oh, Easy Day-oh, at the same time playing the congas like a total pro, dancing about crying and Day-oh-ing until everyone was howling with laughter and clapping to the rhythm.

Just when I thought he couldn't get the crowd any wilder, he picked up a guitar and launched into a perfect impersonation of Elvis Presley's "Blue Suede Shoes." His voice and body language were Elvis and we all clapped and hooted until he shook and Elvised all the way out the entrance to the hall. I looked at Mr. Granville and smiled and he seemed just a little embarrassed to have fallen into Andy's compassion trap and turned a lighter shade of crimson. Years later, I was working as a cheesecake baker at Katz's Cheesecake in Fairfield when Andy showed up at the factory door and I went out to greet him. He said "Rick, can I talk to you?" I said "sure, for a minute or so!" He said "Rick, I have cancer! I'm only telling a few people; I'll be going to the Philippines to see a healer there, do you believe in healers?"

I remembered a healer in Mallorca who was sanctioned by Maharishi; she would sit beside whomever she was working on with one hand on the back of the patient's neck and the other palm up in her lap. By the end of the lecture or meeting, Maharishi would leave and then she would take her hand away. I asked one of her patients if it was helping, and she said "Absolutely!" I think her name was Annalee as the "Beach Boys" recorded a song about her on the "Pet Sounds" album. They had met her on a course with Maharishi in India. After she helped to heal one of them they wrote:

> Annalee, Annalee, the healer
> Healer with the healing hands
> Makes you well as quick as she can
> You'd love to see those smiling eyes
> Of Annalee
> (this is just the first verse)

PSYCHIC SURGEONS

I told Andy that I knew of two very effective healers who had been around Maharishi but that I didn't know about the Filipino healers. He had decided to go to Manila and see for himself and he did. I later learned from the movie about him (Man on the Moon) that when I saw him he was in the last stages of a rare lung cancer and was trying to find a cure to what the Doctors had declared incurable. To me what these Filipino "healers" do is criminal! They travel around the world claiming magical spiritual abilities to cure incurable diseases and through slight of hand, appear to pull tumors and diseased parts out of the body of the patient. They pretend to slip their hand into the body, through the skin and use a little chicken blood to make it look real. Then they throw a glob of chicken guts they had palmed into a pail and everyone assumes that the healer has removed the cause of the disease. Poor Andy barely made it back to the states; his long trip to Manila and it's disappointing results had probably taken months off his short time left on Earth. Perhaps in ancient times there were great Shamans who could actually perform "Psychic Surgery" and there may even be one or two today, just as there are an abundance of fake "Enlightened Spiritual Masters" and only a few truly Realized souls in the world.

THE KARATE KID

My time of playing tape-jockey and babysitter for the Initiators on ATR at Hotel Alexander was done, and it was a sunny brisk early spring morning in front of the Pratschli Hotel where most of the 108 lived with Maharishi. I was standing there looking out at the snow covered mountains to the west when a friend of mine Clifford McGuire, pushed open the big oak and brass door like it was made of balsa wood and joined me there in the sun. He was a strong lad, a college swimmer and totally solid; a Celtic warrior in his past, I thought. He did his usual playful push-punch on my shoulder. I push-punched back and then I told him I had been doing a lot of karate punching and kicking of trees and walls ever since I saw Bruce Lees latest movie. He said "Oh ya, punch me as hard as you can." I said "where?" and he said "anywhere! my stomach, chest, shoulder." I said "OK, but you don't get to punch me back." He was alright with that since he didn't think I was a threat either way, so he could be magnanimous.

He stood there with a rather cynical smile on his face when I said "get ready" and took my stance, did some deep breathing and let a very centered left arm and fist fly with the concentrated prana (chi) of my whole body behind it. "Crack" went the splitting sound of the bone on his sternum. My poor able bodied friend fell back, trying to find his breath and holding his chest, with a sharp pain shooting through it. He grimaced and said "Jesus! Rick you've broken my chest bones, I can't breathe." Somehow, I didn't feel sorry for him, it was like a David and Goliath kind of thing. I mean I was skinny, about 148 pounds at 5'11" and he must have weighed in at around 185 pounds of solid swimmer muscle at 5'11." He ended up going to the hospital and being bandaged up for around six months until his sternum healed. He was never very friendly with me again even though I've always liked him. He's a good guy, humble with a sense of humor.

THE WAKING DREAM

One night in Arosa I had what can only be described as a "Waking Dream;" your body is asleep but your mind is more awake and clear than when your actually awake in the waking state of consciousness. Of course there are only three commonly accepted states of consciousness, waking, dreaming and sleeping but what about transcendental consciousness? The scientific studies on TM have proven over and over again that a fourth state exists and forget about science, what about the scriptures and oral tradition of every culture in the world for thousands of years that describe a state of pure consciousness, samadhi, turiya, void, cosmic consciousness etc. OK, the experience of the fourth state, pure being or consciousness itself is silence! just silent Being. In meditation you only know you were there by the fact that you closed your eyes and the feeling you would normally feel concerning how much time had gone by would pretty much go with what the clock tells you. When you come out of meditation and an hour has gone by, but you would swear it could only have been five minutes, then you know you have been basking in the silence of samadhi, pure awareness.

Now, when you are asleep and you go into a state where you can see your hands and legs and feet and you can smell and touch and taste and hear your environment more sensually real than when you are awake, more memorable than any waking experience, you are clearly having a "Waking Dream." It may be a remembrance of a previous lifetime, a vision of some future experience or even of something that happened in this life. The "Dream," My WD, was from a time in the ancient past. That night in Arosa in the Pratchli Hotel I was suddenly aware that I was in the back of a wooden horse drawn cart. There were about ten of us and judging from the others, we were all around ten years old. We looked like Amazon Indians, that beautiful bronzed brown color and we all had leather head bands and black hair cut about four inches above the shoulder. Our only clothing was a breech cloth.

I was one of the first to get out of the back of the cart and my attention was taken by the light of a large bonfire in a clearing over to my left. There was a very big man standing between me and the fire so that I couldn't make out who he was. I could hear the fire crackling and smell the smoke and feel the cool night air all over my body, I could even taste the smoke in my mouth. I felt to walk a bit closer to the shadowy figure, something drew me to him, something that I knew back then. When I was about twenty feet from him I realized who he was and he held out his arms for me to come to him. An over-powering Love encompassed me and now I could see his smiling face and I could hear his deep melodic voice speaking to me. The Love between us was a love I have only experienced once on this earth, in this life and that was the Divine love that overpowered my heart and soul on the beach at Lompoc California, the love of Guru Dev. The love of God, the Love that God is,cannot be experienced unless God is present.

THIS PHOTO OF TAT WALI BABA LOOKS A BIT LIKE
MY WAKING DREAM GURU

This Lordly being was wearing some kind of headdress with beautiful red and deep blue feathers and he wore only a silk cloth, wrapped Egyptian style, around his waist that looked like the silken garment worn by Krishna in traditional paintings of him. He didn't have a beard but he wore colorful necklaces and leather sandals. I knew who he was! He was Maharishi when Maharishi was ?????? and I knew when he embraced me that he was my father or my master. The other boys had all walked on down the path by the horses with the man who had brought us to this place and I didn't see them again. This experience was from an early time in Atlantis.

The next day I finished meditating late and by the time I got to the kitchen all the food was put away. Turning into the small meeting hall I saw Maharishi having an informal creative session with ten or fifteen 108. I took a seat near the back of the room and watched for any sign from Maharishi that he knew what I had dreamt. What happened was, what always happened whenever I wanted acknowledgement that I was special; I never got it! because there is no "me." Really, the waking dream was more than enough of an acknowledgement

112 WAYS TO TRANSCEND

Not long after or before my Waking Dream, Maharishi was giving a lecture in the Kulm Hotel in Seelisberg on the 112 ways to transcend that his dear friend Swami Laksmanjoo had congnized with the Shiva Sutras. The room was full and I, as usual, sat in the very back against the wall resting my head on the fifteen foot long window drape that provided a pillow as I leaned back in my chair. These lectures could sometimes go on for hours and I liked sitting in a place that provided an escape route that wouldn't offend Maharishi. After an hour or so I began to sink into a meditative state with my eyes open staring, unblinking at Maharishi's face. Back in LA at the Gentle Soul house I would sometimes stare that way at a candle flame and would see the flame take on the shape of a dancing fire elemental, flicking about with sparks popping and hissing. When I was teaching TM, Guru Dev would begin moving and smiling, turning and blinking from his portrait, usually after I had initiated 15 or more people. I didn't have to stare at him, just doing the puja and initiating so many times would put me in the transcendent in action, Cosmic Consciousness. Witnessing through the sense of sight seemed to come easily.

The practice seemed natural to me having done the same thing for years in the Boy Scouts or whenever I would camp out and sit around a campfire. Just as I was locked in this expanded, solidly grounded and powerful awareness; not having blinked for over an hour, Maharishi said "Yes, Tratak" is the technique of transcending through sight, very good!" He was looking right at me as he said this but no one noticed me because, there I was just looking at Maharishi with my eyes open, perfectly attentive and of course, I was at the very back of the room. That was the day Maharishi validated my spontaneous experience of Trataka yoga, the technique of transcending through the sense of sight, a technique I had been doing most of my life without knowing it.

Kids these days stare at computer screens, video games, androids and TV all day, exhausting their eyes with little natural impetus to come upon Tratak spontaneously. Tratak naturally happens when sitting in front of a campfire or a wood stove or even that game of staring into another person's eyes without blinking "to see their soul." I'm glad I grew up before most of the screens took over our sense of sight. Then again, we used to do all that reading and squinting to see the faces of the actors on our 7" black and white TV screen! but only for an hour or two max. (except on weekends at Grammy's house).

MOLLIE MONTCRIEF

"Lady" Viggie, the daughter of the English Lord I mentioned earlier, was coming out of Maharishi's room when she saw me walking down the hall. She said "Rick, come" (most of us talked a bit like Maharishi after listening to him speak for years) I walked over and she said "I've just talked with Maharishi and he said that it was OK to find out some of the most important lives that we lived in the past. There is a lady in England, Mollie Montcriefe, who is able to consult the "Akashic Records" on our behalf and she will find out the seven most consequential lives that you have lived. It can help with understanding your present life; here is her address, just send her something like a ring or other personal item.

"Now, I didn't know for sure that because Maharishi told Viggie she could have her life reading done that it was OK for me or anyone else for that matter. I doubt that he expected her to spread the news so virally, especially, telling me! I must have told at least five others about Mollie myself. I sent off my old wedding ring with my return address and waited, not really expecting much. When the print-out arrived with my wedding ring I was probably more relieved to get the gold ring back than to read who I had been in a previous incarnation! I figured there would be some vague references to completely unknown Native Americans, English musicians or even African slave lives.

I opened up the print-out and read her descriptions of each life that seemed to hold a mysterious hint of the rest of the story; especially when the rest might be too bold, or off color for an English lady to express to strangers. Her descriptions seemed clear at first read but deceptively deep with inuendo which took some scrutiny and reading over and over again to fully fathom. Even when the short paragraph on each life had revealed their secrets, the fact that she never used names but would describe the person by his most evolutionary and defining actions one would still have to do a lot of detective work to find out who the person was; if that was even possible. We weren't all Napoleon Bonepart or Queen Elizabeth.

The two most interesting lives were the third and seventh, many thousands of years apart. The third had me as a disciple or family member of a great Enlightened master during the third epoch of Atlantis. She wrote that I stayed on the fringe of the master's followers. This life was glimpsed in my Waking Dream (WD) and the Love of the Master/Father was fully lived again. The seventh or last life that she cognized through the Akashic Records was described as taking place five hundred years ago in the 16th century. "A soldier who goes on a clandestine political mission from Scotland to Norway in hopes of gaining support for his head of state." Mollie liked to take the romance out of her descriptions so that we don't lose perspective of the realities of life in those earlier times. She also wrote "He was captured and sent to a dungeon in Denmark where he went insane after ten years of frustration at being unable to rescue his Queen as he had promised." Now, she had given me some description that might help me figure out who this guy was.

She also described a meeting that Souls have, before their next life on Earth, with the masters who offer two or three alternative incarnations which the individual can view on a large screen that goes through some of the best and worst scenarios the soul will have to encounter in that particular life. She said I was offered an easy life and a very hard life. The hard one was full of trials and ended in great suffering. I chose this one because they promised that in my next incarnation after this hard one, I would become Realized, Enlightened! Knowing that the goal of life and lives on Earth would be gained and I would never have to incarnate on the Earth plane again, I probably said "sign me up," or "Yippee Kiyo Kiyay! Kemosabee."

Molly didn't go into the fact that I would be reunited with the Great Atlantean master who had since incarnated as the Old Testament prophet Elisha, the New Testament master, John the Baptist and now as His Holiness Maharishi Mahesh Yogi. She didn't mention that he would tell me, as my master Maharishi, that I would attain Self-Realization in this life. Of course Molly's descriptions struck deeper chords of truth in me the more I compared them to my experiences in this life. Over time I discovered who Molly's "Soldier" was and even found two very accurate biographies as well as his autobiography. The popular history of his life and actions in 16th century Scotland were written by his enemies, Queen Elizabeth's cronies and the Scottish Lords, traitors who sold out their country for English gold. Fortunately, the Soldier's true heroism and fearless support for his Queen against all of them has been brought to light by an exacting scholar, Robert Gore-Browne in the biography "Lord Bothwell" 1937.

MARY QUEEN OF SCOTS & JAMES HEPBURN
4TH EARL OF BOTHWELL MARY'S 3RD HUSBAND

Lady Helena Carnegie inspired Browne to take on the challenge of righting the wrongs of 400+ years of prejudice and slander repeated by lazy historians using secondary sources, concerning Mary Stewart and James Hepburn, Mary Queen of Scots and Lord Bothwell. If a lie has been repeated long enough, even supposed scholars will accept it as true without bothering to check the primary sources. Robert Gore-Browne was not a lazy scholar, he studied every Scottish, English, French, Norwegian and Danish court record of the time. Every letter, personal and political from Elizabeth, Mary, James Stewart, Bothwell, Anna Thronsand, the English spy master Cecil and all of the other players in the intrigue were studied.

Even the naive love poems of Anna Thronsand (Bothwell's Norwegian lover) that Elizabeth's fallacious court falsely claimed were written by Mary to Lord Bothwell in an attempt to prove a conspiracy, were examined by Browne who found that they had been corrupted and Mary's signature forged and used as proof that she had conspired with Bothwell to kill Darnley her 2nd husband. The scholar analyzed Mary's masterful poems as well and found no mention of Bothwell at all; the court hadn't bothered to look at the poems she actually wrote. They weren't looking for proof of Mary's innocence and had to manufacture proof of her guilt. After imprisoning the Queen of Scots, for twenty years, her own cousin, Elizabeth I, had the Scottish Queen's head chopped off by an amateur with a dull axe.

"February 8, 1587: Mary, Queen of Scots, executed. 'I forgive you with all my heart, for now, I hope, you shall make an end to all my troubles,' Mary told the executioner. His first blow missed her neck altogether. The second struck her neck, but didn't cut through -- he had to saw through to finish the job. When he held her head aloft by the hair, her wig came off and her head rolled to the ground. Then, a bloody little Skye terrier emerged from her skirts, and refused to leave his mistress." It's a lively story, the tale of Bothwell & Marie, I've written a few ballads about it on the CD "The Ballad of Bothwell & Marie."

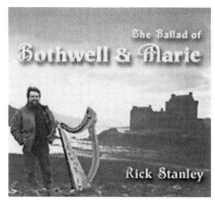

THE BALLAD OF BOTHWELL & MARIE

MAHARISHI & SCOTLAND

Not long after I got the news that my last life was supposed to have been in Scotland over four hundred years ago, Maharishi sent for me and I sat on the soft rug just in front of him. He said "we are going to spend a few weeks in England and Scotland, what will you do?" Somehow, I knew that this was a loaded question, he was really telling me that I could go with him if I chose to. I was always up for going anywhere with Maharishi and the added incentive of the Celtic connection only made things more exciting. I said "Is it possible for me to come?" He said "we will see.

Shortly after that meeting, one of Maharishi's secretaries came up to me and said that I was going to England with the group and that I should be ready to get on the bus for Zurich in front of the Sonnenberg Hotel the next morning at 9:30 am. I didn't bring my guitar on this trip as it would end up being thrown around with the other baggage and might get damaged. Maharishi led the entourage in his own car and I think Vesey Crichton was driving. I looked around the bus to see who my traveling companions were. There was Johnny Gray, Jerry Jarvis, Keith Wallace, the German Doctor, Michael Haig, Jane Prouty, and several others. It seemed only natural that the majority had Scottish ancestry.

We landed at Heathrow in London and Maharishi held meetings with the English TM movement leaders and the press. I think it was this trip that Maharishi gave a lecture at the Royal Albert Hall and it was full to the brim with young people and press. The next thing I can remember is staying at a motel in northern England and talking to one of Lawrence Sheaf's artist girls. She had been one of his proteges when she was on international staff in Mallorca and Fiuggi Italy. She and her fellow English artists, mostly cute girls, had always been quite disdainful of American men; they would either ignore us or turn up their noses when we passed. I don't remember any of them laughing or even smiling. But, they were so cute with their little Harry Potter accents and Laura Ashley dresses.

The one who actually talked with me at the motel was one who had always intrigued me when she worked with Lawrence. She had huge blue eyes like a doll, and when she talked she would hold her head to one side so that her golden blond hair covered one of those blue orbs; then with her eyelash fluttering she would speak with a Monty Python twit-lisp, spittle flitting from her rosy lips. The only reason she lowered herself to communicate with me in England was because she was no longer around Maharishi and I was!

Next, we landed in the highlands near Inverness. I got off the plane with Nankashore (Nan) and the wind was mighty. A huge Highlander immediately walked right up to Nan and in his broadest brogue said "Ahh yer a likely lad, all wrapped up in yer sheets and yer great black beard." He gave Nan a big hug in his massive arms and then grabbed his hand and shook it aggressively and said "I like ye lad! gimme yer bag and ah'll tak ye tae the boos." I couldn't stop laughing and Nankashore was giggling like a little girl. The bag handler behaved as if we had landed in his family croft, so friendly and hospitable.

But now we were in Scotland and Maharishi had said that this would be our vacation; we were going to enjoy. That first evening in our Inverness hotel, Jerry arranged for a Scottish bagpiper to play for us. I had recommended this to Jerry in a mood of hospitality toward everyone. In other words, the Scottish past in me felt compelled to offer the very soul of Scotland, the highland pipes to my guests! This was weird because I felt no need whatsoever to hear them myself. After all, that Bothwell past in me had moved about with at least ten to twenty pipers whenever he was on official duty as Lieutenant of the Borders or escorting the Queen; arriving or departing the city of Edinburgh. Jerry was upset with me for not coming down to hear the piper, he said "Where were you? we had a very hard time finding a piper who would play on Sunday and we got her for you."

I was kind of shocked that he thought that I wanted the piper for myself but he had no idea that it had been a four hundred and sixty year old part of me that had requested the piper for his guests, somehow, I was home and on some level they were all the guests of Bothwell. It's interesting how past lives creep into the present. Even more embarrassing was the fact that I had been upstairs with Jane Prouty checking out our rooms and talking, and I'm sure Jerry thought that we were having sex, something that really never happened, although we came close a few times as I've mentioned more than twice! Both Jerry and Vesey were somewhat perturbed that I was the only one on this trip who wasn't paying his way, except for them, of course. Neither of them had been in a position to know that I never had to pay my way like the other 108's. Michael Dimmick had always been the banker in Switzerland but no one had been informed about my situation on this trip. My musical contribution had paid enough to cover years of trips like this, but they were perplexed! Who was paying for Rick's Piper?

Maharishi wanted to go on a bus trip with all of us, so I brought along my cassette player and some Highland bagpipe music; "The Royal Scots Greys," ten pipers, two kettle drums, four snare drums and a big base, marching drum, all playing in perfect tune and rhythm. The snares sounded like tabla players all playing intricate ratatats, weaving rhythmical beats all around the pipers and kettle drums, very cool! Maharishi loved it, this was the first time he had really heard a masterful pipe band and he wanted me to keep playing it as we waited for the ferry to cross to the Isle of Sky. I put on "The Skyboat Song," that beautiful heartfelt ballad about Bonny Prince Charlie crossing the channel to Sky from the very spot we were sitting. In the middle of the tune Maharishi glanced over at me, I was sitting just across from him in the front of the bus, and he whispered "beautiful, beautiful." He made it quite clear that he knew very well my connection to this land.

BOTHWELL RIDES AGAIN

The ferry was too long in coming so we decided to head for a magical glen deep in the highlands near Glencoe where a tiny medieval castle sat on an equally tiny island in the middle of a lake, probably built for some Clan Chief's children to play in, or maybe an ancient home of the daoine sìdh (fairy folk)? Our bus driver pulled over to the side of the narrow country road. I jumped from my seat and ran down the steps and out of the bus as The Scots Grey's were playing a cavalry charge which spurred my urgency. To my surprise Keith came running down the hill after me. I headed straight for a huge ancient oak by the lake and grabbed onto a rope hanging from the tree and swung high and away and then back toward Keith. When I landed in front of him he immediately grabbed the rope and swung away and as he came back I pulled an imaginary Rapier from my waist and cleaved the air above his head as he ducked and drew his Claymore. We were dueling in full view of Maharishi, who was laughing with great delight as the Royal Scots Greys pipes and drums droned a most appropriate battle charge.

The martial ardor that the Highland Pipes seemed to awaken acted as a revelation to me. I think we were as surprised as any of our company (other than M.) to witness our joyous, child-like play acting of times both of us had lived as warriors in these Scottish Highlands. Both Keith and I had been wrestlers in school and he possessed a regal soul. I could always imagine him being a Scottish King, perhaps Robert the Bruce? I still can remember the old days and the great respect I had for him when we were both young and free.

GLENCOE

We played around this pretty glen for an hour or so and then a Scottish Initiator who spoke the Queen's English wanted us all to get back on the bus. It turned out his father owned a tour-ist shop in Glencoe that he wanted us to visit. As we drove through the mountains and down into Glencoe you could feel an eerie sadness that permeated this remote valley. We un-loaded and filed into the quaint shop that was built like the ancient 16th century Scottish homes with thatched roof and great stone walls. Inside, was some of the coolest stuff I've ever seen in a tourist shop. Real big fluffy sheepskins and deer antlers. Very cool Sgian Dubh, (Scottish Dirk) that are custom-arily worn by bagpipers and were worn by all medieval clans-men. Beautiful bagpipes and kilts; all of very high quality. Piles of tartan wool blankets and all the accoutrements and apparel of the Highlands from Crofter to Earl.

Above are "007" Sean Connery in formal dress kilt and "Rob Roy"
Liam Neeson in a traditional "Highland Great Kilt."

As we milled around the shop we were treated to a high tea with shortbread and scones and oat cakes. Some of us noticed a plaque that gave testimony to a little local history that explained the sad aura that permeated the glen. We asked our host, who I remember as the National leader of the TM movement in Scotland, to give us the whole story of Glencoe. He hesitantly gathered us around and began in almost a whisper with the story of "The Glencoe Massacre."

It isn't the number of casualties that is so shocking, rather, the manner of it, and the treachery of it. The MacDonalds opened their doors of rather modest homes, and generously let the Campbells inside their abodes. The Campbells said they were lost in the snow and asked to stay for a while, warm themselves and rest. Graciously, the MacDonald's agreed to let all the Campbell men and their Highland allies into their humble dwellings, trusting in God, that they were doing the right thing. They fed them their winter preserved meat, their wine, ale, friendship and by some accounts blossoming love among the younger folk. Glencoe is known by most people now, as the site of the massacre."

GLENCOE IN WINTER

These are the words to a song, immortalizing the black deed that some members, under Robert Campbell of Clan Campbell of Breadlabane, carried out on the helpless MacDonalds.

-The year was 1692

{CHORUS}

Oh cruel as the snow that sweeps Glencoe, and covers the graves o' Donald (Donnell), Oh cruel was the foe that raped Glencoe, and murdered the house of MacDonald.

They came in a blizzard, we offered them heat, a roof
for their heads, dry shoes for their feet, we wined
them and dined them, they ate all our meat, and
they slept in the house of MacDonald.

They came from fort William, with murder in
mind, the Campbell had orders, King William had
signed, put all to the sword, these words underlined,
leave no one alive called MacDonald.

They came in the night, while our men were asleep,
this band of Argyles, through snow soft and deep,
like murdering foxes, among helpless sheep, they
slaughtered the house of MacDonald.
Some died in their beds, at the hands of the foe, some
fled in the night, and were lost in the snow, some lived
to accuse him, who struck the first blow, but gone
was the house of'[m ,,,,,,,,,n MacDonald.
Oh cruel as the snow that sweeps Glencoe, and covers
the graves o' Donald, Oh cruel was the foe that raped
Glencoe, and murdered the house of MacDonald,
and murdered the house of MacDonald."

Words: J. McLean

The fact that we were standing on the very ground that this
horrific event took place, listening to a man descended from
the families that suffered the slaughter, made a huge impression on me. I could feel the terror and fear permeating this
misty, sad valley and I wanted to get on the bus and go. As
soon as our host had finished his story there was a rude rush
for the bus and we were on our way across the Highlands to the
Eastern shores of Scotland and Edinburgh.

The Grampian mountains were still blanketed with snow as
we made our way through the beautiful green glens and the
steep ancient hills, fence free and sparsely roamed by woolly
sheep. The sun shone brightly during most of our Highland
holiday. My English and Scottish hosts informed me that this

was highly unusual. We gradually descended into the low-lands and the colorful city of Edinburgh came upon us little by little. The streets were lined with shops from another century but most were stocked with odds and ends that a tourist might find interesting; they didn't appear to be there for the locals.

We stopped in the Old City along the Royal Mile and perused a few of them that still had their centuries-old rusted signs like "H.B. Smith Breeches Maker" and "F. Cooke, Live eel Importer" I couldn't imagine how they made a living? Others, like "Thistle Do Nicely" were selling flea market, nickle and dime junk. The proprietor of one shop told me that in Scotland you didn't go into a store and ogle at their wares unless you intended to buy something; she was a tough middle aged Edinburghian with fire in her eyes. I picked up a plastic pin-on trinket with "Edinburgh" emblazoned in red across it and said "will this do?" I dropped a five pound note on the glass counter and she said "Ah'll nay gaeve ye change fer five pound!" I picked up my five and headed for the door. I could hear her muttering obscenities and "damn Yank" all the way onto the street.

THE IN-HOSPITABLE SCOTTISH MATRON'S STORE

EEL IMPORTERS

TIN SMITH'S

The bus let us out on a busy street in front of a stone edifice which looked more like an office building than a hotel, everything was gray. When I got to my suite I opened the door, and thought I had the wrong room; it appeared to be a small storage space until I noticed the windows were blinded and a dark suited, short haired business type was shuffling about in the dim light. He was stuffing the only closet full with duplicates of the suit he was wearing. The look on his face when I said "hi, room #532?" made it quite clear he was hoping to have the room to himself. He was trying to be polite and friendly but was obviously from a socially reserved family. This was one of the academics who had been helping Maharishi and the other professors with the syllabus for the new Maharishi International University, (MIU) that they were creating on paper. My new roommate and I weren't going to be doing much socializing. Although we were of the same generation,

I felt like I was cohabiting with "The Man", CIA or FBI agent. I wasn't far off, he was a law professor.

Whenever my social environment included professors engaged in academic conversation, in the language of their particular discipline, or in a hall listening to the PhD's as they puffed themselves up trying their best to sound more brilliant than their comrades for Maharishi, I couldn't help feeling out of place. Unless you speak the language of physics you can't be a part of the conversation and the same goes for every one of the academic disciplines. It must be rather lonely, especially for science geeks when they haven't got another geek to talk to. I have often noticed that the moment I find myself alone with one of these over educated types, they seem to become confused, awkward, almost socially inept. They find normal conversation almost like a foreign language, after all, the language of their narrow academic discipline has taken over their lives, their sense of ego and self. Again, I exaggerate but that's just the entertainer in me. I find normal conversation without some color, exaggeration or humor that complements the story-line, boring. That's not to imply that "My Song Of Life" is in any way fictional! No, I just picked the true stories in my life that don't need any more color than they already have; after all the truth is almost always stranger and more interesting than fiction. And yet, I did just exaggerate, didn't I? Well, I didn't change the actual story, I just shared my opinion about academics for a moment.

Until I actually went to University in my early 40's I held on to my college inferiority complex whenever I was around college types. After six years of study and a Masters degree in English with emphasis in creative writing (an added year of intense creative writing and research) I finally realized that all I had learned was how and where to research whatever I wanted to know about, and how to write in my own voice. Of course if Google had been around back in 86' the research part of my college education would have been so much easier. My music reputation and validation was all that gave me confidence back in the 70's, well, that and my usefulness to Maharishi, and of course my direct experience of much of what he was teaching.

EDINGURGH CASTLE

I drew the blinds of my cramped hotel room and almost fell over at the sight of Edinburgh Castle looming over the town on that giant volcanic edifice they call Castle Rock. "Edinburgh Castle is situated on Castle Rock in the city of Edinburgh, Scotland. Castle Rock formed after a volcano erupted over 340 million years ago. The first castle that existed on the rock was known as "The Castle of the Maidens." According to legend, the castle had been a shrine to the "Nine Maidens," one of whom was Morgan Le Fay. You know, the Arthurian legend's Morgan Le Fay. It's interesting that "Arthur's Seat," an enormous "hill" that towers over Hollyrood castle and Edinburgh, suggests that an actual King Arthur once made this area his own, especially when you consider the historical reference of Morgan Le Fay as one of the nine maidens associated with the most ancient incarnation of the castle.

Next morning at breakfast Jerry Jarvis asked who would like to go on a tour of Edinburgh Castle and King Arthur's Seat way up on a hill overlooking the Old Town. As I remember there were several takers, all guys. Jerry, Keith Wallace and me and a few others. The bus that Jerry had ordered had to be canceled and the four or five of us jumped into a large taxi and headed up the Royal Mile to Edinburgh Castle. When we got there we had to walk about five minutes up the ancient cobble stones to Castle-hill and through the Esplanade. We were told we couldn't visit the dungeons and prison cells as they were being improved; I didn't want to see new and improved dungeons, I wanted to see the real thing and then get out fast.

THE SWORD OF WALLACE

Jerry told us we could actually see the Great Sword of Wallace which is almost five and a half feet in length. William Wallace is said to have measured seven feet in height and he wasn't a skinny man by any means. Only he could have wielded a sword this long. We were told that the sword was in the armory. I can only remember Jerry, Keith and I standing in front of a table with a Castle guard behind it. Jerry said "We understand you have Wallace's Sword kept here, we have a Wallace with us who would like to see it." The guard went over to a rack where a line of Claymore's were hanging and said "So! Ya be a Wallace? than heft this laddy." He almost threw the Claymore at Keith and to our surprise and the guard's, Keith grabbed it in midair and swung it round his head in perfect samurai fashion as if he had done this before. The guard gasped, "Aye, ye be a Wallace." He did not expect this, and had let his Scottish pride and disdain for Yanks with his hero's last name to get the better of him. He could have cut Keith's hands or wrists, but even though he's a little guy, I believe Keith Wallace was a warrior many times. Maybe even Robert The Bruce, who followed Wallace's lead in freeing Scotland from England's rule, and was one of the only Kings to rule all of Scotland, not just Edinburgh and the lowlands. Of course I may be wrong, it's an intuition thing, doesn't really much matter now I suppose. Now he's the king of cutting edge scientists.

At the time we didn't know that this wasn't Wallace's Great Sword but one of his normal sized Claymore's. The Great Sword had been housed in the Wallace Memorial near Stirling Castle: "The ancient Wallace Sword is our strongest surviving link to the real William Wallace. Wading into battle with the English in the late 1200s, Scotland's hero would have wielded this extraordinary two-handed weapon. It tells us Wallace was a giant of a man, likely standing almost seven feet tall. For 600 years the sword was kept at Dumbarton Castle. Since 1888, however, it has enjoyed pride of place in the National Wallace Monument in Stirling, overlooking the site of Wallace's most famous victory at the Battle of Stirling Bridge (1297)."

SIR WILLIAM WALLACE

Twenty years later, my wife and I visited Stirling Castle and Wallace's Monument. I stood beside the Sword and imagined how big I would have to be to swing it in battle and I'm afraid I came up short. The life sized Wallace figure in full 13th century battle gear which stands beside the sword looks big enough to heft it. The plaque beside the ancient relic says that Wallace had the blade forged in France, the "Auld Alliance." The French were the medieval masters of sword making and swordsmanship in Europe.

This whole trip with Maharishi was like the vacation with my father that I never had. He seemed to delight in my behaving as if I were finally home after five hundred years, and that's exactly the way I felt. Everywhere we went I couldn't help having an attitude of owning the place and feeling that I should play the part of the hospitable host. It was obvious that these "new" Scots all around us had no idea of the depth of our possible past. Here we were, King Robert The Bruce; Lord Bothwell, husband to Mary Queen of Scots; General Haig; John Gray and several others of us who seemed to have deep ties to this wild land. We flew back to London, and from there to Switzerland. The feeling of the aura of the British Isles as we passed through it, was one that included Wales and Scotland and was a warm and creative, naturally human feeling that I could relate to.

Being around Maharishi would awaken my sensitivity to environmental differences, and would inspire the best from the people and places we traveled to. My first visit to Scotland with Maharishi was like coming home and the Scots were almost as hospitable as the Irish. However, my second trip, without Maharishi, unleashed a dislike for American tourists who visit off-season. We came to feel like unwelcome guests at every bed and breakfast we stayed in. There were two exceptions, an ancient B&B on the shores of Lock Ness and hotel Sligachan on the Isle of Skye. "With the Black Cuillin Mountains towering at its back and the sparkling waters of Loch Sligachan at its foot, the hotel has served mountaineers, walkers and lovers of the wild Highland scenery for nearly 180 years."

SKYE & SLIGACHAN

We crossed the new Skye Bridge from the mainland at Kyle of Lochalsh, it hadn't been there on my first visit with Maharishi; remember, we were waiting for the ferry and I played the Skyeboat Song by the Scots Grey's Pipe Band for him? Anyway, we drove along the shore on A87 looking for a B&B that was open during the off season and couldn't find a place to stay. We were told not to go south to Sleat, known as the garden area of Skye, as the locals speak Scottish Gaelic and don't welcome English speaking outsiders. They embrace their traditional arts and music and I couldn't help feeling rejected since I have been singing Celtic ballads all my life and even building and playing Irish and Scottish Harps for almost twenty years. If I wasn't so shy, so expecting rejection at every turn, I probably would have been welcomed if I had arrived singing an old ballad or playing my harp, but alas, I didn't have a harp or guitar with me.

We kept driving the coast road west until the Cuillin mountains were looming up close and as we rounded a bend and drove the length of a long salt lake, there in front of us was a really cool looking Hotel with "Sligachan" in big letters across it's castle like walls. Even though it looked almost deserted we parked out front and walked into what appeared to be a confrontation between its local management and some Cambridge educated English business type, who obviously had his own ideas about the way he wanted the place run. It was kind of fun listening to the posh bloke and the kilted highlander arguing in front of a pub full of mountain climbers. It turned out that the place was open for the annual Glamaig Hill Race which had been going on since the 19th century and there was a new stout being served called "Black Cuillin" that we were invited to try. I asked what else there was and I obviously asked the wrong question as the creator and Brew Master of the new stout was standing beside me at the bar.

SLIGACHAN HOTEL & THE BLACK CUILLINS

He said, "D'ye nae lack a gude stoot laddy?" and the manager who had moved to his place behind the bar said "thes es tha masterr brooer, gev tha blak Cuillin a try maan, ef ye dinae lak et et's frae." He passed a full pint of the blackest Stout I'd ever seen and when I took a sip I said "Mmm, that's really good, give me one more for my wife." It had just been brewed and seemed so full of life and goodness, it was like eating a hearty meal. We sat by the coal fire blazing in a hearth and couldn't believe how great this whole atmosphere was, the Black Cuillin and the warm fire. I asked the manager if they had any rooms and he said "Aye, fer two?" We were pleased that our large room looked out on the Cuillins and the Lake. The bathtub was built for some giant at least seven feet tall and yet very narrow. This was by far our best B&B or hotel experience in Scotland. We often think fondly of Skye, the Sligachan and Dunvegan Castle, and of the Clan Mcleod with its "Faery Flag & Bridge.

THE FAIRY FLAG, WHAT'S LEFT OF IT!

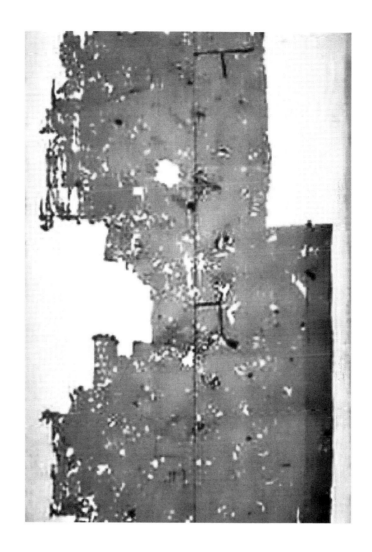

THE FAIRY BRIDGE AT DUNVEGA DUNVEGAN CAS-
TLE OF THE CLAN MACLEOD

Dunvegan Castle

In Alexander Smith's 'A Summer in Skye' (1865), a man named Malcolm tells that author that the "Fairy-Flag is kept in a glass case in Dunvegan Castle, and never shown to strangers, at least when the family is from home." The author asks him how the Macleods came into possession of the flag and he replies "Well the old people say that one of the Macleods fell in love with a faery, and used to meet her on the green hill out there by the Faery Bridge. Macleod promised to marry her; and one night the fairy gave him a green flag, telling him that, when he or one of his clan was in distress, the flag was to be waved, and relief would be certain. Three times the flag was to be waved; but after the third time it might be thrown into the fire, for the power would have gone all out of it.

"I don't know, indeed, how it was, but Macleod deserted the faery and married a woman." This version of the tale ends in tragedy, the faery woman heard of the marriage and was in a great rage. "She cast a spell over Macleod's country and all the women brought forth dead sons, and all the cows brought forth dead calves. Macleod was in great tribulation. He would soon have no young men to fight his battles, and his tenants would soon have no milk or cheese wherewith to pay their rends. The cry of his people came to him as he sat in his castle, and he waved the flag, and next day over the country there were living sons and living calves. Another time, in the front of a battle, he was sorely pressed, and nigh being beaten, but he waved the flag again, and got the victory, and a great slaying of his enemies." He tells that it has not been waved a third time yet, not even during the potato failure when people were starving."

When we were at Dunvegan, the Faery Flag was in a glass covered frame high up on the wall of the banquet hall. It was all tattered and torn and the original crosses and red dots all but worn away. It was recently analyzed and found to be extremely precious and fine middle-eastern silk dating back to pre 3rd or 4th century, before the Crusades.

ENGELBERG TTC

IN THE LAND OF THE BORG

Returning to the 70's, and flying out of the British Isles we started to descend over Germany and into the aura of Switzerland. There was an abrupt mechanistic, almost Borg-like vibe; as if we were landing in the middle of a land of hive people which made me long for the wild Highlands. (Back in Seelisberg) I was there for about three years, running "Advanced Teacher Training" courses, rounding, and teaching a TTC in Engelberg which was over the river and through the woods in a beautiful valley surrounded by snow covered peaks. John Loyd and I basically played video tapes of Maharishi lectures from previous TTC's and we did a lot of organizing of study groups for learning all the various aspects of teaching TM.

We also had to answer questions that always came up after the video tape had ended. This was really supposed to be very straight forward; the questions had to be about what was covered on the tape and we were supposed to stick to a basic answer that used Maharishi's words to clarify what he said. We were just supposed to repeat what he said on the tape, maybe in slightly clearer English. However, sometimes a question would be about what was on the tape, such as the Bhagavadgita, only they wanted an answer that included knowledge from having read the entire Mahabharat as well as the central chapter, the Bhagavadgita.

Having read several of the Vedic texts I couldn't help but answer these questions from my reading because most of the course participants enjoyed my story telling, especially when the subject of Devas and Rakshasas would spice up the tale. John would invariably reprimand me with a pained facial expression whenever I gave my more exotic story answers from Vedic literature. I didn't do this often but probably often enough to get some students interested in reading more Vedic literature and too often for those who wanted to stick to the program of learning to teach TM. Oh well! After watching Maharishi give all those lectures and then watching them again eight times teaching ATR's; then again, teaching TTC, I just needed a creative outlet, I needed to entertain the troops and alleviate my boredom.

John, my fellow course leader, invited me to go for tea and crumpets one afternoon. That was nice except he couldn't imagine that anyone wouldn't have enough money to pay for tea. He ordered tea and all sorts of cakes and dainties before I arrived, expecting me to pay half without letting me in on the plan. John was a multimillionaire from old money, and I wasn't even receiving a stipend at this point; if I needed money I would have to put in a request to Michael D., and I hadn't recently needed any; mostly because I avoided eating out. I kind of figured that since John invited me to have tea with him he was going pay for it. When the check came and he looked at me with a "cough-up" look in his eyes, I said "I don't have any money; I can pay you later when I get some from Michael." He was really upset with this and I realized how his family managed to have so much; they clung to every penny like Gollum clung to "precious."

DR. CRAGFACE

Occasionally, I would have to snoop on the less "one-pointed" people who felt it was fine to behave as if they were at a party college, pairing up, girl and boy for a nite's fun in the middle of rounding. My worst offender was an English initiator/ mathematician who had invaded my course one evening. He was supposed to be helping Maharishi with the MIU catalog. Somehow, he had met a free-loving lady from California in the dining hall who welcomed him to come to her room after everyone was supposed to be in bed with lights out. I was making my rounds before going to bed myself when I heard giggling and a deep male voice emanating from this course participant's room. I knocked on the door and there was sudden silence; I knocked again and the girl came to the door and said I had woken her up, "what's wrong?"

I said you have a man in your room, that's what's wrong! Then Dr. Cragface Fortesque pushed himself passed her and put his face up in mine as he made his way through the door, fastening his pants belt and complaining; "who do you think you are imposing yourself on our privacy?" I said, "I'm the course leader and your imposing yourself on one of my students who is supposed to be following the course schedule. This could get her thrown off the course; she could lose her chance of becoming a teacher of TM because of you, if I were to report this!" The girl looked worried and asked him, if he didn't mind she would see him at the end of her course. He took on an air of apology and said "oh! you're Rick Stanley the course leader; I'm sorry I was about to leave anyway; she's an old friend and I didn't see any harm in catching up on old times." Of course he was full of shit unless meeting someone a half-hour ago can be considered "old times!"

SCANDINAVIAN GIRLS!!!

I must admit that as easy as it was for some of the material scientists to follow their mind/desire appetites with physical actions, many of us shared the mental part of sensual desire, however, through intuitive control of our bodies, through rest and rounding and being with Maharishi, we managed to gain in physical/mental purity, resulting in refined consciousness and empathy for those we may desire. I can attest to my own crushes on two exceedingly cute course participants; Scandinavian girls that my mind haunted me with in meditative un-stressing but whom I could only respect as sisters upon interaction with their actual physical and mental presence in conversation. When talking with these girls in passing, I would feel like a child or young boy with his older sisters even though I was several years their senior. Still, the blond, svelte Swedish girl was so introspective and serious. She never talked to anyone except her Norwegian girlfriend; they always seemed to keep themselves apart from everyone else even though they could both speak perfect English.

One day after the Engelberg TTC, and my course leader responsibility had ended, I was in my room at the Kulm Hotel down the hall-way from Maharishi's room. I had just written a song on my Sitar, both words and music and thought I'd go downstairs for some tea-time bread and cheese. There she was! the girl I had written the song about, the Swedish introvert. I walked up to her and asked if she would like to hear a song I had written for her. She didn't smile, she just nodded her head and I led her up to my room. It was obvious there wasn't going to be any small talk and so I just started singing and picking. She stared at the wall and sometimes out the window and when I finished she stood from sitting cross legged on the floor and started for the door. I asked, "did you like it?" and she said "yes, nice" and opened the door and left.

Later I saw her with the Norwegian girl, smiling and walking hand in hand down in the flower gardens and I realized that not every girl can be won over by music or anything else that has to do with men. I finally figured out she liked girls. I believe the majority of Lesbians and gay men are souls who were the opposite gender in their previous life. It's hard to get over your attraction to the opposite sex in just one life, especially if you are abused in the childhood of your new gender by the opposite sex. Perhaps your wondering how I could go on about being attracted to two of my course participants after blasting the PhD for the same thing...well the TTC was over and the girls were staying at my hotel for a few days before returning home, and Maharishi was out of the country. Also, Maharishi wanted me to get married again so I was looking.

GUATEMALA

At some point lost to memory, we flew to Guatemala. As we broke through the clouds it looked like we had pierced through a time portal into the land that time forgot. We descended over the jungle with active volcanoes hissing up smoke and the smell of rotten eggs; towering above the trees and the pyramids. The pilot deftly carried us between two of these smoking mountains and we could see the airport below, just a long stretch of concrete with forest all around it. I really couldn't see any towns; it was like the airport was the town! When we got off the plane and were making our way through customs I was stopped by one of the inspectors who asked for proof of inoculation. I showed him my small pox scar and with a wave of his hand he motioned me to follow him into a makeshift clinic with open needles and their plastic packaging discarded all over the floor and tables.

I knew right away that he was playing a con-game with me. Pay me a bribe and I'll forego giving you the needless inoculation. It was all too obvious, especially when he rubbed his finger and thumb together, the universal sign language for pay-up! Somehow, I just couldn't give him the satisfaction of succeeding in his illegal hassling of tourists. I just kept smiling and pretending that I didn't know what he wanted other than to give me yet another chance to get small pox. I just kept smiling and pretending that I didn't know what he wanted. He kept messing about with the needle and a cotton swab that he purposely dropped on the floor and picked up with a side glance at me to see just how much he was freaking me out. I just kept on smiling and being unnaturally patient.

Meanwhile, Maharishi and company were long gone to peruse the local market place as they waited for the plane to Rio. Feeling kind of deserted and yet still resolute in my desire to thwart this petty thief's intentions I remained calm like a lamb at slaughter. At last he stopped greedily rubbing his thumb and forefinger, gave me a final look of "this is going to mess you up, I've actually dropped it on the dirty floor Gringo!" and started poking my shoulder with the supposed small pox vaccine. When he had finished his little scam and told me to "vete" I smiled and handed him a tip for all his trouble; he had to think I was either simple minded or that I refused to be a part of his illegal game on the basis of an incorruptible moral code. Ya! I think he just thought I was a half-wit; so much for my righteous stand against wrong action.

When I got to the terminal entrance, someone was waiting there for me. He thought, either I had been kidnapped by some government thugs for ransom or I'd wandered off somewhere. We grabbed a cab and made for the market where we found Maharishi laughing like a child as a local Aztec Indian pulled a hand made, wooden donkey that sounded exactly like a real animal and would stall, lower it's hind end and straighten it's front legs and heehaw, heehaw, as it did this. Then the Indian would walk toward the donkey as the string rewound itself by means of an internal spring. Once he was about three feet away he would again pull the string and the donkey would clipitty-clop along for about ten feet and repeat his performance.

The toy was so life-like it soon had us all laughing every time the donkey did his stall and hee-haw. What really made it so funny was the pantomime performed by the Indian. The guy would walk like he was really going somewhere and when the donkey stalled he would act like the string just about pulled him over backwards. his whole act was beautifully done and we all wanted to buy his wooden donkeys but there was really no room for them on the plane so only one of them was bought for us to play with when we got home.

RIO

Next stop, Rio De Janeiro. Again, we came down through the clouds to see the massive Brazilian jungle below and off in the distance that huge statue of Jesus on the mountain with his arms outstretched as if in blessing. I got to share a large hotel room with Keith Wallace. The hotel was like a hundred foot tall cylinder, like the Capitol Records building in LA only twice as tall and narrow. Inside, you had these wrap around windows that looked out over the endless ocean and the white sand beach. Remember Ipanema? That was the beach we were looking down at and those were the long legged, bikini clad, beauties we watched swaying as they moved with the breezes blowing their long dark hair, and dusky dudes purposely kicking the football to get a closer look.

About ten flights above us was the open air restaurant on the very top of the hotel. I was starving as I'd missed breakfast and lunch time was almost over. I ran up the stairs as the elevator was jammed. When I got to the top I bolted around the staircase and almost ran into a couple having lunch at a table just on the other side of the door that I swung open. I was breathing like a dog and couldn't see any place to sit. Then someone called from across the tables with their sun umbrellas, "Rick, over here." Yes! I had no idea who it was that called me but I quickly made my way over and sat down. They were eating the most beautiful huge plate of fruit I'd ever seen; really good fruit! Not the kind you get in the USA, more like what you might get in Mallorca. I ordered the same thing, fresh ripe mango chunks, big delicious strawberries, yummy pineapple pieces and coconut bites. They even had papaya, Brazilian guava and Mayan bread-nut. To top it all off, I had the most delicious grilled cheddar cheese and tomato sandwich I've ever had.

RIO DE JANEIRO

Keith informed me that we were all to accompany Maharishi to the governor's mansion in support of getting TM into the city school system. There was the usual hike up the granite stairs to the imposing stone edifice where the power lay coiled. We didn't have to wait long, two huge oak doors swung open and the ruler could be seen in whispered discussion with his *aide de camp* and a big dude who looked like a hit man and probably doubled as a body guard. The governor looked like a Mafia Don in his $8,000 black, kiton Napoli summer suit. The big guy was constantly checking us out with an "I'll kill anyone who goes for a hidden gun" kind of intensity. Maharishi was sitting across from the governor, laughing and smiling at him and giving him a very brief introductory lecture through his *aide* and interpreter. The governor smiled back but kept looking around as if to say "what the hell is this? How am I going to get rid of this weird little man? What's he talking about?" He finally realized that the only politically correct way to get rid of us was to agree to accept Maharishi's proposal

423

to leave an initiator in Rio, who, with the governor's help, would organize getting TM into the schools. And that's just what he did. Then he self-consciously made a small curtsy to Maharishi as he had been trained to do as a child to men of the clergy; while simultaneously indicating the way out.

Obviously, Maharishi could see through the guy but he always gives everyone the benefit of the doubt, the chance to rise above. Anyway, he was happy that the creature had at least agreed to implement TM into the schools even if he failed to do so. We found out three weeks later that the governor wouldn't even allow the Initiator to meet with him and canceled anymore association with the TM movement. That afternoon we had another meeting scheduled for Maharishi to meet with the Governor of Sao Paulo a city of ten million. His Palace was four times the size of the one in Rio.

SAO PAULO

SAO PAULO PALACE

Here we received a grand reception in a massive dining hall where the Governor and several of his important people were seated. They all stood and welcomed Maharishi with preferential dignity and smiles all around. We were led to our seats by waiters in white livery with red, yellow and black epaulets; the colors of the Sao Paulo flag. They sat us down and brought us our own individual antique silver coffee pots steaming with fresh brewed java. Then they proceeded to pour and the Governor said "this is my own private store of the finest beans of Columbia, please enjoy." Oh my God! I hadn't drunk coffee since the swill on the all-night watches in the Navy off of Danang, Viet Nam.

The scent of this ambrosia wafted over us and there wasn't a dry cup in the hall. Maharishi gave it a polite sniff test and exclaimed "very good." I looked across the ten foot wide, thirty foot long, walnut table and every eye was sparkling; and coffee pots were being filled as fast as the waiters could get to them. I wonder if they put a little something more in that brew? I don't think I've ever been higher on coffee than that afternoon. I forgot to mention the *"matasadas dois,"* the perfect treat with coffee. These Portuguese doughnuts were large, spongy, lemony and covered in sugar. When the "tea time" finally ended, I think I stood up too fast, and almost swooned like a Victorian lady from all that caffeine; but it was a very joyful meeting and I believe we heard later that the Governor fulfilled his promise to help in establishing TM in the Sao Paulo schools.

MAHARISHI'S SCOUT

Most of us went back to the hotel for evening meditation while the organizers bustled about getting a large auditorium set up for Maharishi's introductory lecture across town. The press were supposed to have been alerted weeks ago and posters and radio and TV as well, but when we arrived as the advanced guard the hall was almost empty. A few people were sitting in the audience and when they saw me they figured "there's one of those TM types in the cream suit, let's ask him when the Guru is coming." One of them did ask and I said "he will be coming soon." I didn't really know if Maharishi would actually come and speak in a huge hall with only ten people in it. This would look very bad if there were any press in attendance; just then, one of the local organizers came up to me looking as if she was on a secret mission and said "Maharishi is parked a couple of streets down to the left when you exit the hall; he asked for you to come.

So, off I went just as a newspaper man came strolling down the aisle with a camera and a cynical look on his face. He immediately picked me out as someone who might know what was going on and before he could ask I darted for the door not wanting to say anything that might get quoted. Off to the left and down two streets through a park I could see Maharishi's car with his driver leaning against it. The sun was going down and the lecture was supposed to have started about now. I slowed down to a trot then a walk and breathing heavily leaned over his open window. He said "how many people?" and I said "around ten or so." "And press? TV?" "there was one newspaper reporter who arrived just as I left." "Go back and see if more come, when half the hall is filled come back." Off I trotted and when I got to the hall a few hundred more had manifested and spread out all over the hall but only the first few rows were actually filled. However, a video crew were setting up and I knew that this might be good enough news to inspire Maharishi to come soon.

The interesting thing about playing spy for Maharishi was what I was learning about how to retain one's dignity and reputation in the face of embarrassing lack of public interest. If he had shown up at the hall with only a few people having come out to hear him and even one press reporter was there, the whole of Brazil would hear about the flagging popularity of the Beatles Guru, or worse the story may not even be written; even bad publicity keeps you in the news and attracts an audience I'm told. By the time I left to report again to Maharishi the hall was about half full and there were several news reporters and the TV news all ready and waiting. I asked one of the Brazilian meditators if it was common for lectures and concerts to start late and she said "Oh yes, always late."

So, I walked briskly to Maharishi's car and leaned down again and he said "It is time? How many have come?" "The hall is about half full Maharishi, and the press and TV are there as well. I think they are definitely ready for you to come." He laughed and said "go and tell them at the door to be ready and I'll come." I ran across the field and up to the front of the building and told the guys to set up his dais with the silk, deer-skin and clock for the table and a stainless steel cup of purified water with a hanky draped over it. They said "is he coming?" "Yes! get going, he's just around the corner." Of course when he arrived everyone stood up and clapped and cheered. There is something about not being absolutely sure if your entertain-ment or enlightened lecturer is really going to show up and your almost ready to give up and leave and then suddenly, there he is, all smiles and flowers with an entourage behind him of well dressed aristocrats, and you feel happy and that all is right with the world again.

JIMMY CARTER

Somehow we ended up meeting with Jimmy Carter when he was Governor of Georgia. We informed a doorman or guard that Maharishi was here for a meeting with the Governor. He scaled the Grecian stone steps to the top and disappeared for twenty minutes. When he returned he asked us to follow him and one of us went and got Maharishi and we led him up the long staircase and into the massive stone monument to the glory of the Roman Pantheon. The guard disappeared again and brought back Jimmy with him. The Governor was behav-ing as if he wished he were invisible and secreted us down a dark hall and into a murky little room where he offered Maha-rishi a seat then squeezed himself against the wall to get be-hind his over-sized desk.

Most of us had to wait back down the hall and those of us who stayed had to stand. He spoke in hushed tones with his big southern smile and polite bearing. I could tell that he was enjoying meeting Maharishi but that he was really worried about anyone seeing him; his run for the Presidency was in full swing and he was being very careful. Maharishi told him about TM and how it has helped so many children to enhance their intellectual abilities, their concentration and intuitive and creative strengths as well as overall health and that we were initially offering it for free to the school systems of every country. Jimmy seemed interested but he was overshadowed by his own grandiose agenda and an even bigger building, the white house!

BRITTANY COAST

BRITTANY WITH MA & THE HALFLINGS

When we got back to Seelisberg a letter was waiting for me from my mother inviting me to come up to Heidelberg and go for a two week holiday with her and her second husband's offspring, five year old Pippa & eight year old Alex Jones. A week later we were bound for Brittany on the Celtic coast of France. We got an early start and made it to Quimper in ten hours; Ma and I traded off on the driving. We fasted on dark German bread and Swiss cheese and only stopped once for crepe's when we crossed into Brittany. It was getting dark When we got to the beach area and we drove up and down the coast looking for a campsite. After avoiding the tourist traps we found one that the French actually go to and pulled up in front of a rusty, tin roofed, ramshackle manager's office which sat in the sand beside a raucous game room with a wild happening foos-ball table.

The burly, bristly campground manager looked like a Parisian "Apache" circa 1904 gang-banger. He flirted with Ma as he showed us a map of the grounds and where our site was; fortunately, my mother speaks French, Italian and German so we didn't get the usual rudeness that the French so enjoy inflicting on people who don't speak their language. We set up the tent between two others in a long line of tents situated near the beach in the rolling dunes. I could hear the ocean pounding on the beach all night, reminding me of Grammy's beach house and camping out on 2nd point, way up on the cliffs looking out on Quincy bay. Ma left a note that she had gone searching for breakfast when we got up but it was getting really hot in the tent with no shade anywhere so I left a note for her to meet us down on the beach where it was always cool with that strong west wind blowing off the ocean.

We waited but no Ma, so the three of us scuffled back through the deep sand to the tent and there she was frying up eggs on her little gas stove. She made toast on it as well, and broke out some cheddar cheese and a big baguette that we tore into equal parts and cut chunks of cheese. She put the coffee pot on and poured some fresh cream into two big cups and filled them with steaming coffee. She had a bottle of limonade for the kids, the fizzy French kind that you have to turn upside down so the lemon bits get dispersed around enough for everyone to get some. It was even hotter in the tent now with the oven going so I ate my food, drank my coffee, took a big swig of limonade and headed for the game room to check out the French foos-ballers.

The place was packed with teens and twenty somethings all engrossed in the foos-ball game. I managed to get closer and leaned against the wall. I could see over most of their heads and could not believe what I saw. I thought I was pretty good at this game, we played it all the time at the community center that my mother ran on the army-base near Mannheim when I was in high school. In 70's Switzerland, around Maharishi, we played it quite often as most of the hotels had a foos-ball table. I thought I was good! But these guys were lifting the ball over the heads of the mechanical soccer players and even putting a curve on the ball so that it would fool the goalie and smash though the goal with a loud pop like a gunshot. These kids were unbelievably good and the two were popping and smashing and their fans were screaming and jumping up and down much like they do at a real European Football game.

NEAR DEATH EXPERIENCE

I didn't stay at the foos-ball game very long, just long enough to feel embarrassed that I had actually thought I might play a game or two with the locals. Back at the tent everyone had gone to the beach so I went down and said "I'm going for a long walk over to the stone cliffs." Ma said she and the kids might head over there as well after awhile. The sun was so hot and the wind off the ocean was so cold that it felt exhilarating and cozy at the same time. I had on this ridiculous white, terry-cloth bathing suit that made my pale white skin look as an-emic as a wet blanched almond but I had noticed that most of the camp-grounder's weren't really into tans. I must have walked for half an hour when I saw the huge rock hills standing in the white sand beach about half a mile around a peninsula that jutted out over the wild pounding ocean. When I stood at the bottom of the rocky hills it was obvious that it would take a mountain climber to go straight up so I looked back along the beach for an access path and found one about half a foot-ball field inland.

There was an easy footpath that led up and into the cliffs and I kept hiking up and up until I was standing on the cliff edge looking out over the vast Atlantic and the huge rolling swells. When I looked down the water was about thirty feet below me smashing about the sharp deadly rocks. I felt safe there and looking up to my left; there was a couple who were stand-ing about fifteen feet above me near a higher cliff edge. They were staring at me with a look of horror on their faces, ges-ticulating and pointing out to sea then back at me. I thought they were paranoid and afraid of a little water when, I looked back over the cliff wall and saw a veritable tidal wave about ten feet over my head coming down on me. I turned to run but the wave hit me and flattened me against the rock, pulling with the strength of a bulldozer. I began sliding backwards on my stomach toward the cliff edge, tearing my finger nails on the rock trying desperately to hold on but the overwhelming power of the tons of water were dragging me ever closer to the edge.

I could hear the couple screaming at me as the barnacles tore the skin from my body. Just as I was about to be pulled over the cliff by the giant wave and onto the rocks below, I felt something gently pressing me against the cold, slick stone, holding me still as the water rushed over me. It was too obvious that a higher power had saved my life, Guru Dev? An angel? Maharishi? I have no idea! "Thank you, thank you" I thought as loudly as a scream. The couple were frozen in place as I picked myself up with the blood pouring down all over me, my white bathing suit red and dripping blood, I looked up at them and smiled as I waved and walked up the rock path and down the other side to the beach. There was Alex, he said "how did you get so muddy?" and I said "you mean bloody?" This was one of several times in my life that someone intervened with the laws of nature on my behalf.

I went for a quick dunking in the salt waves which pretty much removed the evidence of my near demise, except for my now pink instead of white, bathing suit. Ma had been ambling along the long beach hike with little Pippa who kept running to meet the waves then running back up the sand, giggling as the fingers of the sea strove to catch her. When it did manage to get her feet wet, she would scream with the shock of the cold and the sense that it was a living thing. Ma lifted her glasses and exclaimed "you have a pink suit as well? I think the white one was a bit more, ah.. more suitable! Is that blood?

THE FOLK FESTIVAL

When we got back to the tent the sound of bagpipes and drums and Bombards and Violons as well as hundreds of campers singing and dancing greeted us. We found out that it was the annual Breton folk festival which started at the campground and continued that evening at a big hall in the local town with professional musicians from all over Brittany, Scotland and Ireland. This was great! and after an hour of dancing around and trying to sing in Breton (a Celtic language similar to Cornish) we all went back to the tent, me to meditate and Alex, Pippa and Ma to take an afternoon nap before we went to town for dinner and the big concert. Of course, the only way to get the kids to nap was to make it a requirement if they wanted to go to town that evening. Alex was smart enough to know we wouldn't leave them alone at the campsite but he was ready to nod off anyway.

As the sun was sinking into the rough Atlantic, we all piled into Ma's car and headed for town. Neither the kids nor I were in the mood for more crepe's so we looked for a popular restaurant, judging popularity by the number of people we could see sitting in them. There was one we drove by that looked appealing and even appeared to have enough room for us. It took a good ten minutes to find a parking spot but fortunately, there was still room for us when we managed to find our way back. We sat down and ordered grilled cheese and tomato sandwiches on small crispy shelled baguettes with pommes-frites all around; oh ya! with fresh local tomatoes. Someone put a coin in the jukebox and out poured the most beautiful Breton folk-rock ballad, pipes and fiddles and gorgeous vocal harmonies. I looked on the jukebox song list and the one that was playing was the number one hit song in Brittany at the time. This was the early 70's when folk music became popular music in the Celtic nations of Ireland, Scotland, Brittany etc. etc. This phenomenon had already happened in the States in the late 60's.

After a yummy dinner we went to the concert and really had a good time. The thing about Brittany that is sort of interesting, is that they have kept the ancient tradition of blowing the Bombard, the equivalent of the chanter on a bagpipe; the part with holes that you finger the melody - by covering, like a flute. It's a reed instrument like the bassoon or clarinet only much harder to get a sound out of. In other words they blow the bagpipe without the bag, which makes it extremely difficult. In India they do the same thing, they blow the Chennai which is very much like the Bombard or the bagpipe Chanter without a bag. The average Chennai player is expected to live only thirty five years or so, due to the incredible stress involved in playing this instrument. Even the Scottish highland bagpipes take their toll with all the forced breathing involved. The Irish got it right with their Uilleann pipes that require only squeezing the small bellows with the elbow against your side, no blowing at all.

INITIATING THE HALFLINGS

The next day I offered Alex and Pippa instruction in TM, Alex was old enough to get the adult technique, but Pippa would get the walking word of wisdom. They were interested, and I set up a puja table in the tent and we all went looking for flowers and the rest of the essentials for a proper initiation. It all went well and each morning and afternoon we would meditate together and at an appointed time in the evening we would have our three days checking meeting. My mother hadn't started TM yet but she did shortly after our trip; at her home in Viernheim Germany. The evening after I initiated the kids I went for a walk down by the beach looking for another adventure. There was a fire and several twenty somethings sitting and lying about it. Some of them knew each other and of course there was your usual cute/popular girl (Brigitte) that two of the guys were lying within striking distance of. I went over and sat on the side of the fire where bikini Brigitte and her two admirers were, although, I was somewhat removed from the group by about five feet.

MARLON THE APACHE

After a lot of French conversation and Brigitte becoming no-ticeably bored, I became aware of three slumped and dodgy looking figures approaching in the dusk from the other side of the small bonfire. My fellow strangers seemed to be unaware of the intruders until the leader, who had been standing in the shadows with his mates watching, and picking out his poten-tial prey, suddenly burst upon us with a loud "Qu'avons-nous ici?" (what have we here?) then taking several long strides and kicking the sand in the air with every step, he stood over us and basically challenged the group with his leering grin and his knife that he revealed by pushing back his jacket to dramatic effect. I was watching him (Marlon) very closely, looking for weapons, weaknesses, strengths etc. He had on the usual tough guy uniform, black leather motorcycle jacket with the silver chains hanging. Matching boots and the sheath knife on his side. He was about twenty or so and compared to PD (book 1) he was a French pussycat, about 5'8" slight build and all attitude; no Parisian Apache here! Brigitte im-mediately sought his attention and he clumsily dropped him-self down between her and the two suitors and put his hand on her hip. She was delighted! A real man. Meanwhile, his henchmen who stood about thirty feet away on a rise in the sand were doing their best to look threatening even though they appeared to be skinny teenagers, no more than sixteen or seventeen.

Marlon kept up what appeared to be threatening innuendo toward all the males in attendance and I had a very effective looking weapon picked out on the off chance that these guys started doing anything abusive. There was a nice three foot long piece of hardwood in the fire that was burning brightly and was like the handle of an axe. Marlon's knife would never even make it out of his sheath before I'd have whacked him in the face with a firebrand that would send him and his mini-froggy gang crying down the beach. I would be screaming bloody murder like a crazed madman as I went after them... but alas! They never quite went over the edge and I have wished that they had for several decades. Why? Because I felt that I had been insulted, thought of as nothing but a skinny guy in a pink bathing suit. No threat at all! Remember, I had been watching endless Samurai and Kung Fu movies, I had been practicing kicking and punching for years, I fancied myself a warrior hero. I wanted to be a warrior hero. Let's face it, we will never know if I would have grabbed that firebrand and laid waste to the little gang or not but I do have something in me that decides these things on it's own, and if Marlon had triggered that automatic weapon in me, I'm sure Mr. Hyde would have taken over and that's enough for me.

The college boys of summer remained in awe of the pseudo tough guys and I wasn't about to play the hero if the dumb girl was actually enjoying the brute's advances. He never actually did anything more than talk and put his hand on her hip which she liked. Perhaps, if I could have understood what he was saying I might have done otherwise but my three years of high school French had been a complete waste of time. Finally, I got bored and made my way back to the tent where Ma was already asleep and Alex was reading with a flashlight.

I BLOW IT, BIG TIME!

Next morning I walked to the other side of the large peninsula we were on and found a small harbor with boats for rent. They had motor boats, row boats and YES! Sailboats. These sailboats were like the old time 15' foot lobster-man Dorys, "Peapods" in Maine, with a small mast and sail forward and an oar like tiller aft. I walked into the building which had lots of other stuff going on in it, like a soda shop counter and tourist odds and ends, and asked a girl behind the counter where you could rent a sailboat. I would have tried my French but I had never learned the words for rent or sailboat. She could speak a little English and pointed out a door with a nice smile, my first since arriving in Brittany. I opened the door and the guy behind the desk was either deaf, focused or rude. I stood in front of him for a good ten minutes, making a decision with myself that I would stand there like a tree until he acknowledged my humanity.

Finally, he looked up out of sheer curiosity to see who would do such a strange thing as to stand silent for ten minutes without getting upset. When he said *"Quoi?"(what?)* I asked if he spoke English and he made some rude comment about Americans and said, "Non, qu'est-ce que vous voulez? (no, what do you want?) Then he yelled for the girl to come. I told her I'd like to rent a sailboat for the afternoon and he looked at me as if I were joking and said *"Je ne peux que louer à de véritables marins avec beaucoup d'expérience." (I only rent to real sailors with lots of experience)* before she even had a chance to translate for him; he obviously could speak English. She told me what he said and I told him that my father was one of the best sailors on the East coast and that I had sailed with him all my life (In reality, only two or three times). I said that I belonged to the Savin Hill Yacht Club in Dorchester Mass. and that I had been in the Navy as well, which made him laugh, knowing that there are no sail boats in the U.S. Navy.

The girl shrugged her shoulders and I was about to turn and leave when he said in perfect English "you cannot allow anyone else in the boat and you must stay in this harbor the entire time." I said "Great!" and he stuck out his hand for the money and grabbed a life jacket and had the girl show me to the boat. She led me down the boat ramp and pointed to the boat I had rented. She reminded me of the rules, "no other people in the boat and stay in the harbor." At first I was a bit freaked out that she was going to keep standing there until I showed I knew what I was doing, raising the sail and pushing myself out from between the two other sailboats and I even went off balance for a moment trying to push off and jump in the back of the boat but she just chuckled and turned toward the Marina building. As I caught the wind in the sail just enough to pull me out of the dock I thought I could see the Frenchman in his office staring out at me with a look of disgust on his face.

Ma and the kids were probably at the beach on the other side of the peninsula, so without a second thought I headed out of the harbor and around the tip of land toward the campground beach. I must have been a couple of hundred yards from shore and the rollers and swells out there were really rough. I'd be up on the crest of a wave then down in a deep trough where I couldn't see anything but water. Brittany is one of the roughest places to sail anywhere if your close to the coast. When I finally got around the point and could see the beach on the other side, I headed straight for land where I could make out Ma lying on the beach. The boat had a centerboard which I drew up before ramming into the beach. The waves were like eight to ten feet high and pretty much crashed me onto the sand and with the help of my mother and Alex we steadied her and everyone got on board.

Ma was excited and said she hadn't sailed since her college

days when she met my father. We were doing OK until I started to head downwind with the wind at our backs. This works fine on most sailboats but on this old Dory the wind and the weight of all four of us started to drive the bow down into the ocean waves and we began taking on water. I remember at one point we had only an inch or two of gunwale between sailing and sinking, so I hauled the mainsail in a bit, very carefully, and we came back up from the brink of another near death experience, probably by drowning; I mean, at least a few of us wouldn't have survived as both Ma and I would have been trying desperately to save Pippa; I don't even know if Alex could swim! When we were headed back toward the beach I caught sight of that girl from the boat house running up the path toward her boss. She had been spying on me this whole time and I knew that it would be only a matter of a few minutes before an irate Francois the Sailor would be screaming in my face. No wonder the French hate Americans, I'm sure I was not the first yank to inspire his enmity and prejudice.

I was hoping I could make it back to shore and let Ma and the kids off but just as I was heading in, Francois's big motor boat came roaring around the peninsula with an irate, red faced Breton gesticulating for me to take down the sail. He was really pissed off! Not only had I broken the rule of staying in the little harbor but I had done the unthinkable, I had taken on three passengers without even having life jackets for them. When he came along side he ordered Ma and the kids into his motor boat and tied the sailboat up to his stern, ordering me to man it's tiller. Meanwhile, he was cussing out my mother in French and she was as red as he was with embarrassment for my irresponsible behavior. It was a long ride around the point again and I felt bad about it because we really did come close to going under on that scary, rough and tumble coast.

THE GIANT OF CARNAC

My mother was good about not holding on to anything negative; she never mentioned my sailing fiasco again. The next day we were driving down the coast and came upon an active archaeological dig. There were other parts of the site that were open to the public so we parked and wandered about reading plaques that Ma would translate for us; mostly about the time-line of the relics or persons found in the Cairn. There wasn't much to see and we were the only ones there, so we ambled over to the area that was blocked off with police tape. Alex and I lifted the tape over our heads and looked over the edge of the biggest grave sight. "Whoa!" I said, pretty loud actually. Alex's expression of shock and awe was even louder and more like a screech, well he was still pre-pubescent. Anyway, we definitely got Ma's attention but she was hesitant to bring Pippa over, maybe what we saw was still alive or something?

I said, "Ma, it's all right it's just a giant skeleton, a very dead one. Down in that hole were the remains of a man almost ten feet long. He didn't have a plaque or sign that explained his existence but it was clear from the huge Dolmens beside his grave that he must have been a Druid or a great Hero. I pondered the fact that if his bones were over five thousand years old as the rest of the site was supposed to be, with all the rest of his body in tact and the original size of his bones before they had dried up and shrunk, he must have been at least eleven feet tall and who knows how broad his shoulders were. They had found a lot of relics in his grave that they removed to ponder and put them in a museum. This one discovery in my travels of the world remains as vibrant in my memory as the day I wandered into it.

We did lots of other fun things in Brittany. Ma, loved Opera and one evening she took us all to a concert that was taking place in an ancient castle that was still lived in by some Baron, grand seigneur du royaume. He, of course was sitting in the best seat in the hall with his Baroness. There were a couple of string players and a cellist, all in tuxedo's, who were playing some 17th century chamber music. When the singers entered the room; the first thing they did was to walk like ballet dancers, in time with the music, up the aisle to the front of the hall and curtsied and paid *hommage* to their hosts, Le Baron et Baronesse du château. I couldn't help giggling a little when the very large (fat) alto did his curtsy, he almost fell into the lap of the baronesse as he waved his silk scarf, clumsily, across her face. She closed her eyes to avert having her pupils scratched and the poor alto went red and backed gracelessly into the delicate soprano. Ma, grabbed my hand and glared at me, she really didn't want us to appear like ugly Americans but I could hear several other titters in the audience and even the Baron looked back at us with a smile.

Once the singing started we sat back and enjoyed the music. Both singers were good and the string players were really good. Pippa and Alex were bored out of their minds, but soon, Pipps fell asleep and Alex went outside to look around the moat. I think he did some exploring that wasn't really allowed as well, because he mentioned something later about the "basement" having chains hanging on the wall and a large deep pit with a rusted iron-barred cover. I asked if there was a rack or an iron maiden but he didn't get the joke. Ma drove me to Quimper, the largest city around on her way back to Viernheim Germany and I flew back to Switzerland.

Over the years she tried a few times to get me to meet again in Brittany for a family vacation, but I would never go. With two kids and a stay at home wife, I felt that I couldn't afford to put all that expense on my credit card when I needed the money to buy food and pay rent etc. Finally, she asked where I would most like to go for a holiday, thinking I would come if I really liked the place; so I told her, Ireland has these gypsy caravans pulled by ponies that you can rent and travel town to town, sleeping in the caravan at camp sites all over Ireland. My poor, dear mother set up a whole trip, renting and living in a Gypsy caravan on the west coast of Ireland, but I still wouldn't go, so she got her sister, my wonderful Aunt Betty and they had a great time. This was the one trip that I have never stopped feeling bad about. I mean here I was supposed to be a Celtic Bard, singer of Irish and Scottish ballads with a hand made Irish harp no less, and I wouldn't even go to the country whose music I most loved and sang with all my heart. What wonderful music and fun I missed out on, I will never know. When it was really too late and Ma could barely walk up stairs without losing her breath and passing out, I asked her if she would like to meet us in Scotland for a few days together but that's a story for later.

OFF TO FIND A WIFE?

Back in Switzerland, I was getting a haircut from "Ron the barber." Ron was an odd little fellow, very serious, never smiled. Maybe he was gay, and the only reason he seemed odd was that he felt he had to hide it? Or, maybe he wasn't gay but just had a lot on his mind; he was a private kinda guy. I mean, usually hair dressers and barbers are very social beings. They know everything about everyone because we feel we can tell them our most intimate secrets. Maybe this is because they are cutting our hair, fussing about with our heads, touching us, sort of intimate things really. They become a sort-of friend, or short term confidant. But Ron wasn't like that, he would just remain silent the entire time and he was so petite and prissy about his own appearance, every hair in place, clothes fitting perfectly etc. that I often wondered. I really don't care if your gay or not gay, it just seems like it would be a drag if you felt guilty about it.

A few months after returning to Seelisberg and Maharishi, I had just finished lunch and sauntered into the lecture hall when a loud "SHHHH" stopped me in my tracks. I looked up at the stage and there was Ron sitting in a chair getting ready to be interviewed by Cielle Callender with an animated video crew setting up lights and mics and Ron glaring out at anyone who didn't just come in and sit down quietly. After a few more minutes of microphone and make-up adjustments, Cielle began the interview with an introduction to the show. She basically said "good afternoon ladies and gentlemen, meditators and Initiators, Maharishi has asked us to make a video course that will help us become more sophisticated in our manners, etiquette and grooming. It seems that many of us are deficient in these areas of social grace.

I thought, "oh my God this is going to be funny; look at Ron, he is dead serious about all this, this is his moment to shine for Maharishi." Cielle said "I have been involved in the study of proper etiquette all my life and we have with us Ron Nachtway, an expert in cosmetology and a professional hair stylist." This was all very serious stuff to Ron but Cielle, being a veteran Vegas entertainer saw no harm in adding a humorous bent to the show. She was talking about dandruff and proper care of one's hair and Ron was anxious to get his two cents in about healthy hair products when I spoke up from the audience with a Monty Python, "Old English General" accent (keep in mind I had torn bits of paper into very small pieces and put them in my hair).

"General Whitehead here! I say, just what are you on about with all this mambo-jumbo about one's hair? Why, when I was commanding Her Majesty's light dragoons in the Punjab, we had to wear our pith helmets for weeks on end, some of us had maggots crawling down our backs, dandruff would have been a bloody blessing." Ron was horrified and looked at Cielle with his hands out as if to say "shit! We'll have to start all over." But Cielle knew she had a hit on her hands and was almost in hysterics laughing as was the audience and film crew; she said "Oh, sir," I said "General Whitehead" and she said "Oh yes, General, you seem to be a man of rare experience and knowledge would you like to join us on the stage?"

I asked an elderly gentleman at hand, if I could use his cane for a moment and someone else lent me their beret; and a video crewman drew a big mutton chops mustache on my face with a thick sharpie. Then I began a torturous, game legged, wounded soldier's limp up to the stage. The whole time I was making my way up the audience was rolling out of their seats with every-time I'd say, "bloody leg!" and poor Ron was doing his best to adjust. Of course what was so funny was that everyone knew this was supposed to be very serious, everyone except me and Cielle! When I sat down on stage, Ron was just finishing his hair product recommendations and Cielle turned to me and said "welcome General, you must have a deep knowledge of personal hygiene with all the men you have commanded in very rough circumstances. What would you recommend for keeping the scalp lustrous and healthy even in battle conditions?" "You can keep all your Nancy-boy ointments and fancy-man unguents, a man's man, a soldier in Her Majesty's Dragoons makes use of what's at hand. Why, when we fought the Guineas, the greasers, the wops, many's the time I've dipped my hand in a bowl of oil drenched linguine and spruced up my hair, lasts a good fortnight."

Then, as the video camera moved in for a close-up, I took off the beret and shook my head. All the white pieces of paper fluttered about and it looked as if the General had a really bad case of dandruff. As I made this move, Cielle was in mid sentence "oh, yes General show us your lustrous head of . ..Oh my God! Is that dandruff?" She actually thought it might be and was horrified for a moment. I said "what! that? No madam, not on my head, nothing but confetti from my last parade through the streets of London; some years ago I believe."

This went on and I can't really remember all the comedy repartee that Cielle and I spontaneously channeled but it was some of the greatest fun I've ever had. Ron was very disappointed even though he got most of his cosmetology in. Cielle didn't get much of her etiquette and manners on that tape but they scheduled a second taping the next day and completed their mission. Now, however, word got around that the new etiquette tapes were hilarious and everyone wanted to see them. So, Ron and Cielle's show went from something we were all required to see for our social improvement, which meant no one would want to see it, to a show that everyone wanted to see. But really, I don't think anyone would have taken it more seriously had it not been entertaining and funny, they would have simply ignored it or made fun of it. Since I had already had my fun, the audience could laugh at the funny parts and wade through the lesson parts in hopes that there might be more funny parts...naturally being very attentive all the while.

A few days later Ron came up to me in the dining hall, and at first I thought he was going to chew me out for ruining his video debut but instead he said "Maharishi wants me to take you to the Courchevel course in the French alps; I'm driving there to cut hair and show the video and he wants you to sing for them. This was odd! Maharishi usually didn't have me sing for the courses unless he was going as well; something was up and I was curious as to what it was. I won't bore you with our long silent drive. Things picked up as we approached Courchevel, the snow covered mountains and deep valleys with their bright kaleidoscopic, rushing creeks, reflecting brilliant sunshots into our eyes as we wove our way through the Alps.

We found the hotel, got our rooms, and bid adieu until we had to drive back to Seelisberg. The course leader told me I could sit-in on the final classes as they were playing some of Maharishi's most inspiring lectures, so I did. When I walked into the small room I felt as if I was a celebrity, everyone was watching me with big smiles on their faces. Later, I found out that Maharishi had told them that I was coming to sing for them. There was one girl in the room who kept staring at me and I could feel this powerful magnetic attraction, almost like some white-magic, voodoo, love potion had exploded in the room.

ARYA

When the tape was over I left the room but stood outside waiting to see what the magic was all about. I was about to turn and go to my room when the girl who had been staring came out and her face shone like a little sun, still smiling with all those bright teeth and moist eyes that worked like lasers beaming and burning right into mine. She came right up to me and said "hi! Rick Stanley, so when are you going to play and sing for us?" I probably said I didn't know yet, maybe tomorrow evening? She said her name was Arya, and we were both fighting that intense magnetism that forced us together. Finally, after not being able to part from each other, I said I haven't been to my room yet, I have to bring my guitar and bag, want to come?" she said "yes" and we went up and talked for awhile until she had to go and meditate.

The next day Maharishi came through the main hall with his entourage and in a big hurry. I had no idea he was going to be in Courchevel and now he was leaving! I went up to him and said "Maharishi, should I go back with you?" He said "No! You have to sing for the course tonight." I was seriously worried that Arya was going to be too much for me to ignore; I was still under the impression that Maharishi wanted me to be brahamachari and celibate, after all wasn't that the ideal? I thought that this was obviously another one of Maharishi's tests, the way he looked at me when I asked if I could go with him, there was definitely something going on because he had that, don't you get it yet Rick? look in his eyes.

Arya sat with me that afternoon for lunch and we walked and talked for over an hour. I think we were sizing each other up and down for a possible mate. She was lean with ballet-dancer muscles in her arms and legs. She said she had some health problems in the past so I thought "oh, well then this wouldn't be a good idea, the puranas always say to marry a healthy woman." That evening I sang and Ron played his video. No one really knew who General Whitehead was; they actually thought he was a real English general until Cielle began laughing and the white confetti snowed down all over the general and his clothes. Now that some comedy was balancing out the lesson plan, the sullen mood of being treated like school kids quickly left the room and someone said "that's Rick Stanley! The General." It was hard for them to believe it was the same guy who had just sung "Love & God" and "The Holy Tradition;" they kept looking back at me, then at the General on the big TV screen and laughing.

That night Arya came with me to my new room which was about half a mile away in a complex of new chalets that were still under construction. Being a special guest, I think I was the only one assigned to the chalets; it certainly was quiet out there. She wanted me to sing Love & God again which I did, and then we just sat and talked, mostly about me and my spiritual experiences; somehow, I was under the deluded impression that every girl I talked to, one on one, would be interested in my stories. She seemed very interested, probably in spite of my fascination with myself, so it went on until around two in the morning. Her bus was supposed to leave for the airport at ten am and she was almost a mile from her room so I said she aught to stay for the few hours that remained for her to get some sleep and she did. "However, she said, unless you intend to have a relationship with me, please don't take advantage of me being in your bed."

THE GREEN GOBLIN

I had no intention of "taking advantage of her" and said "I'll be good if you will" or something to that effect. So, it was a very large bed and I was on one side, she was on the other. About an hour later she woke me with "I'm cold" and I wasn't sure she was awake, maybe talking in her sleep, so I didn't respond. I went back to sleep and in a lucid dreaming state, I heard her say it again "I'm cold" but this time I saw a little green goblin looking thingy inside of her body with a mischievous grin, he was doing the talking, stretching out his neck as he mimicked her voice. It was obvious that this little prankster was trying to get me to cuddle up to Arya so that a relationship might get ignited.

Even though I saw what was happening and understood it from the lucid dream state, from the waking state, which I drifted into, I felt compelled to help her get warm. The moment I put my arms around her she woke up and said "what are you doing?" I said, "you said you were cold so I tried to warm you up." She said that she never said that and then I knew that the imp had worked his magic well because even though we were both innocent of instigating this intimacy, once it had begun we were both too enchanted to end it. We were like two virgin teenagers not knowing if we should continue or pull away. We didn't embrace for long being confused and unsure what had happened; however, now it was left unsaid, but it was there between us, that I must honor my word of having serious intentions toward her if I initiated any love making.

After all, she had warned me that she would fall in love with me. We felt so comfortable together that before it was time for her to go we enjoyed a bath together and I piggy-backed her around the room on my shoulders like a child. She left for her room and I promised to see her off in an hour. I stood beside the bus and she smiled that same brilliant bright-eyed, innocent smile that she had when I first met her only a day or two before. I could feel her being so convinced that I was totally honorable and good, that I would send for her or come and be with her in California. After she left I thought that it was obvious that Maharishi had sent me to Courchevel to meet Arya and that he had put an enchantment on both of us to assure our mutual attraction.

But then, after a few months of letters from Arya and some convoluted thinking, I erroneously construed the Imp that I saw within her, talking for her, as proof of a test by Maharishi; a test to see if I was able to "see" exactly what was happening on all levels of consciousness and therefore rise above it like a good little brahmachari, which I didn't! So, under a rather large mistake of the intellect, I mailed a letter explaining that I really wanted to commit to M group and to be a monk, that I didn't want to be a householder or family man. She respected my choice and was very understanding about it.

BIG MISTAKE #2

It wasn't long after my *brilliant insight* into Maharishi's intentions that I realized it wasn't a test, it was an inspired hand-fasting attempt to pair two well suited souls. The only problem was mine, I could "see" the little spirit who was meant to bring us together and the fact that it wasn't Arya who was inviting me to warm her, made all the difference to me and my fat little ego. The reason why I couldn't accept the Imp as Maharishi's little helper to get me to make the first move, came to me much too late to make the right decision. The road I had chosen led to decades of heartbreak and hardship and I know it wasn't so great for Arya either.

A FEW DONT'S AROUND THE MASTER

There were a few events that I should probably relate simply to give you Maharishi's take on them or, "what not to do around the Master." These stories took place near the end of my time living and traveling with Maharishi, close to the end of 1975. I returned to him in 1980 for the course at the Express building in Delhi India and got sick as I always do in the land of the great unwashed. After that, Maharishi came to Fairfield once or twice but that's about it!

Anyway, we were back at the hotel Pratchli in Arosa Switzerland and a few us went on a short trip with Maharishi to the highest mountain in the area, the Weisshorn which is about 9000 feet with perpetual snow and a cable car that can take you all the way to the summit. We went to the top and looking down as we ascended in the cable car was scary. You wonder, what if that cable snaps or just detaches from the car or the station at the top? You imagine the car dropping like an elevator at first, and then going so fast that your floating around in the cable car trying to get hold of anything to keep from going through a window or smashing your head against the hard steel walls and floor. We made it! and stepped out into the small station on the summit of the mountain and walked out into the brilliant white snow world where it feels like no man is really supposed to be. I immediately ran for the highest place on the mountain and stood looking up at what appeared as a giant celestial apparition. It was hovering directly above that highest point, shimmering with the sunlight sparkling through it's invisible presence.

When some of the others had joined me at the base of another fifty foot promontory, I shouted "King of the mountain" and sloshed up the hill through the snow. The others made for the top as well and when I reached it first, I pushed whoever managed to get up, slipping and sliding back down to the bottom. No one was able to d-throne me, and as I stood there with my arms raised in mock victory, feeling like a child warrior, I noticed Maharishi watching and realized he was not too pleased. I know he didn't mind the Kshatriya game, what he did mind was the impression we were making on the tourists present. Who was going to take Maharishi and TM seriously when his twenty-something teachers play ugly-American domination games in a place that inspires awe and reverence?

That's how I think of it now, back then I wasn't sure why he gave us that look of concern. I mean, remember how he reacted when Keith and I ran about "air-sword" fighting by the little Highland lock during our Scottish trip? He was almost rolling out of his seat on the bus he was laughing so hard; so maybe I'm right about the reflection on Maharishi and TM thing! When I came down from the mini-summit, Maharishi was in the middle of a discourse and I felt like a real jerk, having missed most of it to play a children's game. Every moment with Maharishi was a moment that thousands of people would have given almost anything to have. Most of the meditators, siddhas and governors that I have known have their story of that one time they had with Maharishi, and he said something or even just looked at them in a particular way that they have clung to, and cherished for decades; some for the rest of their lives. But, I felt privileged, like a spoiled prince who enjoyed the freedom of making mischief, like Ganesha and Loki; I loved to laugh during overly serious moments and play practical jokes on people who took themselves way too seriously.

LEONNA

I SAID "LEONNA WHAT ARE YOU DOING HERE?"

I was so pleased to see someone so dear to me that I felt I could play with her, even in front of Maharishi. What my heart and soul were saying was:

"I LOVE YOU DEAR FRIEND"

But my perverted Boston humor had to tongue-in-cheek my welcome into a cruel joke. It was yet another one of those Boston sarcasm eruptions from my, say whatever comes into your head, spontaneous-combustion-mouth-farts that shot an arrow into the heart of someone I had always respected and loved. To this day she swears that I meant every word I said as she entered the little group of Initiators surrounding Maharishi in the hotel hallway. She had just arrived from the states, I assumed, and she walked so reverently toward the Master that I couldn't help wanting to lighten her mood; I was so happy to see her, I couldn't help but say "what are **you** doing here?" in front of Maharishi and the others.

When I said it, I was play-acting with a disdainful look on my face and a derisive tone in my voice; I have always been too good an actor. I saw the look of hurt on her face and I couldn't believe that she took me seriously. Perhaps, she had never encountered Boston humor before, she mustn't have! She had been Sara's and my favorite person in the world, other than Maharishi, for years. She was our mentor, she inspired us to drive up to Lake Louise when all the other initiators were warning us not to go. For God's sake I loved her! and she really believed I would mean something so rude and nasty as a greeting like that!!! She was the one person there, most deserving of total respect other than Maharishi. That was the very reason it was humorous to me, and I thought it would be to everyone there. She obviously didn't have as lofty an opinion of herself as I had of her, otherwise she would have understood?

I thought she would respond with "Yes Rick, you will have to put up with me I'm afraid." Or, maybe she would just hug me and say, "I love you too." But instead, she has held on to my silly joke like a mortal wound, the scar of which she can show to anyone who brings up my name. I ran into her at a restaurant a few years ago and she reminded me of my regrettable "Boston Welcome." She was almost tearing up remembering it, and I told her that it had actually been meant as a special welcome, I would never presume to say something like that to someone I didn't love, only to someone who I was sure would welcome the familiarity, with a like response. But she insisted that I had meant it in a mean way, and I finally gave up trying to explain the jaded Yankee humor of my upbringing to a sweet Canadian innocent.

I think she must have had too high an opinion of me at the time, but that's the problem with thinking that everyone is going to be uplifting and sweet as honey in an obvious way as they become realized. Maharishi once told me that we should be careful about what habits we cling to as we come closer to Self-Realization, "Once you are realized the habits will remain." The Master that Guru Dev first approached when he was just a boy was enlightened, but still had a bad temper and therefore was rejected by Guru Dev. Guru Dev tested him by asking if he had any fire and the master flew into a rage at the question because Dandi Sanyasis are forbidden to have fire. This was a good example of a realized man with a bad habit, I mean if he got mad when a boy asked him an obvious test question how many other things would set this guy off? Not your blissful guru!

THE YOUNGBLUTH'S

The ATR at the Alexander hotel in Arosa was a fun time with Andy Kaufman, but there was something that was having a negative effect on some of our TM teachers, and one night Maharishi made it known that there was a family of "spiritualists" in the states who were being paid by unsuspecting initiators to clean their auras and remove negative karmic attachments (whatever that means)? We were warned that getting involved with these people could be dangerous. At the time I couldn't imagine doing such a thing and soon forgot about it. A year or two later about 1975, I was rounding at the Seeblick hotel on lake Lucern, not long after my faux-pas with Leona. Maharishi was away at the time but before he went I had asked him if I could round instead of teach another ATR or TTC. He asked if I wanted to take the new Vedic Science course at the Kulm Hotel where he lived. I said "Ok" and attended one boring video lecture then immediately got his permission to join an ATR rounding course at the Seeblick as a course participant. You may ask why the Vedic Science lecture was boring to me? Because I had heard every point Maharishi was making before, many times over. It is always the same basic teaching dressed to fit the occasion, Science or Vedic Science, I don't really care! I wanted the actual experience of what all these lectures were about in a permanent way; I was tired of hearing about it and rounding was the way to actualize it.

OFF THE PROGRAM

I was really "off the program" during that ATR and there was a responsible lady initiator who was running it who tried to get me straightened out; go to all the taped lectures, buddy up, the whole organized structure of an ATR. I was probably really un-stressing at the time and someone gave me a form that I could send to some mediums in the US who would, supposedly, clear me of my problem stress release. I sent off the money and signed my permission for them to work on me in the abstract (astral plane) and didn't really believe anything would come of it. One day when I was meditating I could see two astral figures, one on either side of me; they were moving their hands about my head and I realized that these were the very people I had given permission to work on my aura or whatever they mess with. They were dressed in some kind of flowing robes and I could make out a little crimson color but mostly they looked like ghosts. When I came out of that meditation I felt almost crazy, as if someone else was in my body with me. I looked in the mirror and my face looked frantic, my eyes were staring back at me as if freaked out, a raving, lunatic!

Then something took over my body and I went running down the stairs and outside and up the mountain. I was crazed, trying desperately to get away from whatever it was that was in me. I ran up into the woods smashing branches, falling down and crying out, screaming for it to get out. Finally, exhausted and depraved, I slunk back into my room and tried to round again; asanas, pranayam and meditation. I fell asleep and when I awoke I realized that I had better check the pamphlet I had so thoughtlessly signed and sent off. Oh my God! I had invited the Youngbluth's into my consciousness to do what they wished. A week later I got a letter from them stating that they had taken an alcoholic doctor who had died in the 19th century out of my body!!! What they had really done was put this guy in me. For at least six months after that fateful day, my invading, quack doctor had been influencing me to pre-scribe various crackpot cures for several staff members and initiators; I had become somewhat overshadowed by my un-welcome tenant.

The intensity of my somewhat radical form of "unstressing" passed but I was still overshadowed with the desire to be of more use to Maharishi and the Movement with my music. I wouldn't take no for an answer and kept hounding Maharishi for permission to go to the New York Academy where they had a cutting edge recording studio. "Maharishi I want to go to Livingston Manor and record a new album of TM songs." "You don't have any new songs to record.'" I'll write them in the studio like the Beatles do." "The Beatles!" He exclaimed. This conversation had taken place in front of the newly appointed "Board of Governors" who were about to take charge of all of us, eliminating our one on one relationships with Maharishi. My outburst in front of the Board; Rindy, Kornhaus and the others upset Maharishi who was still feeling the hurt that the Beatles had so callously inflicted on him.

After around two weeks of persistant badgering, Maharishi painfully consented to my plan and ok'd the plane tickets to New York. That's it! The biggest mistake of my life, leaving Maharishi just when he was about to give us all the next stage in evolution, the 6 month courses and the Sidhis in France. I did write the songs in the New York Academy, and I did record them in the new studio but it was all for nothing as Maha-rishi really didn't want anymore western music representing the Movement. So finally I got married again, and ended up in Fairfield Iowa with two beautiful kids.

When Maharishi came to Fairfield in the late 70's he asked all the initiators how we were doing. Some said they had started their own businesses, had achieved a PhD., or that they were running the local TM Center. When it came to me I told him about the new album I was going to record. He didn't seem impressed. Later when he was about to leave in a small Cessna airplane, he was saying his goodbyes sitting in the front seat with the door open to us all. I had my son Brendan with me and I put a flower in his hand and walked under the plane and thrust Bren up in front of Maharishi. Maharishi couldn't see me under the plane but he took the flower from Bren and said "Then you have done very well."

Several years later, in a waking dream, I found myself standing in a line of "Governors" "Ministers" and "Rajas" holding a flower as Maharishi walked down the gauntlet taking flowers and making the occasional comment or greeting, mostly Jai Guru Dev. When he got to me he turned, took my flower, gave me one, and said "You will no longer be with me" which meant that the time period when I could have returned to be a part of his entourage, his immediate disciples, had elapsed. Of course I had two kids to raise, and families had no place around Maharishi. A year or two later I had married Claudine and I sent him a picture of our wedding and my kids via a friend. He immediately recognized the quality of her soul and said "Very good, very good, he is settled." I think it was 2008 when Maharishi passed on to even greater things, and when he did he spoke to me in my waking dream state yet again. Of course it is private but it was very reassuring.

LOVE & GOD

After going over these two books, I've realized that the two most important contributions that I've made in my life haven't been included in either book (aside from my two children). Number one is that having become a teacher of Transcendental Meditation, like many Initiators, I traveled the country teaching the simple but profound technique of TM and I am proud to have taught almost two thousand.

The second contribution, aside from the TM albums, including Maharishi's granting me the unique privilege of singing the Holy Tradition in public to dramatic effect on audiences, is my creation of the music to accompany select parts of Maharishi's divine poem "Love & God." As I stated in the book, Maharishi's poetic description of the experience of the Divine mirrored my own brief yet profound revelation, enough to allow me to cognize the music and melodies to sing this sweet Song Of Life based on direct experience, not mood-making.

How did I "cognize" the music to Maharishi's poem? Well, if you must know, I came down with some bronchial or flu-like illness and Maharishi told his secretary to move me to a room that was situated on the other side of the wall from his. One morning I was inspired to pick up my guitar and open the Love & God book to the God prose. I tried to find flowing lyrics that could hold a repeating melody like iambic pentameter or other rhyming meter; it didn't have to rhyme, it just had to be rhythmically singable.

Finally, I gave up and went to the first part of the book, "Love." Yes! there were several singable pages and they were the most beautiful and most inspiring of my memories of the divine experience. I closed my eyes and meditated for a bit and then began playing chord patterns on the guitar that I thought might fit the innocence and sweetness of the words. Every chord sequence seemed to be too worldly to hip or sophisticated so I closed my eyes and fell asleep for what must have been a couple of hours...I was sick. I woke to the sound of someone on the other side of the wall moving about, probably Maharishi.

Now I decided to just try and sing the words I had chosen without the guitar complicating things. The words and structure of each "verse" became my guides and a natural melody began to form itself. I picked up the guitar and found that to accompany the melody and rhythm I had only to go from D to G to A to G to D with bass string notes forming the transitions between chords. That was perfect, it allowed me to play with the melody but after playing this basic vamp for over an hour I realized with the help of a repeated "My Lord, My Love, My God" that I had a naturally occurring chorus which was ideal for making the song breathe with emotion.

I could actually feel something coming from the other side of the wall, it felt like a powerful creative flow of energy and emotion. To this day I inwardly give most of the credit for the power and beauty of the music to Maharishi's Love & God to the man who wrote the words, to Maharishi Mahesh Yogi.

Jai Guru Dev

I think I'll just end the stories here if you don't mind, and add something I left out of the first book of "My Song Of Life."

Pamela Polland and I were the "Gentle Soul." Our first and foremost professional recording contract with Columbia Records, and the album and singles we created and recorded with Terry Melcher, the producer for the "Byrds," has received quite a few positive reviews over the decades and was even re-released on Sundazed Records not so long ago. Here are a few of the reviews to spark your interest, and hopefully entice your desire to buy the first book of "My Song Of Life" so that you can get an inside view of that golden age of music and spiritual awakening called the 60's.

RECENT REVIEWS OF
"THE GENTLE SOUL"

"Rick Stanley may not be a household name in the world of folk-rock, but he's paid his dues and he's still making wonderful music. As a singer/songwriter back in the 1960s, he joined with Pamela Polland and formed The Gentle Soul, a dreamy and love-drenched musical duo whose inspiration for songs and harmonies came chiefly from the Everly Brothers. The Gentle Soul became somewhat of a legend around the Los Angeles area due to their frequent bookings at the famous Troubadour nightclub in 1966 and 1967. With a contingent of loyal fans and friends like Jackson Browne, Ry Cooder, and Linda Ronstadt, and getting a record deal on Columbia with Terry Melcher as producer (the Byrds and Paul Revere and the Raiders), it looked like The Gentle Soul was going to go all the way to the top of the pops. Alas, it was not to be. The band lasted only until 1969,
when Stanley and Polland split up to pursue new spiritual and musical directions, and The Gentle Soul was no more. Sundazed Records has re-released The Gentle Soul, a 1968 album which is beautiful, ornate and captivating, and certainly captures the optimistic vibe of the time.

The lead-off instrumental track "Overture" is a good example of what TGS could do in the studio. Using some of the best session musicians of the era like Van Dyke Parks, Larry Knetchel, Jerry Cole, Hal Blaine, and Ry Cooder, Melcher and the band arrange harpsichord, flute, string quartet, country guitar, and soft zen cymbals to create a Renaissance/Baroque/hippie soundtrack which is dazzling in its depth of production. "Our National Anthem," which was thought by everyone to be a surefire Top Ten single, fizzled out when it was released due

to lack of promotion and touring. Listening to the song now you can't help but be swept up in the dreams-cape-utopia visions of Stanley and Polland, and their vibrant singing, which sounds at times like the Mamas and Papas blended in with Spanky and Our Gang."
T.J. McGrath

"Once again, Sundazed has uncovered a long-lost, barely remembered classic from the '60s. The band - essentially the singing and songwriting duo of Rick Stanley and Pamela Polland along with the support of such renowned sessioners as Ry Cooder, Van Dyke Parks, Larry Knechtel and Jack Nitzsche - made a single record, and it's a goodie. Combining coffeehouse folk and sunshine pop with a daub of psychedelia, The Gentle Soul recalls a time when innocence did not necessarily mean inane and soft rock did not necessarily mean soft-headed. Terry Melcher's billowy production - all perfectly plucked acoustics, chiming harpsichords and trilling flutes - fully complements Stanley and Polland's close harmonies, which paint bright aural colors on songs like the woozy "Young Man Blue," the delicate "Renaissance" and the soaring "Flying Thing," written by onetime member Jackson Browne. The Gentle Soul is not exactly groundbreaking, but it's certainly as uplifting now in the apocalyptic '00s as it was in the turbulent '60s."
Eliot Wilder of amplifiermagazine.com

"Sundazed have done a fantastic job in reissuing the lost 1960s folk rock gem that is the Gentle Soul. Thriving in the vibrant mid to late 1960s folk rock movement, Pamela Polland and Rick Stanley of The Gentle Soul hung out with the likes of Neil Young, Jackson Browne (there's an early tune written by him as one of the bonus tracks here), The Byrds, and Tim Buckley, and worked with the likes of Terry Melcher, Jack Nitzsche, Ry Cooder (whose incredible guitar playing is throughout this cd), Van Dyke Parks, Larry Knechtel, Jerry Cole and Hal Blaine. Amongst this incredible scene of creativity, The Gentle Soul released one album and a handful of singles, but never had the push they needed or any luck with sales. Their recordings became more and more scarce through the years, the album even becoming a collector's item with a 3 figure price tag.

Thanks to Sundazed, we've got the entire recorded output of The Gentle Soul, as well as three previously unissued sides all on cd for the very first time. The cd has the entire album first, then the singles and unreleased tracks, so it doesn't play chronologically. The singles (tracks 12-14, 17-18) have a slightly more rocking sound then the gently orchestral album, but the singles are by no means rock-n-roll.

Tell Me Love is an incredible single which has an alternate take too, both arranged magically by Jack Nitzsche. Both mixes are quite different and shed a different feel on the melodic Celtic lilt. The single mix has a harder hitting sound, but the alternate version has a fuller, modern sound. The first single's b-side, You Move Me, has that coffee house folk rock sound and Mamas and Papas styled harmonies and is tremendous. The second single, Our National Anthem should've been a hit, and it's astonishing it was not. It's also got that Mamas and Papas anthemic folk rock feel, but maybe it's the fact that the chorus is not as out right sing-a-long-able is what kept it off the charts. It's still a catchy as heck folk rock number. Song For Three, its b-side has a Dylanesque melody about a girl named Wendy. The final single, 2:10 Train has a more country folk sound and is a bit meandering, sort of like Linda Ronstadt and The Stone ponies.

The Gentle Soul album (tracks 1-11) are wonderfully orchestrated folk rock. Pamela Polland and Rick Stanley combine incredible vocal harmonies with some great original tunes, which are only improved upon thanks to the production of Terry Melcher and instrumentation from the likes of Ry Cooder and Van Dyke Parks. Songs like Renaissance or Love Is Always Real (which also has an alternate take as a bonus track) are baroque and orchestrated with harpsichords and flutes. The melodies they came up with just enhance the whole proceedings. Generally speaking the songs with Pamela singing come out on top and remind me at times of the Michelle album Saturn Rings. At times this album reminds me of Belle and Sebastian or their side project Gentle Waves (rather fitting) - if they were more inspired by traditional folk music instead of Nick Drake. If you want to hear Ry Cooder at his most pronounced, check out the instrumental album opener Overture or the haunting song Reelin'. If I were to pick a favorite song, it would have to be See My Love - which to me sounds like it could be straight off a Belle and Sebastian album with it's melody, piano and Pamela's light as air lead vocals. It's the closest they come to rocking out.

I was very glad when I learned that Sundazed were going to reissue The Gentle Soul album. I'm glad that more than just the collectors can hear the magic held in this delightful folk rock album. Hopefully, it can find a place in your collection too."
Patrick of Gullbuy.com

A Review of the Original LP The Gentle Soul:
"The Gentle Soul were the singing-songwriting duo of Pamela Polland and Rick Stanley, and made one LP for Epic in 1968 that bridged the folk-rock and singer-songwriter/soft rock eras. The self-titled album, despite coming out on a major label, is extremely rare, and has never been issued on CD. Produced by Terry Melcher (the Byrds, Paul Revere the Raiders), it had quite a stellar supporting cast of session musicians, including Ry Cooder on guitar, Van Dyke Parks on harpsichord, Paul Horn on flute, and Larry Knechtel (later a founding member of Bread) on organ, plus noted arranger Jack Nitzsche. A nice, though not major, effort, it was indeed a gentle record, usually paced by the close male-female harmonies of Polland and Stanley; they also wrote most of the songs, usually but

not always as a team. The folky and acoustic-flavored, but not totally acoustic, ambiance and harmonies recalled the Stone Poneys. The balance between male and female vocals, however, was naturally far more even than it was with the Stone Ponies, who were dominated by Linda Ronstadt even on the numbers with harmony lead vocals. Another reference point, though far more obscure, would be the Bay Area folk-rock duo Blackburn and Snow, although the Gentle Soul were more subdued, in fact foreshadowing the soft rock of the early 1970s.

Prior to the Gentle Soul, Pamela Polland had already begun to establish herself as a folk-rock songwriter, placing her compositions with the Rising Sons ("Tulsa County") and, as a matter of fact, the Stone ponies, who did her "I've Got to Know" on their second album. ("Tulsa County" was later covered by the Byrds and Jessie Ed Davis.) She and Stanley recorded two singles for Columbia, "Tell Me Love" and "Our National Anthem," prior to the release of the Epic LP. The Gentle Soul were together for about three years, during which they employed various musicians as accompanists, including Jackson Browne (who actually replaced Stanley for a brief period, though he never recorded with the group) and drummer Sandy Konikoff (who had played briefly with Bob Dylan in the mid-1960s). Epic couldn't have promoted them very heavily, though. Not only is the album scarce, but the label did not even list Polland and Stanley's names on the sleeve, although at least there was a picture, and the names "P. Polland" and "R. Stanley" dominated the songwriting credits. Polland recorded solo material for Columbia in the 1970s, and was still recording in the 1990s." Richie Unterberger, All Music Guide

THE 25 MOST INTERESTING OVERLOOKED 1960s FOLK-ROCK LPs

By Richie Unterberger

This feature originally appeared in the August 2005 issue

of Record Collector magazine. For more information about *Record Collector*, the UK's finest publication dedicated to record collecting and rock/popular music history, check out its website at www.recordcollectormag.com.

The 25 Top Overlooked American Folk-Rock LPs of the 1960s
The Gentle Soul
The Gentle Soul
(Epic LP BN 26374)

October 30, 1968 CD reissue: Sundazed SC 11123 (2003) While much folk-rock (and rock in general) was getting noisier and more psychedelic in the late 1960s, a few Los Angeles folk-rockers were moving in a rather calmer, rootsier direction. We've already looked at a few - the Stone ponies, Hearts & Flowers, and Fred Neil - all of whom, un-coincidentally, were produced by Nick Venet for Capitol. Elsewhere in town, the Gentle Soul took a similar approach to their Columbia sessions for another top producer, Terry Melcher, most famous for his work on the first two albums by the greatest folk-rock act of all, "The-Byrds."

Though a few musicians (including, briefly, the young Jackson Browne) passed in and out of the Gentle Soul, the band centered around the male-female harmonizing duo of Rick Stanley and Pamela Polland. Indeed, they're the only two pictured on the cover of this ultra-rare late-'68 release, on which Epic Records thoughtfully forgot to credit them by name on the back, though they did manage to list nearly ten session men (including Ry Cooder, with whom Polland performed live in the mid-1960s). Though there were quite a few musicians involved in the sessions and some orchestration was used, it's quite a low-key record, somewhat in the mold of the Stone ponies.

It took quite a while for Melcher and the band - who had

made their first recordings together back in late 1966 - to get an album assembled, and by the time it finally came out on Columbia's Epic subsidiary, the Gentle Soul had just split. Like several other worthy folk-rockers on Columbia (Cooder's Melcher-produced band the Rising Sons, for instance, never even got to release an album for the label), the group were buried by an avalanche of under-promotion. Barely distributed, copies of "The Gentle Soul" were going for three-figure sums 30 years later. But its recent CD re-issue, which augments the album with eight cuts from non-LP singles and out-takes (including the never-before-heard early Jackson Browne song "Flying Thing"), ensures that the music can be heard without spending half of your next paycheck.

RICK STANLEY Q&A

Q: What qualities do you think made the Gentle Soul LP stand out most from other folk-rock coming out in the late 1960s?

A: I think the music on this album and some of the singles capture the more subtle spiritual essence of that little golden age of creativity called the '60s. This music is the pure expression of kids with little concern for money or fame. We were guileless and wrote from our deepest experience and understanding of love and spirituality. We wanted to give only the highest expressions of ourselves, the most beautiful music we could make. We had no plan or agenda for success and this is probably why we so easily parted, Pamela off to Greece with her Poet and me off to India to write two albums of music for Maharishi Mahesh Yogi, just as the Beatles took their leave. Another quality that obviously helped us out was our love for some of the greatest musicians of the time who were unknown outside of the Troubadour crowd. People like Ry Cooder, who met with me for a couple of weeks as we worked up his guitar parts.

Just for the record, much of the guitar that you hear on Gentle Soul is mine; this is something that I have never been credited with. But I was the guitar picker who did the finger picking and funky rhythmic stuff on the album, like "Young Man Blue." I laid all the basic tracks with my own three-and four-finger style, and Ry added his awesome flat-picking style on guitar and mandolin. Van Dyke Parks on harpsichord, and especially Paul Horn, played an important role as session leader and his flute, of course. Fortunately, Terry Melcher had the same taste in session musicians that we had.

Q: What were Melcher's greatest contributions to the record?

A: Terry had a great foundation of folk-rock experience with the Byrds, and great taste in session musicians as I've mentioned. We hadn't recorded all the songs for the album before we stopped recording. Terry had to bring in Ry and some of the other musicians after he had commissioned Jack Nitzsche to write an arrangement of the themes of all the songs on the album to fill up the record. This compilation made up for the missing one or two songs, and I think it was very well done. What I liked best about him was that he wanted us to love what he did with our music, and would listen and respond to our input. He just wanted to make us sound as good as we possibly could. He kept it simple, just as we wanted it to be. We didn't want the "wall of sound" or any other gimmick of the time, although they did give it a try on one of the singles.

Q: Did your splitting up right before the album's release help account for the rarity of the original LP?

A: You got that right!! I found copies in some of the most out-of-the-way places for several years, so they must have sent it out, but without promotion or any sort of advertising. They did send some copies around for review before it was released. I happened upon a Billboard review years later that said "Gentle Soul, the most beautiful unknown album of the year."

Q: What kind of musical and recording directions do you think you might have been able to explore had you managed to hold together-longer?

A: I like to think we would have gone in the same direction that I went myself when I started recording with Henry Lewy, Joni Mitchell's [engineer], at A&M Records. I studied with Maharishi Mahesh Yogi for seven years, starting in 1968, and wrote and recorded two albums of songs with Maharishi's inspiration; the first one "Song of Life," was really an introduction to Maharishi's teaching. We wrote the songs together at the end of my teacher training in Kashmir India. I think

Pamela would have gone to India as well if we had remained a group. Instead, Paul Fauerso, of the San Francisco group the Loading Zone (with Linda Tillery), teamed up with me on the 2nd [1972] album, "Something Good Is Happening," and we wrote and harmonized much like Pamela and I had done. We had to blend our singing styles a bit - Cat Stevens and Daryl Hall become the Everly Brothers, sort of. The two albums sold at least a couple of hundred thousand copies during the '70s. Paul Horn played some great flute on both albums, as he had done on Gentle Soul; Tom Scott and Doug Dillard added some great parts as well.

So I guess what I'm saying is, if Pamela and I had stayed together we might have done those albums together. If you carry the "if factor" up to the present, we would probably be writing and singing some songs against war like "Bonny Brave Boys" (about my Vietnam experience, on the CD Border Lord) and no doubt, songs about Pamela's love for nature and the environment, and beautiful Celtic-influenced songs like the Gentle Soul's single, "Tell Me Love." We would be singing them in rich, weaving harmonies. I would be playing my self-made Irish harp, guitar and banjo and she would be playing keyboards, maybe harmonium?

It would have been great if it had worked out that way. But she is in Hawaii singing traditional songs as she sways to the hula, swimming with the dolphins and monitoring her environmental website. Me, I'm writing songs when they come through me, sometimes about the distant past and sometimes about the rapidly disintegrating world order. What keeps me writing and performing is the high I get when I can go to the feeling level of the audience and share a communication and upliftment of the heart that heals us all.

Printed in Poland
by Amazon Fulfillment
Poland Sp. z o.o., Wrocław